HOUSE OF
TRUMP
HOUSE OF
PUTIN

www.penguin.co.uk

ALSO BY CRAIG UNGER

House of Bush, House of Saud

The Fall of the House of Bush

Boss Rove

HOUSE OF TRUMP HOUSE OF PUTIN

The Untold Story of Donald Trump
and the Russian Mafia

CRAIG UNGER

BANTAM PRESS

LONDON · NEW YORK · TORONTO · SYDNEY · AUCKLAND

TRANSWORLD PUBLISHERS
61–63 Uxbridge Road, London W5 5SA
www.penguin.co.uk

Transworld is part of the Penguin Random House group of companies
whose addresses can be found at global.penguinrandomhouse.com

First published in Great Britain in 2018 by Bantam Press,
an imprint of Transworld Publishers

Published by arrangement with Dutton, an imprint of Penguin Publishing Group,
a division of Penguin Random House LLC

A CIP catalogue record for this book
is available from the British Library.

ISBNs
9780593080306 (hb)
9780593080313 (tpb)

Typeset in 11/15 pt Minion Pro
Printed and bound in Great Britain by Clays Ltd, Elcograf S.p.A.

Penguin Random House is committed to a sustainable
future for our business, our readers and our planet. This book
is made from Forest Stewardship Council® certified paper.

1 3 5 7 9 10 8 6 4 2

In memory of Paul Klebnikov, Alexander Litvinenko, Sergei Magnitsky, Anna Politkovskaya, and the dozens of other journalists, investigators, and dissidents who lost their lives investigating Putin's kleptocracy.

CONTENTS

It's wonderful that the Iron Curtain is gone, but it was a shield for the West. Now we've opened the gates, and this is very dangerous for the world. America is getting Russian criminals. Nobody will have the resources to stop them. You people in the West don't know our Mafiya yet. You will, you will!

—Boris Urov, former chief investigator of major crimes
for the Russian attorney general, circa 1993[1]

Russia has never tried to use leverage over me. I HAVE NOTHING TO DO WITH RUSSIA - NO DEALS, NO LOANS, NO NOTHING!

—Donald Trump, January 11, 2017, via Twitter

HOUSE OF
TRUMP
HOUSE OF
PUTIN

CHAPTER ONE

(VIRTUAL) WORLD WAR III

A t approximately 9:32 a.m. Moscow time on November 9, 2016, Deputy Vyacheslav Nikonov of the pro-Putin United Russia Party stepped up to the microphone in the Russian State Duma, the Russian equivalent of the House of Representatives, to make a highly unusual announcement.

The grandson of Vyacheslav Molotov—the coolly ruthless Stalinist of Molotov cocktail fame—Nikonov had been involved in Soviet and Russian politics for roughly forty years, including serving a stint on Vladimir Putin's staff. Now, he was about to make a rather simple, understated announcement, that in its way was as historic and incendiary as anything his grandfather had ever done.

"Dear friends, respected colleagues!" Nikonov said. "Three minutes ago Hillary Clinton admitted her defeat in US presidential elections and a second ago Trump started his speech as an elected president of the United States of America and I congratulate you on this."[1]

Even though Nikonov did not add what many in the Kremlin already knew, his brief statement was greeted by enthusiastic applause. Donald J. Trump had just become Vladimir Putin's man in the White House.

————

This book tells the story of one of the greatest intelligence operations in history, an undertaking decades in the making, through which the

Russian Mafia and Russian intelligence operatives successfully targeted, compromised, and implanted either a willfully ignorant or an inexplicably unaware Russian asset in the White House as the most powerful man on earth. In doing so, without firing a shot, the Russians helped put in power a man who would immediately begin to undermine the Western Alliance, which has been the foundation of American national security for more than seventy years; who would start massive trade wars with America's longtime allies; fuel right-wing anti-immigrant populism; and assault the rule of law in the United States.

In short, at a time at which the United States was confronted with a new form of warfare—hybrid war consisting of cyber warfare, hacking, disinformation, and the like—the United States would have at its helm a man who would leave the country all but defenseless, and otherwise inadvertently do the bidding of the Kremlin.

It is a story that is difficult to tell even though, in many ways, Donald Trump's ties to Russia over the last four decades have been an open secret, hiding in plain sight. One reason they went largely unnoticed for so long may be that aspects of them are so unsettling, so transgressive, that Americans are loath to acknowledge the dark realities staring them in the face.

As a result, the exact words for what happened often give way to fierce semantic disputes. Whatever Russia did with regard to the 2016 presidential campaign, was it an assault on America's sovereignty, or merely meddling? Was it an act of war? Did Russian interference change the results of the 2016 presidential election? Was it treason? Is Donald Trump a traitor? A Russian agent? Or merely a so-called useful idiot who somehow, through willful blindness or colossal ignorance, does not even know how he has been compromised by Russia?

President Donald Trump, of course, has denied having anything to do with Russia, having tweeted, ten days before his inauguration, "Russia has never tried to use leverage over me. I HAVE NOTHING TO DO WITH RUSSIA - NO DEALS, NO LOANS, NO NOTHING!"[2]

But as this book will show, over the last four decades, President Donald Trump and his associates have had significant ties to at least fifty-nine people who facilitated business between Trump and the Russians, including relationships with dozens who have alleged ties to the Russian Mafia.

It will show that President Trump has allowed Trump-branded real estate to be used as a vehicle that likely served to launder enormous amounts of money—perhaps billions of dollars—for the Russian Mafia for more than three decades.

It will show that President Trump provided an operational home for oligarchs close to the Kremlin and some of the most powerful figures in the Russian Mafia in Trump Tower—his personal and professional home, the crown jewel of his real estate empire—and other Trump buildings on and off for much of that period.

It will show that during this period the Russian Mafia has likely been a de facto state actor serving the Russian Federation in much the same way that American intelligence services serve the United States, and that many of the people connected to Trump had strong ties to the Russian FSB, the state security service that is the successor to the feared KGB.

It will show that President Trump has been a person of interest to Soviet and Russian intelligence for more than forty years and was likely the subject of one or more operations that produced *kompromat* (compromising materials) on him regarding sexual activities.

It will show that for decades, Russian operatives, including key figures in the Russian Mafia, studiously examined the weak spots in America's pay-for-play political culture—from gasoline distribution to Wall Street, from campaign finance to how the K Street lobbyists of Washington ply their trade—and, having done so, hired powerful white-shoe lawyers, lobbyists, accountants, and real estate developers by the score, in an effort to compromise America's electoral system, legal process, and financial institutions.

It will show that President Trump, far from being the only potential "asset" targeted by the Russians, was one of dozens of politicians—most of them Republicans, but some Democrats as well—and businessmen who became indebted to Russia, and that millions of dollars have been flowing from individuals and companies from, or with ties to, Russia to GOP politicians, including Senate majority leader Mitch McConnell, for more than twenty years.

It will show that the most powerful figures in America's national security—including two FBI directors, William Sessions and Louis Freeh, and special counsel to the CIA Mitchell Rogovin—ended up working with Russians who had been deemed serious threats to the United States.

It will show that President Trump was $4 billion in debt when Russian money came to his rescue and bailed him out, and, as a result, he was and remains deeply indebted to them for reviving his business career and launching his new life in politics.

It will show that President Trump partnered with a convicted felon named Felix Sater who allegedly had ties to the Russian mob, and that Trump did not disclose the fact Sater was a criminal and profited from that relationship.

And it will show that, now that he is commander in chief of the United States, President Trump, as former director of national intelligence James Clapper put it, is, in effect, an intelligence "asset" serving Russian president Vladimir Putin,[3] or, even worse, as Glenn Carle, a former CIA national intelligence officer, told *Newsweek*, "My assessment is that Trump is actually working directly for the Russians."[4]

Then again, maybe James Comey put it best. In January 2017, just a week after Donald Trump was inaugurated, the president invited then–FBI director Comey to the White House for a private dinner. Characterizing Trump as "unethical, and untethered to truth,"[5] likening his behavior to that of a Mafia boss, Comey writes in *A Higher Loyalty* that Trump told him: "I need loyalty. I expect loyalty."

The demand reminded Comey of a Cosa Nostra induction ceremony, with Trump in the role of the Mafia family boss. "The encounter left me shaken," he writes. "I had never seen anything like it in the Oval Office. As I found myself thrust into the Trump orbit, I once again was having flashbacks to my earlier career as a prosecutor against the Mob. The silent circle of assent. The boss in complete control. The loyalty oaths. The us-versus-them worldview. The lying about all things, large and small, in service to some code of loyalty that put the organization above morality and above the truth."[6]

Comey writes as if the Mafia conceit is a metaphor. But in a way it is more than that. What follows is the story of Trump's four-decade-long relationship with the Russian Mafia, and the Russian intelligence operation that helped put him into the White House.

———

On June 23, 2017, six months after his inauguration, President Donald Trump tweeted that his predecessor Barack Obama "knew far in advance" about Russia's meddling in the American election. The tweet was unusual in that it represented a rare acknowledgment by the president that Russia may have interfered in the 2016 election, but it was accompanied by Trump's denunciation of any investigation into the matter as a "witch hunt."

At the time, Russian president Vladimir Putin, who was en route to the Crimean peninsula, which Russia had annexed in 2014 from Ukraine, had reason to be grateful for any cover provided by his American friend. His stopover was not a popular one, rekindling as it did animosity in Ukraine, whose foreign ministry issued a statement saying that Kiev "consider[ed] this visit . . . to be a gross violation of the sovereignty of the State and the territorial integrity of Ukraine."[7] It was an issue that loomed large in the shadow play between the two men: Putin's apparent support of Trump seemingly went hand in hand with the latter's acquiescence on Russian aggression in Ukraine.

While Putin and Trump hogged the headlines, however, something took place in Devens, Massachusetts, that seemed light-years removed from the Trump-Russia scandal, but in fact was closely tied to its origins. John "Sonny" Franzese, the oldest federal prisoner in the United States, was discharged from the Federal Medical Center, after serving an eight-year sentence for extortion.[8]

Thanks to his age—Franzese had just celebrated his one hundredth birthday—his release was duly noted all over the world, from *Der Spiegel*[9] to the *New York Post,* which dutifully called forth Franzese's glory days hanging out with Frank Sinatra and boxing champ Jake LaMotta at the Copacabana.[10] An underboss in the feared Colombo crime family, Franzese had repeatedly dodged murder charges because he was likely so good at making bodies disappear. But after one acquittal he was caught on tape explaining how he'd disposed of the bodies of the dozens of people he had killed: "Dismember victim in kiddie pool. Cook body parts in microwave. Stuff parts in garbage disposal. Be patient."[11]

Franzese was old-school Mafia, a relic from the mid-twentieth-century era of the Cosa Nostra's Five Families, the same warring tribes depicted in *The Godfather,* and his return to Brooklyn evoked that powerful, mythic saga that has been so deeply imprinted in the American consciousness. Yet somehow the most enduring part of his legacy, one that will forever have its place in American history, is virtually unknown today. Through his son Michael, Sonny Franzese supervised a gasoline-tax-evasion scam that turned into a billion-dollar enterprise lasting for six years, until the FBI broke it up in the mideighties. The scandal also had far-reaching geopolitical consequences in that it gave the newly arrived Russian Mafia* its first major score in America and positioned it to play a vital role in Donald Trump's rise to power, such a vital role that it is fair to say that without the Russian Mafia's move into New York, Donald Trump would not have become president of the United States.

Born in Naples in 1917, Sonny Franzese had immigrated to the United States with his family as a child, and in his youth rode shotgun on his father's bakery truck in Brooklyn. As recounted in Michael Franzese's *Blood Covenant,* he began his ascent back when Mafia nightlife meant dining at the Stork Club on West Fifty-Eighth Street in Manhattan, Sherman Billingsley's swanky refuge for café society, where Sonny courted and married the coat-check girl, and spent his evenings hanging out with the likes of Grace Kelly, Marilyn Monroe, Ernest Hemingway, Damon Runyon, and Walter Winchell. Before long, the Franzeses became an integral part of the storied Colombo crime family, the youngest and perhaps the most violent of the Five Families of organized crime,† which were locked in an epic and ongoing internecine war.[12]

---

* The terms "Russian Mafia" and "ROC" (Russian organized crime), though not geographically correct, are widely used by law enforcement authorities to refer to organized crime from all the republics of the former Soviet Union, not just the Russian Federation.

† The Five Families were the Colombos, the Gambinos, the Bonannos, the Luccheses, and the Genoveses.

When it came to bringing in revenue for the Colombo family, Sonny handled bookmaking, loan sharking, prostitution, shakedowns, and tax cheating. A thuggish, bull-necked man known for his boxer's flattened nose—he was said to resemble boxer Rocky Graziano—over time, he became a lean, meticulously groomed don sporting all the requisite sartorial flourishes of his profession—crisp fedora, diamond pinkie ring, pointed black shoes, bespoke suits, and a beautifully tailored overcoat. Meanwhile, he commanded half a dozen lieutenants, each of whom had as many as thirty soldiers in their organizations, and carved out a reputation as a ferocious enforcer. "He swam in the biggest ocean and was the biggest, meanest, most terrifying shark in that ocean," said Phil Steinberg, a close friend of Sonny's who was a major figure in the music industry. "He was an enforcer, and he did what he did better than anyone." As his son Michael put it, Sonny "could paralyze the most fearless hit man with a stare."[13]

Sometimes he went significantly further than that. In 1974, a Colombo soldier who had been a bit too attentive to Sonny's wife was found buried in a cellar with a garrote around his neck. According to *Vanity Fair,* the man's genitals had been stuffed in his mouth, an act that authorities characterized as "an apparent signal of Sonny's displeasure."[14]

As underboss, Sonny was in line to run the entire Colombo organization, and, with Michael under his tutelage, the Franzeses sought opportunities in new sectors of the burgeoning entertainment industry that were opening up to the mob. They financed *Deep Throat,* Linda Lovelace's infamous porno film. They backed Phil Steinberg's Kama Sutra/Buddah Records, which provided opportunities for money laundering and payola—not to mention hits by the Lovin' Spoonful, the Shangri-Las, and Gladys Knight and the Pips, among others.[15]

Before long, Michael had become a Colombo *caporegime* like his father, the youngest person on *Fortune* magazine's "50 Biggest Mafia Bosses" list, and one of the biggest earners in the Mafia since Al Capone.[16] By the early eighties, however, organized crime in New York was undergoing a paradigmatic shift for a reason that was not yet widely known: The Russians were coming. In fact, Russians had begun collaborating with Italian mobsters as early as 1980,[17] when the two crime organizations partnered in one of the most lucrative government rip-offs in American history.

At the time, Michael Franzese, then in his early thirties, was already providing protection to a mobster named Lawrence Iorizzo, who owned or supplied three hundred gas stations in and around Long Island and New Jersey,[18] and was making a fortune by skimming tax revenue from gasoline sales. This scam was possible thanks to the sluggishness with which laggardly government officials collected gas taxes.[19] Together, federal, state, and local authorities demanded on average twenty-seven cents out of every gallon that was sold, but they took their time in collecting—sometimes as much as a year.

Having registered dozens of shell companies in Panama as owners of the gas stations, all Iorizzo had to do was to close down each of his gas stations before the tax man came, and then reopen under new management with a different shell company. By the time the tax men came looking for their money, much of it was in Iorizzo's pocket. When the FBI later investigated the scam, which had spread to six states, they called the investigation Operation Red Daisy.[20]

Iorizzo's scheme was going swimmingly except for one thing: A group of men—Michael Franzese described them as "small-fry associates of another family"—were trying to muscle in on Iorizzo's operation.[21] According to Franzese, the six-foot-four, four-hundred-fifty-pound Iorizzo "ate pizzas the way most people eat Ritz crackers" and didn't exactly look like he needed protection. Nevertheless, he had gone to Franzese for help with these small-time hoods who were trying to shake him down and move in on his territory.

Without missing a beat, Franzese figured out a mutually acceptable solution, and a highly lucrative partnership was born. Soon, so much money was pouring in that Franzese was promoted to *caporegime* in the Cosa Nostra.[22] Then in 1984, three alleged Russian gangsters, David Bogatin, Michael Markowitz, and Lev Persits, approached him with a proposition that was very similar to Iorizzo's. Like Iorizzo, they had their own gas tax scam going on, and like Iorizzo, they needed protection.

Franzese instantly saw the opportunity for another huge score, but he sized up the Russians with a mixture of respect and scorn. Bogatin, with his receding hairline and steel-rimmed glasses, looked more like a white-collar professional than a Russian mobster. His father had spent eighteen years in prison in Siberia because he had been "caught" hanging the key to the office door so that it accidentally covered a portrait of Joseph Stalin—thereby defacing the image of the Soviet dictator.[23] In 1966, Bogatin joined the Soviet Army and served in a North Vietnamese antiaircraft unit, where he helped shoot down American pilots.[24] Then, in the mid-1970s, after leaving the army, he began working as a printer but was fired because he was printing outlawed material for Jewish dissidents.

After being blacklisted by the KGB, in 1977, Bogatin clawed his way out of Russia, came to New York, and worked in a factory. He bought a car, mastered English, and began to run a private cab service. That led to a gas station, then a fuel distributorship,[25] all while he made acquaintances among the Russian diaspora.

Having grown up under communism, Bogatin took to capitalism like a duck to water—which won Franzese's respect. The Russians had been among the pioneers of this spectacularly lucrative scam, and they had about two hundred members working under them.[26] They wanted "to flex their muscles," Franzese said, in testimony before a Senate subcommittee in 1996, "and would not hesitate to resort to violence when they felt it was necessary to do so."

Franzese had a harder time taking Bogatin's partner seriously—thanks largely to his attire. Michael Markowitz wore gaudy jewelry, heavy gold chains, and showy wide-collared shirts unbuttoned to the navel. As Franzese saw it, Markowitz aspired to be John Travolta in *Saturday Night Fever,* but instead called to mind the shimmying "wild and crazy guys" played by Steve Martin and Dan Aykroyd on *Saturday Night Live* in the seventies. The dapper Franzese couldn't stop laughing at him. Markowitz "looked like a rug salesman who had just hit the lottery."[27] Was this really his competition?

In the end, however, money trumped fashion, and so, on a Saturday morning in the fall of 1980, Michael Franzese[28] sat down with Bogatin,

Persits, and Markowitz at a gas station in Brooklyn. "These Russians*
were having trouble collecting money owed them," Franzese recalled.[29]
"They were also having problems obtaining and holding on to the licenses they needed to keep the gas tax scam going."

Franzese could help on both counts. One of his soldiers was a guy
named Vinnie, and as Franzese put it, "Vinnie's job was to say, 'Pay the
money, or I'll break your legs.'"[30]

Vinnie was persuasive—so persuasive that the Colombo family had
become famous for getting people to pay their debts. That wasn't all.
Franzese also had operatives inside the state government who could
provide the Russians with the wholesale licenses they needed to defraud
the government.

The Russians desperately needed Franzese, and he knew just how to
play them. "We agreed to share the illegal proceeds, 75 percent my end,
25 percent their end," he said.[31] "The deal was put on record with all five
crime families, and I took care of the Colombo family share of the illegal proceeds out of my end."

Soon, the money came pouring in—$5 million to more than $8 million a week. As the operation expanded, profits soared to $100 million a
month, more than a billion a year. The Italians were the big winners, but
Markowitz and Bogatin were well on their way to lucrative criminal
careers.

Thus, in 1984, at the peak of his success, David Bogatin went shopping for apartments in New York City. Even though he was a junior
partner with Franzese, after seven years in New York, Bogatin had
stashed away enough money to buy real estate anywhere he wanted. For
roughly a decade, thousands of Russian Jews like him had been pouring
into Brighton Beach, Brooklyn. But Bogatin had his eyes on something
more prestigious.

So instead of shopping for a home in Brighton Beach, Bogatin became fixated on a garish fifty-eight-story edifice in midtown Manhattan
with mirrors and brass and gold-plated fixtures everywhere. A

---

* Though he worked with Russian gangsters and was often identified as Russian, Markowitz
was actually Romanian.

monument to conspicuous consumption, it had an atrium covered with pink, white-veined marble near the entrance and a sixty-foot waterfall overlooking a suspended walkway, luxury shops, and cafés. The *AIA Guide to New York City* described it as "fantasyland for the affluent shopper," but hastened to add that the design was more like a generic "malt liquor" than posh champagne.[32]

The *New York Times* architecture critic Ada Louise Huxtable called it "monumentally undistinguished," while another *Times* writer dismissed it as "preposterously lavish" and "showy, even pretentious."[33] The developer's love of excess was such that he purposely overstated the number of floors in the building. That way, he could say he lived on the sixty-eighth floor—even though it was a fifty-eight-story building. Its address was 721 Fifth Avenue, and it was known as Trump Tower.

CHAPTER TWO

TRUMP'S BEAUTIFUL LAUNDRETTE

According to the late Wayne Barrett, who investigated the Bogatin deal for the *Village Voice*, Donald Trump himself took the unusual step of personally meeting with David Bogatin when the transaction took place. Apparently, Trump found nothing untoward in the fact that Bogatin was buying not one but *five* luxury condos in Trump Tower for a total of $6 million (the equivalent of approximately $14.5 million in 2018),[1] even though it was unlikely he had a legitimate way to get his hands on that much cash and had arrived in America with just $3 in his pockets.[2]

There was also one more element in the deal that was highly irregular. The extraordinary hype enveloping the building's glamour overshadowed the fact that Trump Tower offered a special feature that was exceedingly rare. At the time, according to author David Cay Johnston, Trump Tower was one of only two buildings[3] in New York City that sold condos to buyers who used shell companies, such as limited liability companies, which allowed purchasers to buy real estate while concealing their identities.

"If you are doing a transaction with no mortgage, there is no financial institution that needs to know where the money came from, particularly if it's a wire transfer from overseas," said Jonathan Winer, who served as deputy assistant secretary of state for international law enforcement in the Clinton administration.[4] "The customer obligations that are imposed on all kinds of financial institutions are not imposed on people selling real estate. They should have been, but they weren't."

So, thanks to these lax regulations, Trump began to sell condos in Trump Tower as an ideal vehicle through which criminals could put their dirty money into luxury condominiums while keeping their ownership anonymous. Thus, according to the New York State attorney general's office, when Trump closed the deal for five apartments with David Bogatin, whether he knew it or not, he had just helped launder money for the Russian Mafia.[5]

All of this was happening at an extraordinary time. It was 1984. After nearly forty years, the balance of power in the Cold War had tilted decisively toward the West. The USSR was still embroiled in a costly, bloody, and unproductive war in Afghanistan, the "Soviet Vietnam," as it had been since 1979, leaving the Soviet economy in tatters. President Ronald Reagan had aggressively ramped up the arms race with "Star Wars," the Strategic Defense Initiative, which was intended to shield the US against incoming missiles and succeeded in making the cost of being a superpower prohibitively expensive.

Some people in the KGB were beginning to realize that the Soviet Union's economy was doomed.[6] Finally, with the deaths of Soviet leaders Leonid Brezhnev in 1982 and Yuri Andropov in 1984, and the ascent of aging and ailing Konstantin Chernenko to the top spot in the Soviet leadership, the old party structures were failing.

All of which created a gigantic power vacuum for the Russian Mafia to fill at a time when it had grown to roughly nine thousand criminal gangs with thirty-five thousand members,[7] many of whom, likely including Bogatin, were looking to transfer illicit funds into safe havens in the West.

Two powerful forces in a newly created global underground economy had begun to come together. On the one hand, the disintegration of the Soviet Union had opened a fire-hose-like torrent of hundreds of billions of dollars in flight capital that began to pour forth from oligarchs, wealthy apparatchiks, and mobsters in Russia and its satellites. On the other hand, Donald Trump's zeal to sell condos, no questions asked, to shell companies meant that Russians could launder vast amounts of money while hiding their personal identities. Over the next thirty years, dozens of lawyers, accountants, real estate agents, mortgage brokers, and other white-collar professionals came together to facilitate such transactions on a massive scale.

As the *Financial Times* notes, the fact that the US and the UK, unlike most Western democracies, permit anonymous ownership of real estate facilitates money laundering of roughly $300 billion per year in the United States alone, most of it from Russia.[8] As a result, luxury real estate has provided a haven for Russian oligarchs and their kleptocratic president, Vladimir Putin, son of a factory worker and Russian seaman, to stash billions of dollars.

All-cash purchases through shell companies are not in and of themselves illegal or improper, and they have become more common in recent years in luxury home sales all over the world. Nor are sellers under any obligation to question where a buyer's money comes from. However, Trump in effect had taken advantage of these weak regulations to sell en masse to the Russians.

Because it is so difficult to penetrate the shell companies that purchased these condos, it is almost impossible for reporters—or, for that matter, *anyone* without subpoena power—to ascertain the scale at which such laundering may have taken place in Trump-branded properties. Nevertheless, according to a BuzzFeed investigation by Thomas Frank, more than 1,300 condos, one-fifth of all Trump-branded condos sold in the US since the eighties, were sold "in secretive, all-cash transactions that enable buyers to avoid legal scrutiny by shielding their finances and identities."[9]

The BuzzFeed article added that the total value of these condo sales—sales that match the US Treasury's criteria for possible money laundering—was about $1.5 billion, a figure that actually may understate the amount of dirty money in play. The article did not include Trump's many buildings outside the United States, such as Trump-branded highrises in Canada, the Philippines, Panama, Uruguay, Turkey, India, South Korea, and other countries where President Trump often licenses his name and collects royalties.

As a teenager, Donald Trump had helped out in Trump Village, a Brighton Beach–adjacent development in Coney Island his father had built (in fact, the only Trump real estate development named after Fred Trump rather than Donald), by collecting money from the washing machines in the shared laundry used by Russian émigrés and the like—in the form of nickels, dimes, and quarters. Now he was participating in a very different kind of laundering operation—and this time the scale of the money was monumental.

David Bogatin fled the United States in 1987 to avoid prosecution for his gas tax scam, and was extradited from Poland five years later.[10] When he returned, he was imprisoned for the scam, but it remains unclear whether or not Trump knew about the illicit source of Bogatin's money.

Still, over the next four decades similar transactions took place in Trump Tower and other Trump-branded buildings so frequently that it's hard to imagine Donald Trump had no knowledge whatsoever about what was going on. Bogatin may have been the first Russian to use Trump condos to launder money, but other criminals with ties to the Italian mob had already done the same. Indeed, Lucchese crime family associate Robert Hopkins, who ran one of New York's biggest illegal gambling operations, bought his Trump Tower apartments in 1981—two years before the building opened. When he met Trump at the closing, he opened his briefcase and approximately $200,000 in cash spilled out on Trump's conference table. Similarly, soon after Trump Tower opened in 1983, Italian financier Roberto Polo, who was subsequently jailed for embezzlement, bought six Trump Tower apartments in the names of offshore shell companies.[11] And Jean-Claude "Baby Doc" Duvalier, the brutal and corrupt former leader of Haiti, bought an apartment on the fifty-fourth floor in August of 1983.[12]

Still, Bogatin's purchase of five apartments in Trump Tower was unique in that it did nothing less than link the future president of the United States to murderous Russian mafiosi and their subculture of drugs, money laundering, extortion rackets, prostitution, and more.

Even more important, the transaction may have represented an initial contact from Soviet intelligence to see if Trump was a potential Soviet "asset," or agent of influence. Within the world of intelligence, assets are persons within countries being spied upon who provide intelligence to a foreign power. Different categories of assets include those who elect to work for a foreign government because they prefer its ideology, those who betray their country for monetary gain, those who are being black-mailed, and so-called useful idiots who don't even know they are being used, but who still provide valuable information through security lapses or blind pursuit of their own agendas.

When he was asked about the Bogatin-Trump transaction, Oleg Kalugin, the former head of counterintelligence for the KGB, said he was "not surprised. That's typical."

"Normally, the procedures of major intelligence and secret police organizations are intended to collect sufficient information to see if the guy will collaborate," he added.[13] "If he is willing to collaborate, he may be useful."

At the time, the KGB was deeply concerned about its failure to re-cruit more American assets and had issued instructions to agents abroad to find US targets to cultivate.[14] In Trump, the Soviets had discovered a man who was so intoxicated by a huge new clientele with boatloads of cash that he engaged in dubious transactions without asking questions. Doing business with Trump allowed the Russian Mafia to secure a sig-nificant new foothold in the United States and begin an offensive that continues to assault America's most essential democratic institutions to this day. Moreover, as early as 1984, the Russians had discovered that as long as they had money, Donald Trump was listening.

All of which made Trump, initially at least, a tiny part of an historic conflict that began as blowback from the end of the Cold War. For Vla-dimir Putin, the demise of the Soviet Union had been "the greatest geo-political catastrophe of the century."[15] But even that was exacerbated by what came next: One by one, no fewer than thirteen Eastern Bloc na-tions joined NATO.*

---

* In 1999, Poland, Hungary, and the Czech Republic joined NATO, followed by Bulgaria, Estonia, Latvia, Lithuania, Romania, Slovakia, and Slovenia shortly before the 2004 Istan-bul summit. They were subsequently joined by Albania, Croatia, and, most recently, Mon-tenegro. And that does not count East Germany, which, of course, became part of NATO when it reunited with West Germany.

Putin, however, drew a line in the sand with regard to Ukraine. After the Euromaidan protests against Russian aggression began in Ukraine in 2013, Russia launched a massive global offensive in which its strategic goals were to weaken not only the United States but Britain, NATO, the European Union, and, indeed, the entire Western Alliance.

The battle was against not just the United States but the West itself, as Russia repeatedly interceded in domestic politics in the United Kingdom, where it fueled the successful Brexit campaign, in which UK citizens voted to leave the European Union; in the Netherlands, where it backed Geert Wilders; in France, where it supported Marine Le Pen; in Ukraine, where it backed Viktor Yanukovych and other pro-Putin forces; and in Hungary, Poland, and elsewhere in Eastern Europe as well.

The most striking fact of this massive new global conflict, however, may have been that barely anyone noticed that it was taking place. It was extraordinary. War is generally defined as *armed* conflict. However, Vladimir Putin had attacked the sovereignty of America and other Western nations—a Virtual World War III, if you like—but almost no one reported on it in the newspapers, on TV, on the radio, or on the Internet. That's because this was a war by other means, a war that eschewed the bombs, bullets, and boots on the ground of conventional warfare, and instead relied on a new, sophisticated, asymmetric, hybrid form of "nonlinear" warfare.

Only on rare occasions did Russia resort to old-fashioned military intervention, as it did in 2014 when Russian troops were a prelude to the annexation of the Crimea during the Ukraine crisis. Instead, Putin waged a shadow war, or "virtual" war, consisting of covert operations, disinformation, and cyber warfare. It was a war in which Russia hacked its adversaries; used third parties, such as Julian Assange and WikiLeaks, to make it seem as if leaks had emanated from heroic, highly principled whistleblowers, rather than Russian intelligence; hijacked social media and exploited algorithms to make highly provocative "fake news" go viral; transformed Facebook into one of the biggest purveyors of Russian propaganda on the planet; deliberately used not only "alternative facts" and fake news but bogus websites that pretended to *correct* fake news, and, in the process, upended the very notion of truth, of reality itself, of what is real.

Of course, all of this did not go entirely unnoticed. But in Russia, investigative journalists, rogue intelligence agents, and opposition politicians who revealed the truth inevitably faced brutal reprisals. In 2000, Paul Klebnikov published *Godfather of the Kremlin: The Decline of Russia in the Age of Gangster Capitalism,* in which he compared Russian oligarch Boris Berezovsky to a Sicilian mafioso. Four years later, having just become the editor of *Forbes*'s Russian edition, Klebnikov published a list of the one hundred richest Russians, and was shot and killed by unknown assailants.[16]

Similarly, Russian journalist Anna Politkovskaya; Alexander Litvinenko, a former officer of the Russian Federal Security Service (FSB) and KGB who had blamed Putin for ordering Politkovskaya's assassination; and Sergei Magnitsky, a Russian lawyer and auditor representing Bill Browder's Hermitage Capital Management, are just a few* of the scores of people who died mysteriously after investigating the alleged crimes of Putin and his oligarchs.[17]

As a key component of this battle, Vladimir Putin used a secret weapon that few Americans understood. While the Italian Mafia in the US exists largely to serve its own interests, in Russia things were different. Where Americans cracked down on organized crime, Putin co-opted it. He weaponized it. Russian gangsters became, in effect, Putin's enforcers. This is not merely a metaphor. As Oleg Kalugin, former head of counterintelligence for the KGB, told me, in effect, "the Mafia is one of the branches of the Russian government today."[18]

All of which means that, since coming to power first as prime minister in 1999 and then as president in 2000, Putin's greatest triumph is his extraordinary command over a Mafia state, a political system that is effectively a government of, by, and for organized crime. As author

---

* According to the Committee to Protect Journalists, at least fifty-eight journalists have been murdered in Russia since the demise of the Soviet Union in 1991. The figure goes up to eighty-two deaths if one includes those for which a motive has not been confirmed. These figures do not include the murders of Alexander Litvinenko or other people who were killed outside Russia and who, also like Litvinenko, were investigating corruption in Russia outside the context of journalism.

Karen Dawisha explains in *Putin's Kleptocracy,* the Mafia had come to-gether with former KGB officials and the political and economic elites, combining their money and power to forge the basis for Putin's author-itarian kleptocracy,[19] a kleptocracy that ushered in an era of global theft on an unimaginable level and has reportedly made Vladimir Putin the richest man in the world, with wealth, according to Hermitage Capital Management CEO Bill Browder, approaching $200 billion.[20]

As a result of this unfathomable greed, untold billions that ordinar-ily would have been spent on education, transportation, health care, and other services in Russia and its trading partners have been stashed in offshore bank accounts, hedge funds, and luxury condos for Putin and his cronies who were allowed to make billions through drug trafficking, extortion, elaborate financial schemes, the sex trade, arms deals, and the like on just one fundamental condition: they work within Putin's rules to further his strategic goals. They were then free to compromise persons of influence in the West via various forms of *kompromat* that documented money laundering, illicit sexual trysts, and other potential scandals—provided that they serve his political agenda, that they act as intelligence operatives, that they recruit assets, that they collect intelligence on per-sons of interest. In effect, they became geopolitical weapons against the West.

Putin's ascent is best described not by old-school Kremlinologists but, as former world chess champion Garry Kasparov explains in *Win-ter Is Coming,* "by the achievements of Don Vito Corleone: the web of betrayals, the secrecy, and the blurred lines between what is business, what is government, and what is criminal—it's all there in [Mario] Pu-zo's books . . . a strict hierarchy, extortion, intimidation, a tough-guy image, a long string of convenient deaths among leading critics, elimi-nating traitors, the code of secrecy and loyalty, and, above all, a mandate to keep the revenue flowing."[21]

In other words, it was a Mafia—which was something Donald Trump knew a lot about.

CHAPTER THREE

MARRIED TO THE MOB

Donald Trump was no virgin when it came to organized crime. In fact, the Trump family had a taste for it dating back three generations.*

It began at the tail end of the nineteenth century when a rogue entrepreneur who happened to become Donald Trump's grandfather headed out for Canada's Yukon Territory during the Klondike Gold Rush and sought to make his fortune not by panning for gold, but by providing essential services for gold miners.[1] According to author Gwenda Blair, among the various enterprises owned by Frederick, né Friedrich, Trump, was a restaurant sometimes called the Dairy Restaurant and sometimes called the Poodle Dog, which advertised "Private Rooms for Ladies"—a polite euphemism for prostitution.[2]

A generation later, Fred Trump, the son of Frederick, and Donald's father, started out building single-family houses in Queens[3] and then became wealthy thanks to windfall profits from building government-backed housing in Brooklyn and Queens.[4]

Fred's influence was particularly conspicuous in the Brooklyn

---

* Among the biographers who have explored Trump's ties to organized crime are Gwenda Blair, author of *The Trumps: Three Generations of Builders and a Presidential Candidate*; Wayne Barrett, author of *Trump: The Greatest Show on Earth*; David Cay Johnston, author of *The Making of Donald Trump*; Michael Kranish and Marc Fisher, authors of *Trump Revealed: The Definitive Biography of the 45th President*; and Tim O'Brien, author of *Trump Nation: The Art of Being the Donald*.

neighborhoods of Brighton Beach and Coney Island. Brighton Beach had a marvelous sandy coast looking out on the Atlantic and the adjacent Coney Island amusement park, all just ten miles from Manhattan—everything one could ask for in a delightful seaside resort. Unfortunately, it had become scarred by the egregious urban renewal policies of New York "master builder" Robert Moses, which transformed parts of the healthy middle-class neighborhood into a festering slum.[5]

Much of this decline came from Fred Trump's projects in the area, which were tainted by scandal, misappropriation of funds, and cronyism in one form or another. New developments often led to federal hearings and investigations into Trump's business practices, allegations that Trump defrauded veterans in rental agreements, and allegations of racism. According to Coney Island historian Charles Denson, Fred Trump was so shrewd at exploiting the weak spots in federal regulations that "federal laws had to be changed to prevent the kind of nefarious schemes that Trump excelled in."[6]

Fred usually got his way, but when he didn't, there was hell to pay. After being denied a zoning change in his effort to build Miami Beach–style high-rises at Coney Island's famed Steeplechase Park, Donald's father was so frustrated that he threw a party at the site and invited guests to vandalize the stained glass façade of the Pavilion, knocking out the teeth of the enormous Steeplechase funny face, a local landmark. "This sad event was a vindictive and shameful act by a grown man behaving like a juvenile delinquent. It wasn't business—it was personal," wrote Denson, asserting that it revealed "a twisted personality that was unusual for even the most hard-bitten developers."[7]

Fred's projects often involved people tied to the mob, and he dealt with them with the help of Brad Zackson, a convicted felon who had spent nearly five years in jail after taking a plea to dodge an attempted murder charge,[8] and who served as Fred's consigliere[9] and the exclusive broker[10] for all his properties. (Zackson later worked with Donald Trump campaign manager Paul Manafort as Manafort's "real estate fixer," as the *Real Deal* put it, "a Fred Trump protégé with a checkered past and an appetite for fanciful deals.")[11]

According to the New York State Organized Crime Task Force's investigations in the fifties, a complicated web of relationships tied Fred's partner Willie Tomasello to both the Gambino and Genovese[12] crime families, as well as to Lucky Luciano, a father of modern organized crime in America.[13] In addition, when it came to getting crucial favors from city hall insiders, such as zoning approvals, Fred relied on Kenny Sutherland, an ally of the Lucchese family, which had become enormously powerful in city and state politics.[14]

Meanwhile, even in high school at New York Military Academy, Donald was so obsessed with money that he bragged about his father's wealth—he pegged it at $30 million—and boasted that it doubled every year.[15] "He was already focused on the future, thinking long-term more than present," said his roommate David Smith. "He used to talk about his dad's business, how he would use him as a role model but go one step further."

In his spare time, Donald worked enough with his father to learn the real estate game, running errands, hosing down construction sites, and collecting those coins from the laundry rooms at the seven high-rises his father called Trump Village.[16]

In the end, however, Donald saw his father's vision as severely limited by the humble outer boroughs of New York and desperately wanted to take things further. "I want to be in mid-Manhattan, where all the top stuff is going on," he said early on in his career. "I'll never be involved with the old man's property except when he needs me."[17]

Determined to leave behind the more modest world of Brooklyn and Queens, in the midseventies, Donald, then still in his twenties, reached across the East River for the brass ring—Manhattan.

By that time, however, New York City had hit rock bottom. Manufacturing had fled the city. Crime was soaring. By the spring of 1975, the city had an operating deficit of at least $750 million[18] and a debt level of more than $11 billion, and its credit had been exhausted. In October 1975, President Gerald Ford declared he would veto any bill that called for a federal bailout to save New York from bankruptcy. An unforgettable and iconic headline in the New York *Daily News* put it succinctly: "Ford to City: Drop Dead."

For Donald Trump, the fact that the entire city was on the verge of bankruptcy was good news indeed, because prices could not go much lower. For his option to buy the dilapidated, rat-infested Commodore Hotel on East Forty-Second Street, Trump paid exactly $1.[19] Decrepit though it was, the Commodore had two things going for it: First, it was adjacent to Grand Central Terminal, a spectacular location—if the city came back to life. And second, because the property was so big, the upside was potentially colossal in a city valued by the square foot. It was the opportunity of a lifetime.

Helping Trump navigate the perilous waters necessary to get the political support and legal tax abatements to consummate the deal was none other than Roy Cohn, Trump's mentor and role model, the ruthless, heavy-lidded attorney who served as a brutal and pitiless fixer for establishment fixtures (Richard Nixon, Ronald Reagan, and Rupert Murdoch, among others) and mobsters alike (Anthony "Fat Tony" Salerno, Carmine Galante, and John Gotti).

An iconic figure who truly embodied the dark side of his era, Cohn has been dead for more than three decades but still casts a long shadow over American politics. Cohn won notoriety as the hatchet man for Senator Joe McCarthy, the red-baiting demagogue of the fifties, leading McCarthy's aggressive, prosecutorial witch hunt against alleged communists. One of his most infamous Red Scare triumphs took place during the trial of Julius and Ethel Rosenberg, who were convicted of espionage in 1951. Cohn's great feat was to succeed in bullying David Greenglass to testify against his sister, Ethel Rosenberg. Later, Greenglass admitted he had lied on the stand, at Cohn's insistence, when he testified that his sister typed notes that were sent to the Soviets. As a result of his testimony, Ethel was executed in the electric chair.[20]

One of several cases that led to Cohn's eventual disbarment had him entering the room of a dying multimillionaire client, Lewis Rosenstiel, misrepresenting a document that would have made Cohn executor of his will and emerging with a shakily signed signature that the courts refused to accept.[21]

By the 1970s, Cohn became one of many celebrities hanging out at Studio 54, the epochal New York disco, with Andy Warhol, Bianca Jagger, Liza Minnelli, and the club's owners, Steve Rubell and Ian Schrager.

There, Cohn became known as "the most evil, twisted, vicious bastard ever to snort coke at Studio 54," as described by a character in Tony Kushner's *Angels in America*.[22]

Kushner's play, of course, was fiction, but Cohn was described similarly by those who knew him in real life. "You knew when you were in Cohn's presence you were in the presence of pure evil," lawyer Victor A. Kovner told *Vanity Fair*.[23]

"He was a tangle of contradictions, a Jewish anti-Semite and a homosexual homophobe, vehemently closeted but insatiably promiscuous," wrote Michael Kruse in Politico.[24]

Donald Trump had met Cohn at another Manhattan nightspot, Le Club, a pre–disco era successor to café society haunts like El Morocco and the Stork Club, where the fixers and society swells had drinks and traded favors. Trump was instantly captivated by Cohn's combative, belligerent style and later allowed it to shape his approach to politics. Meanwhile, Cohn helped the Trumps battle a 1973 lawsuit by the Civil Rights Division of the Justice Department alleging that Trump rental properties refused to rent to minority applicants.[25] Cohn advised Donald to tell the government "to go to hell and fight the thing in court."[26]

Which is precisely what Trump did, with Cohn as his lead attorney, suing the United States government for $100 million (roughly $575 million in 2018 dollars) on behalf of Trump Management, asserting that the charges were "irresponsible and baseless."[27] In effect, Donald had adopted Roy Cohn's credo as his own: Always attack. Never apologize. Attack, attack, attack.

As Marie Brenner noted in *Vanity Fair,* by the time he became Trump's lawyer, Cohn had carved out a unique place for himself with his unparalleled mastery of New York's "Favor Bank," that invisible network of tacit understandings through which cops, lawyers, judges, *machers,* influence peddlers, and crooks make the world go round.[28]

Cohn was so adept that Trump sometimes phoned him fifteen or twenty times a day, calling upon his magical ability to win an inside fix on generous but dubious tax abatements, zoning variances, contract disputes, and the like. He had become "a walking advertisement for every form of graft, the best-known fixer in New York," Wayne Barrett wrote.[29]

Years later, in moments of crisis long after Cohn's death, President Donald Trump was known to shout out to the world, "Where's my Roy Cohn?"*[30]

As the Commodore project took shape, Cohn, as consigliere for the two biggest crime families in New York, the Genoveses and the Gambinos,[31] was invaluable in helping Trump traverse otherwise choppy waters with concrete contractors, demolition companies, and the like that were often controlled by the mob.

At the time, most developers who used ready-mix concrete were vulnerable to work stoppages by the Teamsters, construction unions, and mobsters who controlled the unions. But when it came to breaking ground on Trump Tower in 1979, Trump bought his Manhattan ready-mix from a mobbed-up company called S & A Concrete that was secretly owned by Mafia chieftains Anthony "Fat Tony" Salerno, of the Genovese crime family, and Gambino boss Paul Castellano, both of whom were regular visitors to Roy Cohn's East Side town house.[32] According to Wayne Barrett, Cohn may even have arranged a meeting in the living room of his town house between Trump and Salerno.[33]

For carpentry, Trump used a company that also was controlled by the Genoveses.[34] In those days, working with mob contractors wasn't particularly unusual for New York developers because the Five Families controlled both the major construction firms and the unions representing their workers.[35] But thanks to Roy Cohn, who represented both Salerno and Castellano, Trump never had to worry about work stoppages orchestrated by the Mafia to extort more cash.[36] That was just one part of the beauty of being connected.

In the end, Roy Cohn helped Trump save $120 million through tax abatements from the city,[37] which enabled Trump and his partners, the Pritzker family's Hyatt Corporation, to renovate the Commodore for

---

* Notwithstanding Trump's fondness for Cohn, their relationship did not end well. Toward the end of his life, Cohn, who was gay, asked Trump for a favor: His lover was dying of AIDS. Could Trump get him a hotel room? As *Vanity Fair* reported, a room was found, but a few months later, Cohn got the bill and refused to pay. More bills followed. At some point, according to the *New York Times*, Trump presented Cohn with a pair of diamond cuff links as a thank-you gift for their friendship. But the diamonds turned out to be fakes. Toward his last days in 1986, the dying Cohn said, "Donald pisses ice water."

$100 million, put a façade of mirrored glass on its skeleton, and transform it into the 1,407-room Grand Hyatt. In 1996, twenty years after he optioned it for $1, Trump sold his share for $140 million.[38]

Cohn died in 1986, and whether or not he was the genius who orchestrated the use of anonymous shell companies to launder money through real estate is unclear. At the time Trump Tower was being planned, though, Cohn was in fact Trump's lawyer and represented Robert Hopkins,[39] the Lucchese crime family associate who Cohn had recruited[40] to pay almost $2 million to buy two units in the still-unfinished building as a way of establishing a high market value. Finally, Cohn clearly did have experience with creative accounting: He represented Studio 54 owners Ian Schrager and Steve Rubell when they were accused of skimming nearly $2.5 million in unreported income. In the end, they pleaded guilty, only admitting to skimming $366,000, and went to jail.*

As for how he felt about Cohn's mob connections, in *The Art of the Deal*, Trump wrote, "I don't kid myself about Roy. He was no Boy Scout. He once told me that he'd spent more than two-thirds of his adult life under indictment on one charge or another. That amazed me. I said to him, 'Roy, just tell me one thing. Did you really do all that stuff?' He looked at me and smiled. 'What the hell do you think?' he said."[41]

In the end, Trump said he never really knew what the answer was. Besides, all that actually mattered was that Trump's first deal in Manhattan had been a success, no matter what it took.

---

* Cohn's bark was ferocious, but it was often far worse than his bite. As a senior editor of *New York* magazine in 1979, I had a run-in with Roy Cohn over a story written by Henry Post that exposed the Studio 54 tax evasion scam. Before publication, Cohn called me, yelled at me, and threatened to sue the magazine unless we killed the story. In the end, we ran the story, Cohn's clients went to jail, and he never sued.

CHAPTER FOUR

BRIGHTON BEACH

At the same time Trump was learning about wiseguys from Roy Cohn, the Russian Mafia began invading Brighton Beach. It had started as an unintended consequence of legislation dealing with the Cold War. In 1974, Senator Henry M. "Scoop" Jackson of Washington and Representative Charles A. Vanik of Ohio, two Democrats who were concerned about Soviet anti-Semitism, had passed a bill that allowed the Soviet Union to enjoy normal trade relations with the US, but only if it let Jewish refugees immigrate to America.

In the aftermath of the Jackson-Vanik Amendment, more than six hundred thousand Soviet Jews emigrated from the USSR, but the KGB made certain that emigration was not limited to innocent victims of anti-Semitism. Instead, the Soviets opened the gates of their gulags, just like Fidel Castro did later, during the Mariel boatlift of 1980, and released thousands of hard-core criminals, among them convicted murderers, psychopaths, thieves, and the like, many of whom settled in Brighton Beach.[1]

A Yiddish-inflected world that was sentimentalized and satirized in Neil Simon plays and Woody Allen movies, Brighton Beach had long been a place where people strolled the boardwalk, scarfed down hot dogs at Nathan's Famous, rode the famed Cyclone roller coaster, and enjoyed other rides at Luna Park, Steeplechase Park, and Dreamland, in nearby Coney Island.

Even before the Russians arrived, however, the neighborhood had been in a steep decline. Heavy manufacturing had abandoned Brooklyn en masse. With the huge loss of jobs, more than three hundred thousand middle-class people had already fled the borough.[2] Now, with the wave of émigrés, there were new meat markets, vegetable pushcarts, Russian bakeries, and specialty stores selling knishes, blintzes, herring, and borscht. Russian restaurants proliferated, their menus written only in Cyrillic.[3] Storefronts under the elevated train on Brighton Beach Avenue offered marriage brokerages, immigration assistance, and other services to a largely Russian clientele.

There were late evenings that went on into the early morning hours at vast, gaudy supper club/cabarets like the Odessa and the National and, later, Café Tatiana and Rasputin, featuring loud, festive nine-course dinners with massive amounts of borscht, sturgeon, sable, beef Stroganoff, and iced bottles of Stolichnaya. There were dancing and garish, over-the-top Vegas-style floor shows, replete with gold lamé gowns and sequins, sequins, sequins. For music, there was a mix of techno, disco, and Russian songs, including those by the renowned Iosif Kobzon, aka the Russian Sinatra, who happened to be notorious because of his Mafia ties. If you were lucky, he'd be there live, in person, crooning "Strangers in the Night."

In some quarters, Brighton Beach became known as Little Odessa, after the Ukrainian city on the Black Sea. And criminals were not the only dubious characters among the new émigrés. There were also spies. According to Oleg Kalugin, the former head of counterintelligence for the KGB, at least two hundred Jews from Leningrad (now St. Petersburg) alone went to the US, and many of them promised to report back to the KGB once they were settled. The KGB's goal was to place them in sensitive positions in the American government or the military-industrial complex.[4]

Once these agents were installed, many of them, including Kalugin himself, began to recruit more spies for the Soviets. "Brighton Beach was one of the places I would look for potential sources of information," Kalugin told me.[5] "I had one guy who I used to meet late at night at Rasputin. That's where I used to go. I would look around, pick up some people, and check their backgrounds with Moscow to see if they were good enough that I should promote a relationship with them."

Even though Brighton Beach was Fred Trump's territory, Donald began developing his own contacts among the new Russian émigrés, including a man named Semyon Kislin. When it came to equipping his newly renovated Grand Hyatt Hotel, née the Commodore, with TV sets in the late seventies, Trump reached out to Kislin to buy a few hundred on credit. "I gave him [Trump] 30 days, and in exactly 30 days he paid me back," said Kislin.*[6]

For Trump, it was the beginning of a long association, and the first of many relationships to people who were close to Russian mafiosi.[7] Kislin and his partner, Temur Sepiashvili, aka Tamir Sapir,[8] both of whom had mob connections, started an electronics store that was well-known among Soviet citizens[9] in the United States and, according to the *New York Times*, became a wholesale outlet from which Soviet diplomats, KGB agents, and Politburo members bought their electronic equipment.[10]

Another émigré of note was Michael Sheferovsky (aka Michael Sheferofsky and Mikhail Sater), who had been a major player in the black market with the mob in Moscow until he moved to Baltimore with his family in the early seventies. In 1977, he moved to Brighton Beach with his wife and kids, and worked with Ernest "Butch" Montevecchi, a soldier in the Genovese crime gang,[11] which had begun to forge a partnership with the newly arrived Russians. Sheferovsky's specialty was extortion: his targets included restaurants, food stores, and a medical clinic in Brighton Beach.[12]

Sheferovsky had a son, Felix (who changed his last name to Sater), who went into the family business but had grand dreams for the future that led to a working relationship more than two decades later with Fred's son Donald that was full of intrigue.

In addition, petitioners in a court case regarding Felix referred to Sheferovsky as "a Mogilevich crime syndicate boss."[13] That last

---

* The FBI investigated Kislin in the 1990s for allegations including mob ties and laundering money from Russia. He was never charged, and he maintains his innocence.

name—Mogilevich—may be unfamiliar to many readers, as it is to the vast majority of Americans. For crime buffs, however, the name is all too recognizable as a reference to Semion Mogilevich, "the boss of bosses" of the Russian Mafia, as the FBI has called him, a man who graced the FBI's "Ten Most Wanted" list for many years—and a man who surreptitiously played an extraordinarily powerful role in the ascent of Donald Trump.

———

To the ordinary working people of Brighton Beach, there were plenty of signs that the new arrivals were not always on the right side of the law. On the back streets of adjacent Manhattan Beach, it was not unusual to see two adjoining houses knocked down and replaced by a multimillion-dollar McMansion replete with elaborate landscaping, marble finishes, and extravagant furniture. Older people on food stamps and social security had to make way for rich young Russians driving Lexuses, BMWs, even Rolls-Royces, loaded with suitcases full of money.

More ominously, many of the new Russians sported foreboding gulag tattoos. Forged passports, social security cards, or driver's licenses could be had easily—for a price. Taxi drivers and émigrés in other modestly paid fields suddenly emerged as billionaires, with no real explanation. Rasputin, the gaudy restaurant/nightclub on Coney Island Avenue, boasted an amenity that was certain to raise questions about security with even the most hardened Manhattan restaurant patron—toilet stalls with bulletproof doors.[14] Before long, virtually every business in Brighton Beach was either connected to the mob or had to weigh carefully the danger of not paying them off.

One of the first journalists to penetrate this new outlaw subculture was Robert I. Friedman, who chronicled the lurid Brighton Beach underworld of tattooed gangsters engaged in money laundering, extortion, prostitution, drugs, and murder as it evolved into a multibillion-dollar international criminal enterprise. Today, for reasons he could not possibly have predicted, the world portrayed in his book *Red Mafiya* has more resonance than ever because it presents a richly textured picture of the Russian mobsters—money launderers, con men, extortionists, and murderers—who initiated ties to Donald J. Trump.

The Russian Mafia's exotic and colorful history dates back more than three hundred years to the time of the tsars, when Russia's toughest hard-core criminals first banded together[15] through imperial Russia's vast network of gulags* and gave birth to a special breed of elite criminal known as *vory v zakone,* which is variously translated as "thieves professing the code" or the more widely used "thieves-in-law."[†]

Though sometimes compared to the "made men" or "godfathers" of the Italian Mafia, the *vory* are a uniquely Russian product of Soviet[16] reality. They grew out of the Stalinist era, when the gulags were flooded with political prisoners and criminals, giving birth to a clandestine subculture, with its own code of ethics and hierarchy, that ruled the criminal underworld within the prison camps and governed the darkest sectors of Soviet life beyond the reach of the KGB.[17]

The *vory* were governed by a strict code that forbade working a legitimate job, paying taxes, fighting in the army, cooperating with authorities, or participating in officially sanctioned political activities.[18] A criminal caste that swore allegiance to its own brand of criminal ideals, the *vory* subsisted on petty theft and black-market profiteering when not in jail. They developed their own secret language that officials were unable to figure out, their own slang, their own nicknames. They set up a communal fund, called *"obschak,"* to bribe authorities, finance criminal business enterprises, and help fellow criminals.

The story of their lives was written on their bodies in tattoos. This was a subculture that fetishized brutality and it was spelled out through images that signified the exploits, rank, occupation, and status of the bearer. A giant eagle with huge, menacing talons tattooed on someone's chest proclaimed his status as *vor.* Stars tattooed on the knees meant the

---

* The term "gulag" refers to Russia's forced labor camps that date back to the seventeenth-and-eighteenth-century era of Peter the Great and the tsars who first developed the idea of exile in Siberia as a punishment, but the word is an acronym derived from the phrase Glavnoye Upravleniye Lagerej (Chief Administration of [Corrective Labor] Camps), a government agency created under Vladimir Lenin.

† In Russian, the word *vor* is singular for "thief." *Vory* is plural.

bearer kneeled before no one. On the shoulders, stars signified a man of standing—perhaps a captain in the *vory v zakone*.*[19]

In the thirties, their numbers increased by leaps and bounds thanks to Joseph Stalin's Great Purge, which resulted in millions of people being sent to gulags. World War II, however, marked a new era for the Bratva. Thousands of thieves joined the Soviet Army, an apparent violation of the Thieves' Code, so a new breed of criminal emerged with an "every man for himself" attitude that meant they could occasionally cooperate with the government if necessary.

Then, when Stalin died in 1952, as many as eight million prisoners were released from the gulags. As the Cold War continued, thievery in Russia became so deeply institutionalized that corruption effectively became the business of the state. Illegal small businesses proliferated everywhere in the Soviet Union. Then the Bratva began to migrate to the West.

The first great boss of the Russian Mafia in America was Evsei Agron, a *vor v zakone* from Leningrad via the gulags, who arrived in 1975. An extortionist, black marketer, and killer,[20] Agron had served seven years for murder in the Soviet prisons, and had run gambling and prostitution rackets in Germany,[21] before coming to New York.[22] Though he declared himself to be a jeweler on his immigration papers, upon his arrival Agron began to put together a rudimentary criminal organization with about twenty people.[23] He worked out of El Caribe Country Club, a banquet hall and restaurant in Brooklyn in the name of Dr. Morton Levine, who shared ownership of it with his relatives, including his young nephew Michael D. Cohen, who later became Donald Trump's attorney both in business and as president. (Dr. Levine was never charged with any wrongdoing.)[24]

Agron, whose short, grandfatherly appearance belied his rapacious nature, ran a lucrative extortion ring that terrorized Russian émigré doctors, lawyers, and shopkeepers,[25] netting him about $50,000 a week.[26] Known for his brutality, he carried a cattle prod under his arm as a highly effective means of persuading debtors to pony up.[27] Among his

---

* According to a 2016 report of Project Millennium citing Interpol Moscow, 1,086 "thieves-in-law" were registered in the files of Interpol Moscow's office. Other sources say there were six to seven hundred registered thieves-in-law.

many infamous exploits, he extorted $15,000 from a man by threatening to murder his daughter at her wedding.[28]

Overseeing a motley crew of con men, thieves, extortionists, and swindlers, Agron was often accompanied by the ferocious Nayfeld brothers, Benjamin and Boris. According to *Red Mafiya,* the former, a steroid-enhanced ex–Olympic weight lifter who boasted a twenty-two-inch neck, once killed a Jewish teenager in a local parking lot "by picking him up like a ragdoll with one hand and plunging a knife into his heart with the other."*[29]

Agron also relied on Emile Puzyretsky as another enforcer. Known as the Technicolor Killer because of his colorful tattoos, "Puzyretsky had a great contempt for life. He killed his enemies with force, fury, and no mercy," a Russian militia colonel told Friedman.[30]

Locals "were scared shitless of [Agron and his men]," said FBI agent William Moschella.[31]

And so, having put fear in the hearts of his Brighton Beach supplicants, Evsei Agron adopted the life of a Mafia don, holding court in local restaurants, making collection rounds in his chauffeured limousine, and pausing on street corners to dispense favors. Unfortunately, Agron performed his daily rituals with the kind of phony theatrics that convinced locals that for Agron, being godfather was merely an act. "He would go round in a car with two big guys, they would open the door for him," said one Brighton Beach resident. "Everything was staged."[32]

Worse, Agron had failed to establish a code of honor. He had done little to foster the sense that he was a legitimate authority to resolve disputes or solve problems. In the end, he was nothing more than a ruthless neighborhood extortionist who ran a gang of thugs that terrorized the émigré community.[33] By the eighties, he had angered so many people that it was simply a matter of time before one of them struck back.

Finally, on the morning of May 4, 1985, after he had already survived two assassination attempts, Agron pushed the elevator button in his

---

* According to Benjamin Nayfeld, the victim had allegedly insulted Benjamin's girlfriend and reached for a weapon. Eighteen witnesses backed up Benjamin's version of events, insisting the stabbing was a justifiable homicide, and the case was dropped.

apartment building to go downstairs, only to be met by a man in the hallway, who shot him twice in the temple.[34]

———

Soon afterward, Marat Balagula, Agron's successor, moved into his former office in El Caribe Country Club. Balagula was widely suspected of having ordered the hit on Agron[35] but was never charged.

Agron's stewardship of the Brighton Beach Mafia had been all about thuggery and torture and physical violence, but Balagula was different. He had moved to the United States in 1977 and begun working as a textile cutter in upper Manhattan for $3.50 an hour.[36] But just a year later, he had won control over fourteen gas stations, formed two fuel dealerships, and begun buying gasoline from the Nayfeld brothers—all of which enabled him to team up with David Bogatin on the Red Daisy fuel tax scam.[37]

Balagula bought the Odessa Restaurant, a Russian/Ukrainian cabaret that was said to be Brighton Beach's answer to the Moulin Rouge. The Odessa served immense portions of Russian delicacies, accompanied by background music from the Motherland by Iosif Kobzon.

Late at night, when the entertainers had finished, the cabaret/disco upstairs transformed itself into a people's court of sorts, in which Russian mobsters adjudicated local disputes, in the tradition of the Russian Mafia, with Balagula and his goons taking a piece of the action.[38]

When it came to recreational activities that were obligatory for mobsters, Balagula held all-night sex and drug orgies on lavish yachts circling Manhattan. He was chauffeured all over town in a white stretch limo with a stocked bar. He tried to buy an island off the coast of South Africa to set up a bank.[39]

But in the end, Balagula, unlike Agron, was a modern don. Intellectuals and political power fascinated him. For the first time, the Russian Mafia had a vision of taking the *organizatsiya* into the world of white-collar crime. From the start, Balagula had cultivated ties with powerful figures in the legitimate world. Even before he came to the United States, on his thirtieth birthday, he had thrown himself an extravagant bash at his dacha in the Crimea. It was attended by none other than Mikhail Gorbachev, then a regional Communist Party boss.[40]

Balagula sought out doctors, lawyers, engineers, and professionals of all stripes. He was a businessman in the sense that he realized if the Russians were to be in the business of skimming taxes from gas sales, they might as well have a vertically integrated operation with oceangoing tankers, terminals, a fleet of gasoline trucks, and scores of gas stations, all of which could be run by émigrés from the Soviet Union. Balagula was even able to bring on as a client a midsize $160-million-a-year company on Long Island called Power Test to buy its bootleg gas. As a result, the Bratva was on its way to creating a multibillion-dollar-a-year criminal enterprise.[41]

The gas tax scam that the FBI called Operation Red Daisy was so successful that over time it spread beyond the New York–New Jersey market to Pennsylvania, Ohio, Texas, California, Georgia, and Florida.[42] Still, there were major differences between the Italians and the Russians. "When the Russians arrived, they came from a world where they didn't have toilets," says author (*Wiseguy*) and screenwriter (*Goodfellas, Casino,* etc.) Nicholas Pileggi, who covered the Italian mob for *New York* magazine in the eighties. "But they knew calculus. They had no deodorants. But they had an education. All of this made them beautifully suited to do financial frauds like the gas tax scam, Medicaid fraud, and pump-and-dump stock scams."[43]

Having come of age in a country that had no investor class and no Wall Street, Russians took their considerable financial acumen and devoted it to crime. Whether it was tax distribution, Medicaid fraud, pump-and-dump stock scams, auto insurance fraud, tax fraud, or money laundering, if there was a loophole or a systemic weakness in the American governmental or corporate infrastructure, the Russians would seek it out and find it. Balagula's gang pursued forgery and counterfeiting as well.

Nevertheless, they had the advantage of being off the FBI's radar screen, relatively speaking. "At the time there were as many as three hundred FBI agents in New York assigned to each of the Five Families of the Italian Mafia," says Pileggi. "Fifteen hundred in all. The FBI had almost no one on the Russians. For one thing, they didn't speak the language."

Plus, Pileggi says, there were political reasons not to take on the Russians. "They turned a blind eye to it because so many of the Russians were Jewish. They didn't want to make problems for legitimate Jews in Brooklyn, and the overwhelming majority was legitimate. If they went off against the gangsters, they were afraid it would hurt Soviet Jewry, so there was no real effort."

From the beginning, the Russians didn't give a moment's thought to the FBI. "They feel we are pussycats," said one New York detective who was monitoring them, "and the United States is one big candy store."[44]

———

With the advent of Ronald Reagan's presidency in the eighties, the center of gravity in America shifted dramatically away from its post-Watergate hangover. Thanks to Reagan's sunny optimism, every day, as if by edict, was a new morning not just in America, but in New York City as well. New York's fiscal crisis receded to the rearview mirror. Wall Street was booming. The Dow soared. Men in suits donned power ties and red suspenders and reemerged as Masters of the Universe. Junk bonds and leveraged buyouts became sexy. *The Predators' Ball, Barbarians at the Gate, Liar's Poker,* and *The Bonfire of the Vanities* dominated the bestseller list by chronicling a new world of stupendous wealth, glamour, and conspicuous consumption, and how it came to be. *Manhattan, Inc.,* a now-defunct glossy monthly magazine, deified the big swinging dicks of Wall Street as the new rock stars of the era.

Suddenly, "greed—for lack of a better word—[was] good," as Michael Douglas's Gordon Gekko put it in *Wall Street.* Greed was right. Greed worked. Greed clarified.

No one embodied the new zeitgeist more than Donald Trump, who,

from his Fifth Avenue aerie, had transformed himself into an international tabloid celebrity who personified a spectacularly luxurious lifestyle and was pumping it for all it was worth. Trump Tower was his
defining moment, the point at which Trump invented himself as a
dream maker, as the epitome of luxury and success.

And so, he set off in half a dozen directions simultaneously, after his
success with the old Commodore—sports, publishing, gambling, real
estate, airlines, and more—marketing himself nonstop, like a latter-day
P. T. Barnum, as the creature most emblematic of this new age of celebrity, grandiosity, and conspicuous consumption.

Trump always said his building had the "Tiffany location," and, on
that score at least, he was correct. The building was surrounded by the
most exalted names in the luxury marketplace—Bergdorf Goodman,
Henri Bendel, Bulgari, Van Cleef & Arpels, and Tiffany. Over the years,
the building was also home to Steven Spielberg, Michael Jackson, Sophia
Loren, Johnny Carson, Bruce Willis, Liberace, and, of course, the man
whose fame ultimately exceeded theirs—Donald Trump himself.

At the heart of his success was a no-holds-barred approach to PR
that Trump once explained to casino executive John Allen. "Here's
how I work," he said. "I call the society editor [of one of the New York
tabloids] and tell them that Princess Di and Prince Charles are going to purchase an apartment in Trump Tower. And they, in turn, investigate the source, call Buckingham Palace. And the comment is 'No
comment.' Which means that it appears to the public that Princess
Di and Prince Charles are going to purchase an apartment in Trump
Tower."[45]

Of course, Prince Charles never had the slightest intention of buying
a condo in Trump Tower. Nevertheless, with the success of Trump
Tower, Trump was suddenly able to make "Trump" the brand name for
a class of products that had never before had brand names—luxury
apartments. It was, *Fortune* magazine said, "a textbook marketing strategy. That name indisputably adds value . . . There is undeniably a Trump
mystique. Some people love him, others despise him, but everybody
talks about him. He has become a cult hero for many people around the

world who seem to regard this flamboyant billionaire as the most heart-ening example of the American dream come true since [Texas computer king] Ross Perot."[46]

As if to prove the wisdom of this marketing strategy, in 1982, Trump began construction of the thirty-six-story Trump Plaza on Sixty-First Street and Third Avenue. Then he bought the iconic Plaza Hotel (not to be confused with the aforementioned Trump Plaza), which, he pro-claimed, was not a building but "a masterpiece—the Mona Lisa."[47]

He announced never-realized plans to build "the world's tallest and greatest building,"[48] a 150-story tower on Manhattan's West Side. In 1984, he bought the New Jersey Generals in the USFL football league. Later, he bought Eastern Airlines' New York–Boston–Washington routes for $365 million and transformed it into the Trump Shuttle, mak-ing sure its flight attendants were accessorized with pearls.[49]

When it came to flamboyance, Trump had no equal. In 1985 he bought Mar-a-Lago, the 128-room, 100,000-square-foot mansion that heiress Marjorie Merriweather Post hoped would one day serve as a winter White House. Trump bought a Boeing 727; a "Darth Vader" he-licopter; a huge estate in Greenwich, Connecticut; and a massive yacht, the *Trump Princess*.[50] And in 1987, he told the world all about it when Random House published his bestseller *Trump: The Art of the Deal*, which was written by Tony Schwartz and stayed on the *New York Times* bestseller list for nearly a year.

Real estate developer, casino operator, football team owner, bestsell-ing author: Trump had transformed himself into a marketing phenom-enon in which his brash self-promotion, however distasteful, generated a self-perpetuating, larger-than-life aura of success, wealth, status, and opulence.

But less visibly, Trump was also going through a highly improbable transformation into becoming a new kind of political figure. It was a transformation that grew out of Trump's 1977 marriage to Ivana Zelníčková, a Czech national who had worked as a model in Canada and whose father was under surveillance by the Czech secret service, which, in turn, as a Soviet satellite, was in league with the KGB; his political education at the feet of Roy Cohn, New York's most notorious fixer; and his unbridled ambition to top his father not just by crossing the river into Manhattan, but by staking out his own place on the world stage. All of which made him a tempting target of operatives of the Soviet Union and the Eastern Bloc.

CHAPTER FIVE

HONEY TRAP

On a frigid December day in 2017, Oleg Kalugin opens the door of his house in Rockville, Maryland, an upper-middle-class suburb of Washington, DC, to meet me. Nothing in particular distinguishes his split-level suburban home from those of the other professionals in the neighborhood, but the man who lives there is very much out of the ordinary, a former KGB spymaster who is now an American citizen.

Born in St. Petersburg (then Leningrad), Kalugin, at eighty-three, now lives just half an hour's drive from the White House, which for decades was dead center in the crosshairs of the KGB, the dreaded secret security forces he served as head of counterintelligence. Some twenty-five years later, he still has "the razor-sharp features and icy glare of a movie spy," as David Remnick described him in *Lenin's Tomb*.[1] A genial host, Kalugin gives a guided tour of his sprawling library spread over three rooms and reveals himself to be a man of history, a veritable Zelig of the Cold War.

A fierce critic of Vladimir Putin, Kalugin, who was sentenced to fifteen years in jail for treason[2] in Russia, moved to the United States in 1995 and accepted a teaching position at Catholic University in Washington. A professor at the Centre for Counterintelligence and Security Studies, where he teaches FBI and CIA officers, he also serves on the board of the International Spy Museum in Washington.[3]

Kalugin's work as a spy began in 1959, when he was a twenty-four-year-old student at Columbia School of Journalism from Russia—who, unbeknownst to his classmates, was already undercover as a fair-haired golden boy of the KGB. But that was just the beginning. In 1960, when Nikita Khrushchev infamously startled the world by banging his shoe on the podium during the United Nations General Assembly, that was Kalugin nearby, then as Radio Moscow's bureau chief in New York—or at least that was his KGB cover. "This country was always a paradise for spies," he told me.[4]

In 1970, Kalugin returned to KGB headquarters in Moscow, where he eventually headed the K branch of the First Chief Directorate, which was responsible for foreign operations and intelligence collection. If you're familiar with the infamous Cambridge Spy Ring,* the group of posh, highly educated Brits who caused an international scandal in the 1950s when they went over to the Soviets, that too was Oleg Kalugin in Moscow, handling Kim Philby and Donald Maclean, in the seventies, long after they had defected. In 1974, Kalugin was promoted to general, the youngest in the history of the powerful Russian spy organization.[5]

When it comes to Soviet leaders Yuri Andropov, Mikhail Gorbachev, and Boris Yeltsin, Kalugin knew them all and can regale you for hours with stories about them. He was even the boss of a promising young KGB officer named Vladimir Putin.

Of medium height, immaculately groomed, clad in dark blue slacks, a striped shirt, and a light blue jacket, Kalugin was congenial and utterly disarming when I met him. As John le Carré wrote, when he interviewed Kalugin nearly twenty-five years ago, he is "one of those former enemies of western democracy who have made a seamless transition from their side to ours. To listen to him you could be forgiven for assuming that we had been on the same side all along."[6]

---

* The Cambridge Spy Ring has been featured, fictionally and otherwise, in countless books, movies, and plays about espionage, including John le Carré's *Tinker, Tailor, Soldier, Spy* and *A Perfect Spy*; Frederick Forsyth's *The Fourth Protocol*; *The Innocent* by Ian McEwan; *Blunt: The Fourth Man* with Anthony Hopkins and Ian Richardson; the BBC series *The Hour*; *The Jigsaw Man* with Laurence Olivier and Michael Caine; three plays by Alan Bennett, *A Question of Attribution*, *An Englishman Abroad*, and *The Old Country*; and many others.

But we weren't. Gracious and amiable as Kalugin is, one has only to remember the 1978 assassination of Bulgarian writer Georgi Markov—a brave and widely loved émigré who was murdered when a KGB operative wielded a specially designed umbrella that fired a tiny poison pellet filled with ricin into Markov's thigh—to remind oneself of the KGB's dark and murderous legacy.

That was Kalugin's work. "We're not children," he told le Carré. "I was the head man for all that stuff, for Christ's sake! Nothing operational could be done unless it went across my desk, O.K.? Markov had already been sentenced to death in his absence by a Bulgarian court, but the Bulgarians were terrible. They couldn't do a damn thing. We had to do it all for them: train the guy, make the umbrella, fix the poison."[7]

Hoary tales of the Cold War aside, Kalugin is of special interest these days because his experience as head of counterintelligence for the KGB makes him a master of the tradecraft that was used to ensnare Trump. The operation began during a 1978 trip to Czechoslovakia not long after Trump's marriage to Ivana, in which the newlyweds piqued the interest of the Czech Ministry of State Security (also known as the StB) enough that a secret police collaborator began observing Ivana and met several times with her in later years.[8]

Keeping tabs on Czechs who had left the country was standard operating procedure for the StB. "The State Security was constantly watching (Czechoslovak citizens living abroad)," said Libor Svoboda, a historian from the Institute for the Study of Totalitarian Regimes in Prague.[9] "They were coming here, so they used agents to follow them. They wanted to know who they were meeting, what they talked about. It was a sort of paranoia. They were afraid that these people could work for foreign intelligence agencies. They used the same approach toward their relatives as well."

According to the German newspaper *Bild*, starting in 1979, encrypted StB files say, "the phone calls between Ivana and her father were to be wiretapped at least once per year. Their mail exchange was monitored."[10] The agent who reported on Ivana used the code names of "Langr" and "Chod."[11] The StB files are stamped "top secret," bear the code names

"Slusovice,"* "America," and "Capital," and indicate an ongoing attempt to gather as much information about Trump as possible.[12]

"The StB thought there was a chance that the U.S. intelligence agencies could use (Ivana Trump). And also they wanted to use Trump to gather information on U.S. high society," said Svoboda.[13]

The StB archives also show that Ivana's father, Miloš Zelníček, was monitored by the secret services and that during his 1977 trip to the US for Ivana's wedding, Zelníček was subject to an StB-ordered search of his possessions at the airport. "He provided information that the secret police found out anyway from other sources," said Petr Blažek of the Institute for the Study of Totalitarian Regimes,[14] who suggested that the search was a warning shot telling Zelníček that cooperation was the only way such trips would be permitted in the future.

Far from handing over compromising materials, Zelníček may have simply delivered the minimal amount of information necessary to keep the StB off his back. "Ivana's father was registered as a confidant of the StB," Czech historian Tomas Vilimek told the *Guardian*.[15] "However, that does not mean he was an agent. The CSSR authorities forced him to talk to them because of his journeys to the US and his daughter. Otherwise, he would not have been allowed to fly."

In the end, we do not know exactly when the KGB first opened a file on Donald Trump. But it would have been common practice for the Czech secret police to share their intelligence on the Trumps with the KGB. More to the point, Trump was so highly valued as a target that the StB later sent a spy to the US to monitor his political prospects for more than a decade.[16]

––––––

It's unclear how much Trump himself knew about his in-laws' encounters with Czech intelligence, but when Mikhail Gorbachev, the last leader of the Soviet Union, rose to power in 1985, and put forth the policies of perestroika (literally "restructuring" in Russian) and glasnost ("openness"), which eased the tensions of the Cold War, Trump became deeply infected with a severe case of Russophilia.

––––––

* Slusovice is the name of the Zelníček family's village.

In the past, his participation in politics had been confined to getting Roy Cohn to push through tax abatements, changes to zoning restrictions, and the like—or making political donations to accomplish such goals. Suddenly, Trump reinvented himself as a pseudo-authority on nuclear arms and asserted that he could play a key role in strategic arms limitations.[17]

Trump took the issue up in an interview with journalist Ron Rosenbaum in the November 1985 issue of *Manhattan, Inc.* magazine, in which he asserted of nuclear proliferation, "Nothing matters as much to me now"—an extraordinarily unlikely passion for a man who personified conspicuous consumption.

Trump started by telling Rosenbaum about his late uncle John Trump, an MIT professor, who explained that nuclear technology was becoming so simplified that "someday it'll be like making a bomb in the basement of your house. And that's a very frightening statement coming from a man who's totally versed in it."[18]

What was taking place was decidedly un-Trumpian. Rosenbaum, who was anything but a Trump enthusiast, said the real estate developer "seemed genuinely aware of just how much danger nukes put the world in." He even passed up a chance to tout the glories of Trump Tower. Instead, Rosenbaum told me, Donald Trump preferred to be seen as being in "on some serious stuff. The fact that his uncle was a nuclear scientist gave him the right to make these pronouncements."[19]

Trump made a similar pitch to the *Washington Post*. "Some people have an ability to negotiate," he told the paper.[20] "It's an art you're basically born with. You either have it or you don't."

Lack of confidence was not his problem. "It would take an hour-and-a-half to learn everything there is to learn about missiles," he said. ". . . I think I know most of it anyway."

Which did not mean Trump was above seeking out expertise. A few months later, according to the *Hollywood Reporter*, in 1986, he insisted on meeting Bernard Lown, a Boston cardiologist best known for inventing the defibrillator and sharing the Nobel Peace Prize with Yevgeny Chazov, the personal physician for Mikhail Gorbachev.[21]

After accepting their Nobel medals in Oslo, Drs. Lown and Chazov went to Moscow and spent time with Gorbachev, the new Soviet leader. Not long after he returned to the United States, Lown got a message from Trump. At the time, Lown had never even heard of him but secretly hoped Trump might contribute to the Lown Cardiovascular Research Foundation, which was low on funds at the time.

They met in Trump's offices on the twenty-sixth floor of Trump Tower. "I arrived totally ignorant about his motives," Lown told me.[22] "We sat down for lunch and Trump was very grim looking, very serious."

"Tell me everything you know about Gorbachev," Trump said.

After twenty minutes or so recounting his experience with the Soviet leader, however, Lown became painfully aware that Trump wasn't listening. "I realized he had a short attention span," Lown said. "I thought there was another agenda, perhaps, but I didn't know what that was."

Lown cut to the chase. "Why do you want to know?" he asked Trump.

At that, Trump revealed his grand plan. "If I know about Gorbachev, I can ask my good friend Ronnie to make me a plenipotentiary ambassador for the United States with Gorbachev."

"Ronnie?" Lown asked.

Lown was unaware that Trump had retained the powerful lobbying firm of Black, Manafort & Stone shortly after it opened shop in 1980,[23] and its three name partners—Charles Black, Paul Manafort, and Roger Stone—had just played vital roles in Ronald Reagan's 1984 landslide victory.

"Ronald Reagan," Trump explained.

Then he clapped his hands together, Lown says, and went on to say how within one hour of meeting Gorbachev, he would end the Cold War.

"The arrogance of the man, and his ignorance about the complexities of one of the complicating issues confronting mankind! The idea that he could solve it in one hour!"[24]

———

Thanks to Gorbachev, the Russian bear had finally put on a friendly face, but the KGB had not. It remained the most effective and most feared intelligence-gathering organization in the world with more than four hundred thousand officers inside the Soviet Union and another two hundred thousand border guards, not to mention an enormous network of informers.[25] And that didn't even include the First Chief Directorate (FCD), the relatively small but prestigious division in charge of gathering foreign intelligence. It had about twelve thousand officers and was headed by General Vladimir Kryuchkov, a hard-liner who seemed to be swimming against the tides of history.

Gorbachev's dovish overtures to the West notwithstanding, Kryuchkov, according to ex-KGB general Oleg Kalugin, was still very much "a true believer until the end, eternally suspicious of the West and capitalism."[26]

Kryuchkov is of special interest not simply because of his unreconstructed hard-line views.* Thanks to a compendium of his memos during this period entitled *Comrade Kryuchkov's Instructions: Top Secret Files on KGB Foreign Operations, 1975–1985,* we know that by 1984 he was deeply concerned that the KGB had failed to recruit enough American agents.[27] To Kryuchkov, absolutely nothing was more important, and he ordered his officers to cultivate as assets not just the usual leftist suspects, who might have ideological sympathies with the Soviets, but also various influential people such as prominent businessmen.[28]

And so, as if orchestrated by Kryuchkov, the political education of Donald Trump began in March 1986, when he met the Soviet ambassador to the United Nations, Yuri Dubinin and his daughter Natalia Dubinina. Dubinina, who was part of the Soviet delegation to the UN, was an interesting figure herself in that the Soviet mission was widely known to harbor KGB agents.[29] As she told the Russian daily *Moskovsky Komsomolets,* when her father arrived in New York City for his very first visit, she took him on a tour, and one of the first buildings they saw was Trump Tower on Fifth Avenue. "I met my father and invited him to show New York," she said, according to a Google Translate version of the article. "After all, I lived there for a long time, and he came for the first time in my life."[30]

Natalia said her father "never saw anything like [Trump Tower], that

---

* As it happens, Kryuchkov also had a spy in the KGB's Dresden station reporting to him—Vladimir Putin.

he was so impressed that he decided he had to meet the building's owner at once." And so, Soviet ambassador Yuri Dubinin and his daughter Natalia, in a highly unusual breach of protocol, went into Trump Tower, took the elevator up to Trump's office, and paid him a visit.

It is unclear whether prior arrangements were made to set up this extremely irregular meeting between a highly placed Soviet diplomat and Trump. But a few months later, at a luncheon given by cosmetics magnate Leonard Lauder, Trump happened to be seated next to Yuri Dubinin,* who proceeded to flatter the young real estate mogul shamelessly.

Trump later rhapsodized about the conversation in *The Art of the Deal*. "[O]ne thing led to another," he wrote, "and now I'm talking about building a large luxury hotel across the street from the Kremlin, in partnership with the Soviet government."[31]

For the KGB, Kalugin told me, recruiting a new asset "always starts with innocent conversation" like this.[32]

As Natalia Dubinina explained, the Russians were off to an auspicious start. "Trump melted at once," she said. "He is an emotional person, somewhat impulsive. He needs recognition. And, of course, when he gets it he likes it. My father's visit worked on him [Trump] like honey on a bee."[33]

As to what Trump was really after in his quest to reinvent himself as a statesman/politician, he may have revealed part of the answer when he told the *Washington Post* that the man who was egging him on was none other than the mentor he so looked up to, a man for whom motives were simple. Primal. There was always money. There was always a deal. There was always an angle, and a fix.

"You know who really wants me to do this?" Trump asked rhetorically. "Roy [Cohn]."[34]

———

In the meantime, Trump was wheeling and dealing much closer to home. In New York, he was in the midst of an ongoing war over special

---

* A few months later, Dubinin was transferred from his post at the UN and was appointed Soviet ambassador to the United States.

zoning and tax benefits for his massive West Side project with New York mayor Ed Koch, with Koch calling Trump "piggy, piggy, piggy" and Trump calling Koch "a moron."[35] And in New Jersey, he was moving ahead with his third casino in Atlantic City, the $1 billion plus Trump Taj Mahal, the largest casino in the world, with more than 2,000 rooms and 67,000 square feet of gaming space.*

Putting the Taj together was no simple matter. For roughly thirty years, from the 1910s until 1941, Atlantic City had been at the mercy of the Republican political machine formerly run by Enoch "Nucky" Johnson, the apparent inspiration for the character Nucky Thompson, played by Steve Buscemi in HBO's *Boardwalk Empire*. This was a world peopled by major criminal figures such as Charles "Lucky" Luciano; Meyer Lansky; Arnold "the Brain" Rothstein, who famously fixed the 1919 World Series; and Al Capone.

By the eighties, however, attorney Patrick "Paddy" McGahn[†] had become the new boss of Atlantic City, and, with his brother, state legislator Joseph McGahn, brought legalized gambling and Donald Trump to New Jersey. Trump, it turned out, was lucky to have them on his side.

One of the first problems Trump encountered was that part of the land he wanted was owned by Salvatore "Salvie" Testa and Frank Narducci Jr., two Mafia hit men[‡] who worked for Atlantic City mob boss Nicodemo "Little Nicky" Scarfo and were known as the Young Executioners.[36]

If Testa and Narducci found out that their prospective buyer was named Donald Trump, it went without saying that they would demand top dollar. So instead the title was temporarily put in the name of Paddy McGahn's secretary so the Executioners wouldn't know they were

---

* The Riviera in Las Vegas disputes the Taj Mahal's claim that it is the largest in the world.

† Some of Trump's acquaintances who were close to individuals associated with the New Jersey Mafia proved to be valuable allies in the future. Don McGahn, the nephew of both Paddy and Joseph McGahn, later became a White House counsel in the Trump administration. In addition, White House counselor Kellyanne Conway, who also served as Trump's campaign manager, is the granddaughter of Jimmy "the Brute" DiNatale, an associate of Little Nicky Scarfo.

‡ Testa was shot to death in 1984 just weeks after a fight with mob boss Nicky Scarfo, according to the *Philadelphia Inquirer*. As for Narducci, he was sentenced to life in prison in 1989 for his role in a mob murder.

selling to Trump.[37] Later, Trump showed his appreciation by naming the bar at the Taj Mahal "Paddy's Saloon."

———

The more Trump expanded his business and saw the spotlight, the more he sought a bigger stage. In January 1987, Trump received a letter from Ambassador Dubinin that began, "It is a pleasure for me to relay some good news from Moscow." The letter added that Intourist, the leading Soviet tourist agency, "had expressed interest in pursuing a joint venture to construct and manage a hotel in Moscow."[38] Vitaly Churkin, who later became ambassador to the UN, helped Yuri Dubinin set up Trump's trip.[39]

On July 4, Trump flew to Moscow with Ivana and two assistants. He checked out various potential sites for a hotel, including several near Red Square.[40]

He stayed in a suite in the National Hotel where Vladimir Lenin and his wife had stayed in 1917. According to Viktor Suvorov, an agent for the GRU, Soviet military intelligence, "Everything is free. There are good parties with nice girls. It could be a sauna and girls and who knows what else."

All of which sounded great, except for one thing: Everything was subject to twenty-four-hour surveillance by the KGB.[41]

———

After the trip, the *New York Times* reported that while Trump was in Moscow, "he met with the Soviet leader, Mikhail S. Gorbachev. The ostensible subject of their meeting was the possible development of luxury hotels in the Soviet Union by Mr. Trump. But Mr. Trump's calls for nuclear disarmament were also well-known to the Russians."[42]

But in fact, Trump's meeting with Gorbachev never really took place.[43] The report, apparently, was merely Trumpian self-promotion. Moreover, there are many unanswered questions about exactly what transpired during Trump's visit. It is not clear whether Trump understood that Intourist was essentially a branch of the KGB whose job was to spy on high-profile tourists visiting Moscow. "In my time [Intourist] was KGB," said Viktor Suvorov.[44] "They gave permission for people to visit."

Nor is it clear if Trump was aware that Intourist routinely sent lists of prospective visitors to the first and second directorates of the KGB based on their visa applications, and that he was almost certainly being bugged.

As to what activities the KGB may have captured in its surveillance, Oleg Kalugin, as the former head of counterterrorism for the KGB, is well versed in the use of video to produce *kompromat*, particularly of a sexual nature. At the time, it was a widespread practice for the KGB to hire young women and deploy them as prostitutes to entrap visiting politicians and businessmen, and to use Intourist to monitor foreigners in the Soviet Union and to facilitate such "honey traps."[45]

"In your world, many times, you ask your young men to stand up and proudly serve their country," Kalugin once told a reporter. "In Russia, sometimes we ask our women just to lie down."[46]

Which, according to Kalugin, is what probably happened during Trump's 1987 trip to Moscow, during which he would have "had many young ladies at his disposal."[47]

To be clear, Kalugin did not claim to have seen such material or have evidence of its existence but was speaking as the former head of counterintelligence for the KGB, someone more than familiar with its tradecraft and practices. "I would not be surprised if the Russians have, and Trump knows about them, files on him during his trip to Russia and his involvement with meeting young ladies that were controlled [by Soviet intelligence]," he said.

———

On July 24, 1987, almost immediately after Trump's return from Moscow, an article appeared in a highly unlikely venue, the *Executive Intelligence Review*,* that strongly suggested something mysterious was going on between him and the Kremlin. "The Soviets are reportedly

———

* *Executive Intelligence Review* is a weekly newsmagazine founded by Lyndon LaRouche, a cultlike political activist who has run for president eight times. The magazine has promoted a number of unlikely conspiracy theories, including one asserting that Queen Elizabeth II runs an international drug cartel and that the British royal family ordered the assassination of Diana, Princess of Wales.

looking a lot more kindly on a possible presidential bid by Donald Trump, the New York builder who has amassed a fortune through real-estate speculation and owns a controlling interest in the notorious, organized-crime linked Resorts International," the article said. "Trump took an all-expenses-paid jaunt to the Soviet Union in July to discuss building the Russians some luxury hotels."[48]

Were the Soviets really supporting a Trump run for the presidency? Was Trump seriously considering it? Answers to the second question began to materialize less than two months after his return from Russia, when Trump turned to Roger Stone, a Nixon-era dirty trickster then with the firm of Black, Manafort & Stone, for political advice. Trump had met Stone and his colleague Paul Manafort through Roy Cohn. Although they worked in somewhat different spheres—Cohn was a hardball fixer, Stone a political strategist and lobbyist—to a large extent, they were cut from the same ethically challenged cloth.

Under Stone's tutelage, on September 1, 1987, just seven weeks after his return from Moscow, Trump suddenly went full steam ahead promoting his newly acquired foreign policy expertise, by paying nearly $100,000 for full-page ads in the *Boston Globe, Washington Post,* and *New York Times* calling for the United States to stop spending money to defend Japan and the Persian Gulf, "an area of only marginal significance to the U.S. for its oil supplies, but one upon which Japan and others are almost totally dependent."[49]

The ads, which ran under the headline "There's nothing wrong with America's Foreign Defense Policy that a little backbone can't cure," marked Trump's first foray into a foreign policy that was overtly pro-Russian in the sense that it called for the dismantling of the postwar Western Alliance and was very much a precursor of the "America First" policies Trump promoted during his 2016 campaign.

"The world is laughing at America's politicians as we protect ships we don't own, carrying oil we don't need, destined for allies who won't help," he wrote.[50] ". . . It's time for us to end our vast deficits by making Japan and others who can afford it, pay. Our world protection is worth hundreds of billions of dollars to these countries and their stake in their protection is far greater than ours."

Given the extraordinary success of the Western Alliance as the underpinning of American foreign policy since World War II, one can only wonder who, if anyone, helped Trump come up with policies that were so favorable to the Soviets. Even more startling, an article published the next day in the *Times* suggested that Trump might enter the 1988 Republican presidential primaries against George H. W. Bush, then the incumbent vice president. "There is absolutely no plan [for Trump] to run for mayor, governor or United States senator," said a Trump spokesman. "He will not comment about the Presidency."[51]

That tease—a refusal to comment on a question that no one had asked—did not take place in a complete vacuum, however. Earlier that summer, a Republican activist named Mike Dunbar from Portsmouth, New Hampshire, had approached Trump with a proposal to speak before the Portsmouth Rotary Club, an obligatory stop for presidential candidates in the first presidential primary state.*[52] After proclaiming that Vice President George H. W. Bush, the odds-on favorite to be the GOP nominee, and Senator Bob Dole, another contender, were "duds,"[53] Dunbar said that he raised money and collected one thousand signatures to put Trump on the 1988 primary ballot.

Trump's top casino executive, Steve Hyde, later told Wayne Barrett that going to New Hampshire, far from being a stunt, represented "a serious test of the political waters."[54]

"If things shake out," Hyde added, "I wouldn't be the least bit surprised if he decided to do it." New York GOP leaders had tried unsuccessfully to draft Trump to run against Mayor Ed Koch or Governor Mario Cuomo.[55]

But on October 22, 1987, Donald Trump's chopper set down in Portsmouth, New Hampshire, so he could deliver a luncheon address sponsored by the Portsmouth Rotary Club, at Yoken's restaurant, an obligatory rite of passage for candidates running in the New Hampshire primary.

---

* The Iowa caucuses precede the New Hampshire primary, but they consist of precinct caucuses to select candidates, not statewide elections.

———

In many ways, the event eerily prefigured those of more recent years. Wearing a scarlet "power" tie, and flanked by a surly personal body-guard, Trump spoke before a crowd of five hundred, more than that of other candidates who had appeared, and served up the same kind of red meat he has delivered in recent years to those who became his base.

"[Our allies] are ripping us off left and right," he said. "They knock the hell out of the United States. Do they say, thank you? No. Do they like us? Not particularly."[56]

A tax increase should not be the answer to the federal budget deficit, he said. Instead, Trump said, "We should have these countries that are ripping us off pay off the $200 billion deficit." That's why, he explained, we needed "a tough, smart cookie" running the United States so it would not be pushed around.[57] The crowd loved it.

Trump's promising reception notwithstanding, Vice President George Bush had a commanding lead in the race for the Republican nomination, and Trump himself had another issue he needed to deal with. Trump had felt Ivana's awkward English and heavy Czech accent would be liabilities on the campaign trail.[58] It was not a happy relation-ship and in fact his marriage was an issue he wanted to resolve before making a serious presidential run. Nevertheless, Donald Trump's presidential quest was under way.

Trump's White House ambitions did not make an especially deep impression on American voters in the 1980s, but foreign agencies took notice. Several months after Trump's visit to New Hampshire, Ivana returned to her homeland, where the Czech StB continued to keep a close eye on her. StB agents suggested Ivana was nervous throughout the trip because she believed US embassy officials were following her at a time when she was supposed to be meeting with Czech security opera-tives.[59] Twice, the American ambassador to Prague, Julian Martin Niemczyk, invited her to visit the embassy. But Ivana declined.

Meanwhile, the Czech secret police filed a classified report dated Oc-tober 22, 1988, saying that "as a wife of D. TRUMP she receives constant attention . . . and any mistake she would make could have immense consequences for him."

In addition, the StB report made two noteworthy revelations. For the first time, it was clear that Trump had decided he would run for president. The question was timing. "Even though it [his presidential prospects] looks like a utopia," the awkwardly translated report said, "D. TRUMP is confident he will succeed."[60] Only forty-two, the report added, Trump planned to run as an independent candidate in 1996, eight years hence.[61]

Finally, the StB file made one more curious observation about Trump's political future: It said he was being pressured to run for president. And exactly where was the pressure coming from? Could it have been *kompromat* from the honey trap in Moscow? Unfortunately, the answer was unclear.

CHAPTER SIX

GANGSTER'S PARADISE

S emion Mogilevich is not well-known to most Americans, but to the FBI, the five-foot-six, three-hundred-pound[1] "boss of bosses" of the Russian Mafia is a legend. Said to be worth more than $10 billion,[2] "the most dangerous mobster in the world," as the FBI calls him, is renowned as the "Brainy Don" thanks to his mastery of sophisticated financial crimes and a vast array of transgressions in other sectors. Even the British press, which is notoriously skittish about libel suits, doesn't mince words when it comes to Mogilevich, with the *Independent* calling him "the most evil gangster in the world."[3]

In real life, however, Mogilevich has maintained an extraordinarily low profile. Fans of John le Carré's spy fiction may get a sense of him in the author's portrait of Dima—Dmitri Vladimirovich Krasnov, the money-laundering Russian banker in *Our Kind of Traitor,* who people have speculated is based on Mogilevich. Sometimes referred to as a real-life Keyser Söze, the mythical and legendary villain in the 1995 movie *The Usual Suspects,* Semion Mogilevich has survived investigations by the FBI, Interpol, and other law enforcement agencies, not to mention multiple assassination attempts.[4] It is a safe bet that he knows secrets that men have died for, but it is also clear that he has no intention of sharing them.*

---

* When I asked to interview Mogilevich, his attorney Ze'ev Gordon told me, "He doesn't want to give an interview . . . He has nothing to do with President Trump and he doesn't know anybody who has business with him . . . The last time he was in the United States was more than twenty years ago."

So it is not surprising that Mogilevich's media appearances have been few and far between—with the notable exception of "The Billion Dollar Don," a 2002 episode of the BBC documentary series *Panorama*.[5] There, and in other interviews, Mogilevich reveals himself only to be a gruff and opaque presence with a brush mustache and pockmarked face who dodges questions with sardonic, dismissive responses. "Once I accidentally washed $5 I'd left in my shirt pocket," he told the *Moskovsky Komsomolets*, when asked about his mastery of money laundering. "I must say they looked a lot cleaner and brighter after that."[6]

Such false modesty, of course, only serves to disguise a man who is said to have played a key role in transforming organized crime through globalization. "Mogilevich typifies the new global criminal," said Jeffrey Robinson, an author who specializes in international financial crime.[7] "These men don't rob banks. They buy them."

Taking full advantage of ill-equipped law enforcement and lax money-laundering laws, Mogilevich has become, the FBI says, a strategic threat on the geopolitical playing field, a man who "can, with a telephone call and order, affect the global economy."[8]

The Semion Mogilevich Organization, as his operation is known, has allegedly sold weapons to al-Qaeda,[9] financed the sale of enriched uranium to terrorists, laundered money through companies on the New York Stock Exchange, and is said to have assembled a private army of brutal killers.[10] It has launched business operations in Austria, Canada, France, Hungary, Israel, Russia, Ukraine, the United Kingdom, the United States, and at least eighteen other countries[11] and has been active in areas as disparate as furniture and armaments, gambling and energy, art theft, extortion, drug trafficking, and prostitution. Mogilevich allegedly smuggled more than six hundred thousand gallons of vodka out of Hungary. And in Southeast Asia, Mogilevich provided money laundering services to heroin suppliers, the FBI said, and bought a bankrupt Georgian airline to help make their deliveries.[12]

More worrisome is the fact that, according to classified Israeli and FBI documents, Mogilevich sold $20 million worth of stolen Warsaw Pact weapons, including ground-to-air missiles and twelve armored troop carriers, to Iran. As if that weren't enough, he bought major companies that dominated the Hungarian armaments industry, in the process putting at risk NATO and the war against terrorism.[13] He has won a spectacularly lucrative share of the Russia-Ukraine energy trade, provided *krysha* (literally a "roof," or protection) for billionaire oligarchs, and laundered countless billions of dollars.

To get a sense of the magnitude of his power, one has only to name two people with whom he has had long-term business relationships: Vladimir Putin and Donald Trump.

———

Born in Kiev, Ukraine, in 1946, Semion Mogilevich was the son of a podiatrist mother and a father who managed a large state-owned printing company.[14] In the early seventies, after he graduated from the University of Lviv, Mogilevich* reportedly ran with the Lyuberetskaya crime group in the Moscow suburb of Lyubertsy, and was involved in petty theft and fraud.[15] That led to two jail sentences totaling more than four years for infractions involving illegal currency.[16]

These initial transgressions were small-time, relative to what was in store for Mogilevich, but one thing was clear: Money was his medium. Mogilevich started to make his fortune in the early eighties by approaching fellow Jews who were emigrating en masse to Israel and the United States and were trying to get market value for art, antiques, jewelry, and other collectibles at a time when there were strict limits on what assets could be taken out of the Soviet Union.[17] Mogilevich came to their rescue—or so it seemed—by buying their possessions cheaply and promising to send more money once he had resold their property. In the end, however, he simply kept the money and used it[18] to help finance a petroleum import-export company called Arbat International

---

* According to FBI files, Interpol's Millennium Project, and other sources, Mogilevich's name has appeared in many different forms, either as an alias or as an alternative spelling. Among them: Semion Mobllerltsh, Seva Magelansky, Sergei Schneider, Seva Moguilevich, Semon Yudkovich Palagnyuk, Semen Yukovich Telesh, Simeon Mogilevitch, Semjon Mogilevcs, Shimon Makelwitsh, Shimon Makhelwitsch, Sergei Yurevich, Seva Schnaider, Mogiletin Senior Mogilevich, Semion Mogeilegtin, Semion Mogleritis, Semion Mogrilets, Sergei Magrilets, Semyon Teles, Sergei Palagniuk, Semyon Palagniuk, Shimon Makelvitsh, Shimon Makelvich, Seymon Mogilevsk, Lev Fisherman, Simeon Teles, Semyon Yudkovich, Sergei Mangriyats, Sergei Yuryevich Schneider, Moguilevich, Mogilevitch, and many others.

that was registered in the Channel Islands, an international center for money laundering and other financial crimes.

Arbat was Mogilevich's first foray into serious finance and his partners were men who would become some of the biggest names in Russian organized crime. At the time, in the early eighties, Mogilevich had been hanging out at the Legendary Hotel Sovietsky, a grandiose example of Soviet classicism that had become a celebrated watering hole in the Moscow suburb of Solntsevo.

A rare nightspot that served alcohol after hours, the Sovietsky was notorious for its clientele of tracksuit-wearing mobsters, cardsharps, black marketeers, "shadow capitalists," ex-wrestlers and ex-boxers, and other denizens of the dark side, including Alimzhan Tokhtakhounov, a businessman from Uzbekistan,[19] and a gangster named Vyacheslav Ivankov.[20] Both men were thieves-in-law.

It was here that Mogilevich—his friends called him "Seva"— met a waiter named Sergei Mikhailov, aka Mikhas, who was just getting his first taste of the Bratva, on his way to becoming head of the Solntsevskaya organization, which, according to a report by Interpol's Millennium Project, "is considered the most powerful criminal organization in the world," with control of the Moscow region and significant influence in Europe, North America, and Israel.[21] Mikhailov, in turn, was friendly with two brothers who were ex-boxers, Viktor and Alexandr Averin.

No one knew it at the time, of course, but these were historic early meetings of a new generation of leaders in the Russian Mafia, of men who shared a vision beyond the Soviet Union. Nor could anyone have known that over the next thirty years they would be tied to both Donald Trump and Vladimir Putin.

At a time when hundreds of Russian mobsters were engaged in open gang warfare, Mikhailov and his Solntsevskaya associates also transitioned to the white-collar, legitimate business world, through their ownership of casino Maxim in Moscow; Sistema Holding, a large conglomerate with insurance, telecom, oil, and banking interests;[22] and SV Holding, a firm that manages real estate, casinos, restaurants, and hotels, and served as the first legal cover for the activities of Solntsevskaya group.[23] Within that context, Mogilevich carved out a unique position as the financial genius behind Mikhailov's huge Solntsevskaya organization, the biggest Russian gang of all, with a thousand men engaged in extortion, drug trafficking, arms trafficking, and prostitution.[24]

For all that, it is possible that the FBI and the Western media have overstated Mogilevich's power. "I understand that the American press makes Mogilevich out to be the big don, but he is not," said one knowledgeable source who has considerable experience in the Russian underworld.[25] "He never was. The real boss was Mikhas and then Avera [Viktor Averin]. It is very clear. Mikhas was and is the boss of the Solntsevskaya Bratva. But all of them were too stupid to make business. For that they needed Seva. They could not make the business without Seva. He was the only one who had the brains. Mikhas and Avera, they are the ones with the muscle."

According to Interpol,[26] Mogilevich was a member of Solntsevo's "board of governing members" with Mikhailov, and participated in crafting a "criminal community strategy," resolving internal and external conflicts, laundering money, distributing profits among the leaders, distribution of "*obshakom*" (collective funds used to bribe authorities or finance new ventures), and other shared issues. Finally, the Interpol report said, Mogilevich was also "responsible for [Solntsevo's] relations with Ukrainian criminal organizations."

While he partnered with Solntsevo, Mogilevich also ran his own smaller 250-person gang,[27] the Semion Mogilevich Organization, which allegedly became a launching pad for criminal enterprises that included arms dealing, drug running, prostitution, contract murder, financial crimes, and more all over the world. Much of this was done through Arbat, which Mogilevich controlled, while Mikhailov and his pal Viktor Averin co-owned 25 percent and Vyacheslav Ivankov owned the remaining quarter.

But in the end, it was Mogilevich's expertise at laundering money that made him so invaluable to other mobsters. He had mastered a skill that was deeply coveted by the most formidable gangsters on the planet: He took dirty money and made it clean.

Mogilevich's ascent happened to coincide with a period during which Soviet leaders had been dying in such rapid succession* that Vice President George H. W. Bush, who represented the US at state funerals, was said to have a new motto: "You die, I fly."[28]

The replacement of the sclerotic old hard-liners of the Soviet Union by Mikhail Gorbachev and his energetic new younger generation signaled a tectonic shift in global affairs. Gorbachev's policies were successful in easing tensions with the West and providing a relief valve to its repressed citizenry. But they also weakened Soviet control of its satellites. Before long, Moscow lost control over Soviet republics in the Baltic and the Caucasus. In November 1989, the Berlin Wall fell.

All of which was widely celebrated in the West. But Trump's views were slightly different. "Russia is out of control and the leadership knows it," he told *Playboy* in 1990.[29] "I predict [Gorbachev] will be overthrown, because he has shown extraordinary weakness. . . . Yet Gorbachev is getting credit for being a wonderful leader—and we should continue giving him credit, because he's destroying the Soviet Union."

Which wasn't far from the truth. In 1991, Boris Yeltsin, the newly elected president of the Russian Soviet Federative Socialist Republic, turned against Gorbachev, whom he had initially supported. In August, there was an aborted coup, which temporarily removed Gorbachev from power. He returned a few days later, but, for all practical purposes, the Soviet Union was dead.

On December 23, Gorbachev met with Yeltsin. Two days later, on Christmas Day, he resigned, and Yeltsin then became the first president of the Russian Federation. In an effective heartbeat, the world's oldest and most powerful communist state had ceased to exist.

———

This was everything the Mafia had longed for. When it came to property, criminals, and illicit funds crossing borders, the floodgates had

---

* Leonid Brezhnev died in 1982; Yuri Andropov in 1984; and Konstantin Chernenko in 1985.

opened. "As soon as the Berlin Wall came down, there was no border," said James Moody, former deputy assistant director of the FBI.[30] "Criminals were just flowing. Once they got into Europe, they could do anything they wanted."

The hermetically sealed, closed world of the Soviet Union was dead and gone for good. Under communism, the Bratva had had to make do with relatively small-time crime such as extortion rackets and black marketeering. Now it emerged with an explosive force to fill the vacuum left by the failed Soviet state.

Yeltsin had vowed that a market economy would replace communism, but the shift was so abrupt that cash-rich gangsters rushed in to join forces with corrupt apparatchiks—including those in the KGB— and loot newly privatized state-held assets. Once that happened, the die had been cast. Instead of creating a truly democratic infrastructure and a market economy, Yeltsin essentially was allowing a handful of oligarchs to become enormously wealthy, in return for which he demanded their political support.[31]

Russia was a poor country but it had an enormous amount of natural resources—oil and natural gas, iron ore, chromium, copper, tin, lead, aluminum, wheat, timber, and more. Massive industries that had been held by the state were now up for sale—all for mere kopeks on the ruble. Russia had become a gangster's paradise. It was the birth of a new age of unimaginable greed, in which organized crime was about to become a powerful geopolitical force.

Mogilevich approached the post–Cold War era like a general surveying a battlefield with a grand strategic vision. As early as 1985, he had set up offices in Switzerland, Nigeria, and the Cayman Islands.[32] In 1990, according to the FBI, Mogilevich acquired Arigon Ltd., which sold clothing in the former Soviet Union and oil to Ukrainian Railways, and registered it in the Channel Islands,[33] then began using it as a corporate base for his growing empire and as the main legal entity for laundering funds from Solntsevskaya when he received money-laundering assignments from Mikhailov.[34]

He reportedly cultivated a relationship with Czechoslovakia-born Robert Maxwell, the powerful British press lord who had bought control of the Bulgarian Cooperative Bank. That became another vehicle through which Mogilevich could launder money for Solntsevskaya.[35]

Now was the time to go global. Thanks to Israel's Law of Return,* the easiest route for Mogilevich, one favored by countless Russian mobsters, was to get Israeli citizenship.[36] "There is not a major Russian organized crime figure who we are tracking who does not also carry an Israeli passport," said Jonathan Winer, the former money-laundering czar in the Clinton State Department.[37] Many of them, Winer added, such as Sergei Mikhailov, were not even Jewish. It was not unusual for Russian gangsters to suddenly discover a Jewish grandmother lurking in their family tree.

Not long after his arrival, according to an Israeli intelligence report, Mogilevich "succeeded in building a bridgehead in Israel . . . [and] developing significant and influential [political and business] ties" by forging relationships with both Russian and Israeli criminals to run businesses in tourism, real estate, and catering through proxies. That included opening bank accounts in Israel, attending gatherings in Israel with other criminals, and, according to a classified FBI document, the "alleged purchase" by Mogilevich of an unnamed Israeli bank, with branches in Moscow, Cyprus, and Tel Aviv, for "laundering money for Colombian and Russian Organized Crime groups."[38]

Still, Mogilevich found something in Israel that he didn't like. "There are too many Jews," he told the *National Post* of Canada. "Too much arguing. Everybody is talking all the time and their voices are so loud."[39]

And so, in 1991, he married Katalin Papp, a Hungarian national, and moved to Budapest, where he established a new international base of operations.[40] There, Mogilevich bought the Black and White[41] nightclubs, a chain of strip joints in Budapest, Prague, Riga, and Kiev, and

---

* Israel's Law of Return gives Jews the right to come and live in Israel and to gain Israeli citizenship. In 1970, the right of entry and settlement was extended to people with one Jewish grandparent and a person who is married to a Jew, whether or not he or she is considered Jewish under Orthodox interpretations of Halakha.

turned it into a global hub for prostitution and money laundering.*[42] He
worked with the Italian Camorra, a leading Neopolitan crime syndicate,
in drugs, arms sales, and money laundering.[43]

Before long, according to Interpol's Project Millennium, Mogilevich's activities included "trade in oil, weapons and military strategic
materials and human trafficking on an international scale."[44] As his organization grew, Mogilevich remained partners with Mikhailov in
Solntsevskaya, which was also growing rapidly. According to the Russian crime blog *Russian Mafiozi,*[45] Mogilevich partnered with Mikhailov
in at least eight other companies in addition to Arbat.† Solntsevskaya
had begun to acquire real financial power, both in Russia and abroad.

But Mogilevich had not yet made his mark in the US. To do that, he
turned to one of his partners in Arbat, Vyacheslav Ivankov, one of the
most brutal and murderous gangsters in the history of Russian crime.

———

Starting off in the sixties in the back alleys of Moscow,[46] Ivankov began
his career as a gangster in a highly unusual way. In his youth, according
to the *Moscow Times*, he had trained to be a circus performer, which led
to a brief career working as a stuntman and training others for Mosfilm,
the largest film studio in the Soviet Union.[47] According to the memoirs
of Nikolai Vashchilin, a well-known Soviet stuntman who appeared in
the 1967 adventure film *The Elusive Avengers* (*Neulovimye mstiteli*),
when Ivankov turned to crime, he put together his first criminal gang
consisting largely of athletes and stuntmen.

Vashchilin adds that Ivankov had ties to Leonid Usvyatsov, who allegedly ran a similar gang of mobsters who were stuntmen with Lenfilm, the Leningrad film studio. Usvyatsov, in turn, happened to have
another job in Leningrad, teaching judo to young men, and among his
prized students was someone named Vladimir Putin.[48]

When Ivankov wasn't gracing the silver screen, he made a name for

---

* In an interview with *Moskovsky Komsomolets*, Mogilevich explained, "In the eyes of the
FBI, any disco that contains Russians is a brothel."

† Maxim, SV Holding, Emire Bond in Israel, Arigon, Magnex in Hungary, MAB International in Belgium, YBM Magnex in the US, and Benex.

himself as a ruthless practitioner of extortion who went after black marketeers, bureaucrats, and store managers with such cruelty that his victims were paralyzed with fear. Using fraudulent militia documents, he would search the homes of wealthy Russians, take whatever he wanted, and leave.[49] A fairly typical outing had Ivankov and his gang breaking into the home of a wealthy black marketeer, handcuffing him to the radiator, and threatening to pour acid all over him unless he signed a promissory note for 100,000 rubles.[50] "As a rule, his victims did not contact the police," wrote Galina Odinokova, a crime specialist in the Ministry of Internal Affairs, in *Russian Militia Gazette*, a police publication, in 1992. "They preferred to part with their wealth than with their lives."[51]

Inevitably, however, Ivankov's wild gun battles and daring getaways led him to jail, psychiatric hospitals, and finally a remote and frigid penal colony in Siberia where he was inducted into the brotherhood of the *vory v zakone*. Even imprisoned in a Siberian gulag, in the eighties, Ivankov managed to cultivate a mystique as an enforcer, as one of the top *vory*. He took on the name Yaponchik, which means "the little Japanese" in Russian and was made famous by a folk hero–like gangster named Mishka Vinnitsky, who had run the underworld in prerevolutionary Odessa.[52]

Those who crossed Ivankov in jail sometimes paid for it with their lives. According to *Red Mafiya*, he stabbed one inmate in the back and used a metal stool to club a prison guard over the head.[53] As his reputation for brutality grew, Ivankov became one of the top *vory*, and, with the help of accomplices on the other side of the world, was able to control criminal activities in the Russian Far East, persuade banks to buy millions of dollars of stocks in a phony Siberian mining company, and send out a hit man in Toronto, Canada. In other words, he was exactly what Mogilevich was looking for.

And so, in late 1990, Mogilevich bribed a Russian judge to secure Ivankov's early release from a Siberian prison where he was being held for robbery and torture. When Ivankov was freed, Soviet authorities tasked him with the daunting assignment of taking on the ferocious Chechen Mafia, an undertaking Ivankov embraced with such fervor that rivers of blood soon were flowing from gangland shootouts, car bombings, and the like. Before long, Ivankov's excesses had enraged the very politicians who had helped free him: Now that the Soviet Union had collapsed, Russia desperately wanted Western investors, and Ivankov was scaring them away.[54]

As a result, in early 1992, the so-called Circle of Brothers, the ruling council of the *vory,* gave Ivankov his marching orders: "Go to the New Land and invade America!"[55]

Meanwhile, Donald Trump was opening a new chapter in his life. His marriage to Ivana had produced three children—Donald Jr., Ivanka, and Eric—but Trump had begun a highly publicized tabloid relationship with Marla Maples. Trump and Ivana were headed toward divorce. At the same time, his massive losses in Atlantic City had made it very difficult for him to get financing, which paralyzed any future development.

In the past, Italian Mafia associations had been crucial to his family's success. They had helped his father's projects. They had helped Donald develop Trump Tower, giving him secure access to ready-mix concrete. Mob-connected lawyers like Roy Cohn had always been there for him.

It is not clear how much Trump knew about Mogilevich's expansion into New York or the imminent arrival of Vyacheslav Ivankov and the Russian Mafia. But he was not wanting when it came to bravado. "I've always been blessed with a kind of intuition about people that allows me to sense who the sleazy guys are," he wrote in *Trump: Surviving at the Top,* "and I stay far away."

CHAPTER SEVEN

THE BILLIONAIRE BOYS' CLUB

As early as 1990, Trump's casinos were in so much trouble that, far from being a multibillionaire, as he claimed, Trump actually had a negative net worth. Indeed, at a time when payments on more than $1 billion worth of bonds on his casinos came due every ninety days, he was down to his last $1.6 million.[1]

Then, in 1991, the Trump Taj Mahal, the $1.2 billion casino Trump touted as the "eighth wonder of the world," became the first of six Trump bankruptcies. As these fiascos took place, Trump structured his bankruptcies so he could sell off his stocks and reap millions while investors lost their shirts.[2] But even that wasn't enough to allow his empire to remain intact. Thanks to personal liabilities exceeding $900 million, one after another, Trump's three Atlantic City casinos and the Plaza Hotel slipped out of his grasp. Other assets, such as the Trump Shuttle and his 282-foot yacht, the *Trump Princess,* were casualties as well.[3]

Whether the Russians had been using Trump casinos to launder money was never established in court, but there was more than enough reason to be suspicious. The Taj Mahal had become a favorite destination for the Russian mob because Trump made a point of giving high rollers "comps" for up to $100,000 a visit, an amenity that casinos often offered big-time gamblers.[4] Later, two other Trump casinos, the Trump Castle Hotel and Casino, and the Trump Plaza Hotel and Casino, agreed to pay fines for "willfully failing to report" currency transactions over $10,000 and failing to comply with laws designed to prevent money laundering.[5]

———

As it happened, Donald Trump wasn't the only future president who had vital business relationships with the Russian Mafia. In Russia at roughly the same time, in the early and midnineties, the deputy mayor of St. Petersburg was also working with them. His name was Vladimir Putin.

Born in 1952, Vladimir Vladimirovich Putin grew up in war-ravaged Leningrad (now St. Petersburg), the only child of parents who had both suffered badly in World War II. His family was not particularly well off, and one of its most notable marks of distinction, revealed in a two-hour documentary called *Putin* that was released in 2018, was that Putin said his paternal grandfather had been a cook for both Vladimir Lenin and Joseph Stalin in their dachas in the Moscow area.[6]

Impulsive, angry, and undisciplined, Putin was so uncontrollable as a schoolboy that he was initially rejected by the Pioneers,[7] the Soviet youth movement that was roughly the Russian equivalent of America's Boy Scouts, but with a communist twist.

Despite his rebellious streak, Putin had already begun cultivating two passions to which he would remain deeply committed for the rest of his life—the KGB and judo. Inspired by *The Shield and the Sword,* a popular book/miniseries that romanticized Soviet espionage and its heroic KGB agents, he dreamed about becoming a Soviet spy. In ninth grade, Putin actually went to the offices of the KGB directorate in Leningrad to enlist, only to be told that he was too young and should probably go to law school before applying.[8]

Knowing that the KGB expected its adherents to be proficient in hand-to-hand combat,[9] he also took up both sambo* and judo as sports he practiced his entire life. "Judo is not just a sport," Putin said. "It's

———

* Sambo is a Soviet martial art that was created by Red Army officers in the 1920s. The word "sambo" is derived from an anagram of a Russian phrase for "self-defense without weapons."

a philosophy. It's respect for your elders and for your opponent. It's not for weaklings . . . You come out onto the mat, you bow to one another, you follow ritual."[10] Later, once he was in power, Putin would follow a judo-like practice of turning his adversaries' greatest strength against them.

Judo also shaped Putin in ways that are not widely recognized.[11] For starters, there's the matter of his coach, Leonid Ionovich Usvyatsov. Putin had other judo coaches who are frequently cited in the media, but Usvyatsov may have been the most influential. In *First Person,* Putin speaks fondly about Leonid Ionovich, or Lyonya, Usvyatsov's nickname, but he would often omit the last name of the beloved coach who was such an influential force in his life. The reason for that apparent oversight may be that he did not want people to know his beloved coach was a mobster. Usvyatsov's epitaph on his tombstone in St. Petersburg suggests the depth of his ties to the mob. "I may be dead," it reads, "but the mafia is immortal."[12]

Whatever talents Usvyatsov had in the martial arts, few people realized that Putin's coach was also a key figure in the Tambovskaya[13] crime gang (aka Tambov), based in St. Petersburg, which has been referred to as "the Russian Goodfellas"[14] and became known for smuggling heroin from Afghanistan to St. Petersburg and Western Europe.[15]

In the late sixties, while still in his mid-teens, Putin also began going to judo workouts at the Trud athletic club at 21 Decembrists Street in Leningrad, with Usvyatsov as his coach. Still a highly impressionable teenager, for the first time, Putin encountered a world that was a precursor to the kleptocracy he later created, complete with wannabe oligarchs and Bratva mobsters.

Indeed, when Putin first began training under Usvyatsov, his coach had already served a ten-year prison sentence for rape.* In addition to

---

* Usvyatsov's prison record didn't seem to interfere with mentoring Putin, as Usvyatsov is sometimes credited with helping the future president win admittance to the law school of Leningrad State University, a considerable feat, if true, given Putin's lackluster academic record. The suggestion that Usvyatsov helped Putin get into college has been written about in various blogs in Russia, but Putin gives a somewhat different version in *First Person*. (See https://pressimus.com/Interpreter_Mag/stream/2712.)

his criminal record, Usvyatsov, according to a fellow stuntman, had close ties to Mogilevich henchman Vyacheslav Ivankov.[16] Their connection was an unusual one: Just as Ivankov had an aboveboard career as a stuntman at Mosfilm in Moscow, so Usvyatsov had a similar career as a stuntman at Lenfilm in Leningrad. That made them both gangsters who happened to moonlight as stuntmen for the silver screen.

Moreover, Usvyatsov and Ivankov were not the only judokas who actually got screen time. Many of Putin's judo pals were stuntmen at Mosfilm or Lenfilm, and, according to Vasily Shestakov, president of the International Sambo Federation, Putin himself sometimes appeared as an extra in films, notably in *Blockade* and in *Izhorsky Battalion*.[17] Shestakov said he even played a Nazi soldier in one.[18]

And it was at the Trud where Putin met the men to whom he has been forever loyal, including not just coach Usvyatsov, but also two judo pals who became his lifelong friends and sparring partners, the brothers Arkady and Boris Rotenberg.*[19] (The Rotenberg brothers were sanctioned in 2014 by the US Treasury Department for "acting for or on behalf of or materially assisting, sponsoring, or providing financial, material, or technological support for, or goods or services to or in support of, a senior official of the Government of the Russian Federation.")[20] In essence, the Trud athletic club—whose members included a big-time mobster in Usvyatsov, at least two men who became billionaire oligarchs, and the future president of Russia—was to Putin as Manhattan's boardrooms and back rooms were to Trump: the place where they met the men who built them and gave them power.

———

One of Putin's most noteworthy qualities, as the title of Masha Gessen's *The Man Without a Face* suggests, was not so much any single easily recognizable characteristic as the *absence* of such traits. Vladimir Putin was faceless. Opaque. He revealed nothing. All admirable qualities in

---

* In the wake of the 2014 Crimean crisis, President Barack Obama blacklisted the Rotenberg brothers, among other friends of Putin.

the world of espionage that, no doubt, he put to good use when he joined the KGB in 1975.

Nevertheless, Putin's career as a spy is reported to have been far less glamorous and exotic than he might have imagined as a young boy.[21] After a series of dreary assignments monitoring foreigners and foreign officials in Leningrad, in 1984, Putin spent a year in spy school in Moscow,* where he became a great proponent of the use of "active measures," including disinformation, both within Russia and abroad, by disseminating conflicting accounts of events to create the impression that there are no reliable facts.

But in 1985, Putin was transferred to Dresden, East Germany,[22] a drab Cold War backwater where, for the most part, he was reduced to collecting press clippings with useless information for the KGB. More to the point, Putin had little to show for his years of service in the KGB. Soviet leader Mikhail Gorbachev, as part of his policies of détente, had vowed to dismantle the KGB. After the Berlin Wall came down in 1989, Putin's friends were banned from working in law enforcement, as teachers, or for the government.[23]

In these final days of the Soviet Union, however, Putin may have taken away one enduring lesson. In December 1990, KGB chief Vladimir Kryuchkov ordered his subordinates to create hundreds of front companies as a safe haven for money for party leaders.[24]

In some ways, there was nothing particularly new about this strategy. Throughout the eighties, Soviet operatives had been more or less regularly expelled from France, Italy, Portugal, Sweden, the United States, and other countries[25] for industrial espionage and the like. One of the most notable of those companies was Seabeco SA,[26] which was founded in 1982,[27] according to Belgium's *Le Soir*,[28] "as a cover for the

---

* Putin attended what is now known as the Academy of Foreign Intelligence or the SVR Academy, and was previously known as the Yuri Andropov Red Banner Institute or Red Banner Institute, one of the primary espionage academies of Russia, and, before that, the Soviet Union, serving the KGB and its successor organization, the Foreign Intelligence Service or Foreign Security Service. Known as the Federal'naya sluzhba bezopasnosti Rossiyskoy Federatsii in Russian, it is most frequently referred to in English as the FSB. But the historic power of the KGB is such that it is often referred to by those initials as well.

Soviet services" by Boris Birshtein*, who had a close business relationship with the Solntsevskaya Bratva's Sergei Mikhailov.

But now that the Soviet Union was dying, desperate measures were called for. After all, what would happen if their embassies were shut down? "The Russians wanted to have intelligence officers in country even if the embassy was down," says John Sipher, who spent twenty-eight years in the CIA's clandestine service, which included serving in Moscow and running the CIA's Russian operations.[29] "So in addition to having legal residents who were intelligence officers in embassies, they had illegal residents who might appear to be French citizens living in France or Finnish citizens in France, but they were fake. They were really Russians. It was an incredible amount of work to give these people real backgrounds, languages, passports, and real businesses. But as the Soviet Union fell apart, Kryuchkov wanted to make sure he had Russians in other countries working for Russian businesses that were self-supporting and could support intelligence activities."

So in March 1991, after the Baltic States and other republics split off from the USSR, Kryuchkov created a plan to launch about 600 companies run by "retired" KGB officers, often as joint ventures in the Baltics or Israel. All agents in the operation were instructed to do whatever they could to gain a commercial foothold that would enable them to be self-sustaining. The companies were there not merely to provide cover for intelligence operatives. They were there to function as real companies, as major corporations, to make money, to finance operations against the West, to launder money, and to gather intelligence that could be used against the West. This was the kind of expertise that would serve Putin well in the future as it became clear what shape the new Russia would take.

Meanwhile, after the Wall fell, Putin moved back to Leningrad in 1990, continued with the KGB, and kept a low profile.[30] According to Oleg Kalugin, who was one of his bosses, within the KGB, Putin was something of a cipher. "He would knock on my door, and say, 'Please sign this,'" Kalugin recalled.[31] Otherwise, Kalugin said, Putin did not make much of an impression.

---

* Birshtein, through his lawyer, has denied any KGB connection. (See https://ft.com/trumptoronto.)

His prospects were bleak. "He came from Germany with no job," said Kalugin. "He had to be a cab driver with his own car he brought from East Germany, a Trabant probably.* And he drove for a few months, six or eight months, just earning money."†32

Everything had changed. Conventional wisdom had it that the Great Game was over. The West had won. A classified ad in the *International Herald Tribune* told the story: "FORMER KGB agent seeks employment in similar field," it read, accompanied by a phone number.33

For a brief period that year, Putin took an administrative post at Leningrad State University—a fairly standard cover for a KGB operative.34 Then, just as the Soviet Union was dissolving, Anatoly Sobchak, a former law professor of Putin's at Leningrad State, became mayor of Leningrad.‡

In sync with the changing times of the Gorbachev era, Sobchak had positioned himself as a strong pro-democracy politician, but he also knew that the KGB was scrambling to take charge of whatever institutions might survive—including the municipal government in Leningrad. In addition, he was wise enough to realize that he'd be better off if he picked his own deputy from the KGB rather than allowing the KGB to choose the man who would work directly under him.35

As a result, Sobchak asked Kalugin whom he should hire from the KGB. "I mentioned a couple of names, but he said they were too highly placed," Kalugin recalled.36

Sobchak wanted someone who was not immediately identifiable as a high-profile, hard-line KGB operative, so instead, he hired Vladimir Putin, a mere lieutenant colonel, whom he had known when Putin worked at Leningrad State. Putin was still on active reserve with the KGB, which was monitoring the ascent of the new "democratic" leaders in Russia,37 and, his low profile notwithstanding, the hiring of a KGB

---

* With its two-cylinder engine and plastic body, the Trabant was referred to as "a spark plug with a roof" and came to symbolize the demise of the Eastern Bloc.

† In *First Person*, Putin disputes Kalugin's account, saying, "[Kalugin] doesn't remember a thing. He couldn't remember me. I had no contact with him, nor did I meet him. It is I who remembers him, because he was a big boss and everybody knew him."
  "Kalugin is a traitor," Putin added. "I saw Kalugin during my time in Leningrad when he was deputy head of the Directorate. He was an absolute loafer."

‡ Leningrad changed its name back to St. Petersburg in 1991.

bureaucrat by Sobchak was seen as a betrayal. "Sobchak portrayed himself as a crusader for freedom and cursed the KGB," said Alexander Schelkanov, who served as chairman of the executive committee of the Leningrad city council at the time. "He then went out and hired a professional KGB operative as his closest deputy. He openly violated his own principles."[38]

With the country still very much in crisis, KGB men began turning up at the sides of newly minted oligarchs, government ministers, at the highest levels of power. In Moscow, that included President Boris Yeltsin, who, from the first moment he succeeded Gorbachev, found that wherever he went, KGB bodyguards were watching his every move.[39]

Similarly, Putin's new job may have been part of a carefully orchestrated KGB operation to penetrate Sobchak's inner circle and that of other pro-democracy politicians. "This really means that [Putin] acted on orders [from the KGB] and was part of an operation that I would call 'Trojan Horse,'" said Leonid Dobrovolsky, deputy chairman of the city's food committee.[40]

Even though Putin saw the collapse of the Soviet Union as a disaster, it was the best thing that could have possibly happened to his career. At an extraordinary moment in its history, Russia's newfound lawlessness became a mission worthy of his enormous ambitions, as well as a gigantic opportunity.

At the time, hyperinflation had wiped out the savings of millions of people[41] just as hundreds of billions of dollars' worth of Russia's natural resources—gas, oil, metals, timber, and more—were about to be sold off by the state.[42] Food shortages necessitated launching a temporary system of barter operations in which the city of St. Petersburg traded raw materials—oil, timber, rare metals, and the like—with foreign companies for food.

Because St. Petersburg was the first Russian city[43] in which property was privatized, Putin led the way. From his relatively unimpressive perch as deputy mayor of St. Petersburg and chair of the External Affairs Committee (KVS), he was given the mandate of encouraging, regulating, and licensing foreign investment in huge formerly state-owned enterprises. Now that the centralized command structures of the Soviet era were gone, authorities desperately needed new mechanisms to put goods into stores. Putin had acquired the power to determine who could become wealthy.

According to Marina Salye, a former city council member who chaired a commission that investigated missing food imports, Putin made a killing by signing export licenses, despite lacking the proper authority to do so, for various dubious companies. In the process, she said, he doled out more than $120 million in goods to highly suspect people—and the city received nothing in return.[44]

Outsiders who were unwilling to go to the dark side didn't stand much of a chance. "This began in an era when selling blue jeans was an economic crime," explained an American businessman who was doing deals in Moscow at the time. "You could go to jail for that. Now, suddenly there was oil. So I was working with bankers who rose to the top during this period. We had to hire security, thuggish guys who like to fight. You had your security and the other guys had security.[45]

"It was the Wild West. You had no idea of what was going on. There was the Mogilevich gang and Chechen gangs all fighting gang warfare. I was trying to comply with the Foreign Corrupt Practices Act, but we didn't really know whom we were dealing with or how the system might change. And if you wanted to take over the really big enterprises, you needed the Mafia's help. You needed protection."

Various Mafias stepped in to fill the breach—Azeris, Chechens, Solntsevo, the Mogilevich Organization, and, in St. Petersburg, the Tambov crime gang. The criminals needed export licenses, tax exemptions, below-market-rate loans, business visas, and freedom from arrest and prosecution for their crimes. All of this and more was available from Putin and corrupt bureaucrats under him.

Money could not go abroad without the approval of Putin's KVS. The same was true for businesses that wanted to be licensed and registered. He also was able to control the movement of money across international borders. All of which put an enormous amount of power in Putin's hands—not Sobchak's.[46]

Like Donald Trump, Putin had been well acquainted with mobsters long before he had a political career, thanks to judo coach Leonid Usvyatsov.[47] In 1994, Usvyatsov was killed[48] in a gang dispute, but Putin cemented ties with Tambov through its leader, Vladimir Kumarin,*[49] aka Vladimir Barsukov, who also served as an executive at the Petersburg Fuel Company, which Putin had chosen to be the sole supplier of gasoline for the city.[50] In return, Tambov helped Putin and his cronies control the airport, the seaport, rail stations, and various other choke points through which flowed 20 percent of all Russian imports and exports.[51]

Kumarin was also on the board of directors of a subsidiary of SPAG, a German company that had huge real estate holdings in St. Petersburg and, according to the BND (Bundesnachrichtendienst, the German Federal Intelligence Service), was laundering money for Russia's organized crime and also for Colombian drug dealers.[52] According to *Newsweek*, SPAG executives were indicted for laundering more than $1 million in cash for Colombia's Cali cocaine cartel.[53] Putin served on its advisory board at the time.[†]

By 1994, the Russian economy was in such disarray that a plan called "loans for shares" was instituted through which Russian banks lent the government money in exchange for temporary stakes in the state-owned companies that were to be auctioned off.[54]

But once the auctions began, the *New York Times* reported, "it became all too obvious that a fix was in. Foreign investors were barred from bidding for the most desirable assets, and the same banks that were assigned by the Government to organize the auctions ended up winning them, and usually at only a fraction over the minimum bid."[55]

A tiny elite began to acquire control over a vast number of public enterprises. Oligarch Mikhail Khodorkovsky got a 78 percent share of ownership in Yukos, the oil and gas giant, worth about $5 billion, for

---

* Kumarin is serving a fourteen-year sentence for money laundering and organizing the illegal takeover of companies in St. Petersburg.

† A Liechtenstein court found two men associated with SPAG, Rudolf Ritter and Eugen von Hoffen, guilty of fraud, but acquitted them on charges that they laundered money for the Cali cartel.

just $310 million. Boris Berezovsky bought Sibneft, another oil giant, worth $3 billion, for a mere $100 million.[56]

A majority stake in Gazprom, the state-owned energy company that controlled a third of the world's gas reserves, was sold for just $230 million, according to an article by James Henry, former chief economist at McKinsey & Company, in the *American Interest*. Russia's entire national electric grid was privatized for just $630 million. Natural resources such as oil, iron and steel, and aluminum; high-tech arms; airline industries; diamond mines; and most of Russia's banking system went for next to nothing.[57]

In all, Russia privatized 150 state-owned companies for just $12 billion. Anatoly Chubais, Russia's first deputy prime minister and the so-called father of Russian privatization, framed the dilemma in stark terms. "We did not [at first] have the choice between socialism and ideal capitalism," he said.[58] "The choice in Russia . . . was between a criminalized transition and civil war."

What Russia faced was nothing less than the looting of its natural resources, the betrayal of a capitalist revolution, and the birth of Putin's kleptocracy, an era of unimaginable corruption and greed. It was as if a virus had been injected into the system, spreading and institutionalizing corruption throughout a Mafia state run by a kleptocrat who ruled over a web of crooked patronage networks.

Before long, the money began to flow. There were real estate transactions, arms sales, shady bank deals, illegal exports, and much more.[59] From the beginning, Putin's friends did well. His judo pals Arkady and Boris Rotenberg ended up being co-owners of SGM (Stroygazmontazh) Group, the largest construction company for gas pipelines and electrical power lines in Russia. *Forbes* estimated Arkady's wealth at $2.6 billion, and Boris's at $1.16 billion. Gennady Timchenko, another judoka pal of Putin's, fared even better as chairman of the Gunvor oil-trading firm, with a net worth of $15.6 billion.[60] Anatoly Turchak, yet another judo sparring partner of Putin's, served as deputy to Putin in St. Petersburg.[61] He ended up being the main owner of the Leninets defense plant, and was worth hundreds of millions of dollars.[62]

Others who remained loyal to Putin over the years were rewarded with enormous wealth and key positions during his presidency—among them, Igor Sechin, who ended up as CEO of Rosneft, the huge Russian oil company;[63] Alexei Miller, CEO of Gazprom; Herman Gref, CEO of Russia's largest bank, Sberbank; Dmitry Medvedev, who became prime minister and subsequently president; and many others.

In their very different ways, Trump and Putin were assembling networks that were essential to their political ambitions. In Trump Tower, Donald had put together a glamorous refuge for celebrities and the super-rich that enabled him to project a highly marketable persona all over the world. As for Putin, he took the idea of the dacha, the seasonal or second home that is so popular among Russians, and personalized it for his own inner circle by assembling the Ozero dacha cooperative on the shores of Lake Komsomolskoye as a relaxing weekend retreat for the new privileged Russian elite, including Yeltsin and his family; Tambov crime boss Vladimir Kumarin, who served as the Ozero co-op's vice president; and a number of oligarchs in the making.

Over time, the Ozero cooperative became so emblematic of Putin's inner circle that in 2014, when the United States and the European Union imposed economic sanctions on Putin's closest associates, no fewer than eight shareholders in Ozero were sanctioned.[64]

———

Putin's tenure in Sobchak's office was so rife with scandal that it led to a host of investigations into illegal assignment of licenses and contracts by Putin as head of the Committee for Foreign Liaison; collaboration with criminal gangs in regulating gambling; a money-laundering operation by the St. Petersburg Real Estate Holding Company, where Kumarin was involved and Putin served on the advisory board; Putin's role in providing a monopoly for the Petersburg Fuel Company, then controlled by the Tambov criminal organization; and much, much more—virtually all of which was whitewashed.[65] But according to Kumarin himself, while he was in St. Petersburg in the nineties, Putin signed many hundreds of contracts doling out funds to his cronies.[66]

One KGB/FSB agent who tracked Putin's corruption relentlessly during this period was Alexander Litvinenko, a lieutenant colonel then in his midthirties who later wrote about his findings in *The Gang from Lubyanka*.* An avid athlete, Sasha, as his friends called him, had joined the KGB as a young lieutenant to be "part of a real team fighting a common enemy—and on the right side, so you think."[67]

"I thought I was going to be protecting people from harm," he told a friend.[68] "That the Agency had a dark past—the Gulag, you know, millions of victims—I didn't learn until the 1990s."

In the end, Litvinenko discovered that Putin's "relationship with the criminal Kumarin-Barsukov is currently the number one state secret in Russia." He added that "the whole of St. Petersburg knows that Putin is linked to this man by personal friendship and financial ties."[69]

When St. Petersburg prosecutors investigated Putin's corruption, they concluded, "In 1994, the humble clerk [Dmitry] Medvedev† owned 10% of Europe's largest pulp‡[70] and paper mill. . . . And this was only Medvedev, Putin's advisor. Can you imagine what kind of money was already owned by his boss?"[71]

Putin himself mysteriously ended up with a villa in Biarritz that was registered to Gennady Timchenko for many years.[72] But that was merely the beginning of a wealth that includes huge stakes in Russia's massive private energy and commodities companies and that is so vast and so secretive that it could not reliably be calculated.

While much of the world thought post-Soviet Russia was struggling with the birth pangs of creating a new democracy, in fact something very different was going on: A kleptocracy was being born. Putin had put himself at the nexus of three worlds—the Chekists (agents of the

---

* Lubyanka, of course, is the home of the KGB/FSB, and the title is meant to suggest that agents such as Putin were in fact nothing more than gangsters.

† Medvedev became president of Russia in 2008 after having served as Putin's chief of staff and then as first deputy prime minister. When Putin retook the presidency in 2012, Medvedev became prime minister.

‡ At the time, Medvedev was a consultant to the city hall's External Affairs Committee, which was headed by Putin. In November 1993, Medvedev became the legal affairs director of Ilim Pulp Enterprise, Russia's largest lumber company, with annual revenues of $500 million. According to Daniel Treisman's *The Return: Russia's Journey from Gorbachev to Medvedev*, Medvedev actually received 20 percent of the company's stock—not 10 percent.

KGB, FSB, and other state security organizations), the bureaucrats with whom he worked who were in charge of licensing and regulating companies that had been controlled by the state but were being privatized, and alleged Russian mafiosi such as the Tambov gang's Vladimir Barsukov, also known as Kumarin.

Altogether, Putin's three-legged stool formed a base of operations that was capable of propelling its creator to the highest reaches of power in the new Russian Federation that was rising from the ashes of the Soviet Union. But if Putin was truly to achieve his grandest ambitions, he would need something more—namely, an ally who had the power and reach to recruit assets and agents among people of influence deep inside the United States.

CHAPTER EIGHT

MOGILEVICH'S BIG MOVE

Far from sitting idly by as the Soviet Union crumbled, Semion Mogilevich had quickly forged extremely close ties at the highest levels of Boris Yeltsin's new Russian government and become a highly valued adjunct to Russian intelligence.

Indeed, according to secretly recorded conversations between Leonid Kuchma, the second president of newly independent Ukraine, and Ihor Smeshko, the head of Ukraine's secret service (the SBU), Mogilevich was still living in Budapest, but had bought property in Moscow and had already begun delivering valuable intelligence to Yeltsin's highest-ranking security officers—all in an apparent effort to strengthen his ties to the intelligence establishment in the chaotic Russian capital.

Kuchma: "He [Mogilevich] has bought a dacha in Moscow, he keeps coming."

Smeshko: "He has received a passport already. By the way, the passport in Moscow is in a different name. And . . . [Alexander] Korzhakov [the head of Boris Yeltsin's personal security] sent two colonels to Mogilevich in Budapest in order to receive damaging information on a person . . . He himself did not meet them. His organization's lieutenant, [Igor] Korol, met these colonels and gave them the documents relating to 'Nordex.'*[1]

---

* In 1996, then-director of the CIA John Deutch called Nordex, a Vienna-based multinational company, "an example of an organization associated with Russian criminal activity moving out of Russia."

Mogilevich has the most powerful analytical intelligence service. But Mogilevich himself is an extremely valuable agent of KGB, PGU. . . . When one colonel . . . tried to arrest [Mogilevich] . . . they told him 'Stop meddling! This is PGU elite."*[2]

Being tightly wired with the Kremlin, however, was not enough for Mogilevich. By 1993 or 1994, according to Litvinenko,[3] Mogilevich had also made contact with Deputy Mayor Vladimir Putin. Little is known about how they met or exactly what transpired, but some insight into their relationship might be gleaned from transcripts of secret tape recordings made several years later in which Ukrainian president Kuchma inquires about Mogilevich in conversation with secret service chief Leonid Derkach.

Kuchma: "Have you found Mogilevich?"

Derkach: "I found him."

Kuchma: "So, are you two working now?"

Derkach: "We're working. We have another meeting tomorrow. He arrives incognito."

Later in the discussion Derkach revealed a few details about Mogilevich.

Derkach: "He's on good terms with Putin. He and Putin have been in contact since Putin was still in Leningrad."

This apparent budding relationship with Semion Mogilevich tied Putin to a man whose money-laundering virtuosity was vital now that a torrent of flight capital had been unleashed in post-Soviet Russia. For both men, it was Mogilevich's burgeoning operation in the United States that held so much promise. As Putin's ascent began, the Mafia moved into a powerful strategic position on the geopolitical chessboard from which it would be able to compromise powerful political figures and businessmen in the United States, undermine financial markets, and exploit the weaknesses in a wide array of political institutions such as campaign finance, Washington lobbying, and more.

---

* PGU is the First Chief Directorate of the KGB/SVR, which is responsible for overseeing all aspects of acquiring and managing foreign intelligence.

———

When Vyacheslav Ivankov landed at JFK airport in March 1992, just after the fall of the Soviet Union, he was met by an Armenian *vor* who handed him a suitcase packed with $1.5 million in cash. According to *Pravda*, he soon married an American woman, to legalize his stay.[4]

Before long, however, he discovered that the Brighton Beach Mafia was riven by turf wars and in complete disarray. In the late eighties, Marat Balagula had used the Red Daisy gas tax scam as the basis for a vertically integrated operation that included a fleet of gasoline trucks, more than one hundred gas stations, oceangoing tankers, refinery terminals in Eastern Bloc countries, and the like. But after being convicted of credit card fraud in 1986, Balagula fled the country. He was finally apprehended in Frankfurt in 1989,[5] and served years in jail.

Meanwhile, David Bogatin, likely the first Russian to launder money through Trump Tower, fled first to Austria and then Poland after the Red Daisy scam. His partner, Michael Markowitz, had been shot to death in his Rolls-Royce after assisting authorities in the investigation.[6]

Short and wiry, Ivankov was stern faced and bearded with a strong jaw, sparse eyebrows, and strikingly unusual eyes that sloped noticeably downward. His slight stature—five foot four, maybe 140 pounds—notwithstanding, he projected the intense ferocity and the daunting aura of the *vory v zakone*. Even when he was spruced up for a court appearance—a blue blazer with a handkerchief in his pocket, an Oxford shirt concealing the menacing eight-pointed stars tattooed on his shoulders—Ivankov was right out of central casting as a fearsome Russian mobster. "One felt as if in the presence of Ivan the Terrible, or Joseph Stalin," said one observer who saw him in New York.[7]

Before long, Ivankov became known as the most powerful Russian mobster in the United States,[8] and oversaw the mob's growth from a local extortion racket in Brooklyn's Brighton Beach to a multibillion-dollar-a-year criminal organization.[9]

Ivankov's mandate from Mogilevich was to consolidate the Russian Mafia in the US, to form alliances with the Cosa Nostra and other

Mafias, to take over smaller gangs, and to bribe politicians as part of a plan to infiltrate governments in the US and elsewhere.[10] Ruthlessly systematic, the Russians began scrutinizing the vulnerabilities of America's campaign finance system, the K Street lobbying system, Wall Street, and more.

To that end, Ivankov launched a two-pronged offensive. On the one hand, with his foreboding tattoos and fearsome visage, he was the man who brought the *vory* from the gulag to Brighton Beach. The old-school Mafia scams, shootouts, car bombs, and murders were still an important part of their operations. To help fight these gang wars, Ivankov recruited two brigades composed of 250 athletes and Special Forces veterans of the Afghan war who were put on $20,000-a-month retainers to kill his enemies and establish ties connecting thieves-in-law to the United States. Monya Elson, the brutal killer who had been Marat Balagula's bodyguard, was still working for Ivankov in New York,[11] and Ivankov also used a man named Alexander Inshakov in "five or six murders of top ROC [Russian organized crime] figures who 'got in the way.'"[12]

Even after he was locked up for extortion in 1996, Ivankov continued to order the murders of his underworld adversaries from his prison cell. Witnesses who dared testify against him were forced to take new identities in the Federal Witness Protection Program. FBI agents who investigated him ended up on his hit list.[13]

The same was true for journalists. When Ivankov found out that Robert Friedman was on his trail, he went so far as to send a message crafted especially for the occasion inside a Hallmark Valentine's Day card that teased, "It was easy finding a Valentine for someone like you": "Friedman! You are a dirty fucking American prostitute and liar! I WILL FUCK YOU! And make you suck my Russian DICK!" America's most fearsome *vor* signed the affectionate missive "Vyacheslav Kirillovich Ivankov."[14] Later, Friedman found out that a $100,000 contract had been taken out on his life—by Semion Mogilevich.

———

But to a certain extent, Ivankov's colorful depravities masked a bigger story. Just as Russia had effectively become a gangster state whose political system was governed by organized crime, so the Russian gangsters who emigrated and ran the Russian mob were now poised to infect and infiltrate a vast array of power centers in the more open, more easily manipulated corporate and political America.

So it was with Ivankov, who also had steered the post-Soviet Bratva into the white-collar professional world of lawyers, stockbrokers, accountants, and the like with offshore shell companies comprising a vertically integrated corporate empire all over the world. As a classified FBI report put it, "Ivankov brings with him the tradition of hard-core Russian criminals. . . . While not abandoning extortion, intimidation and murder, Ivankov also incorporates more subtle and sophisticated modern methods which enable cooperation with other groups."[15]

Over time, thirty Russian crime syndicates began operating in New York, Miami, San Francisco, Los Angeles, Denver, and at least a dozen other cities, orchestrating insurance scams, pump-and-dump stock rip-offs that inflated stock prices, complex schemes to launder millions of dollars in flight capital pouring out of Russia, medical fraud, and jewelry heists.[16] Ivankov used a consulting firm in Vienna to launder tens of millions of dollars.[17] He tried to steal diamonds in Sierra Leone. In New York, the FBI suspected that Ivankov was engaged in money laundering.

———

Meanwhile, throughout most of the nineties, Mogilevich was based largely in Budapest, but traveled regularly to Vienna, Munich, Rome, and Athens under several different names and passports. However, he and Ivankov also kept a keen eye on developing operations in the US. According to FBI files, in North America, Mogilevich traveled to Toronto, Philadelphia, Miami, and New York, and went to LA at least five times between May 1992 and November 1994. There, he met with Vladimir Berkovich, a key Mogilevich lieutenant who, according to FBI files, "arrange[d] contract murders, bringing in 'hitmen' from Russia under tourist visas, out of the Palm Terrace restaurant."[18] There were deals for a Russian restaurant in Denver, real estate in the Rocky Mountains, a

dimir Putin *(left)* and Donald Trump *(right)* during the G8 meeting. Putin has denied
rference in the 2016 US presidential election, while the state media he controls has claimed,
ump is ours." *(Evan Vucci/AP)*

Donald Trump and his mentor Roy Cohn in 19[..] "I don't want to know w[..] the law is," Cohn famo[..] said, "I want to know w[..] the judge is." *(Bettmann/G[..] Images)*

The Torturers' Lobby: Back in 1985, Paul Manafort and Roger Stone were young political operatives who reveled in taking on dictators as clients. Trump was an early client for the duo. Many years later, Stone advised Trump during the 2016 campaign while Manafort became Trump's campaign manager. *(Harry Naltchayan/The Washington Post/Getty Images)*

Political operative Roger Stone spl[..] with the Donald Trump campaign but allegedly played a major role in WikiLeaks' leaking of the DNC's hacked emails during the presiden[..] election. *(Jesse Dittmar/The New York Tim[..] Redux Pictures)*

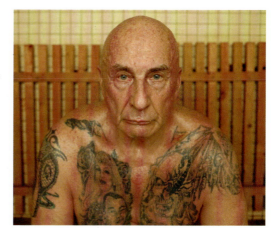

ghton Beach Russian mobster Boris
~feld, one of the last of the old-time
~y, provided muscle for both Evsei
~on, who was murdered, and his
~cessor, Marat Balagula, in the eighties.
~ Wenig/AP)

Brutal mobster Vyacheslav "Yaponchik" Ivankov
was a high-level associate of Semion Mogilevich, a
"thief-in-law," and a Trump Tower resident. Ivankov
made frequent visits to Trump's Taj Mahal. *(TASS/
ZUMA Press/Newscom)*

Left to right: Semion Mogilevich, Sergei Mikhailov, and Viktor Averin.
According to Interpol, Mikhailov and Averin ran the huge Solntsevo crime
gang, but Mogilevich was the "Brainy Don" who introduced sophisticated
finance to the Russian Mafia. *(Courtesy of* The Insider)

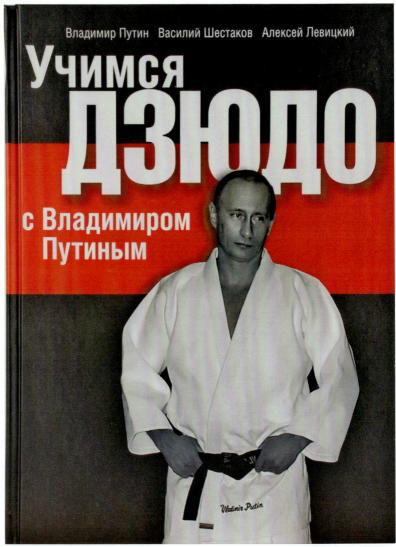

Russian president Vladimir Putin on the cover of a judo book he coauthored in 2014. Putin uses the principles of judo as a political philosophy. "Judo teaches self-control, the ability to feel the moment, to see the opponent's strengths and weaknesses, to strive for the best results." *(Sergey Ponomarev/The New York Times/Redux Pictures)*

Russian president Vladimir Putin *(left)* and billionaire Arkady Rotenberg *(right)* at the funeral of Putin's former judo trainer Anatoly Rakhlin in August 2009. Rotenberg and his brother Boris were childhood judo sparring partners of Putin's who became billionaire oligarchs. *(Sasha Mordovets/Getty Images)*

yor Anatoly Sobchak *(right)* and his assistant Vladimir Putin *(left)* attend a meeting of the Petersburg city legislature in 1993. At a time when billions of dollars' worth of Russia's ural resources were being privatized, Putin had a low-profile but powerful position. *(Mikhail uvaev/Kommersant/Sipa USA)*

Oleg Kalugin, former head of foreign counter-intelligence for the KGB and Putin's former boss, says Russian intelligence probably had *komprom* on Donald Trump from Trump's visit to Russia i 1987. *(© RIA Novosti/The Image Works)*

Donald Trump and his ex-wife Ivana Trump in Leningrad in 1987, during Trump's first trip to the Soviet Union. The trip was arranged by Soviet ambassador Yuri Dubinin through Intourist, a Soviet travel agency said to have had KGB ties. *(Maxim Blokhin/ ZUMA Press/Newscom)*

…tin assumed power in 2000 and has tightened his grip on Russia by rewarding his inner circle …d eliminating anyone who poses a threat to him. *(Sergei Ilnitsky/AFP/Getty Images)*

Russian president Vladimir Putin *(left)* and Chief Rabbi of Russia Berel Lazar at a flower-laying ceremony at Red Square, November 4, 2015. Lazar's Chabad-dominated Federation of Jewish Communities of Russia, which was funded in part by two Putin confidantes, Lev Leviev and Roman Abramovich, also had direct ties to Trump. *(© RIA Novosti/The Image Works)*

President Donald J. Trump meets with a delegation organized by the American Friends of Lubavitch (Chabad), March 27, 2018. Jared Kushner, Felix Sater, and many other Trump associates provide a link to Putin via Chabad. *(SMG/ZUMA Pres Newscom)*

car dealership in Houston which the FBI asserted was for money laundering, diamond thefts in Sierra Leone.[19]

When the Russians moved into Miami, Ivankov allegedly became a silent partner in Porky's, a Miami strip club owned by Russian mobster Ludwig Fainberg, also known as Tarzan thanks to his muscled torso and long mane of hair. Fainberg helped strike a deal with the Cali cartel in Colombia to provide heroin and money laundering in exchange for Cali's cocaine.[20]

These were not small-time transactions. At the time, Russian military hardware was absurdly easy to come by if you knew the right people in the former Soviet empire—and that meant everything from armored personnel carriers to submarines. At one point, Fainberg was in talks with Colombian drug lords to sell them a submarine to help smuggle the illicit drugs and money—complete with a Russian crew of eighteen men. Before it could be finalized, however, the deal was busted by the Drug Enforcement Administration.[21]

———

In large part, Mogilevich's success grew out of the fact that he had cultivated close ties to the powers that be in the post-Soviet world. He had operatives who infiltrated the Hungarian National Police, and in Prague, where he also had a major presence, the Czech police. He was wired into the intelligence services of both Russia and Ukraine at the highest levels.

One of the key people helping Mogilevich in Budapest was Dietmar Clodo, a longtime associate of Mogilevich with a colorful history as a mercenary in Rhodesia and as a supporter of the mujahideen in Afghanistan against the Soviets. A suspected international arms and drug trafficker, Clodo was sentenced to ten years in prison for his role in a series of bombings in Hungary in the 1990s and was extradited to Germany in 2005, where he was wanted on charges of murder, bank robbery, and other serious crimes.

According to an article by Russian journalist Anastasia Kirilenko on a website called Hungarian Spectrum, in 1994, Clodo said he was entrusted by Mogilevich with the delivery of large sums of money to various top political officials in Hungary.

On one such occasion, Clodo received a suitcase with approximately one million deutschmarks with instructions to give it to an unnamed political figure who was coming by to pick it up. As Clodo recalled, when the man arrived, he "didn't want to come into my house. I told him, 'Listen to me, I have that damned money in a suitcase. I don't want to go out on the street with this suitcase. I don't care. If you refuse to come in, I will give it back to Mr. Mogilevich. I don't care.'"

Of course, Clodo did not tell the man why he wanted the transaction to take place indoors—namely, that there was a hidden camera among his books that would record the transfer.

"I wasn't interested in who this man was," said Clodo. "It was only after the elections that I understood that this was a young man who became a powerful nationalist politician."

For a master of money laundering like Mogilevich, banks were essential, and in 1994, he infiltrated and later took over Inkombank, one of the largest private banks in Russia, allegedly via a secret deal with its chairman, Vladimir Vinogradov.[22]

In the UK, he had first staked out turf in the early nineties, laundering large sums of cash allegedly from activities ranging from arms dealing to prostitution, extortion, and drug trafficking, through Arbat and Arigon, the companies he had launched with Ivankov and Mikhailov in the Channel Islands. In 1995, however, after large amounts of money started going to the companies' lawyers, London's Metropolitan Police raided their homes and seized millions from the Royal Bank of Scotland.[23] No charges were filed, but the companies were dissolved and Mogilevich was banned from Britain.

Increasingly, Mogilevich focused his energies on the corporate world—and not just in Russia and Ukraine, but also the United States. To make his dreams a reality, he put together a network of white-collar professionals who would propel the Semion Mogilevich Organization to another level entirely. He cultivated young Russian businessmen who had expertise in creating shell companies to launder money. He found bankers who made it possible to launder money on a multibillion-dollar level on an ongoing basis.

A decade earlier, the Russians had deconstructed the system of gasoline tax distribution in the United States, zeroed in on its vulnerabilities, and put together a virtually foolproof scheme to steal billions of dollars. Now they prepared to take on Wall Street, America's campaign finance system, the world of K Street lobbyists, and any politicians who were ready for hire, all in a widespread effort to have as much power and money in their pockets as possible.

But Mogilevich's ascent was not without setbacks. By 1994, Mogilevich's Inkombank was able to have "virtually daily interaction"[24] with the Bank of New York (BONY), one of the largest banks in the United States,[25] meaning that he finally had direct access to mainstream international banks to launder billions of dollars.* But a British investigation code-named Operation Sword revealed that Arbat International, one of the Channel Island firms Mogilevich had started in the early nineties, was at the center of a web of companies in London and New York through which Mogilevich laundered as much as $10 billion.[26]

Meanwhile, by 1995, Mogilevich was in the midst of a heated dispute with longtime ally Sergei Mikhailov. The reason, according to Interpol files, was that Mikhailov had "ordered Mogilevich to transfer about 5 million US dollars to the general security of the Solntsevo group."[27] The matter came to a head at a meeting in the Czech Republic on May 31 of that year, the purpose of which, according to Interpol files, was to split up "newly discovered routes for smuggling gold and jewelry, a new route of cocaine smuggling from South America to Moscow and heroin from the CIS countries to Western Europe and the United States."[28]

---

* Through Inkombank, Mogilevich separately acquired a substantial interest in Sukhoi, a large manufacturer of Russia's military aircraft.

It happened to be Averin's birthday, and in true Bratva fashion, the "meeting" took place at the V Holubu, a Prague restaurant Mogilevich owned and used as a money-laundering center, with strippers, hookers, and a guest list that included Mikhailov, Averin, Mogilevich, and everyone who was anyone in the Russian Mafia.

"They were having an elaborate dinner and entertainment," Special Agent Robert Levinson of the FBI told the BBC.[29] "They had a Russian singer and a comic and they had some cabaret entertainers, and everyone was having a very good time for themselves."

Then, while the performances were still under way, the Czech Republic's organized crime SWAT team suddenly came into the restaurant, jumped on the stage, and, armed with machine guns, ordered the crowd not to move.[30]

At first, everyone was transfixed, thinking it was part of the show. According to FBI files, what they didn't know, however, was that before the festivities got under way, "an unidentified Russian delivered an anonymous letter to the chief of police in Budapest, Hungary, in which it was alleged that Semion Mogilevich was to be assassinated that evening at the 'summit meeting' in Prague."[31]

Slowly, the partygoers realized that the SWAT team had foiled an assassination attempt on Mogilevich. As for Mogilevich, he had been tipped off and was nowhere to be found.[32] "Mogilevich knew he was dealing with some very, very treacherous people," said Levinson. "They'd kill him in an instant."

———

In the wake of the Prague fiasco, Mogilevich, Mikhailov, and other alleged Russian mobsters were banned from the Czech Republic, effectively shutting down operations there. In June 1995, Ivankov had been nabbed for extortion and held without bail. He was later sentenced to nine years and seven months in jail.[33] On occasion, there were shootouts between rival gangsters and internecine warfare. But all that was the price of doing business. By some accounts, Mogilevich was already said to be worth over $100 million—and money was rolling in.

At the same time, with Ivankov overseeing operations from his cell in upstate New York, Mogilevich had begun to consolidate operations in the US while maintaining major business interests in Europe. He had major holdings in the Hungarian arms industry. He had managed to steal millions of dollars of Soviet military equipment that had been left behind in East Germany when the Soviet Union dissolved.[34] Between weapons trafficking, assassinations, prostitution, drug trafficking, dealing in precious gems and stolen art, extortion, and money laundering, cash was pouring in from all over the world.

In the history of the American Mafia, there have been a handful of summit meetings at which rival gangs sort out how to divide operations such as loan sharking, drug dealing, gambling, prostitution, and, of course, the resulting spoils. Among the most famous is the 1957 meeting in the sleepy hamlet of Apalachin, New York, that was raided by state and local cops, resulting in more than sixty underworld bosses being detained and indicted.

The Bratva meeting in Prague had played out differently for Mogilevich than the Apalachin meeting did for the American mob. He and his allies had been forced out of the Czech Republic, but they lived to fight another day. Moreover, vital issues were still unresolved. So in October 1995, Mogilevich attended a summit meeting of Russian crime figures in the Tel Aviv office of Boris Birshtein, a flamboyant, politically connected Russian-Canadian businessman who ran Seabeco SA and had close ties both to the KGB[35] and Sergei Mikhailov,[36] with whom he partnered in a Belgian company called MAB International.

Others who were present included Mikhailov partner Viktor Averin; Ukrainian media mogul Vadim Rabinovich, who had ties to the arms trade and had spent seven years[37] in jail for black market ventures; several other Ukrainian businessmen; and, of course, Semion Mogilevich.[38]

While they were in Israel, the group traveled around the country, "including a visit to a shooting range." Israeli officials had telephone coverage of their hotel rooms and detected calls to Russia, Hungary, and Paris. According to the FBI, they "did not appear to practice communications security, freely discussing business over the telephone."[39]

Now that the Soviet Union was dead and gone, they had gone global. Hundreds of billions of dollars in natural resources were there for the taking, but they had to figure out how to split their booty. And so a settlement was reached whereby Mogilevich paid Mikhailov the disputed $5 million, but in return got something far more valuable.

The key subject of the meeting in Tel Aviv, and subsequent gatherings of the Russian mobsters, was how to divide spoils in Ukraine among the criminal gangs, especially Ukraine's energy trade. With more than fifty million Ukrainians overwhelmingly dependent on Russia for such an essential commodity as gas, especially given Ukraine's frigid winters, an intermediary would be in a strong position to dictate whatever terms he liked. Of course, that meant asserting real political power at the highest levels of government in Ukraine and Russia. Even more important, in the long run, it also necessitated having access to power in the United States.

CHAPTER NINE

TURN OF THE SCREW

I n the fall of 1996, after years of nonstop wrangling with creditors over billions of dollars in debt, Donald Trump's comeback began. One of many reasons for the delay had been Trump Castle, one of the most troubled properties among his Atlantic City casinos. All of them were failing, but the Castle was the ugly stepmother. It had been that way for years.

In 1990, after Trump built the stupendously extravagant Trump Taj Mahal, with its minarets and carved elephants, the Taj began to cannibalize the nearby Trump Castle so much that it almost fell into the hands of bondholders. It was saved only when Fred Trump, Donald's father, famously bought $3.3 million in poker chips and didn't use them—thereby giving his son's casino a questionable loan.[1]

The following year, however, the Castle's decline in revenue was so dire that the New Jersey Casino Control Commission ruled that the resort was at risk of losing its license. Trump's casino empire had so much debt, at such high interest rates, there was almost no chance he would succeed.

Then came the bankruptcies, with four trips to bankruptcy court. In the end, bondholders had to accept more than a $1.5 billion[2] loss while Trump continued to collect a big salary, bonuses, and other payments. Through it all, Trump managed to stay in the game and persuade bankers and bondholders to refinance his casinos in a way that allowed him to keep majority ownership.

Then, finally, on September 30, stockholders of Trump Hotels and Casino Resorts, his publicly traded company, agreed to buy Trump Castle, the weakest of his Atlantic City properties, for $485.7 million. That meant stockholders paid Trump more than $130 million in stock and nearly $1 million in cash, and assumed $354.8 million in debt.[3]

"It took two years of hard work, but now everything is put together into one beautiful, simple, lovely, substantial company," Trump said. "People are shocked when they look at the numbers because the numbers are terrific, the numbers are just huge."[4]

Even his critics were impressed. "His turnabout is a classic," casino analyst Marvin Roffman told Playboy. "It is the biggest comeback I've ever seen. Donald Trump, financially speaking, has come back from the dead."[5] Roffman had been fired from his Wall Street firm under pressure from Trump for refusing to apologize for a report critical of Trump.[*6]

"He was worse than broke," Stephen Bollenbach, a corporate salvage expert who helped rescue Trump's empire, told Playboy's Mark Bowden.[7] "He was losing money every day, and he was already hundreds and hundreds of millions of dollars in debt."

"This time," Roffman said, "he has real net worth."[8]

––––––––

But cash never lasted long in Donald Trump's hands. As if to prove that he hadn't lost his taste for profligacy, less than a month later, in October 1996, Trump bought three beauty pageants—Miss Universe, Miss USA, and Miss Teen USA—from ITT.[9] As is often the case with Trump, the exact amount of the transaction is unclear. In The Art of the Comeback, he wrote that his winning bid was $10 million. But later, he couldn't

––––––––

* Immediately after reading Roffman's analysis of the Taj Mahal, Trump had sent a letter to Janney Montgomery Scott, the investment firm that employed Roffman, and demanded that Roffman issue a public retraction of his assessment of the Taj, or, in the absence of such a retraction, that Janney fire Roffman.

resist changing the narrative to make reporters think he had gotten a steal and paid only $2 million.[10]

Regardless of the price, less than a week later, with this new calling card in hand, and whatever cachet came with it, Trump returned to Moscow for the first time in nearly a decade, with visions of yet another Trump Tower still in his head.

Even though there's no evidence that Trump had direct contact with Ivankov or Mogilevich, throughout his three-day stay in Russia in November 1996, Trump and his entourage were escorted around Moscow by people with alleged connections to them.

This time, Donald was accompanied by his friend, New York real estate developer Howard Lorber,* and Lorber's business partner Bennett LeBow. Lorber was the president of the Brooke Group,† whose holdings included Liggett-Ducat Ltd. (formerly known as Liggett & Myers), America's third-largest tobacco company, and major real estate assets in both New York and Moscow; LeBow was founder and chairman.

Having started out in the early Wild West days of post-Soviet privatization, the duo had already forged some interesting relationships. LeBow had begun partnering[11] with Vadim Rabinovich, the pro-Russia Ukrainian oligarch who had spent seven years in jail for embezzlement.‡[12] Only a month before Trump, Lorber, and LeBow's Moscow visit, Rabinovich had participated in the Tel Aviv summit meeting at which Mogilevich was granted control of the Ukraine energy trade.[13]

Once Trump and his entourage arrived in Moscow, they were shown

---

* Though relatively low-profile among Trump's associates, Lorber was an important figure in the Trump administration in that he introduced Trump to David Friedman, who became Trump's ambassador to Israel. In addition, Friedman's former partner Marc Kasowitz became Trump's lawyer.

† In 2000, the Brooke Group was renamed the Vector Group.

‡ Even though Rabinovich says he was jailed on trumped-up charges, the US has barred his entry into this country. "You will find accusations against me in the U.S.," Rabinovich told the *Forward*. "In Israel, some say I am connected to the mafia. In Ukraine, they say I am Mossad agent, if you find this kind of nonsense interesting. I don't."

around town by its mayor, Yuri Luzhkov. As John Beyrle, the American ambassador to Russia, saw it, Luzhkov was the embodiment of the Russian "political dilemma" in that his political power was both marred by and fueled by "the shadowy world of corrupt business practices"[14] and a system in which "almost everyone at every level is involved in some form of corruption or criminal behavior."[15]

As reported by the liberal newspaper *Novaya Gazeta*, Mayor Luzhkov was alleged to be deeply in bed with Mogilevich, Ivankov, and company. In fact, according to a classified cable Ambassador Beyrle wrote, "Luzhkov used criminal money to support his rise to power and has been involved with bribes and deals regarding lucrative construction contracts throughout Moscow. [Source redacted] told us that Luzhkov's friends and associates (including . . . crime boss Vyacheslav Ivankov and reputedly corrupt Duma Deputy Joseph Kobzon) are 'bandits.'"[16]

Luzhkov also had ties to Sistema, a company that privatized Moscow real estate and gas,[17] and, according to *Novye Izvestia*, was tied to Mogilevich's companies[18] in the Channel Islands and the Solntsevo crime gang. According to the *Guardian*, he vehemently denied the accusations as "total rubbish."[19]

On the occasion of Donald Trump's return to Russia, Mayor Luzhkov was effectively giving Trump the keys to Moscow as part of a serious overture from the Yeltsin government to build a Trump Tower–like complex in the Russian capital. According to TASS, the Russian press agency, Trump began negotiations with first deputy mayor of Moscow, Vladimir Rezin, to build a $300-million luxury residential complex.[20] Over time, Mayor Luzhkov reportedly changed his approach and asked Trump about possibly renovating the run-down Rossiya and Moskva hotels in the style of the Commodore in New York.

In the end, talks stagnated, and once again, nothing came of the project. Nevertheless, this was a period during which post-communist powers were desperately courting business leaders and politicians of every stripe as a way of winning favor with American power brokers.

David Geovanis, Liggett-Ducat's director of real estate, who was also on the trip, played a role in promoting Trump's project[21] and may have helped make sure Trump was lavishly entertained during his sojourn, as he had been on his earlier trip. At least, that is one of the suggestions that is made in a controversial "dossier" that Devin Nunes, the Republican chairman of the House Intelligence Committee and congressman from California, produced in an attempt to discredit allegations of a conspiracy between Donald Trump and Russia. The document essentially consists of unfinished notes that have been neither corroborated nor confirmed and were part of an ongoing investigation by journalist and investigator Cody Shearer, a longtime ally of Bill and Hillary Clinton.

Before leaving Russia, Trump held a press conference in Moscow's Hotel Baltschug Kempinsky, a magnificent, palatial nineteenth-century building overlooking Red Square, the Kremlin, and the Moskva River—which, FBI files allege, happened to be owned by Semion Mogilevich.

At the press conference, Trump announced he planned to invest $250 million to build two "super-luxury" residential towers, to be called Trump International and—surprise—Trump Tower, both of which he said "Moscow desperately wants and needs."[22]

"Moscow is going to be huge, take it from the Trumpster!" he later told *Playboy*.

But, as in the eighties, the project remained eternally stalled, a public face that masked a constantly changing network of clandestine relationships.

———

One reason those relationships changed so frequently was that the political situation in Russia was still quite volatile. In June 1996, Anatoly Sobchak lost his reelection bid as mayor of St. Petersburg, leaving his protégé Putin without a highly placed mentor. But two months later, in July, Putin was invited to Moscow by Nikolai Yegorov, Boris Yeltsin's chief of staff, and offered a job as a deputy.[23]

These were days of chaos in the Kremlin. Yeltsin, then sixty-five, was tired beyond his years, erratic and incoherent, beset by alcoholism and serious health problems. He had had open-heart surgery and multiple heart attacks. The hawks among his advisers were perpetually at war with neoliberal reformers. Things weren't stable in the short term for Putin, either. Just days after Putin moved in as deputy chief of staff, his job was eliminated. His patron, Chief of Staff Yegorov, had been fired in the internal warfare.[24]

For all the palace intrigue, Putin was playing a longer game, and by August he had finagled a position as a public liaison to the Presidential Property Management Directorate. That meant his new job was to oversee hundreds of palaces, dachas, hospitals, spas, yachts, aircraft, state factories, and more.[25] It was not what he wanted, but he had finally found a foothold in the Kremlin.

At a time when the knives were certain to come out in internal turf battles, Putin was a marginal figure whose greatest asset was his unobtrusiveness.[26] It was the key to his survival and upward trajectory. By March 1997, after just seven months on the property job, Putin was promoted to deputy chief of staff in the presidential administration. A week later, he was given broader authority to investigate abuses in government spending.[27]

For an intelligence operative who had been a promulgator of such abuses himself, what more could one ask for? The fox had been given keys to the proverbial henhouse. Putin launched inquiries into dozens of regions and took disciplinary action against hundreds of officials. As one scandal after another unraveled, Putin unspooled the narrative exactly as he saw fit, attacking his enemies while whitewashing and protecting potential allies who would surely pay back his favors with interest. He drew up a report on corruption at a foundation created by Anatoly Chubais, the deputy prime minister who had rejected him for a job a year or so earlier.[28] But he publicly absolved President Yeltsin and his former defense minister, General Pavel Grachev, of allegations regarding illegal sales of $1 billion in weapons to Armenia earlier.[29] Before long, he had burnished his reputation as a powerful campaigner against corruption and had strengthened his position politically.

Then, in July 1998, at a time when the Russian economy was in free fall and his administration was lurching wildly about, Boris Yeltsin decided he needed to instigate a complete overhaul of the Russian security apparatus. At the time, Putin had been a highly disciplined model of discretion. His written reports were said to be "a model of clarity."[30] While countless other bureaucrats were groveling for advancement, Putin's relative "coolness" was attractive to Yeltsin.

And so, Lubyanka, the massive neo-baroque building in the Meshchansky District of Moscow, headquarters of the FSB (formerly KGB) and the site of its affiliated prison, with its dark, dark history of torture and executions, now had a new boss. Lubyanka was where Nikolai Bukharin, the Bolshevik revolutionary and foe of Joseph Stalin, was wrongly charged in 1937 with plotting to kill Vladimir Lenin, and was sentenced to death in a show trial.[31] It was where Lavrentiy Beria, Stalin's bloodthirsty executioner and the architect of Stalinist purges, sent countless victims to their graves. Beria was himself shot by a firing squad in 1953.[32]

And now, Vladimir Putin, a mere lieutenant colonel in the KGB, had leapfrogged over scores of multistarred generals to take charge of the Russian secret service and reshape it in his image. He moved into a relatively modest office on the third floor of Lubyanka and turned the official executive office, which had been occupied by KGB chiefs from Beria to Yuri Andropov, into a shrine of sorts, with a small statue of Felix Dzerzhinsky, aka "Iron Felix," the Bolshevik revolutionary who was the founder and director of the Soviet secret police, on the desk.[33]

Just as Donald Trump had risen from the ashes of Atlantic City, Putin began a second act as well. He started by completely restructuring the agency he loved, bringing in confederates from his old days at the KGB, and purging his enemies. Among the latter were two key agencies, the Directorate for Economic Counterintelligence and the Directorate for Counterintelligence Protection of Strategic Sites, both charged with investigating high-level economic crimes, which inevitably involved Putin and his allies. In the hands of his political foes, these agencies, not unlike the Special Counsel's Office in the United States, potentially posed a serious threat to Putin. Now that he had the power, Putin made sure that both agencies were swiftly eliminated.[34] Having control over agencies that had the power to investigate you was just one perk that came with Putin's new position and it was indispensible to anyone who wanted to retain power for long periods of time. In the United States, of course, the separation of the judiciary from the executive branch made that impossible—theoretically at least. If, for example, the president were to fire a special counsel who was investigating the White House, that could not happen without causing a grave Constitutional crisis.

––––––

On August 20, less than a month after Putin's appointment to head the FSB, Russians got a serious taste of the treatment facing his critics when Anatoly Levin-Utkin, a journalist for a newly launched paper called *Legal Petersburg Today* (*Yuridichesky Petersburg Segodnya*) left his office and returned to his apartment on Rednova Street.[35]

Levin-Utkin's newspaper had only published its first three issues but it had already provoked controversy thanks to its investigations into the corruption surrounding privatization by the deputy mayor of St. Petersburg who had just become head of the FSB. One of the paper's articles was headlined "Vladimir Putin Became Head of the FSB Unlawfully." Levin-Utkin had not written the article, but he had contributed to it.

When Levin-Utkin got home and checked his mail, two men assaulted him from behind, shattering his skull in several places, and left him unconscious on the floor. He died on the morning of August 24.[36]

No one was convicted of the murder, nor, for that matter, was it clear that there was ever any serious investigation. As a result, no evidence surfaced linking Putin to the crime. Nevertheless, the murder of Anatoly Levin-Utkin sent a signal about the value of loyalty to Putin and his allies, and was a harbinger of things to come.

On November 17, 1998, four months after Putin became head of the FSB, six men, four of whom wore masks and two of whom were unmasked, held an extraordinarily dramatic press conference in Moscow. All six had investigated organized crime for the FSB, and, as they told the assembled journalists, the organized crime unit they worked for had been transformed into a brutal and corrupt criminal enterprise itself.[37]

The unmasked leader of the group, Alexander Litvinenko, was a lieutenant colonel, the same rank, ironically, as Putin, and took the lead in revealing how his superiors in the FSB were involved in kidnapping, extortion, and the like. But the most sensational disclosure of all was Litvinenko's revelation that he had been ordered by the FSB—now headed by Putin—to assassinate Boris Berezovsky.[38]

An engineer and mathematician by training, Berezovsky had become a billionaire oligarch in the nineties through the privatization of automobiles, television, Aeroflot, and other state assets. He had met Putin in the early nineties, when Berezovsky wanted to open a car dealership in St. Petersburg. Stunned to see Putin turn down a bribe, Berezovsky put in a good word for him with Yeltsin. "He was the first bureaucrat who did not take bribes," Berezovsky said. "Seriously, it made a huge impression on me."[39]

Berezovsky was influential enough that his remarks to Yeltsin were widely seen as a factor behind Putin's ascent to the top of the FSB. He had already used his money and power to promote Yeltsin's 1996 reelection, and, as a result, had become a member of Boris Yeltsin's inner circle, known as the Family.[40]

But that didn't mean Berezovsky was in a secure position. Having come to wealth through the automobile industry initially, Berezovsky switched to the media when he took the remnants of Soviet television— Channel One Russia, the only Russian broadcaster with a nationwide reach, spanning eleven time zones—and turned it into a powerful tool promoting Yeltsin's reelection in 1996.

Like many state-owned industries, Channel One, also known as ORT, had been steeped in corruption. By some estimates, advertisers paid five times as much as the network received, with the difference going into the pockets of gangsters and various middlemen, all of whom were now at risk with Berezovsky orchestrating a massive restructuring.[41]

In 1995, Berezovsky had declared a moratorium of a few months while he built a new in-house sales department and cut out the middlemen. But nine days later, on March 1, Vlad Listyev, the new director general at Channel One, and a popular broadcasting personality, was gunned down at his Moscow home.[42]

Clearly, Berezovsky was the next in line. Not only was he cutting off the livelihood of scores of gangsters, he also controlled a political tool of immense power.

Meanwhile, Litvinenko had done something unheard of—he had taken on Putin and the *kontora* (the company) on national TV. Putin's response to the sensational press conference was twofold. Publicly, he held a press conference in which he announced that there would be internal investigations into all the accusations made by Litvinenko and company. "We are not afraid to wash our dirty linen in public," he said.[43]

But privately, he called Litvinenko in for a meeting at Lubyanka Square. Litvinenko arrived accompanied by two colleagues and a hefty dossier documenting his allegations. But Putin refused to accept the dossier and insisted that Litvinenko come into his office alone. Their encounter was chilly and brief. Later, Litvinenko described the meeting to his wife, Marina. "I could see it in his eyes that he hated me," he told her.[44]

He was right.

Shortly afterward, Putin met with President Yeltsin and argued that Litvinenko had betrayed the FSB. Rather than investigate Litvinenko's allegations, he gave Yeltsin documentation suggesting that Litvinenko and his allies had betrayed their oath of office as intelligence officers. Then, he fired them.[45]

But removing Litvinenko from the hunt was not enough. An even more serious threat to both Yeltsin and him was in the works from Russia's prosecutor general, Yuri Skuratov, whose investigation went so far as to target Yeltsin and the Family about millions of dollars of dubious transactions surrounding the restoration of the Kremlin and the renovation of Yeltsin's dacha. Members of the Duma had already raised the question of impeachment.[46]

Skuratov's investigation had also begun probing corruption in St. Petersburg under Mayor Sobchak, including the privatization of apartments by a company called Renaissance, some of whose apartments went to Putin.[47] Now was the time for Putin to prove his loyalty to Yeltsin—and save his own skin in the process.

On March 17, 1999, the newscast on RTR state television broadcast a caveat that the report to follow might not be suitable for young viewers.[48] What followed were clips from a black and white surveillance video taken inside a Moscow apartment. The segment, titled "Three in a Bed,"[49] featured two young women, partially dressed, who were described as prostitutes, moving in and out of the frame, and a man appeared who, the narrator said, "very much resembles the Prosecutor General."[50]

And so Yuri Skuratov was forced to resign. His ouster had all the hallmarks of having been orchestrated by a master of KGB tradecraft and the arts of *kompromat* and honey traps.

And what role, if any, did Putin play? According to an article by authors Yuri Felshtinsky and Vladimir Pribylovsky* on Garry Kasparov's website,[51] Putin's agents rented and paid for the apartment in which the video was shot. Putin's agents videotaped the evening. "A man who looked like the head of the FSB"—i.e., Putin—personally delivered the video to the head of RTR. And, finally, it was Putin who publicly announced President Yeltsin's demand for Skuratov to resign.

But was the man in the apartment actually Skuratov? Former KGB general Oleg Kalugin maintains that the whole episode "was a special FSB operation to discredit an official with the help of a video featuring a person who resembled the prosecutor-general."[52] It was classic KGB work that had been transformed into a riveting media spectacle for maximum political impact.

———

Ousting Skuratov solidified Putin's relationship with Yeltsin, but it was unclear exactly what that meant for the ambitious young FSB director. It would be an understatement to say that at the time, the Yeltsin administration was on shaky ground. The ruble had collapsed the previous

---

* In January 2016, Pribylovsky, a prolific Putin critic, was found dead in his Moscow apartment at the age of fifty-nine. The cause of death was unclear. His colleague Yuri Felshtinsky also cowrote *Blowing Up Russia* with Alexander Litvinenko, who died of polonium poisoning in London in 2006.

year, leading to a nationwide financial crisis. Impeachment proceedings in the Duma were now under way against Yeltsin. It was unlikely impeachment had enough support to pass, but incessant reports in the media about corruption in Yeltsin's "Family" left him deeply wounded politically at a time when he sorely needed to put together a parliamentary majority in the Duma. Prime ministers came and went with alarming regularity. By the summer of 1999, he had already fired seven prime ministers and acting prime ministers.

Finally, on August 5, 1999, Yeltsin called Putin to his dacha outside Moscow. "I've made a decision, Vladimir Vladimirovich," Yeltsin told him, "and I would like to offer you the post of prime minister."[53]

Putin wanted the job, but he had no desire to be a sacrificial lamb like so many short-lived previous prime ministers. He needed political capital because Yeltsin and his "Family" were still facing possible criminal prosecution and wanted protection. But to the public at large, he was a nonentity.

Thus, according to historian David Satter, a plan called Operation Successor was implemented to resolve precisely those problems.[54] It began on the night of September 4, when a huge explosion rocked a five-story building in Buynaksk, a town of about sixty thousand in the Russian republic of Dagestan, killing sixty-four people. Five days later, another explosion destroyed a nine-story apartment building in Moscow. This time, ninety-four people died.[55]

On September 13, yet another explosion rocked another Moscow apartment building. This time the death toll was 118. And a fourth bombing took place on September 16 in the southern city of Volgodonsk, killing seventeen.

To tens of millions of Russians, these bombings were roughly the equivalent of 9/11, and were widely blamed on separatist rebels from Chechnya, the tiny, largely Muslim republic near the Caspian Sea that had been part of the Soviet Union. In the aftermath of the bombings, with all of Russia crying out for vengeance, Putin, who had just been appointed prime minister, appeared on national television night after night, the one man who could assuage their fears and stave off the collapse of the Russian state.

A new hero had been born.

But then, on the evening of September 22, 1999, something happened in Ryazan, a medium-sized city about 120 miles southeast of Moscow, that reversed the narrative entirely. Many questions about the episode remain unanswered, but according to a book that was banned in Russia, *Blowing Up Russia: The Secret Plot to Bring Back KGB Terror,* by Yuri Felshtinsky and Alexander Litvinenko, at about nine fifteen p.m., a man named Alexei Kartofelnikov called authorities and told them he had seen two men and a woman carrying three large sacks into a twelve-story apartment complex.

By the time the police arrived at 9:58 p.m., all three had gone, but officials discovered three fifty-kilogram sugar sacks that were stacked on top of each other in the basement. It was soon determined that instead of sugar, the sacks contained a powerful explosive known as hexogen or RDX, for Royal Demolition Explosive. There was a slit in the upper sack through which one could see an electronic device with wires, insulating tape, and a timer.[56] When the sack was cut open, the police found batteries, an electronic timer, and a detonator. It was set for five thirty the following morning.

In the end, the authors conclude that this failed effort to bomb yet another apartment building produced compelling evidence that the real perpetrators were not Chechen terrorists at all but an elite team from the FSB. In other words, the heinous bombings that killed nearly three hundred innocent Russians were likely the product of a "false flag" operation that enabled Putin to consolidate power, much as Adolf Hitler did after the Reichstag fire.

"To blow up your own innocent and sleeping people in your capital city is an action that is almost unthinkable," writes Karen Dawisha. "Yet the evidence that the FSB was at least involved in planting a bomb in Ryazan is incontrovertible [. . .] and it strikes at the heart of the legitimacy of the Putin regime."[57]

But few Russians were aware of what had really happened. As the newly appointed prime minister who had been put in charge of the war, Putin won popularity overnight.

On December 31, 1999, the last day of the millennium, Boris Yeltsin resigned and appointed Putin acting president. He became president having pledged to chase Chechen terrorists everywhere, famously promising to "rub them out in the outhouse," if necessary.[58] He had promised to stop the plundering of the Russian state by rich oligarchs. But very few Russians knew that Putin had been a primary actor in the same kind of activity in St. Petersburg. And as for cleaning up corruption, one of Putin's first acts as president was to pardon Boris Yeltsin, thereby guaranteeing immunity from prosecution to the outgoing president.[59]

Across the ocean, it was unclear whether or not Trump took notice of Putin's act of clemency—one that would become very important to him years later. Nevertheless, the 2000 election cycle was just getting under way, and Donald Trump had made a very important decision: He wanted to be president of the United States.

CHAPTER TEN

THE MONEY PIPELINES

On October 7, 1999, on CNN's *Larry King Live*, Trump formally announced that he would form a presidential exploratory committee, in hopes of winning the Reform Party's presidential nomination. Over the next six months, he jousted with fellow Reform Party candidates, principally pundit and strategist Pat Buchanan, in the closest approximation of a political campaign he had ever had.

But close was not good enough, and on February 14, 2000, Trump dropped out, and blamed the Reform Party itself, noting that it was dominated by a "fringe element" that he didn't particularly care for. More specifically, Trump complained that at a reception in California for the party, "the room was crowded with Elvis look-alikes."[1]

Meanwhile, in Moscow, Vladimir Putin had a very different set of issues to deal with. When he took office as acting president on January 1, 2000, he was essentially a blank slate to the Russian people, a man who was known largely for being inscrutable. A Russian newsmagazine headlined a profile of him "Magician Without a Face."[2] Russian political analysts referred to him as a "black box."

"He is a grey man, an invisible man," said Ruslan Linkov, a liberal politician from St. Petersburg. "He was always in the shadows. He has psychological skills, and he uses his KGB skills in the political structures. Nobody quits the KGB forever. If someone works there, he works there until his death."[3]

To the West, Putin was little more than an enigma whose ascent elicited anodyne critiques. "He's a smart, cool customer who is one of those solution-oriented problem solvers and virtually unflappable," said Bill Clinton's national security adviser, Samuel "Sandy" Berger. "The next three months (before March 26 Russian presidential elections) will reveal much about where his instincts lie."[4]

The most telling clue to Putin's real views came in an essay he wrote as he was about to take office. "Russia has been and will continue to be a great country," he wrote, ". . . [but it] is never going to be another USA or England, where liberal values have deep historical traditions," because Russians are more attracted to "collective forms of life."[5]

Perhaps the most revelatory moment in his essay was his use of a somewhat archaic term that had an imperial ring to it: *derzhavnost*, a word dating back to tsarist times that indicates belief in the greatness of the state. The word is derived from *derzhava,* the orb that was part of the tsarist regalia, which signified Russia's imperial reach.[6]

At a time when the once-formidable Eastern Bloc was vanishing before his eyes, was Putin truly serious about resurrecting Russia's imperial past? Hungary, the Czech Republic, Poland, and East Germany (which had reunited with West Germany) had already joined NATO. Estonia, Latvia, Lithuania, Slovenia, Bulgaria, and Romania were next in line, ready to go.

If Putin were to reverse the course of history, where would he possibly begin?

The unspoken answer, now that both the Soviet Union and communism were dead, lay in the fact that the Russian security forces and the Mafia had rushed in to fill the power vacuum. Under the new, emerging Putin paradigm, the Kremlin operated hand in glove with the Bratva, to the benefit of both, with the Mafia adhering to guidelines established at the top.

For Mogilevich, having Putin as an ally meant he was now in a position to make a major move. Instead of arbitrating turf battles in Brighton Beach or Budapest, he was now poised to begin rearranging multibillion-dollar pieces on the geopolitical chessboard. The upshot of the 1995 Mafia summit meeting in Tel Aviv had been that Mogilevich would be allowed to make a move on the Ukraine energy trade. Implementing that agreement, however, required cooperation from the powers that be in both Moscow and Kiev. Everything was possible so long as Mogilevich played by Putin's rules—namely, that Putin now provided *krysha* (protection) for Mogilevich, just as Mogilevich did for his underlings. "Nobody would survive in Moscow without the roof of the FSB," said a highly knowledgeable Mafia source.[7]

Meanwhile, Mogilevich's plans for globalization continued apace. Having set up an industrial magnet firm in Budapest called YBM Magnex, he expanded into Canada and the United States, and dispatched Dr. Jacob (Yakov) Bogatin, a trained metallurgist who happened to be David Bogatin's brother, to its Newtown, Pennsylvania, branch to become CEO.[8]

But on May 13, 1998, the FBI raided YBM's Newtown offices and found its huge site littered with thousands of pages documenting sales, purchase orders, invoices, and the like. However, they did not find any actual magnets.[9] Instead, they discovered that Mogilevich had been using some extraordinarily creative accounting—and hyperbolic PR about a nonexistent product—to send YBM's stock price skyrocketing from less than ten cents a share to $20.15.[10]

After the raid, trading of YBM shares on the Toronto Stock Exchange was halted. In December 1998, YBM went into receivership.[11] By then, however, according to the Toronto *Globe and Mail*, Mogilevich had personally made $18.4 million from stock sales and other compensation, while partner Jacob Bogatin had made $10 million,[12] all from a company that, according to the FBI, did not actually make magnets and "was created for the sole purpose of committing securities fraud."[13] In 2003, Mogilevich, Jacob Bogatin, and Igor Fisherman, YBM's European operating manager, were indicted on forty-five felony counts for the $150 million stock fraud. But because there is no extradition treaty between the United States and Russia, they were never brought to trial in the United States.

———

In the course of its investigation, the FBI took the unusual step of starting the FBI–Hungarian National Police Organized Crime Task Force in Budapest to dismantle organized crime groups in the very city that Mogilevich had chosen as his base.[14] As soon as the task force began investigating, Mogilevich realized that if he stayed in Budapest, he risked extradition because Hungary did have such a treaty with the United States. So in June 1999,[15] he fled to Moscow, where he was safe.

In a rare newspaper interview a few months later at the Moscow Marriott, with Sandra Rubin of Canada's *National Post*, Mogilevich made no secret of the contempt he had for the United States as a result of the FBI's investigation, refusing even to take a sip from a sealed bottle of mineral water, lest it be poisoned. "This is an American hotel," his translator explained. "He does not eat or drink in the house of the enemy."

The problems all went back, Mogilevich said, "to some low-life FBI agent who pretended he was an expert on Russian matters and made up a file of people who were supposedly 'known' to Russian authorities. It was just made up."[16]

Since the FBI started investigating him, he said, "I wouldn't say my life has changed—it has disappeared. My son comes home from school with bruises all over his body. He has been fighting with everyone who calls him the son of a killer, the son of that guy involved in drugs."

With that, Mogilevich's eyes filled with tears. He looked down at his ashtray. "I used to smoke True because it expressed what was inside me," he said, as he chain-smoked Davidoffs. "But I switched brands because I found out there is no such thing as 'true' in America."[17]

———

Meanwhile, in Budapest, American officials had put together a very different picture of Mogilevich, and were dumbfounded by the fealty of the Ukrainian secret service (SBU) to him. Even though the Ukrainians knew the FBI was hot on his trail, SBU director Leonid Derkach rhapsodized about Mogilevich as a great entrepreneur to a reporter, asserting that he had created "a scientifically unique mini-magnet that would revolutionize industry and transport."[18]

Of course, that was nonsense. The so-called mini-magnets didn't even exist. It was another magnificent scam. Mogilevich and his associates had just cheated investors out of $150 million.[19]

In response to Derkach's homage to Mogilevich, US ambassador to Ukraine Steven Pifer, accompanied by an FBI agent, met with Ukraine's secretary of state for security and defense, Yevhen Marchuk, and gave him the FBI file on Mogilevich, who had made it to the FBI's vaunted "Ten Most Wanted" list.

But that changed nothing. In February 2000, Derkach met secretly with Mogilevich in Kiev to finalize a business deal whereby Mogilevich would sell the Ukrainian SBU an electronic intelligence-gathering system.[20] Mogilevich had become so close to Derkach and Ukrainian intelligence that he was actually the vendor for the SBU when it came to sensitive intel gathering. And even there, Mogilevich was able to make out like a bandit. The SBU paid Mogilevich almost $4 million for a system that cost just over $2 million in America.

————

Strategic relationships like these were vital to Mogilevich if he was to insinuate himself into the lucrative Ukraine energy trade, a subject, no doubt, that seems extraordinarily arcane and dreary—until one realizes that it is a great way to siphon off huge sums of money. A key figure in helping make that happen was Dmitry Firtash, an up-and-coming Ukrainian oligarch who had been bartering consumer goods in Ukraine, Turkmenistan, and Russia in the nineties when he won permission from then–Ukrainian president Leonid Kravchuk to buy gas for the Ukrainian market.[21]

The deal was worth billions, thanks to Ukraine's historic role as a transit point for Western European gas imports from Russia and Turkmenistan and as a major consumer of gas in its own right. Poland, Germany, and other European countries also relied heavily on Turkmen gas, which Ukraine bought through the barter of food, chemicals, and machinery, rather than cash. Then Ukraine sold the extra gas for hard currency.[22]

Given Ukraine's high rate of inflation, there was a certain logic to doing business that way, but there was one drawback: Barter as a form of trade is highly susceptible to tax evasion and corruption.

Enter Semion Mogilevich.

Putin's reputed alliance with Mogilevich now effectively enabled the Russian Mafia to participate in multibillion-dollar trade deals that appeared, on the surface, to be entirely legitimate. Among those deals, the most significant involved establishing "opaque intermediary companies," whose ownership and roles were often unclear, to be key players in the lucrative Ukraine energy trade. In principle, the scam was simple. Once the gas had been transferred by Moscow to Ukraine at low, low prices to Mogilevich and company, they could immediately resell it at market prices in Europe and pocket the difference, thereby siphoning off untold millions—perhaps billions.

As Mogilevich's partner, Dmitry Firtash was emblematic of the new breed of oligarchs. Having grown up in a small village in western Ukraine, in his youth, Firtash worked as a tomato grower and trained to become a fireman. Then, after the Soviet Union collapsed, he began to sell canned goods, dry milk, and other foodstuffs to Central Asia through barter arrangements.[23]

At the time, Firtash said, he felt he was living "between two countries— one that had ended and one that was beginning" and was still "a country with no laws and no taxes."[24]

His description was absurdly accurate. When he traveled to Turkmenistan trying to collect on a $3 million debt from a state-owned company, the cash-poor government offered to pay him in natural gas instead.[25] Getting involved in the Ukraine gas business in the early days of cowboy capitalism was a high-risk, high-reward undertaking. One had only to look at the track record of Prime Minister Pavlo Lazarenko, who had embezzled $200 million during his thirteen months in office starting in 1996, and, in June 2000, was charged by Ukrainian prosecutors with ordering the assassinations of at least two prominent officials in Kiev who didn't go along with his larcenous business practices.[26] No conviction followed.

As Firtash later told an American official, there were dinners with mobsters—Mogilevich and Sergei Mikhailov from the Solntsevo Bratva, among others—at which he did not know "if he would be beaten up or even killed."[27]

Then, in 2001, Firtash joined a Cyprus-based company called High Rock Holdings LLC that became a key part of his relationship with Mogilevich. According to a classified "Secret" cable by the US ambassador to Ukraine, William Taylor, which was published by WikiLeaks, Firtash acknowledged but downplayed his ties to Mogilevich, "stating he needed Mogilevich's approval to get into business in the first place. He was adamant that he had not committed a single crime when building his business empire, and argued that outsiders still failed to understand the period of lawlessness that reigned in Ukraine after the collapse of the Soviet Union. . . ."[28]

"He noted that it was impossible to approach a government official for any reason without also meeting with an organized crime member at the same time. Firtash acknowledged that he needed, and received, permission from Mogilievich [sic] when he established various businesses, but he denied any close relationship to him. . . . If he needed a permit from the government, for example, he would invariably need permission from the appropriate 'businessman' who worked with the government official who issued that particular permit. He also claimed that although he knows several businessmen who are linked to organized crime, including members of the Solntsevo Brotherhood, he was not implicated in their alleged illegal dealings."[29]

Firtash denies having made the remarks to the ambassador.* But files from the FBI, Interpol, and the US State Department assert that Firtash's ties to Mogilevich were very real indeed. His most important link to Mogilevich came through a Cyprus-based company he joined in 2001 called High Rock Holdings LLC. High Rock's financial director, Igor Fisherman, had served as a high-level aide to Pavlo Lazarenko, the former Ukrainian prime minister, but was better known as Mogilevich's right hand,[30] and had also been a principal at YBM Magnex[31] in Newtown, Pennsylvania, as

---

* In 2016, Shaun Walker reported in the *Guardian*, "Firtash fiercely disputes the contents of the cable and claims he never said this to the ambassador. 'I knew Mogilevich, but so did half of Ukraine. I never had any dealings with him.'"

part of Mogilevich's pump-and-dump stock scam.* As a result of such connections, the Department of Justice has identified Firtash as an "upper-echelon [associate] of Russian organized crime."[32]

And those weren't Firtash's only alleged ties to Mogilevich. According to the US ambassador to Ukraine's cable, "34 percent of High Rock was owned by a firm called Agatheas Trading Ltd," which Galina Telesh, Mogilevich's ex-wife, reportedly directed from 2001 to 2003.[33] Thanks to all of this, a reporter from the *Financial Times* concluded, Firtash had become "the new face of the Mogilevich group."[34]

And so began a series of opaque intermediaries, corporations that siphoned off billions of dollars from the Ukrainian energy trade. By 2002, a new intermediary called Eural Trans Gas (ETG) had been founded in Hungary by Israeli attorney Ze'ev Gordon,[35] to transport gas from Turkmenistan through Russia to Ukraine. As an investigation by Reuters concluded, its ownership structure was "unclear,"[36] but Gordon happened to be Mogilevich's longtime attorney and Firtash seems to have played a major role in the company. Moreover, the day after the tiny company was founded—its startup capital was a mere $12,000—it got a massive contract to transport gas from Turkmenistan to Ukraine that was worth as much as $1 billion on the European markets.[37]

According to "It's a Gas," an investigation into the Turkmen-Ukraine gas trade by Global Witness, an NGO, the ownership papers for ETG listed three hard-up Romanians with no connection to the gas industry, one of whom was an out-of-work actress who says she allowed her name to be used in order to pay her phone bill. The following year, ETG cleared $760 million in profits.

In 2004, RosUkrEnergo (RUE) replaced Eural Trans Gas and became the go-between for gas deals between Turkmenistan and Ukraine. Once again, the ownership was hazy initially, but in the end it became

---

* According to a RICO indictment drawn up by the Eastern District of the State of New York against Fisherman, Jacob Bogatin, Anatoly Tsoura, and Semion Mogilevich, Fisherman served as chief operating officer of YBM and was on its board of directors. He was also president of Arigon, a YBM subsidiary in which Mogilevich was a principal.

clear that Firtash and Gazprom, the giant Russian gas company, owned nearly the entire company.[38]

Through all these deals, Reuters concluded, Firtash's "success was built on remarkable sweetheart deals brokered by associates of Russian leader Vladimir Putin, at immense cost to Russian taxpayers."[39]

Indeed, the price Firtash paid for the gas was so low that companies he controlled made more than $3 billion on the arrangement, at the same time that bankers close to Putin gave Firtash up to $11 billion in credit, much of which went to back pro-Putin political factions in Ukraine.[40]

Billions of dollars were pouring out through the Ukraine energy trade, but that wasn't the only pipeline for flight capital coming out of Russia. In New York, one telltale sign that everything wasn't kosher could be found in the dazzlingly unlikely rags-to-riches stories that abounded about Russian émigrés arriving penniless in New York and ending up enormously wealthy.

One of them was Tamir Sapir, né Temur Sepiashvili, an immigrant who came to America with the proverbial $3 in his pocket, started driving a cab, and a few years later had become a billionaire owning an apartment in, of all places, 721 Fifth Avenue, Trump Tower. His journey was not without intrigue.

After his taxi days were over, Sapir partnered with fellow immigrant Semyon "Sam" Kislin to open a small wholesale electronics store whose clients included Soviet diplomats, Politburo members, and KGB agents.[41] Kislin had sold hundreds of TV sets to Donald Trump back in the seventies for his first major project, the transformation of the Commodore Hotel.

According to *Newsday*, the store was extraordinarily popular with the Soviets, so much so that Sapir somehow managed to parlay its success into getting licenses to ship Soviet oil to US refineries, a serendipity that led to great wealth.[42]

But a small electronics store is an unlikely path to massive fortune, and their real secret may have been their ties to organized crime through an Uzbek businessman named Mikhail Chernoy.* Like many oligarchs, Chernoy had gotten his start via immensely profitable and sometimes imaginative barter deals in which he traded iron ore pellets in exchange for Lada cars, coal for food and sugar, and the like. "Basically, I converted rubles to dollars by exporting coke and importing consumer goods," he told the *Observer* (UK). "I approached Russian factories, which were operating only at 30 to 40 per cent capacity. They were on the point of collapse without the coke to run the furnaces."[43]

That wasn't all. In the early nineties Chernoy and his brother Lev emerged with a fortune of more than $100 million, according to a report by Pulitzer Prize–winning reporter Knut Royce for the Center for Public Integrity.[44]

The Chernoys then used the funds to seed their London-based holding company, Trans-World Group, through a convoluted maze of offshore companies, and "rapidly gained control of Russia's aluminum industry and acquired a large stake in processing and distribution of other metals and petroleum products."[45]

In the meantime, the Chernoys had begun working with Semyon Kislin's firm, Trans Commodities, Inc.[46] A 1994 FBI file characterized Kislin as a "member/associate" of the mob organization headed by Vyacheslav Ivankov, the "godfather of Russian organized crime in the United States", a connection Kislin denied.

In the "Aluminum Wars" that followed, many businessmen who opposed the Chernoys ended up dead.[47] But perhaps that's not so surprising, given the players and the enormous stakes. In the end, Royce's report said, "The brothers obtained licenses to buy the aluminum for $10 and sell it for $1,500 by bribing top Russian officials." Just one of many ways that billions were made.

———

In addition to overseeing the massive flow of flight capital that resulted from "privatization," Putin had a deft touch when it came to

---

* At various times, Chernoy has been transliterated as Chorny, Chornoi, Chorney, and Chornoy, among other spellings.

consolidating his power. That became apparent when, just after becoming prime minister, Putin recruited two oligarchs who were among his closest confidants, Roman Abramovich and Lev Leviev,[48] to undertake the highly unlikely mission of creating a new religious organization called the Federation of Jewish Communities of Russia. The idea was to bring together various Orthodox Jewish communities in Russia through an Orthodox Hasidic sect known as Chabad.

To anyone familiar with the long and bitter history of anti-Semitism in Russia, Putin's outreach on behalf of Jews was extraordinarily unusual. Even though the 1917 revolution theoretically ended official tsarist policies that persecuted Jews, Stalin instituted anti-Semitic policies that sent tens of thousands of Jews into the gulags and, in the long run, gave birth to the Russian Mafia. But anti-Semitism endured even after the demise of the Soviet Union, and the rise of the Russian Mafia and the new oligarchs, many of whom were Jewish, provided fodder for anti-Semites.*[49] As a result, the Russian Mafia was sometimes referred to as the Jewish Mafia or the Kosher Nostra.

On the surface, at least, Putin differed from previous Russian leaders in that he openly celebrated and rewarded his friendships with his Jewish high school teacher and Jewish sparring partners from judo practice.†[50] But Putin's professed philo-Semitism, however genuine, was also vital to his political agenda. One of the imperatives of power in post-Soviet Russia was that the Russian chief of state had to keep the oligarchs under his control—and that included Jewish oligarchs.

Until Putin's ascent, the leading Jewish organization in Russia had been the Russian Jewish Congress, or Rossiiskii Evreiskii Kongress

---

*According to a report by the Israeli website Ynetnews, forty-eight out of the two hundred richest people in Russia are Jewish. In some ways, however, the disproportionate wealth of a few dozen Jewish oligarchs can be seen as the unintended consequence of anti-Semitic Soviet policies that gave all the best career slots to ethnic Slavs and forced Jews into the black market. That meant when communism collapsed and free-market capitalism replaced the black market, Jewish entrepreneurs had a head start.

† In 2005, on a visit to Tel Aviv, Putin dropped by the home of Mina Yuditskaya Berliner, who had taught him German in high school some forty years earlier, and before he left, gave her a new apartment in Tel Aviv. Two of his judo sparring partners, the brothers Boris and Arkady Rotenberg, fared even better—much better. They ended up being worth about $2 billion each, thanks, in part, to $5.5 billion in construction contracts awarded to them by Putin for the 2014 Sochi Winter Olympics.

(REK), which had been cofounded by Vladimir Gusinsky. A former theater director turned media mogul, Gusinsky was unique among the oligarchs in that his wealth was created from the ground up rather than from taking over formerly state-run properties.[51] With the REK, Gusinsky succeeded beyond all expectations in winning recognition from the state of Israel and bringing together a vast array of Jewish organizations and leaders. The Israeli daily *Haaretz* called him "the No. 1 Jew in Russia."[52]

None of which was good news for rival oligarchs Roman Abramovich and Lev Leviev, both of whom were strong Putin supporters, and, like Putin, felt "that Gusinsky was exploiting not only his businesses and ties, but also REK to further his standing at their expense," according to *Haaretz*.[53]

As a result, in 1999, Putin got Abramovich and Leviev to create the Federation of Jewish Communities in Russia, under the leadership of Rabbi Berel Lazar, a leader in the Hasidic movement called Chabad-Lubavitch.

Founded in the late eighteenth century, the tiny, Brooklyn-based Chabad-Lubavitcher movement is a fundamentalist Hasidic sect centered on the teaching of the late Rabbi Menachem Schneerson, who is sometimes referred to as a messiah—*moshiach*—a savior and liberator of the Jewish people. It is antiabortion, views homosexuality as a perversion, and often aligns itself politically with other fundamentalist groups on the right.[54]

Its biggest donors included Leviev, an Israeli billionaire who was an Uzbek native and was known as the "King of Diamonds" thanks to his success in the diamond trade, and Charles Kushner,[55] an American real estate developer who was later jailed for illegal campaign contributions, tax evasion, and witness tampering. Kushner is also the father of Jared Kushner, who married Donald Trump's daughter, Ivanka, and later became a senior adviser to President Trump.

Leviev's friendship with Lazar dates back to 1992 and, according to *Haaretz,* made Leviev "the most influential, most active and most connected person in the Jewish community of Russia and made Lazar the country's chief rabbi."[56]

With Abramovich as another powerful ally, Leviev strengthened his alliance with President Putin and in May 2000 Lazar was awarded Russian citizenship[57] and became known as Putin's rabbi—pushing aside Gusinsky and his rabbi in the process.[58] As for Putin, by putting loyalists in charge of a new national organization for Jews, he had come up with a unique way of consolidating power among the oligarchs.

But there was one other unintended consequence that grew out of this alliance that proved to be most important of all: Oddly enough, at the end of the day, the tiny Hasidic sect called Chabad would provide some of the richest and most unexpectedly direct sets of connections between Putin and Donald Trump.

CHAPTER ELEVEN

EASY PREY

America was different from Russia in so many ways that initially many Russians were baffled by the unusual business practices they encountered in the West. Which is precisely what an American businessman in Moscow discovered while talking to a rich Uzbek cotton trader about the pay-for-play K Street lobbyists in Washington.

The Uzbek, an aspiring oligarch who was all too familiar with the dark practices of the Bratva, listened patiently to a long explanation about how corporate America uses lobbyists to get access to Congress. Then it was as if a light bulb went off. "You mean you have firms with highly paid professionals who are *paid* to bribe congressmen?" he asked.

He couldn't get over it. He had spent years navigating the perilous world of Bratva protection rackets, and here the Americans had sanitized corruption, institutionalized it, and made it into part of the white-collar, professional world! Not only was it legal, it was a highly paid profession.

After decades carrying water for Big Oil, Big Pharma, and Wall Street, K Street lobbyists were ready, willing, and able to jump in bed with anyone who could write a big check—including Russians.

Among the first wave of lobbyists willing to play ball with them was Jack Abramoff, aka "Casino Jack," the notorious super-lobbyist who wined and dined DC's most pliable politicians, made deals all over town, and reaped huge paydays from casino-rich Indian tribes, which he spent in fancy restaurants and stadium skyboxes and golf trips to Scotland and the Pacific island of Saipan.[1] Jack Abramoff worked in the margins and loved it.[2]

Abramoff eventually served more than four years for mail fraud, conspiracy to bribe public officials, and tax evasion and was at the center of a pay-for-play scam that led to the conviction of twenty-one other people, including Republican majority leader Tom DeLay of Texas. A high point in the scandal came when DeLay and Abramoff took a six-day trip to London and Moscow, played golf, and met Prime Minister Viktor Chernomyrdin, among other Russian leaders.

Though Abramoff billed the trip to a client in the Pacific, the Commonwealth of the Northern Marianas, the money was really coming in from a shell company controlled by Russian oligarchs Marina Nevskaya and Alexander Koulakovsky of NaftaSib, a huge Russian oil company.[3]

At one point, the two oligarchs said they "wanted to contribute to DeLay." One of them even asked, "What would happen if the DeLays woke up one morning" and found a luxury car in front of their house?[4]

That would have been illegal, of course. It would have been bribery. Everyone concerned would have ended up in jail, so the car never came.

Instead, a $1 million check mysteriously made its way to the US Family Network, a DeLay slush fund. DeLay had initially opposed a foreign aid bill that would help the International Monetary Fund bail out Russia's weak economy. But after the $1 million check arrived, he had a change of heart, although he later denied the payment had influenced his vote.

Other Russians joined in. Alfa, the multibillion-dollar Russian conglomerate,* paid Barbour Griffith & Rogers, the influential GOP lobbying firm cofounded by former Mississippi governor Haley Barbour, nearly $2 million in lobbying fees. Barbour Griffith also received $820,000 from a United Kingdom shell company called Foruper Limited, which had no assets or employees, but which the US Justice Department was investigating.[5]

---

* The Alfa Group has interests in oil and gas, commercial and investment banking, asset management, insurance, retail trade, telecommunications, water utilities, and special situation investments.

In Congress, Representative Curt Weldon, a Republican from Pennsylvania, began touting a Russian arms control group called the International Exchange Group, which, according to ProPublica, happened to employ the head of the FSB as well as the Russian army's chief of staff.[6] According to the *Los Angeles Times*, Weldon also helped round up thirty fellow congressmen for a dinner to honor the chairman of the Itera International Energy Corporation, a Russian natural gas company. As it happened, Itera had agreed to pay $500,000 a year for public relations to a firm run by Weldon's daughter, then an inexperienced twenty-nine-year-old lobbyist. Itera was the intermediary that Firtash and Mogilevich pushed aside to move into the Russian-Ukraine energy trade.[7]

Whether it was lobbying or finding lawyers, the Russians went straight to the top, as they had since the early days in Brighton Beach. When David Bogatin got busted in the Red Daisy gas tax scam, he took on as his attorney Mitchell Rogovin,[8] the highly placed former special counsel to the CIA. When Bogatin's brother, Jacob, needed representation for his role in Mogilevich's YBM Magnex pump-and-dump scam, he hired Eric Sitarchuk,[9] who later ended up representing Trump himself in a suit filed against him as owner of the Trump International Hotel in Washington.[10]

Bob Dole, the former Senate majority leader and 1996 Republican presidential nominee, accepted a $560,000 fee to help Russian billionaire Oleg Deripaska obtain a visa to visit the US, after Deripaska had been accused by rivals of bribery, which he denied.[11]

Even William Sessions, director of the FBI from 1987 to 1993, was not above doing a complete about-face when it came to Russian organized crime. In 1997, after he returned to private practice, he traveled to Moscow and alerted the world to the horrifying dangers of the brutal Russian Mafia. A few years later, however, Sessions had no qualms about taking on as a client a Ukrainian-born mobster whom the FBI had put on its "Ten Most Wanted" list. His name was Semion Mogilevich.*[12]

---

* William Sessions is not related to Attorney General Jeff Sessions. He is, however, the father of Representative Pete Sessions (R-TX) who, interestingly, given his father's representation of Russia's most powerful Mafia boss, was one of the most vocal opponents in the House of

Still, Russia's relationship with Trump was unique. One measure of that was discovered by FBI agents who were on the trail of Vyacheslav Ivankov but couldn't figure out where he lived. "[Ivankov] was like a ghost to the FBI," said Gregory Stasiuk, an investigator with the New York State Organized Crime Task Force.[13]

Ivankov, of course, had been spotted frequently at the Trump Taj Mahal in Atlantic City and was widely thought to be based with other Russian mobsters in Brighton Beach. But whenever the FBI was ready to pounce, he vanished. When they finally found him, he wasn't in Brooklyn at all. Instead, they discovered that the head of the Russian Mafia lived in a luxury condo in Manhattan—at 721 Fifth Avenue, in fact—Trump Tower.[14] (Ivankov was eventually convicted of extortion and sentenced to nine and a half years in jail.)

———

Meanwhile, Russians continued to court Trump, even though his political prospects seemed middling at best. In 2000, with trickster Roger Stone as his strategist, Trump had made a stab at winning the presidential nomination on the Reform Party ticket, but dropped out when he found out that the Reform candidate, no matter who it was, would not make the cutoff for the presidential debates. For the most part, Trump was still relegated to the bin of novelty celebrity candidates like professional wrestler turned governor of Minnesota Jesse Ventura.

Nevertheless, Trump had a unique résumé for someone on a presidential track. By this time his ties to Russian money stretched back more than two decades. When it came to laundering money, casinos and real estate were the vehicles of choice, and the Trump Taj Mahal* in Atlantic City seemed to be a favorite destination for Russian mobsters,

Representatives of sanctions against Russia. It is worth pointing out that, according to Canada's *National Post*, earlier, Mogilevich had hired another important figure in American law enforcement as his attorney, namely, Richard Crane Jr., former head of the US Justice Department's Organized Crime Strike Force for the Western United States.

* Trump's bankruptcies notwithstanding, the Trump Taj Mahal continued to operate in what is known as a "prepackaged bankruptcy" in which Trump gave a 50 percent stake in the business to its bondholders in exchange for lowered interest rates and a longer payoff schedule.

who frequently arrived in Ferraris and Rolls-Royces with stacks of $100 bills.[15]

If money laundering was going on, the Taj seems to have done everything within its power to keep it secret. In 1998, the Financial Crimes Enforcement Network (FinCEN) assessed a $477,700 civil penalty against the Trump Taj Mahal for currency transaction reporting violations—namely, failing to report each time a gambler cashed out with more than $10,000 in a single day.[16] FinCEN added that the casino admitted to "willful and repeated" Bank Secrecy Act violations, including violations of AML (anti–money laundering) program requirements, reporting obligations, and record-keeping requirements.

But that didn't tell the whole story. At a time when it was very much the preferred spot of the Brighton Beach Mafia, the Taj Mahal was also short on cash, on the verge of bankruptcy, and not likely to cause trouble for such a free-spending clientele. Modest though it was, at the time, FinCEN's fine was the biggest in history by the federal government for violating the Bank Secrecy Act. Moreover, it represented no fewer than 106 violations of the act.

All of which left key questions unanswered. How much was laundered is unknown. In addition, as CNN reported, the names of parties suspected of money laundering had been scrubbed from the report, as were the identities of Trump employees involved in the transactions.[17]

"Trump Taj Mahal received many warnings about its deficiencies," said FinCEN director Jennifer Shasky Calvery.[18] "Like all casinos in this country, Trump Taj Mahal has a duty to help protect our financial system from being exploited by criminals, terrorists, and other bad actors. Far from meeting these expectations, poor compliance practices, over many years, left the casino and our financial system unacceptably exposed."

———

As the Russians knew, real estate was a far more efficient way to launder billions in flight capital, and Trump's newest projects were perfectly suited to their needs. In 1999, when the Russian economy was in a tailspin and scores of oligarchs were looking for a safe haven, construction was already under way on Trump's biggest project yet.

Rising to seventy-two stories in midtown Manhattan, Trump World Tower, overlooking the United Nations, was touted as the tallest residential building on the planet. Before long, one-third of the units on the tower's highest and priciest floors, floors seventy-six to eighty-three,* had been snatched up, either by individual buyers from the former Soviet Union, or by limited liability companies connected to Russia or countries that had been part of the Soviet Union. "We had big buyers from Russia and Ukraine and Kazakhstan," sales agent Debra Stotts told *Bloomberg Businessweek*.[19] Ukrainian billionaire Semyon "Sam" Kislin assisted the sales effort by issuing mortgages to buyers of Trump's latest luxury condos.[20]

Among the new tenants was Eduard Nektalov, a diamond dealer from Uzbekistan who had bought a condo on the seventy-ninth floor of Trump World Tower, directly below Trump's future campaign manager, Kellyanne Conway.[†21]

With his multimillion-dollar condo and a $300,000 Bentley, Nektalov, who was related to Lev Leviev, the billionaire pal of Putin's known as the "King of Diamonds," had been making a good living in the diamond world, but now he was being investigated by a Treasury Department task force for mob-connected money laundering. He and his father, Roman Nektalov, had been targeted in Operation Meltdown, a two-and-a-half-year sting operation that uncovered a scheme through which diamond merchants laundered $8 million in Colombian drug proceeds.[22]

On a pleasant evening in May 2004, after reports circulated that he might soon start cooperating with federal investigators, Nektalov closed

---

* As with other buildings he developed, Trump deliberately mislabeled the floors in Trump World Tower to make it seem higher. As a result, it was possible for Eduard Nektalov to live on the seventy-ninth floor of the seventy-two-story Trump World Tower.

† According to the *Washington Post*, the Conways caught Trump's attention during a condo board battle in which various residents wanted Trump's name stripped from the building's exterior. George Conway was one of the pro-Trump leaders, and his wife, Kellyanne, took a seat on the condo board and became friendly with Trump as a result.

Like so many Trump associates, Kellyanne was not without ties to the Mafia. According to the New York *Daily News*, her late grandfather Jimmy "the Brute" DiNatale was described by law enforcement authorities as a "significant criminal associate" of Nicodemo "Little Nicky" Scarfo, the heir apparent to a Philadelphia-based crime family.

his store in New York's Forty-Seventh Street Diamond District and began walking to the garage where he kept his Bentley. When he neared Forty-Eighth Street, a long-haired man pulled a .45 out of his pants and fired once in the back of Nektalov's head. Nektalov collapsed. Then the shooter pumped two more bullets into his back and fled.[23]

"Everybody on 47th Street knew if you had stolen stuff, you could bring it to the Nektalovs," said David Ribacoff, a fellow Uzbek and a veteran of the Diamond District.[24] "I knew someday something was going to happen with these people. If you play with fire, you're going to get burned."

This was Trump's market. "Early on, Trump came to the conclusion that it is better to do business with crooks than with honest people," said Anders Åslund, a Swedish economist and senior fellow at the Atlantic Council.[25] "Crooks have two big advantages. First, they're prepared to pay more money than honest people. And second, they will always lose if you sue them because they are known to be crooks."

All Trump needed to do, it seemed, was slap his name on a big building, preferably in gigantic, bold, brass, upper-case lettering, and high-dollar customers from Russia and the former Soviet republics were guaranteed to come rushing in—gangland shootouts among his residents notwithstanding.

After Trump World Tower opened, Sotheby's International Realty teamed up with a Russian real estate company to make a big sales push for the property in Russia. Dolly Lenz, a New York real estate broker, spoke to *USA Today*. "I had contacts in Moscow looking to invest in the United States," Lenz said.[26] "They all wanted to meet Donald." In the end, she said that she sold some sixty-five units in Trump World Tower to Russians.

————

There was one more factor that helped Trump evolve toward a new business model. Disastrous as his Atlantic City bankruptcies had been, one serendipity had come out of the experience: Banks that were on the hook for his gigantic losses decided that the Trump name had real market value.

This was not merely the wishful fantasy of an egomaniacal once-and-future billionaire. "Ironically, the fact that he was so overextended worked to his benefit when the real estate market collapsed," said Stephen Bollenbach, a corporate salvage specialist who helped structure Trump's Atlantic City rescue operation.[27] "He already had his financing. They were stuck with him."

Bollenbach's epiphany came after a cash-strapped Trump failed to make an $800,000 quarterly insurance payment for his prized yacht, the *Trump Princess*, and assumed the bank would seize the boat.[28] But Bollenbach had argued to the bank that the yacht was more valuable as the *Trump Princess* than as just another big boat—and to his astonishment, the bank agreed. They even paid the insurance premium. That meant the banks realized they were in better shape if Trump was back in business.

It also meant that Trump could implement a completely new business model that allowed him to stay in real estate without having to deal with the onerous chores of financing and of actually being the developer. The model was simple: Because his name had brand value, he would license it to developers who would do all the work and give him a piece of the action. Then, he would sit back and collect royalties, which were often 18 percent or more.

It was also the perfect solution for both Trump and the Russians. On the one hand, Russians had billions of dollars from illicit sources that needed to be laundered. On the other hand, Trump, who was in dire need of financing, had the ideal vehicles for laundering their money—real estate and casinos—and a history of not asking too many questions of his buyers.

To capitalize on this new business model, Trump struck a deal with a Florida developer to attach his name to three high-rises in Sunny Isles Beach, just outside Miami. Without putting up a dime of his own money, Trump would receive a cut of the profits. "Russians love the Trump brand," Sunny Isles developer Gil Dezer told Bloomberg.[29] A local broker added that one-third of the five hundred apartments he'd sold went to "Russian-speakers." So many bought the Trump-branded apartments, in fact, that the area became known as "Little Moscow."

Many of the units were sold by a native of Uzbekistan who had emigrated from the Soviet Union in the 1980s; her business was so brisk that she soon began bringing Russian tour groups to Sunny Isles to view the properties. According to a Reuters investigation, at least sixty-three buyers with Russian addresses or passports spent $98 million on Trump's properties in South Florida.[30] What's more, one-third of the units—more than seven hundred in all—were bought by shell companies that concealed the true owners.

And over the next few years, roughly 20 percent of Trump-branded condos—more than 1,300 luxury[31] condos in all—repeatedly went to anonymous shell companies. Far from being a comprehensive tally, this number represents a conservative estimate of the amount of Russian flight capital that came through Trump property in the late nineties alone: $1.5 billion.*

And, mind you, that figure refers only to the sale of Trump condos in the United States. It does not include his buildings in Turkey, Panama, the Philippines, India, Toronto, Baku, or elsewhere.

———

A key part of the model was that Trump appears to have defined his target market as Russian money. "Trump specifically marketed his Sunny Isles, Florida, apartment units in Moscow, St. Petersburg, and other venues designed to attract Russian organized crime money,"[32] said Kenneth McCallion, a former federal prosecutor and New York attorney who specializes in human rights, money laundering, and civil racketeering cases. A Reuters investigation did not find any wrongdoing by Trump or his real estate organization.

In response to media inquiries, Trump Organization lawyer Alan

---

* The estimate comes from a BuzzFeed investigation that concluded that more than 1,300 of Trump's 6,400 condos sold in the US had the characteristics of money-laundering deals (all cash, bought through a shell company). The condos sold for an average of $1.2 million.

Garten commented that the firm did not track nationalities of buyers and that the company rarely plays a role in recruiting buyers.

However, the dubious character of Trump's clientele was so obvious that the *Financial Times* suggested that the Russian American Chamber of Commerce, headed by Sergei Millian, who claimed to be Trump's exclusive broker for Trump properties in Russia and the former Soviet Union, was the kind of Russian operation that harkened back to Cold War–style espionage.[33]

Konstantin Borovoi, who was president of Russia's first commodities exchange, agrees that Millian's chamber of commerce is reminiscent of the kind of practices one saw from the secret services at the height of the Cold War. "These institutions have been revived and developed," he said. "The chamber of commerce institutions are the visible part of the agent network . . . Russia has spent huge amounts of money on this."[34]

In Moscow, of course, since the demise of the Soviet Union, the KGB had been replaced by the FSB, but that did not mean its vaunted tradecraft had been lost or in any way diminished. To the contrary, the Kremlin was now being run by a career KGB operative—in fact, one whose life's goal was to revive Russia's shattered dreams of empire. To that end, at almost every turn there is evidence of the Russians throwing the KGB textbook at Trump, trying to entangle him and compromise him in as many ways as possible. And in Trump, the Russians seemed to have found the perfect mark.

As Comrade Kryuchkov's notebooks had made clear, the KGB wanted to know about the "level of subject's truthfulness and sincerity. Is he hypocritical in double dealing?"

They wanted to know about compromising information regarding the subject, "including illegal acts in financial and commercial affairs, intrigue, speculation, bribes, graft, trading in narcotics, and exploitation of his position to enrich himself."[35]

They wanted to know if "pride, arrogance, egoism, ambition, or vanity [were] among [the] subject's natural characteristics."[36]

Then there was the question of the subject's relationships with women. "Is he secretly fascinated by them? Is he in the habit of having affairs with women on the side?"[37]

By this time, of course, Russian intelligence already knew exactly where Trump fit in terms of such questions. According to Oleg Kalugin, Trump likely had his first taste of sexual *kompromat* in 1987. There were similar reports, unconfirmed, about possible comparable incidents in 1996.

And then there was the fact that, after years of promoting himself as a billionaire, Trump was still anathema to Western banks, and was desperate to climb back to the top of the heap. Using his name as a brand was an inspired idea. But it was coupled with his apparent eagerness to turn a blind eye to practices that allowed the Russian mob to launder money through his real estate on a massive scale.

Getting to that level, however, required a third party—not unlike Bayrock Group LLC, a real estate firm that was largely staffed, owned, and financed by émigrés from Russia and the former Soviet Union, and had moved into the twenty-fourth floor of Trump Tower.[38] With its ties to the Kremlin, Russian intelligence, and possibly the Mob, Bayrock's looming presence in Trump Tower should have had American counterintelligence agents on high alert. To Russian operatives, one can only imagine, Trump was such easy prey.

CHAPTER TWELVE

INTERNATIONAL MAN OF MYSTERY

Whatever the Russians may have thought about Trump, when the ratings came in for the last week of the 2004 TV season, American television viewers clearly had a very different opinion. The final episode of *The Apprentice,* Donald Trump's wildly successful new show on NBC, had been seen by an estimated twenty-eight million viewers and ranked as the number one show of the week. It was the most popular new show of 2004.

To outside appearances, Trump was back on top after his failures in Atlantic City. Earlier that year, he had launched the new show in typical Trumpian fashion. "My name's Donald Trump," he had declared in his opening narration for *The Apprentice,* "the largest real estate developer in New York. I own buildings all over the place. Model agencies. The Miss Universe pageant. Jetliners, golf courses, casinos, and private resorts like Mar-a-Lago, one of the most spectacular estates anywhere in the world."[1]

But it wouldn't be Trump without a better story than that. "It wasn't always so easy," he confessed, over images of his cruising around New York in a stretch limo. "About thirteen years ago, I was seriously in trouble. I was billions of dollars in debt. But I fought back, and I won. Big league. I used my brain. I used my negotiating skills. And I worked it all out. Now my company's bigger than it ever was and stronger than it ever was. . . . I've mastered the art of the deal."

The show, which reportedly paid Trump up to $3 million per episode,[2] instantly revived his brand. "*The Apprentice* turned Trump from a blowhard Richie Rich who had just gone through his most difficult decade into an unlikely symbol of straight talk, an evangelist for the American gospel of success, a decider who insisted on standards in a country that had somehow slipped into handing out trophies for just showing up," journalists Michael Kranish and Marc Fisher observe in their book *Trump Revealed*.[3] "Above all, *Apprentice* sold an image of the host-boss as supremely competent and confident, dispensing his authority and getting immediate results. The analogy to politics was palpable."

Unfortunately, much of what Trump said simply wasn't true. He wasn't the biggest developer in New York, the *New York Times* pointed out. Nor did he own the Trump International Hotel and Tower at New York's Columbus Circle, which was featured in his promo.[4]

Nevertheless, there was no denying that he was back. Critics derided his show as a cheesy, Vegas-like caricature of what business was really like,[5] but *The Apprentice* was a huge hit and provided a prime-time platform that Trump used to further enhance his brand, and to unveil another big project.

Over time, ratings sagged, but the show was still a powerful marketing tool for Trump. On the 2006 season finale of *The Apprentice*, as more than eleven million viewers waited to learn which of the two finalists was going to be fired, Trump prolonged the suspense by cutting to a promotional video for his latest venture. "Located in the center of Manhattan's chic artist enclave, the Trump International Hotel and Tower in SoHo is the site of my latest development," he narrated over swooping helicopter footage of lower Manhattan.[6] The new building, he added, would be nothing less than a "$370 million work of art . . . an awe-inspiring masterpiece."

What Trump didn't say in the video was that Trump SoHo was the brainchild of two development companies—Bayrock Group LLC and the Sapir Organization—run by a pair of wealthy émigrés from the former Soviet Union who had done business with some of Russia's richest and most notorious oligarchs.

Together, their firms had made Trump an offer he couldn't refuse:

The developers would license Donald Trump's name for branded luxury high-rises Bayrock would finance and develop. Without a financial investment, Trump was back in action, phoenix-like, with his name on yet another gleaming luxury hotel/condominium development. In return for lending his name to the project, Trump would get an 18 percent equity stake.[7]

In the wake of his massive debts and multiple bankruptcies, Wall Street had said no to Trump. The banks had said no to Trump. New York had said no to Trump. But Bayrock had said yes, and thanks to them, Donald Trump was back in business.

———

No one at Bayrock was more important in working with Trump than Felix Sater, its managing director. One of the most enigmatic figures in the entire Trump-Russia saga, Sater was Bayrock's international man of mystery, a stocky, olive-complexioned, Porsche-driving super salesman straight out of *Glengarry Glen Ross* who was always on, pushing a pump-and-dump stock scam, or going undercover for the CIA, the DIA, the FBI—whomever—to try to buy Stinger missiles from al-Qaeda or undertake other mind-boggling feats of derring-do.

Born in Moscow, Felix had come to the United States with his family, then known as the Sheferovskys,*[8] in the early seventies, when he was a young boy, and settled with the first waves of Soviet émigrés in Brighton Beach's "Little Odessa." They left Russia with few regrets. According to Howard Rosenberg, a producer at CBS's *60 Minutes* who interviewed Sater, Felix's father, Mikhail Sheferovsky, is said to have watched the communists execute *his* father—Felix's grandfather—in the courtyard of their apartment building.[9]

There long have been allegations that Mikhail Sheferovsky had ties to organized crime, including Mogilevich, but much of his past is

———

* Sater's father is most frequently referred to in the press by the name Sheferovsky, but there are many conflicting spellings of his real name. According to an article by Vladimir Kozlovsky for BBC's Russian Service, the real family name in Russia was actually Saterov. As for Felix, court documents show that he also went by the names of Satter, Slater, Sader, Haim F. Sater, Hai Ying Sater, and his putative birth name of Sheferovsky.

shrouded in mystery. Sater's attorney, Robert S. Wolf, told me, in an email, that Sheferovsky "never met nor had anything to do with Semion Mogilevich. Mikhail Sater [Sheferovsky] has never been a named accomplice of Semion Mogilevich, nor are there any court documents that so indicate. This is a complete fabrication."[10]

Nevertheless, according to a certified US Supreme Court petition, Felix Sater's FBI handler described Felix's father, Michael Sheferovsky (aka Mikhail Sater), as "a (Semion) Mogilevich crime syndicate boss."[11] Exactly what that meant was not defined. As Richard Lerner, the lawyer who wrote the Supreme Court petition, explained, "The Russian Mafia doesn't exactly hand out business cards."[12]

Sheferovsky's ties to the Italian mob were more clear-cut. After he got to Brighton Beach, Sheferovsky partnered in various extortion scams with Ernest "Butch" Montevecchi, a soldier in the Genovese crime family, which had joined with the Russian Mafia in the Red Daisy gasoline tax scam in the eighties and had been represented by Roy Cohn. Sheferovsky made the rounds of his victims accompanied by a six-foot-nine, three-hundred-pound giant nicknamed King Kong[13] whose intimidating presence could be rather persuasive. In 2000, Sheferovsky pleaded guilty to charges that he ran an extortion ring that targeted grocery stores, restaurants, and other establishments.[14]

His son Felix grew up near Brighton Beach and, as a teenager, counted among his friends Michael D. Cohen, who later became President Trump's personal attorney. At the time, Cohen was dating Laura Shusterman, a Ukrainian girl Sater knew and whom Cohen later married,[15] but the two men came from distinctly different worlds. Sater's Brighton Beach/Coney Island neighborhood, of course, had its rough spots. "I was one of the white kids on the block, which led to lots of beatings," he told Talking Points Memo.[16] By contrast, Cohen lived in the tonier, more suburban precincts of Long Island's Five Towns in Nassau County.

Sater took classes at Pace University but dropped out, and before long was a Wall Street hotshot working at shops like Bear Stearns and Shearson Lehman Brothers.[17] A charismatic but volatile man, and an unrelenting salesman, Felix, then in his midtwenties, loved the high life.

He collected expensive watches and thought nothing of going into Er-
menegildo Zegna and spending $30,000 on suits. Felix's father had
wanted his son to go straight, but, as his friend Salvatore Lauria put it
in his autobiography, *The Scorpion and the Frog*,* Felix "would rather go
through the back door than the front door of any deal."[18]

Sater also had a quick temper, and on October 1, 1991, when he was
having drinks at a bar in midtown Manhattan, he got into a fight over a
girl. "[I]ntoxicated and inebriated as a result of excessive drinking,"[19]
according to court records, Sater grabbed a margarita glass, broke it on
the bar, and smashed the stem into his foe's face. Then, according to the
trial transcript, Sater picked up another piece of broken glass and lunged
at the victim's friend. "I'm going to kill you, motherfucker," he said.
"You faggot. Your mother's a whore. Some black nigger fucked your
mother."[20]

The man's injuries required 110 stitches.[21] Sater was convicted of felony assault, served a fifteen-month sentence, and was barred from le-
gally selling securities. "I had great plans for myself which were all
shattered with that stupid drunken night in a bar," Felix later told
ABC.[22]

But that wasn't the end of it. Even though Sater had lost his license to
trade stocks, in 1993, he and two associates got control of White Rock
Partners, a brokerage firm that later changed its name to State Street
Capital Markets. Felix had rented a penthouse office suite[23] at 40 Wall
Street—a seventy-one-story neo-Gothic skyscraper in downtown Man-
hattan, owned by Donald Trump.

According to the *New York Times,* the three men secretly used offshore accounts to gain control of large blocks of penny stocks in four
companies so they could inflate the value of the shares. Once the price
went up, Sater and his friends sold the stocks at a steep profit, in an illegal pump-and-dump scheme that left ordinary investors holding the

---

* In an email to the author, Sater's attorney Robert S. Wolf disputed allegations made in *The
Scorpion and the Frog*, and asserted that it was "a work of fiction" and that "Mr. Sater was
not a character in the book." However, David S. Barry, the book's coauthor, has said the
book is entirely factual, and its publisher, New Millennium, has marketed the book as non-
fiction.

bag when prices collapsed[24] and was somewhat similar to Mogilevich's YBM Magnex scam.

With the help of Sater's father, the firm got protection from the Genovese family, and Sater used an alias, "Paul Stewart," to launder the proceeds through a network of Caribbean shell companies, Swiss and Israeli banks, and associates in New York's Diamond District.[25] In the end, it was a mob operation that ended up cheating unsuspecting investors out of $40 million.[26]

Then, in 1995, everything changed for Sater. He quit the business because, he told BuzzFeed, he "didn't want to do dirty shit anymore."[27] Before long, Sater was given an opportunity to take part in a telecommunications deal for AT&T in Russia, and while he was there, he entered the world of espionage.[28]

It happened one night in Moscow when an American defense contractor named Milton Blane* noticed Sater dining with "high-level Russian intelligence agents," got his number, and set up a meeting for the next day.[29]

They met at an Irish pub in Moscow,[30] and Blane, clearly impressed by Felix's mastery of Russian and his easy access to Russian military officials, proceeded to tell Sater that he worked for the US government— the Defense Intelligence Agency.[31]

The people Sater had been sitting with the previous night were, Blane said, "extremely high-level Russian intelligence operatives . . . very strong people, people who can deliver the things that America needs. They seem to like you. You speak Russian. You blend in there. And your country needs you."[32]

Blane then asked Felix to work as a confidential source for the Defense Intelligence Agency, but gave him a stern warning. "I want you to understand," he said, "if you're caught, the USA is going to disavow you and, at best, you get a bullet in the head."

Felix thought about it for five seconds. "Having the opportunity to

---

* Blane died in 2016.

serve my country and do anything in its defense was a no brainer. It was, 'where do I sign up?'"[33]

And so began Felix's second career.[34] His most notable early operation took place in 1998, when he went on the hunt for Stinger antiaircraft missiles that the CIA had originally given to the mujahideen for use against the Soviets during their occupation of Afghanistan, but which were at risk of falling into the hands of radical jihadists.

Felix went to work. His attorney Robert Wolf called David Kendall, then President Bill Clinton's lawyer, and told him that Sater had serial numbers for the Stinger missiles the Clinton administration had sought. After President Clinton was informed, Wolf then spoke to CIA general counsel Robert M. McNamara Jr. and read out the serial numbers of the Stingers.[35]

But the CIA was still skeptical. Next, Felix provided photographs of the missiles with their serial numbers and a copy of a daily newspaper to show the photo was contemporaneous.[36] Meanwhile, Wolf began extended talks with two men in the CIA's clandestine division about al-Qaeda, Osama bin Laden, and the Stinger missiles.

When President Clinton authorized the August 1998 bombing strike against al-Qaeda in retaliation for the terrorist bombings of the US embassies in Kenya and Tanzania, BuzzFeed reported, no fewer than ten current and former intelligence and law enforcement officials said Sater "supplemented US intelligence by providing location coordinates for al-Qaeda camps that the US military ultimately bombed in Khost, Afghanistan."[37]

There was much more. Sater reportedly helped the FBI find dealers in New York's Forty-Seventh Street Diamond District who were laundering money for al-Qaeda, and took part in other daring spy missions. After he started trying to track down the Stinger missiles, he began developing sources in Afghan intelligence and Russian intelligence.

He is even said to have been involved in North Korea's nuclear program. "I was given photographs of the North Korean military intel operative who was out there buying various components to build a nuclear weapons program," said Sater. "He sent me intel photos, surveillance photos, as well as photos of him sitting in restaurants, of him sitting in front of the North Korean Army choir, with the instructions that this is the man that needs to be put a tail on."[38]

––––––

Meanwhile, in late 1998, the FBI responded to a tip from New York police and broke into a Manhattan storage locker, where they discovered a shotgun, two pistols, and a gym bag full of documents tied to Sater.[39]

Immediately, the FBI's Russian organized crime task force began hunting for Sater, who happened to be vacationing in Italy. He already had developed close ties to an intelligence officer with the Northern Alliance, the anti–al-Qaeda Afghan militia led by Ahmad Shah Massoud, who, BuzzFeed reported, called him with precious information: He had five satellite phone numbers belonging to Osama bin Laden,[40] and he wanted Sater to pass the numbers along to US intelligence.

Then the FBI found Sater and told him he was under investigation for the pump-and-dump scam. "I never intended on fighting and I surrendered," he said. "I knew I was going to cooperate."

And so, Felix Sater became an informant not just for the CIA and DIA, but for the FBI as well, providing, according to former attorney general Loretta Lynch, information crucial to the conviction of more than twenty people. Moreover, in return, Sater managed to negotiate an immunity deal that allowed him to stay out of jail, pay a small fine of $25,000, and emerge relatively unscathed with a sealed criminal record. Sater was not even forced to pay restitution.[41]

The terms of the deal were so favorable that the matter came up during Loretta Lynch's confirmation hearings for attorney general in 2015. Lynch explained that Sater had provided "information crucial to national security and the conviction of over 20 individuals, including those responsible for committing massive financial fraud and members of the Cosa Nostra."[42]

Then, on September 11, 2001, everything changed. Terrorists hijacked four airliners, crashing two of them into New York's World Trade Center and one into the Pentagon. Nearly three thousand people were dead.

The FBI, which had focused so much attention on the Italian Mafia in the past, now shifted its attention to a new enemy. The Italian Mafia was yesterday's news, and resources were now directed to fighting radical Islamist terrorism. As for the Russian Mafia, it was barely on the FBI's radar screen.

Meanwhile, the tragedy of 9/11 had made Felix's contacts far, far more valuable than ever before. From now on, Felix Sater would be the FBI's best friend.[43] But to the rest of the world, by 2002, he had moved on and become managing director of a New York–based real estate development company called the Bayrock Group. Finally, with Felix Sater, there was always the possibility that the best stories of all were still untold.

CHAPTER THIRTEEN

BAYROCK

Officially, Bayrock was the heartwarming immigrant success story of its Kazakhstan-born founder and chairman, Tevfik Arif, who graduated from the Moscow Institute of Trade and Economics[1] and worked in the Soviet commerce and trade ministry before running an export-import business, building hotels in Turkey,[2] and moving to New York, where he developed property in Brooklyn.

With the flags of the United States, Turkey, and Kazakhstan conspicuously on display in his office, Arif projected the image of a cosmopolitan international businessman who had fulfilled the American dream.[3] Boasting more than $2.5 billion in investments in luxury waterfront resort, hotel, residential, retail, and office space developments, Bayrock had hired renowned architects to design new projects in New York, Europe, the Mediterranean, and elsewhere. The icing on the cake in terms of Bayrock's marketing identity could be articulated in one word: Trump. Trump was ready to license his name to Bayrock and other developers to build luxury condos in Panama City, Panama; Toronto, Canada; Baku, Azerbaijan; Kiev, Ukraine; Moscow; and many more places all over the world.

Judging from its twenty-eight-page presentation materials, one would think Bayrock was one of the most successful real estate development companies in the world. Among its projects, Bayrock planned to build the Trump SoHo in New York, the Trump International Hotel and

Tower in Fort Lauderdale, the Trump Las Olas in Fort Lauderdale, and the Trump International Hotel and Residences in Phoenix. And that was just the United States. As a coda to its presentation, its star-studded list of strategic partners was topped with the name "The Trump Organization" and a photo of Bayrock founder Tevfik Arif standing shoulder to shoulder with Donald Trump.[4]

That was Bayrock—or, at least, the image Bayrock projected. But the reality was much more complex. Bayrock through its business practices brought into Donald Trump's orbit a host of oligarchs and alleged mobsters involved in laundering money, the trafficking of underage women, feeding intelligence to the Russians, and more. In court records from a lawsuit by former employees, it is alleged Bayrock was "covertly mob-owned and operated," "backed by oligarchs and money [the oligarchs] stole from the Russian people," and "engaged in the businesses of financial institution fraud, tax fraud, partnership fraud, human trafficking, child prostitution, statutory rape, and, on occasion, real estate."[5]

Bayrock is no longer active as a real estate development company and now exists only as a legal entity engaged in ongoing litigation, of which a spokesperson said the firm disputes all such allegations. Nevertheless, Bayrock had many of the attributes that one might find in a center of operations affiliated with the Russian Mafia. That was of special interest, given that its key partner was the future president of the United States.

———

Trump was first introduced to Bayrock by the late Tamir Sapir,[6] the penniless Soviet émigré turned billionaire who became, in Trump's words, "great friends" with Trump himself,[7] and who introduced Trump to Tevfik Arif, the founder of Bayrock, aka Tofik Arifov.[8] On paper, at least, Arif's story was another stirring rags-to-riches saga. In 2002, after becoming a successful real estate developer in Brooklyn, he moved Bayrock's offices to Trump Tower, where he and his staff of mostly Russian émigrés set up shop on the twenty-fourth floor.[9]

When Arif and Sater helped put together several prospective Trump Tower licensing deals for sites including Moscow, Warsaw, Istanbul, and

Kiev, Trump was ecstatic. Thanks to Bayrock, he could bring franchising to high-end condos. He could be the Colonel Sanders of luxury high-rises. "It was almost like mass production of a car," Trump crowed.[10]

For some projects, he boasted, he would get up to a 25 percent stake, plus management fees and a possible percentage of the gross—without having to invest a dime.

Trump worked closely with Bayrock on real estate ventures in Russia, Ukraine, and Poland. When it came to financing them, however, he was still so toxic after Atlantic City that he left matters of funding to his new partners. "Bayrock knew the investors," he later testified.[11] Arif "brought the people up from Moscow to meet with [Trump]."

Altogether, Bayrock's leadership, as portrayed in its presentation materials, was a cozy family of billionaire oligarchs from the former Soviet Union. In fact, the extent to which various Bayrock partners actually came through with financing is unclear, but according to Bayrock's promotional literature, Arif turned to fellow Kazakh billionaire Alexander Mashkevich and his Eurasian Natural Resources Corporation (or Eurasian Group, as it is called in Bayrock's promotional literature), which he controls with Patokh Chodiev and Alijan Ibragimov, among others, to finance Bayrock. (Even though he was referred to on Bayrock's website, Patokh Chodiev has denied any connection to Donald Trump, the Trump Organization, or Bayrock Group. Similarly, a person close to Mashkevich told Bloomberg that Mashkevich never invested in Bayrock.)[12] Together, the three men—known as "the Trio"—are major stockholders in the Eurasian Natural Resources Corporation and control chromium, alumina, and gas operations in Kazakhstan,[13] which adds up to about 12 percent of the industrial production in the entire country.[14]

In June 2005, many of them came together when Arif celebrated his fifty-second birthday at the grand opening of the "seven-star" Rixos hotel in Belek on the Turkish Riviera near Antalya. Guests came from all over the world—St. Petersburg, the Côte d'Azur, Ukraine, Latvia, Israel, and Moscow, traveling by yacht and private jet.[15]

This was no run-of-the mill gathering. There were huge mounds of caviar, food, drink, and song. Among the honored guests was then-prime minister of Turkey Recep Tayyip Erdoğan, who later became president.[16] There were professional hockey stars, Moscow restaurateurs, and billionaires from all over the world.

In all, Bayrock's promotional literature boasted that it had seven billionaires affiliated with the company, in one way or another. Among them was Tamir Sapir, who arrived on the *Mystère,* his 160-foot yacht, which has been described as the most beautiful private vessel in the world.[17] Alexander Mashkevich cruised in on his yacht, the *Lady Lara,* which was nearly twice as big, at 299 feet.[18] Not all the Bayrock billionaires could make it, but one extremely high-profile tycoon in New York who couldn't attend made sure that his presence was felt anyway. So on Tevfik Arif's birthday, the familiar image of Donald Trump suddenly appeared on a big-screen videoconference call for the entire party to see.

"Tevfik is my friend," Trump said. "Let's drink to Tevfik!"[19]

———

By this time, Trump was indeed in the midst of a phoenix-like rebirth, both personally and professionally. His turbulent tabloid marriage to Marla Maples, his second wife, had come to an end, and he had married his third wife, Melania Knauss, a model from Slovenia, in January 2005, in a suitably extravagant wedding on his Mar-a-Lago estate that was attended by celebrities including Shaquille O'Neal and P. Diddy, then-senator Hillary Clinton, and former president Bill Clinton.

And when it came to real estate, Trump's new paradigm was taking off like wildfire. He was all over Bayrock's promotional literature, but he had nothing to do with financing and few development responsibilities. The larger point was that Trump had created a new model where he was paid to put his name on major development projects. "He's a marketing genius," Adam Rose, president of Rose Associates, which manages more than fourteen thousand apartments, told the *New York Times.*[20] "He's gotten to the point where he can license his name."

And license he did, lending his name to projects like Trump University,[21] a "real estate training program" that turned out to be not a university at all but a gigantic high-pressure bait-and-switch scam* that "preyed upon the elderly and uneducated to separate them from their money," as one affidavit from a former salesman for Trump University put it.[22]

In addition to various projects in development with Bayrock, Trump signed a deal to license his name for an 813-unit condo project[23] called Trump Towers in Sunny Isles Beach, Florida, a barrier island north of Miami Beach. In 2005, he built a thirty-five-story Trump Tower in White Plains, New York. He pursued licensing his name to a Trump Tower development in Tampa, but it never got off the ground.[24] Trump made plans to build what became Trump Tower Chicago—a ninety-eight-story condo-hotel tower.[25] In Hawaii, he licensed his name to the Trump International Hotel Waikiki. In Las Vegas, a sixty-four-story Trump International Hotel was on the drawing board. And his name was in play with Bayrock for a tower in Phoenix.[26]

As usual his clientele had had its share of run-ins with the law. In Florida, at least thirteen buyers of Trump Towers condos in Sunny Isles Beach had been the subjects of government investigations, either personally or through their companies, including members of a Russian-American organized crime gang, the *Miami Herald* reported. When interviewed about the Sunny Isles condos, Trump Organization lawyer Alan Garten stated that it was "completely unfair and completely misleading to suggest we had anything to do with those people" and called shady buyers an industry-wide problem for luxury real estate. But the larger point is that in these ways and more, Donald Trump was bigger than ever.[27]

———

When it came to having fun, Trump's partners spared no expense. Tev-fik Arif flew Bayrock employees out to the Rixos hotel in Antalya, Turkey, for an all-inclusive vacation.[28] On another occasion, both Arif and

———

* In 2016, Trump denied wrongdoing but agreed to pay $25 million to Trump University students who had filed a class action suit. New York attorney general Eric Schneiderman called it "a major victory for the over 6,000 victims of his fraudulent university."

Alexander Mashkevich rented the *Savarona*—a 446-foot yacht that had once been owned by the Father of the Turks, Mustafa Kemal Atatürk.

For a week-long party in September 2010, when Mashkevich rented the yacht, nine young "escort girls" were allegedly supplied for businessmen attending the party on the *Savarona*.

A search by police, the report said, turned up "a huge amount of contraceptives and a file with escort girls' pictures and hotel receipts."[29]

Ten suspects, among them two Turkish billionaires, were arrested immediately and investigated for solicitation and trafficking in women. Mashkevich and Arif denied the accusations against them,[30] and in April 2011 Arif was acquitted of all charges.[31] The court judgment also recorded that all women aboard the yacht were over eighteen.

According to Mashkevich's lawyer, Ronel Fisher, Turkish authorities made no claims against Mashkevich, nor was he interrogated by police.[32] A spokesman told the British daily the *Telegraph* that he was on board the yacht when it was raided but he was not in any way connected to criminal or immoral acts on it.[33]

Nevertheless, the indictment paints a salacious picture of a sordid and extraordinarily decadent[34] world of spectacular yachts, Mediterranean villas, and private planes, in which batches of teenage girls are shipped in to have sex with wealthy businessmen, while their underlings wrangle over whether to pay top dollar for a virginal sixteen-year-old and the bother of having to "send that unpretty back."[35]

The level of decadence was unparalleled. Every oligarch had to have a yacht, each one bigger than the next. And who among them could be the most transgressive? Tamir Sapir won notoriety for furnishing his yacht with bar stools covered in python skin, a stuffed lion, and the carcasses of twenty-nine different endangered species.*[36] As the *New York Post* put it, "It was just like Noah's Ark, except everything was dead—and illegal."[37]

Bayrock never seemed short of funding. In the nineties, Arif had worked in Kazakhstan for the UK-based Trans-World Group, a

---

* Sapir agreed to pay $150,000 for violations of the Endangered Species Act.

company run by David and Simon Reuben and the Chernoy brothers—all big players in the highly lucrative but spectacularly dangerous metals industry, which was beset by "Aluminum Wars".[38]

Similarly, Alexander Mashkevich and his partners in the Trio who may have been investors did business with Mikhail Chernoy and had huge holdings in chromium, alumina, and gas operations in Kazakhstan. When it came to having ties to the Kremlin, Tamir Sapir had high-level connections through Rotem Rosen, his son-in-law and the CEO of the Sapir Organization. Rosen was also a lieutenant of Israeli diamond magnate Lev Leviev, who was a major donor to the Putin-supported Chabad sect and had been close to Putin since the early nineties.

Given that his control over the oligarchs was crucial to maintaining power, Putin needed to be able to keep tabs on their whereabouts and where their money went. If hundreds of millions of dollars from the Russian Mafia or other forms of flight capital were funding a Trump-branded project, Putin wanted to know. If oligarchs were buying scores of Trump condos in SoHo or Panama or Toronto, Putin wanted to know.

––––

And Bayrock would have had the answers. Indeed, in many ways, Bayrock resembled an updated version of the initiative launched by KGB general Vladimir Kryuchkov at the end of the Cold War, when the KGB had founded scores of front companies that appeared to be self-sufficient independent corporations but were staffed by operatives tied to the KGB and the GRU. Far more than merely providing phony identities as cover for intelligence operatives, these companies were meant to be multibillion-dollar corporations that would trade the natural resources of the former Soviet Union on the global market, make billions of dollars, and simultaneously launder money, gather intelligence, and grow through relations with Western partners and Western banks.[39]

One of the models for those companies was Boris Birshtein's Seabeco SA.[40] Over the years, Birshtein, who hosted the famous Tel Aviv meeting with Mogilevich, had worked with Colonel Leonid Veselovsky,[41] an intelligence operative who, during the Soviet era, had specialized in starting front companies for the KGB all over the world—in Antwerp, Toronto, Winnipeg, Panama, Zurich, and Delaware.[42] Along the way, through the Soviet foreign ministry, Birshtein also met and began working with Patokh Chodiev and Alexander Mashkevich, who comprised two-thirds of Eurasian Natural Resources Corporation's Trio.[43] He also had ties to Solntsevo head Sergei Mikhailov, with whom he started a business in Antwerp called MAB International.[44]

Birshtein seemed to have followed the dictates of the KGB under Kryuchkov's guidelines to set up enterprises abroad,[45] but it was unclear how successful this initiative was. Colonel Veselovsky himself maintained that most of the ideas for shifting communist assets overseas never got beyond the planning stage.[46] Regardless, many of the apparatchiks chosen by the KGB went ahead and launched their careers as independent businessmen. Moreover, Birshtein understood the importance of having mutually beneficial relationships with strategically placed bureaucrats. And so it was that Birshtein hired Veselovsky and introduced him to the world of private jets, immense limousines, and extravagant mansions.[47]

In 1991 and 1992 alone, Seabeco gave birth to at least six highly profitable joint ventures, and went on to create many more all over the world. "You shouldn't think that people like Birshtein and Veselovsky are financial geniuses," Sergei Sokolov, a journalist for *Komsomolaskaya Pravda*, told the *Washington Post*.[48] "What mattered in the old days—and what matters now—is personal connections."

And so, a decade later, those connections resurfaced in ventures tied to Trump. In the early 2000s, Alexander Shnaider, a former Seabeco executive who was Birshtein's son-in-law, began to develop the tallest building in Canada, the sixty-five-story Trump Tower and Hotel in Toronto. When it came to financing the skyscraper, Shnaider, a billionaire of Russian extraction, turned to Raiffeisen Bank International AG in Vienna,[49] a bank whose affiliate has been linked to the gas company Semion Mogilevich controls, RosUkrEnergo. Which raises the question, was funding from the Mogilevich-Firtash money pipeline behind the Trump project in Toronto?

In addition, the *Wall Street Journal* reported,[50] Vnesheconombank, or VEB, at the time, bought $850 million of stock in a Ukrainian steelmaker from Shnaider, about $15 million of which went into the Trump Toronto project. At the time, the chairman of VEB's supervisory board was Vladimir Putin.

Later, Symon Zucker, Shnaider's lawyer and the initial source of that information, changed his statement and said he was not able to confirm that VEB funds went into the project. "Trump was never a partner," Zucker told Business Insider. "He never had an equity interest. We licensed his name and there was a contract for him to manage the hotel."[51]

Once again, an arrangement in which Trump was merely licensing his name was used to exculpate him. Nevertheless, the VEB deal did go through, and Trump did collect fees from the project.* (Shnaider did not respond to messages left for him.)

———

Trump fostered similar relationships all over the world. In 2003, Trump had whetted Latin American interest in the Trump brand by staging the Miss Universe pageant in Panama City, Panama.[52] Three years later, he struck a deal in Panama to develop the Trump Ocean Club International Hotel and Tower, a sail-shaped seventy-story waterfront complex that included residential apartments and a casino. According to an investigation by Global Witness,[53] an anticorruption watchdog, Trump was entitled to a licensing fee, 1 percent of any financing he secured, and a cut of every unit sold—all of which would add up to more than $75 million.[54]

Many of the problems behind the project led to a man named Alexandre Ventura Nogueira, the tower's primary broker. According to a report by Reuters, Nogueira, who, with his partners, sold more than half the apartments in the project, marketed the condos largely to Russians

---

* Four years after the building was finished in 2012, it went into receivership due to poor sales. Trump's name was later removed from the building.

because, a colleague said, "Russians like to show off. For them, Trump was the Bentley" of real estate brands.[55]

But the Reuters investigation also found Nogueira did business with a Colombian who was later convicted of money laundering; a Russian investor in the Trump project who was jailed in Israel in the 1990s for kidnapping and death threats; and a Ukrainian investor who was arrested for alleged people-smuggling while working with Nogueira and later convicted by a Kiev court. In addition, Reuters reported, he was alleged to have "either failed to pass on all the deposits he collected to the project's developers, or sometimes sold the same apartment to more than one client, with the result that, on completion of the project, some clients had no clear claim on a property."[56] Nogueira said that half of his buyers were Russian, and that some were allegedly part of the Russian Mafia.[57]

According to conversations secretly recorded by a former business partner, in 2013 Nogueira said he had laundered tens of millions of dollars through real estate. "More important than the money from real estate was being able to launder the drug money—there were much larger amounts involved," he said in the recording. "When I was in Panama I was regularly laundering money for more than a dozen companies."[58]

Nogueira told Reuters that he became the leading broker for the project thanks in part to the support of Trump's daughter Ivanka, who appeared in a promotional video with him.[59]

The Trump Organization went into overdrive with the new model. Why not? Since Trump did none of the financing and almost none of the development, its risks were minimal and the upside was high. The Trump Organization's role in the Panama project "was at all times limited to licensing its brand and providing management services," said Alan Garten, the company's chief legal officer. "As the company was not the owner or developer, it had no involvement in the sale of any units at the property . . . No one at the Trump Organization, including the Trump family, has any recollection of ever meeting or speaking with this individual [Nogueira]."[60]

Similarly, one Trump-branded project after another was beset by corruption, lawsuits, and the like. In Baku, Azerbaijan, the *New Yorker* reported, Trump licensed Trump Tower Baku to close relatives of Ziya Mammadov, a transportation minister who was described in a diplomatic cable as "notoriously corrupt even for Azerbaijan."[61]

Now Trump licensing projects got under way all over the world, from White Plains, New York, to Kolkata and Pune, India; from Vancouver to Washington to Jersey City and more. Which did not necessarily mean that they did well. Though it was almost completed, Trump Tower Baku never opened. Likewise, one after another, Trump Tower projects were launched and then either canceled or never completed—in Fort Lauderdale, Tampa, Charlotte, Phoenix, New Orleans, Dubai, Rio, Stuttgart, Tel Aviv, Baja, and more.

In the face of such chaos, most organizations would fail or be forced to change their approach. But not Trump's operation. In fact, what would become Trump's most significant new real estate ventures were being hatched on the twenty-fourth floor of New York's original Trump Tower, where Felix Sater had taken charge of Bayrock and had his sights set on Russia.

Russian president Vladimir Putin hands over a medal to singer Iosif Kobzon, aka "the Russian Sinatra," during an awards ceremony in the Kremlin in Moscow, August 29, 2012. Kobzon is said to be a longtime favorite of Russian mobsters, often providing entertainment at events attended by members affiliated with the Russian Mafia. *(Misha Japaridze/AFP/Getty Images)*

sian prime minister Vladimir Putin *(center)* with two of his closest confidantes, aluminum arch Oleg Deripaska *(left)* and finance minister Viktor Vekselberg. Deripaska was promised mp campaign briefings during the 2016 US presidential election by Paul Manafort, Trump's paign manager. Vekselberg met Trump lawyer Michael Cohen after the election, and made a e contribution to Trump's inaugural fund shortly thereafter. *(Konstantin Zavrazhin/Getty Images)*

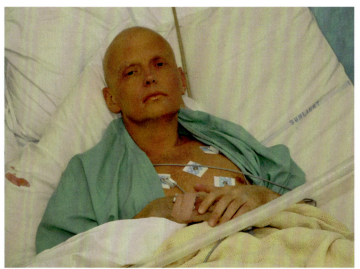

Alexander Litvinenko in the intensive care unit of University College Hospital in London, England, on November 20, 2006, three days before his death. The 43-year-old former KGB spy exposed Russian president Putin's ties to Semion Mogilevich and was poisoned with radioactive polonium-210 shortly afterward. He accused Putin of involvement in poisoning him. *(Natasja Weitsz/Getty Images)*

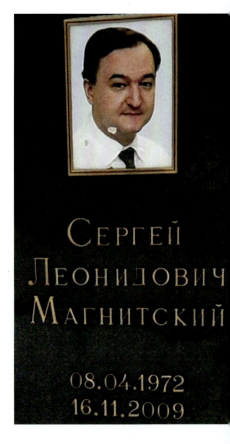

СЕРГЕЙ
ЛЕОНИДОВИЧ
МАГНИТСКИЙ

08.04.1972
16.11.2009

The tombstone of Russian lawyer Sergei Magnitsky, who was hired by Hermitage Capital's Bill Browder to investigate a $230 million tax fraud. For his efforts, Magnitsky was jailed, tortured, and killed while in a Russian prison—leading the US Congress and European Union to pass sanctions that targeted Russian human rights abusers. *(Andrey Smirnov/AFP/Getty Images)*

l Klebnikov, the editor of *Forbes* magazine's
sian edition and author of a book about
on Boris Berezovsky. Klebnikov was shot
eath in Moscow in 2004. Despite pressure
n the US government, Russia has failed to
y investigate the murder. *(Misha Japaridze/AP)*

People light candles next to a portrait of Russian journalist Anna Politkovskaya
during a rally in St. Petersburg on October 8, 2006. Politkovskaya, an outspoken
critic of President Vladimir Putin, was shot dead at her apartment block in central
Moscow. *(Alexander Demianchuk/Reuters)*

Russian president Dmitry Medvedev *(left)* speaks with his Ukrainian counterpart, Viktor Yanukovych, and Prime Minister Vladimir Putin on September 24, 2011. Paul Manafort help get the pro-Putin Yanukovych elected and remained with him for years. *(Sergei Karpukhin/AFP/Ge Images)*

Ukrainian president Viktor Yushchenko listens to Prime Minister Tymoshenko during a meeting with representatives of local governments in Kiev. President Yushchenko suffered dioxin poisoning while running against Yanukovych during the presidential election of 2004. *(Mykhailo Markiv/Reuters)*

ice officers lead former Ukrainian prime minister Yulia Tymoshenko out of the courtroom
er a court upheld her conviction, which was condemned as politically motivated by the West.
moshenko was found guilty of abuse of office and overstepping her authority while negotiat-
; a natural gas contract with Russia in 2009. *(Efrem Lukatsky/AP)*

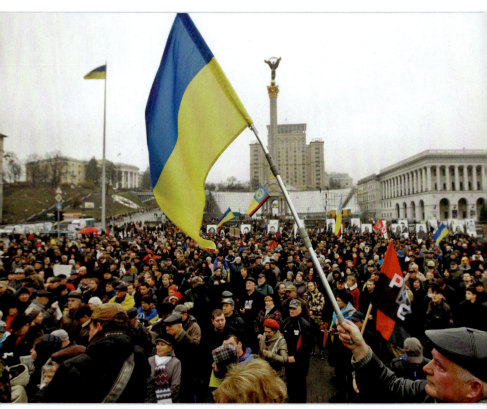

Ukrainians mark the second anniversary of the Euromaidan Revolution, which resulted in President Yanukovych's fleeing Ukraine to Russia under the protection of the Kremlin. One hundred thirty civilians and eighteen police officers were killed during the protests. *(NurPhoto/ Getty Images)*

Dmitry Firtash *(right)*, one of Ukraine's richest men, with Ukrainian president Viktor Yanukovych *(left)*. Allegedly associated with Semion Mogilevich, Firtash made millions off the Ukraine energy trade, some of which went to Trump campaign manager Paul Manafort. *(Mykhailo Markiv/Reuters)*

Former Trump campaign manager Paul Manafort worked for Ukrainian president Viktor Yanukovych and the pro-Putin Party of Regions for nearly a decade to help implement Russian interests. *(Yuri Gripas/Reuters)*

Donald Trump, Tevfik Arif, and Felix Sater attend the Trump SoHo launch party on Septemb[er] 19, 2007, in New York. Bayrock Group, the developer of Trump SoHo, was cofounded by Arif and Sater. The latter was a convicted felon who was involved in a money-laundering scam wit[h] the Mafia prior to Bayrock. *(Mark Von Holden/WireImage/Getty Images)*

Left to right: Eric Trump, Tevfik Arif, Donald Trump Jr., Ivanka Trump, Donald Trump, Tam[ir] Sapir, Alex Sapir, Julius Schwarz, and Zina Sapir attend a press conference at the Trump SoH[o] construction site on September 19, 2007. Trump SoHo was involved in a lawsuit claiming it wa[s] partly funded from "questionable sources" in Russia and Kazakhstan. *(Clint Spaulding/Patrick McMullan/Getty Images)*

CHAPTER FOURTEEN

MOTH, FLAME

During his years in Moscow, former CIA agent John Sipher, who worked undercover in the US embassy, heard all about businesses like Boris Birshtein's Seabeco and came to the conclusion that the United States had absolutely nothing like them. Both the KGB and CIA had long staffed embassies with undercover operatives as a standard practice.[1] In addition, the CIA also provided "non-official cover" for operatives such as Valerie Plame, whose association with the agency was famously leaked to the press by the George W. Bush administration. However, such "cover" was largely limited to providing false identities—in Plame's case, that she was an energy trader in Brussels.[2]

But, Sipher told me, launching actual profit-making companies like Seabeco was a different story entirely. "It's very hard for us in the West to distill the idea that you also have a cloudy group of people with ties to the Kremlin, who have intelligence training, and who have made a bunch of money that can support intelligence operations," he said. "Those of us who worked in the [American] embassy [in Moscow], we instinctively stayed away from it because it was dirty. We knew there was an overlap of crime and assassinations and surveillance and money in Cyprus and real estate in London."

If Bayrock was a latter-day version of Seabeco, getting to the heart of it meant dealing with Felix Sater, its most visible, charismatic and authoritative presence. "He has a talent for drawing people in," said Bayrock's former finance director Jody Kriss, who later sued the company,[3] alleging that it was "covertly mob-owned and operated." Kriss's suit claimed that Bayrock had defrauded Kriss and another Bayrock employee and "never intended to honor" promised payments. The real purpose of the company, it said, in addition to marketing expensive condos, was to launder millions of dollars and evade taxes.[4]

Bayrock contested Kriss's claims and described him as a disgruntled employee. The case was later settled on undisclosed terms.

"Felix knew how to be charming and he knew how to be brutally nasty," said Kriss.[5] "He has charm and charisma. But that's what con men do."

On the one hand, that meant Felix could out-Trump America's most famous real estate magnate and convince him that he, Felix Sater, had an opportunity no one could possibly pass up. "How did I get to Donald?" Sater asked. "I walked in his door and told him, 'I'm gonna be the biggest developer in New York, and you want to be my partner.'"[6]

On the other, Felix was also the kind of guy who was accused of threatening to attach live-wired electrodes to the testicles of a colleague, cut off his legs, and leave him dead in the trunk of a car—as Sater allegedly promised a business associate in Arizona.[7] Robert Wolf, Sater's lawyer, denies these allegations and stated that the claim that Sater had threatened violence was "an outright fabrication."

Which was the real Felix Sater? His work with Bayrock as a partner of Trump's and later his work on behalf of Trump himself raised a number of unanswered questions.

Sater's biggest project at Bayrock was the troubled Trump SoHo, the forty-six-story, $450 million hotel-condominium in downtown Manhattan that was beset by one lawsuit after another.* From the start, the mere fact that Sater was a principal in Bayrock created a very serious quandary as it was trying to raise $1 billion for Trump SoHo and other

---

* In November 2017, the Trump Organization announced that it was going to end its affiliation with the Trump SoHo by the end of the year. The building was subsequently renamed the Dominick.

projects. Sater was a twice-convicted felon; no banks would lend to Bayrock if they knew about Sater's convictions. In fact, when Trump SoHo got under way, Sater began spelling his name "Satter," as he told the *Times,* to "distance himself from a past" and to throw off anyone searching his name on Google.[8]

Another complication was the fact that Sater was also a "cooperator" with the FBI and other federal agencies. As a result, he had an immunity deal and, he later asserted, was still carrying out various daring missions for the CIA, the DIA, and the FBI, such as helping the FBI investigate scams run by the Italian Mafia on Wall Street.

For his help, Sater was given extraordinary latitude by the FBI—so much that Frederick Oberlander, an attorney who represented Jody Kriss in his lawsuit against Bayrock, and other attorneys and journalists sometimes referred to Felix as "another Whitey Bulger." Bulger, who had been the crime boss of the Winter Hill Gang in Boston, became an FBI cooperator and used his immunity as cover for an ongoing crime spree. He was later convicted of involvement in eleven murders.

At the very least, it seemed, Sater had a double life. He was a felon, but he was working undercover for America's secret services. That much was clearly established. But what if he was really working for the Russians? What if he really had a triple life? The answers were difficult to find—in part because the records of Sater's convictions had been sealed as a result of his immunity deal.

No one seemed to know the whole story about Sater—especially Donald Trump. That became clear later, when Trump gave a deposition in a court case filed against him, Bayrock, and several other parties, and was asked, under oath, about working with Sater. First, an attorney showed Trump a copy of a December 17, 2007, story in the *New York Times* headlined, "Real Estate Executive with Hand in Trump Projects Rose from Tangled Past," and asked if he was familiar with it.

"Very vaguely," Trump replied. "Long time ago . . . I just vaguely remember the article, but we weren't dealing much with him."

How many times had Trump conversed with Sater?

"Over the years?" Trump asked. "Not many. If he were sitting in the room right now, I really wouldn't know what he looked like. . . . If he

would call, I'd take his call because he was representing Bayrock. . . .
You should ask those questions to Bayrock. He worked for Bayrock, he
didn't work for me."[9]

Trump was obviously perturbed by the line of questioning, but his
testimony was crystal clear about Sater. He barely knew the guy—or so
he said.

Yet there was plenty of evidence to the contrary. In the beginning,
Sater and Tevfik Arif had been thrilled to be situated on the twenty-
fourth floor of Trump Tower precisely because residents on the upper
floors had to get off at the twenty-fourth-floor landing and change eleva-
tors to reach street level. That made it easy for Felix to bump into Trump
"accidentally" and pitch him new projects—and he took full advantage
of their proximity. Others at Bayrock talked to Trump on occasion, but
it was a relationship that Felix jealously kept to himself—with considerable success.

Once they got to know each other, Felix thought nothing of going up
a flight of stairs to Trump's office to chat about business ideas—"just me
and him."[10]

After returning from a trip to Russia, Sater said, he'd "come back,
pop [his] head into Mr. Trump's office and tell him, you know, 'Moving
forward on the Moscow deal.'"[11]

In 2005, when Trump flew to Colorado to give a motivational speech,
he and Melania brought Felix with them.[12] Trump and Sater were interviewed and photographed together in Denver and Loveland, Colorado;
Phoenix; Fort Lauderdale; and New York.[13]

A former colleague of Sater's told Politico, "Trump called Felix like
every other day to his office. . . . They were definitely in contact always.
They spoke on the phone all the time."[14] And they occasionally dined
together at a restaurant in Manhattan's Meatpacking District called Kiss
& Fly, with what *New York* magazine described as "a quasi-Roman-
bathhouse feel" for its "young, rich, and overwhelmingly European"
patrons.[15]

Back in Trump Tower, as an inducement for Donald to drop by their
twenty-fourth-floor offices, Felix became so fixated on the appearance

of female employees that the firm was referred to as Baberock. Taking the bait one day in 2006, Trump ran into Bayrock secretary Rachel Crooks, then twenty-two, on the elevator landing, who introduced herself and then saw him go into action.[16] "He took hold of my hand and held me in place like this," Crooks said. "He started kissing me on one cheek, then the other cheek. He was talking to me in between kisses, asking where I was from, or if I wanted to be a model. He wouldn't let go of my hand, and then he went right in and started kissing me on the lips."[17]

Crooks has since joined several other women in demanding a congressional investigation into Trump's alleged sexual misconduct.

Meanwhile, Trump entrusted Felix with accompanying his children to Moscow to work on Trump projects in the Russian capital.[19] On one of the trips, Felix took Ivanka on a tour of the Kremlin and later said he arranged for her to sit in Vladimir Putin's chair. "It would be bizarre for him to take her into the president's personal office—presumably while the president was absent—unless Putin and his security service advisers knew about it and viewed the relationship with the Trumps as worth developing," Daniel Treisman, a UCLA political science professor and an expert on Russian politics, told Business Insider.[20]

The Trumps began spending more and more time in Russia. Starting in 2006, Donald Jr., executive vice president of development and acquisitions for the Trump Organization, made about half a dozen trips to Russia over the course of a year and a half. "[I]n terms of high-end product influx into the US, Russians make up a pretty disproportionate cross-section of a lot of our assets," he later told a Manhattan real estate conference.[18] ". . . We see a lot of money pouring in from Russia."

Trump himself said he was looking forward to the realization of a major project in Moscow. "We will be in Moscow at some point," he said in a deposition.[21] He added that he had met with Russian investors at Trump Tower to pursue the Moscow deal, and that Donald Jr. was working on it.

As for Felix Sater's role, Trump said nothing. In fact, Alan Garten, the Trump Organization's general counsel, later asserted to *Forbes* that

Sater's presence in Moscow while Ivanka and Donald Jr. were there was merely a coincidence.[22]

As Donald Jr. saw it, the stumbling block in Russia was corruption. "Several buyers have been attracted to our projects there," he told a trade publication.[23] "It is definitely not an issue of being able to find a deal— but an issue of 'Will I ever see my money back out of that deal or can I actually trust the person I am doing the deal with?' As much as we want to take our business over there, Russia is just a different world. . . . It really is a scary place."

Of course, how scary Moscow was depended on what kind of company you kept. In addition to his work for Trump, in 2007 Sater began working as an "adviser" to real estate oligarch Sergei Polonsky, a flamboyant, longhaired six-foot-four[24] billionaire developer whose company, Mirax Group, had been making a name for itself in Moscow.[25]

Polonsky had won both fame and notoriety for a number of reasons, the former for developing Moscow's ninety-seven-story Federation Tower, which for several years was the tallest building in Europe, and the latter for becoming an icon of excess who declared "anyone without a billion dollars should fuck off."[26]

In 2008, Polonsky spoke at a real estate conference in Moscow at which Donald Trump, Jr., was the keynote speaker.[27] Since then, Polonsky was convicted of fraud in 2017, after having been charged with stealing 3.2 billion rubles (about $51 million).[28] He and other principals at Mirax, including two board members and its board president, Maxim Temnikov, fled Russia and were being sought for allegedly appropriating 2.4 billion rubles (about $39 million) from a Moscow real estate development.[29]

Sater wasn't exactly a big hit with everyone at Mirax. "You can't trust him in any way, not in a professional setting, not in a personal setting," Mirax's chairman of the board, Alexey Kunitsin, told the *Atlantic*.[30] "You could see it very clearly. He was telling constant crazy stories, wild fantasies about all the people he knew. He was not a balanced dude. He's very emotional and gets into conflicts very easily."

Nevertheless, Sater had begun to forge ties in the treacherous world of Russian business. Polonsky and Mirax had had an extended working relationship with Moscow mayor Yuri Luzhkov and had partnered with the Mogilevich-linked company Sistema.[31] In addition, Sater joined with Maxim Temnikov to buy a $4.8 million condo in affluent Fisher Island, Florida.[32]

———

Exactly how much Trump knew about Sater and the inner workings of Bayrock was unclear—which is exactly the way he seemed to want it. But on December 19, 2007, Trump gave a deposition in a lawsuit he filed against author Timothy O'Brien. Two days earlier, *New York Times* reporter Charles Bagli had revealed that Felix Sater had a hidden past, and now that Trump was under oath it was possible to determine the extent of his knowledge. When asked about Sater's criminal history, Trump testified, "[I'm] looking into it because I wasn't happy with the story. So I'm looking into it."[33] In other words, under oath, Trump had admitted that he knew about Sater's run-ins with the law.

Because the deposition was marked "Confidential" and kept under seal, Trump may not have expected it to become public. Regardless, Trump's knowledge of Sater's past was now a matter of court record. According to Jonathan Winer, the former money-laundering czar in the Clinton administration, if someone in Trump's situation failed to investigate such allegations he would be "open to charges of 'willful blindness' in terms of the knowledge he had."[34]

"The responsible course of action would have been to have Sater resign and disclose Sater's past to interested parties," says Richard Lerner, who, with Frederick Oberlander, filed a *qui tam* lawsuit against Bayrock in 2015—that is, a civil suit that rewards private entities working to recover funds for the government.[35] In this case, they charged Bayrock with laundering $250 million in profits from Trump SoHo and other projects, and setting up elaborate mechanisms to evade more than $100 million in state and federal taxes. Sater's attorney, Robert Wolf, characterized the allegations of "their extortionate litigations" as "baseless and highly defamatory."[36]

But rather than extricate himself from the deal with Bayrock and a partnership with a convicted felon, Trump kept silent about Felix, continued working with Bayrock, and ultimately profited from the arrangement. Indeed, according to Bayrock's internal emails, rather than disclose the truth, Trump even saw the predicament as an occasion to renegotiate his fees—upward, of course. "Donald . . . saw an opportunity to try and get development fees for himself," Sater emailed investors a few days after the deposition.[37]

In the end, Sater remained managing director of Bayrock through 2008. Trump also continued to participate in the venture and enjoy its profits. "Inducing a bank to lend money based on a fraudulent loan application—i.e., concealing Sater's criminal past—is bank fraud," said Fred Oberlander.[38] "If you know that the loans were procured by fraud yet stay involved, it's a conspiracy to violate money laundering and racketeering statutes."

"It's certainly a question for [special counsel Robert] Mueller to look into," said Jonathan Winer.[39] "What anyone in Trump's position should have done is investigate those allegations [about Sater's criminal past] to ensure that there was not a money-laundering operation."

But Trump wasn't charged with any crime at the time. Nevertheless, once condos in the building were finally put up for sale, the project suffered more than its share of problems. The building's no-man's-land neighborhood—not really SoHo—with its grand entrance beside Varick Street and the chaotic approach to the Holland Tunnel, made it a difficult sell. In addition, in order to circumvent restrictive zoning laws, the project was explicitly marketed to prospective buyers overseas as a second or third home, with the highly challenging proviso that owners could live in their apartments only 120 days a year, and never for more than 29 consecutive days in any 36-day period. In 2010, 15 condo buyers filed suit, charging the Trumps and Bayrock with "an ongoing pattern of fraudulent misrepresentations and deceptive sales practices." According to the Daily Beast,[40] among the claims made to spur sales were Ivanka Trump's proclamations to Reuters and to the London *Times* in June 2008 that 60 percent of the 391 units in the building had been sold.

Documents later submitted to the New York attorney general showed that only 15 percent had found buyers.

The suit was eventually settled, and the plaintiffs received 90 percent of their deposits back.[41] But in 2014, four years after its opening, more than two-thirds of the building's condos remained unsold. The website Curbed headlined a story "Trump SoHo Heads to Foreclosure Due to Unsellable Condos."

As other lawsuits unfolded, more charges about Bayrock came forth, among them allegations that the condos themselves were being used as vehicles for money laundering. According to the *Financial Times*,[42] lawyers for Almaty, the biggest city in Kazakhstan, charged that Viktor Khrapunov, a former Kazakh energy minister and the city's ex-mayor, and his family "conspired to systematically loot hundreds of millions of dollars of public assets . . . and to launder their ill-gotten gains through a complex web of bank accounts and shell companies . . . particularly in the United States."[43]

Khrapunov and Mukhtar Ablyazov, another Kazakh oligarch, have been accused of embezzling about $10 billion from a Kazakh bank and laundering it through shell companies, which purchased real estate all over the world.[44] With regard to Trump SoHo, the lawyers charged that Khrapunov's network used dozens of shell companies, among them three limited liability companies—whose ownership could be easily concealed—called Soho 3310, Soho 3311, and Soho 3203, which corresponded to apartments of the same name in Trump SoHo. The vendor of the apartments was Bayrock/Sapir LLC, which was named after the developers of the building, Bayrock and Tamir Sapir's Sapir Organization. The *Financial Times* also reported that, according to regulatory filings, Bayrock/Sapir had a third co-owner—Donald J. Trump.*

---

* In response, Jan Lawrence Handzlik, an attorney for Khrapunov, issued a statement saying, "These allegations are more than a decade old. . . . For seven years ending in 2004, Viktor served with honor and distinction as administrator, or akim, of Almaty, a political subdivision of the Nazarbayev government. He then served as Nazarbayev's administrator of the East Kazakh Region until 2007. It was then that Viktor had a political falling-out with the Nazarbayev regime. Since then, Viktor has been relentlessly pursued by the regime, which has sought to discredit him in the eyes of the Kazakh people. Now persona non grata in their own country, Viktor and his family look forward to refuting these old allegations

Initially, Sater had helped the Khrapunov family buy apartments in Trump SoHo, but he later turned on the family and began cooperating with lawyers and private investigators who were pursuing multiple cases against them on three continents.[45] According to the New York *Daily News,* Sater pocketed at least $21.5 million from related deals with Khrapunov and Mukhtar Ablyazov.[46] Sater's lawyer, Robert Wolf, denied that Sater ever worked with Ablyazov or that he knew whether or not Ablyazov was involved in any wrongdoing.

The Oberlander and Lerner lawsuit alleged Bayrock's projected profits were "to be laundered, untaxed through a sham Delaware entity" to the FL Group,[47] Iceland's largest private investment fund,[48] the first major firm to collapse in 2008 when Iceland's financial bubble burst, and a favored financial instrument for loans to Russia-connected oligarchs who were, court papers claim, in favor with Vladimir Putin.[49] (The Kremlin has denied that Putin has any connection to the FL Group or Bayrock.)[50] According to Bloomberg, Eva Joly, who assisted Iceland's special prosecutor in the investigation of the financial collapse, said, "There was a huge amount of money that came into these banks that wasn't entirely explained by central bank lending. Only Mafia-like groups fill a gap like that."[51]

———

But Iceland was only one of Bayrock's many connections to Russian money, Russian intelligence services, and the Russian mob. In the Soviet era, Arif had spent seventeen years working for the USSR Chamber of Commerce and Industry, an agency run by KGB officers that had long been systematically engaged in commercial espionage in the West.[52] As for Alexander Mashkevich and Patokh Chodiev, who were named in Bayrock's promotional material, both had worked for Boris Birshtein's KGB-linked Seabeco[53] and were allegedly tied up with the Russian Mafia through their alliance with the Chernoys in the Aluminum Wars. In

———

in a fair public trial in a country that guarantees justice to those who come before its courts." Ablyazov maintains that the allegations are false and he is the victim of a vendetta.

the early 2000s Mashkevich, Chodiev, and Alijan Ibragimov were accused of money laundering in Belgium, where prosecutors believed
their funds to be of "criminal origin." In the end, however, the cases
were settled, with the Trio paying a fine to the Belgian government and
not admitting their guilt.[54]

Another significant Bayrock partner, the Sapir Organization, had,
through its principal, Tamir Sapir, a long business relationship with
Semyon Kislin, the commodities trader who was tied to the Chernoy
brothers and, according to the FBI, to Vyacheslav Ivankov's gang in
Brighton Beach.[55] A generous donor to former New York mayor and
future Trump attorney Rudy Giuliani, Kislin* happened to have considerable political capital after Giuliani appointed him to be a member of
the New York City Economic Development Corporation. (At a 1999
press conference, Kislin denied any ties to the Russian mob, insisting,
"I have done nothing evil."[56] Kislin did not respond to an email request
for comment.)

In addition to being wired into the Kremlin, Sapir's son-in-law,
Rotem Rosen, was a supporter of Chabad along with Sater, Sapir, and
others at Bayrock, and, as a result, was part of an extraordinarily powerful channel between Trump and Putin.

After all, the ascent of Chabad in Russia had been part of Putin's plan
to replace older Jewish institutions in Russia with corresponding organizations that were loyal to him.[57] When they began, Russia already had
a chief rabbi, Adolf Shayevich, who was recognized as such by the Russian Jewish Congress. But when Abramovich and Leviev installed
Chabad rabbi Lazar at the head of their rival organization, the Federation of Jewish Communities of Russia, the Kremlin recognized Lazar as
Russia's head rabbi and removed Shayevich from its religious affairs
council.[58]

Consequently, the Federation of Jewish Communities of Russia, the
voice of Chabad in Russia, became so close to Putin that he even made

---

* In his attempt to win influence, Kislin's donations were not partisan, and he contributed
to Democrats as well, including New York senator Chuck Schumer.

a point of attending the dedication of their center in Moscow's Marina Roscha neighborhood in 2001.[59] With Chabad's Rabbi Berel Lazar leading the way, the Federation of Jewish Communities of Russia was now providing Putin with a Jewish "umbrella" that allowed him to battle Vladimir Gusinsky, whose media properties had become critical of him and who even dared to back candidates opposed to Putin. "I said openly," Lazar said, "that what Gusinsky was doing was not desirable and would hurt the Jewish community."[60]

But another reason for the close ties between Chabad and Putin was that both Lazar and Leviev had promised Putin that they would make their connections available to the Kremlin and "open doors to the corridors of power in Washington."[61]

At the time, Trump's comeback in real estate and his ascent in TV were in full swing, but his political prospects were still dicey at best. However, his role in Bayrock and its real estate deals with Russian oligarchs were real and provided a connection to Moscow.

That's what made the Chabad channel so mysterious. First and foremost, the biggest contributor to Chabad in the world was Leviev, the billionaire "King of Diamonds" who had a direct line to Rabbi Berel Lazar, aka "Putin's rabbi," to Donald Trump, and to Putin himself dating back to the Russian leader's early days in St. Petersburg. Leviev would make major real estate transactions with Jared Kushner, including selling the retail space in the former New York Times Building to Kushner for $295 million.[62] As an undergraduate at Harvard, Jared had been active at the campus Chabad House at Harvard.[63] Jared later married Ivanka Trump and became a senior adviser to her father in the White House. Jared and Ivanka were also close to Chabad donor Roman Abramovich and his wife, Dasha Zhukova.

Another major contributor was Jared's father, Charles Kushner,[64] an American real estate developer who was eventually jailed for illegal campaign contributions, tax evasion, and witness tampering. But that is just the beginning of Chabad's ties to Trump. Indeed, one of the biggest contributors to Chabad of Port Washington, Long Island, was Bayrock founder Tevfik Arif, a Kazakh-born Turk with a Muslim name who was not Jewish, but nonetheless won entry into its Chai Circle as a top donor.[65]

The Port Washington founder and head rabbi, Shalom Paltiel, happened to be an acolyte of Rabbi Berel Lazar, Paltiel's "dear friend and mentor,"[66] as he referred to Lazar. But he was also close to Felix Sater and later named Sater "man of the year" for Chabad of Port Washington. At the ceremony honoring Sater, Paltiel recalled how Sater recounted his daring adventures as an intelligence operative. "I only recently told Felix I really didn't believe most of it," Paltiel said.[67] "I thought perhaps he watched too many James Bond movies, read one too many Tom Clancy novels. Anyone who knows Felix knows that he can tell a good story. I simply did not put too much credence to them."

In addition to Sater, Daniel Ridloff, a fellow Bayrock employee, was a member of the Port Washington Chabad house.[68]

Chabad supporters Rotem Rosen and his bride, Zina Sapir, of course, were tied to Bayrock through Zina's father, Tamir Sapir, and they were such close personal friends of Trump that he let them have their 2007 wedding at Trump's Mar-a-Lago, with Lionel Richie and the Pussycat Dolls performing.[69]

A few months later, Leviev met with Trump in Moscow to discuss potential deals for Trump in Russia.[70] Then, in June 2008, after Zina and Rotem's son was born, Lev Leviev arranged for the bris, the Jewish ritual of circumcision, to take place at the grave of Rabbi Menachem Mendel Schneerson, the renowned Hasidic rabbi who was the spiritual leader of the Chabad-Lubavitch movement.[71]

Touting the event as "the best *bris* invite ever," *New York* magazine opined that the "invite list for this particular penis-chopping" was as chic as it gets, including hotelier André Balazs, restaurateur Giuseppe Cipriani, New York nightlife empress Amy Sacco, various real estate moguls, and, of course, Donald Trump and his future son-in-law Jared Kushner.

———

In the midst of these efforts, something took place that seemed entirely unrelated to Trump's interactions with Russia but ended up creating one of the most significant links of all between him and the Kremlin. In 2006, a group of apartment owners at Trump World Tower, his seventy-two-story skyscraper overlooking the United Nations, had taken control of the condo board and were accusing Trump of financial impropriety. For help, Trump turned to a sympathetic condo owner named Michael D. Cohen, who was such a devotee of the Trump brand that he had bought a number of Trump apartments himself, and had his parents, his in-laws, and a business partner buy apartments in Trump World Tower.[72]

Cohen was the same Michael Cohen who knew Felix Sater when he was growing up in Brighton Beach. Initially, when Sater was first asked about his ties to Cohen, he downplayed their relationship. "[Cohen] wasn't one of my close friends," Sater told Talking Points Memo in 2017,[73] "just a guy dating a girl in the neighborhood and we had a bunch of mutual friends."

Later, however, on MSNBC, Sater referred to Cohen as "an old and dear friend,"[74] which was likely closer to the truth.

His suburban roots notwithstanding, Cohen had his own ties to the wiseguys of Brighton Beach. Most notably, through his uncle Dr. Morton Levine, there was his family's shared ownership of Brooklyn's El Caribe Country Club catering hall, the well-known hangout for both Russian and Italian gangsters.[75] According to the New York Times, Dr. Levine was a family practitioner, and one of the families for whom he provided medical services was the Lucchese crime family. In the process of providing those services, according to a sworn affidavit in 1993 from an FBI special agent, Dr. Levine "aided their illegal activities." The affidavit added that a Lucchese underboss, Anthony "Gaspipe" Casso, "regarded Levine as someone who would do anything for him."[76]

In addition to having served as headquarters for Evsei Agron and his gangsters, El Caribe was where John Gotti held his Christmas party in 1988, when he was at the height of his power as head of the Gambino family.[77] Among other notable mob festivities at the restaurant, Genovese crime family soldier Ernest "Butch" Montevecchi, who partnered with Felix Sater's father, Michael Sheferovsky, hosted a reception at El Caribe for a mob subordinate who happened to be the nephew of Charles "Lucky" Luciano.[78]

But El Caribe was just the beginning of Cohen's mob ties. After college, Cohen got a law degree from the Thomas M. Cooley Law School (now known as Western Michigan University Cooley Law School), at the time, a notorious diploma mill, which, according to Reuters, has been repeatedly sued for misrepresenting employment and salary data about its graduates.[79] In addition, Cohen got involved in an offshore casino business in Florida based on a 196-foot yacht, the *Atlantic,* a "failed gambling operation," as BuzzFeed described it, that allegedly did not pay its debts and did business with people tied "to accused and convicted criminals" in both the Italian and Russian mobs. The casino was managed by Tatiana Varzar, the owner of the eponymous Russian nightclub in Brighton Beach, and her husband, Michael Varzar, who had been sent to prison for his role in the gasoline tax scam in the nineties.[80]

Representative Peter King, a Republican congressman from New York's Second District, observed that Cohen had cultivated a tough-guy pose that is "a main part of who he is. He talks about it. He likes to play up the act that he's a guy who was not raised in Manhattan . . . 'I'm from Long Island, we don't take crap from anyone.'"[81]

According to an investigation of Cohen by ProPublica, after law school Cohen worked with a series of small firms that defended clients accused of participation in various medical malpractice scams, phony auto accident cons, and the like that were similar to Russian Mafia swindles in the eighties and nineties. One of his first jobs after law school was working for a personal injury lawyer named Melvyn J. Estrin, who pleaded guilty to bribing insurance adjusters to inflate damage estimates.[82] He subsequently drew up incorporation papers for a number of dubious medical practices and medical billing companies, one of which had filed nearly three hundred lawsuits. In one of the clinics Cohen incorporated, the principal doctor pled guilty to writing phony prescriptions that allowed clients to get 100,000 pills they ordinarily would not have been able to obtain.[83]

In 1994, Cohen had married Laura Shusterman, daughter of Fima Shusterman, a taxi entrepreneur who had pleaded guilty to defrauding the IRS.[84] Meanwhile, Cohen's younger brother Bryan had also married a Ukrainian woman, and Bryan's father-in-law, Alex Oronov, was seeking investors for an ethanol business Oronov co-owned with Viktor Topolov.

According to the FBI, Topolov's conglomerate, Kiev-Donbas, employed three executives who were part of the Russian Mafia, including one enforcer who was tied to Mogilevich and admitted to taking part in at least twenty murders.[85]

In New York, Cohen followed his father-in-law, Fima Shusterman, into the taxi medallion business, where they registered more than fifteen companies—Sir Michael Hacking Corp., Lady Laura Hacking Corp., Smoochie Cab Corporation—and ended up working with Simon Garber and Evgeny Freidman, two Soviet-born New York taxi barons, who managed part of Cohen's fleet.[86] By 2003, he claimed he controlled a fleet of two hundred cabs.[87] Before the advent of Uber and similar services, taxi medallions sometimes sold for more than $1 million.[88]

"Cohen associated himself with the most reckless and greedy players in the industry," said Bhairavi Desai, the executive director of the Taxi Workers Alliance, a group that represents cabdrivers.[89] "They have simultaneously worked to inflate the value of their medallions and rip off their drivers."

In 1999, Cohen received a check for $350,000 that was written by star hockey player Vladimir Malakhov.[90] Under a sworn deposition, Cohen said he did not recall receiving the check and did not know why Malakhov might have paid him that sum. When Cohen was deposed and asked under oath if the signature endorsing the check was his, he replied, "I don't know but it could be."

Then, asked why someone would have sent him the check, Cohen said, " I have no idea."[91]

Meanwhile, Cohen assembled a mini real estate empire of his own, part of which involved his and his family's buying up numerous Trump apartment units, with his Ukrainian father-in-law buying at least four units and Cohen buying five.[92] According to Rolling Stone, during a five-year period, Cohen and people close to him bought $17.3 million in Trump properties.[93]

In February 2007, Trump complimented Cohen on the wisdom of his acquisitions. "Michael Cohen has a great insight into the real-estate market," he told the *New York Post*.[94] "He has invested in my buildings because he likes to make money—and he does."

Indeed, Trump was so impressed by Cohen's insight that by May, he hired Cohen as an executive vice president at the Trump Organization, the same title held by three of Trump's children, Donald Jr., Ivanka, and Eric.[95] Now Cohen was working in the same building as his old buddy Felix Sater.

Once Cohen began working for Trump, his pronouncements only enhanced his reputation as a hard-nosed fixer—as Roy Cohn 2.0, his new pit bull. "If somebody does something Mr. Trump doesn't like, I do everything in my power to resolve it to Mr. Trump's benefit," he told ABC News in 2011. "If you do something wrong, I'm going to come at you, grab you by the neck and I'm not going to let you go until I'm finished."[96] Fittingly, perhaps, on Twitter, his hashtag would become #secretaryofloyalty.[97]

———

And so, all the strands had started to come together: There was a booming real estate market. There was Vladimir Putin's festering bitterness about his country's humiliating Cold War defeat. There were Putin's dreams of reviving Russia's imperial glory. There was the newly globalized post–Cold War version of the Russian Mafia, still very much a state actor in league with Russian intelligence. There were untold billions of dollars in flight capital in anonymous shell companies in Cyprus, the Channel Islands, Panama, and other havens for dark money. There were sumptuous chateaux, villas, dachas, and estates, one bigger than the next; gigantic yachts; private jets; and all the rest, all part of a new culture of unimaginable greed.

And finally there was Donald Trump, emerging from a decade of litigation, multiple bankruptcies, and $4 billion in debt, to rise from the near-dead with the help of Bayrock and its alleged ties to Russian intelligence and the Russian Mafia. "They saved his bacon," said Kenneth McCallion,[98] a former federal prosecutor who filed suit against Mogilevich, Paul Manafort, Ukrainian oligarch Dmitry Firtash, and others on behalf of former Ukrainian prime minister Yulia Tymoshenko.

But Trump's rescue by the Russians was not cost-free. By working with Bayrock, McCallion says, Trump may well have been performing gigantic favors for Vladimir Putin without even knowing it. Indeed, in 2016, Trump's political adversaries commissioned Christopher Steele, a former MI6 agent, to dig up opposition research on Trump, and among the most astonishing allegations in the infamous thirty-five-page Steele Dossier, which alleges Trump has been severely compromised by Russia, is that Trump unknowingly regularly supplied intelligence to Vladimir Putin.

On the face of it, Steele's allegation seems absurd to anyone familiar with Trump's insistent tweeting, impulsive outbursts, and scores of outrageous indiscretions. Who could possibly believe he had the discipline necessary to carry out such a daring intelligence operation?

On the other hand, Steele's dossier specifically said the intelligence in question was about "the activities of business oligarchs and their families' activities and assets in the US, with which PUTIN and the Kremlin seemed preoccupied." That kind of intel was crucial to Putin, because his relationship with the oligarchs often seesawed back and forth. Putin oversaw them with an iron fist, and when they fell out of favor, they either toed the line or ended up being purged (media executives Vladimir Gusinsky and Boris Berezovsky), being jailed (Yukos Oil's Mikhail Khodorkovsky), and/or dying under mysterious circumstances (Berezovsky).

Thanks to Bayrock, McCallion suggests, the future president was indirectly providing Putin with a regular flow of intelligence on what the oligarchs were doing with their money in the US. "I believe that Christopher Steele was right," says McCallion. "Initially, Trump wasn't that important to Putin. But now that Trump was getting investments from the Russians, Putin could keep track of where their money went because Bayrock kept a ledger that Moscow likely had access to. It was not just about buying condos, which was the tail wagging the dog. It was direct capital investment into various Trump projects."

In other words, for example, if capital came in to Bayrock from Iceland's FL Group, as it did for Trump SoHo, Putin would likely know. "Putin didn't stop the expatriation of billions of dollars because he benefited from it," said McCallion,[99] "but it was a serious problem for the Russian economy. Billions of dollars were going out and he really wanted to keep track of it for a variety of reasons, to see what the financial strength was of the oligarchs."

If the Sapir Organization, or the Trio behind the Eurasian Natural Resources Corporation—Mashkevich, Chodiev, and Ibragimov—or Lev Leviev invested a few hundred million or so, Vladimir Putin would know. He would know if Felix Sater was trying to strike a deal with Mirax's Sergei Polonsky. He would know about money that was being laundered through the purchase of condos in Trump SoHo and other developments. He would know about Tevfik Arif's various adventures. And, through Chabad, he would have access to even more information about his oligarchs.

Nor is McCallion the only one who believes Steele might be right about Trump's inadvertent funneling of intelligence to Putin. "If you read the Steele Dossier about Trump providing information on Russian money and oligarchs," says John Sipher, "maybe that is Felix Sater finding out where Russian money is coming in from and relaying it back to Russia. Maybe he is the go-between. I don't know." Of course, Sater has repeatedly denied any such allegations.

Regardless, Sipher and other undercover CIA operatives in Moscow were told that the Russian Mafia was simply not in their purview. "In fact, when you arrived in Moscow, agents were given operational directives that explicitly told them to stay away from them," Sipher said.[100] "To Trump's people, it was like a moth to a flame."

That left the FBI as the most powerful remaining bulwark against the Russian Mafia. But the FBI was infatuated with Felix Sater, raving about his contributions to national security.

Many questions about the FBI's interaction with Sater remain unanswered, but one gauge of its relationship to the Russian Mafia can be seen in the trajectory of former FBI director William Sessions. Once one of the premier law enforcement officers in the nation, in 1997, Sessions had gone to Moscow to address the issue of the Russian Mafia. "I believe we can beat organized crime," he told the assembled crowd.[101]

But ten years later, back in private practice, Sessions had moved in another direction. Just as Bob Dole and Jack Abramoff and Tom DeLay and Barbour Griffith & Rogers had jumped on the Russian gravy train, William Sessions decided to take on a Russian client. In this case, the client had been charged with racketeering and was trying to negotiate a deal with the US Department of Justice, and was so powerful that he not only had made the FBI's "Ten Most Wanted" list, but had now gotten a former FBI director, William Sessions, to represent him.[102] Sessions's client, of course, was Semion Mogilevich.

In the end, Mogilevich did not get the plea deal he wanted. But the mere fact that the former head of the FBI had a client who, according to the US Department of Justice, represented an enormous national security threat provides a sense of how close the Russian Mafia had come to America.

What would be worse, of course, was if the Russian Mafia somehow managed to go even further and breach the White House. All of which seemed extraordinarily far-fetched. Even though Trump had expressed his presidential ambitions by this time, no one took him terribly seriously.

As for what Trump thought when he took stock of Putin's presidency in Russia, that was open to speculation, but increasingly it looked as if he liked what he saw. "He saw a guy who a) can be president for life basically, and b) is worth about $200 billion," said Kenneth McCallion. "So Trump had to be thinking, 'Why not here?'"[103]

CHAPTER FIFTEEN

PUTIN'S REVENGE

On April 25, 2005, in his annual address to the nation, Vladimir Putin called the demise of the Soviet Union "the greatest geopolitical catastrophe of the twentieth century."[1] More than a mere sound bite that romanticized the deceased communist state, Putin's pronouncement could be seen as his reassertion of the idea that Russia must fulfill its great imperial destiny. All of which portended renewed conflict—in one form or another—with the West.

Which should have surprised no one. Even before the Soviet Union took its last breath, Eastern Bloc satellites had started to abandon Russia. First, in 1990, what had formerly been East Germany reunited with the Federal Republic of Germany and became part of NATO. That included Dresden, Putin's old haunt. In 1999, three former communist countries—Hungary, the Czech Republic, and Poland—joined NATO. After that, Western officials repeatedly assured Russia that NATO would not expand to the east[2] but broke their pledge. By the time of Putin's speech in 2005, seven more Eastern Bloc countries—Bulgaria, Estonia, Latvia, Lithuania, Romania, Slovakia, and Slovenia—had joined NATO. Albania, Croatia, and Montenegro followed.[3]

For Putin, however, the red line was Ukraine—a nation of more than forty million people that is Russia's breadbasket, an essential trade partner, and Russia's biggest buffer with the West. Under no circumstances would Putin allow it to fall to the West. Yet Ukraine's Orange Revolution of 2004 had posed a grave threat to Putin's control.

The protests had their genesis in a crisis that began in September 2000 when Georgian politician and journalist Georgy Gongadze, a prominent critic of President Leonid Kuchma's administration and its close ties to Putin, wrote a story, "Everything About Oleksandr Volkov," published on the Ukrayinska Pravda website, tying Volkov, a top Kuchma adviser, to the Russian Mafia.

A high-level oligarch himself, Volkov was one of several people close to Kuchma who had helped Dmitry Firtash get established in the Ukraine energy trade. And now, Gongadze was reporting that Volkov had foreign bank accounts with $15 million in them.[4]

But on September 16, 2000, after his exposé of Volkov was published on Ukrayinska Pravda, Gongadze disappeared. Shortly afterward, Deputy Interior Minister Mykola Dzhyha announced that, among other theories, authorities thought Gongadze might have staged his own abduction.[5] That turned out to be incorrect. Two months later, his decapitated body was found about seventy miles outside Kiev.[6]

Gongadze's murder has never been solved, but there is reason to believe someone at the highest levels of the Ukrainian government orchestrated his assassination. One key piece of evidence comes from clandestine tape recordings made by Mykola Melnychenko, a former bodyguard to President Kuchma, who secretly recorded five hundred hours of conversations in Kuchma's office between 1999 and 2000.[7] Among them is a conversation with Ukrainian secret service chief Leonid Derkach.[8] As reported by Radio Free Europe/Radio Liberty, in the Melnichenko tapes President Kuchma says, "I'm telling you, drive him [Gongadze] out, throw him out. Give him to the Chechen's [expletive], have him become a hostage, let them pay a ransom for him."

To which another voice, believed to be that of Interior Minister Yuriy Kravchenko, replies, "We will think it through. We will do what is needed. . . . I was told today that we are preparing a program for him. We are studying his movements, where he goes. We need to learn this and then we will act."

President Kuchma denied that any such surveillance of Gongadze took place, and maintained that the Melnichenko recordings made in the president's office are fakes.[9] However, in 2001, a former FBI forensic expert at Bek-Tek, a private audio lab in Virginia, determined that the audio recordings regarding the surveillance of Gongadze were genuine. Later, in 2002, according to Radio Free Europe/Radio Liberty, the FBI came to the same conclusion when it examined a different segment of the recordings.

———

Gongadze's murder was the first of dozens, many of which remain unsolved, in which journalists and others who were investigating Putin's kleptocratic tribute system were mysteriously killed. According to the Committee to Protect Journalists, no fewer than seventy journalists have been murdered in Russia and Ukraine between 1992 and 2018.[10] These were the men and women who had been reporting on how Putin's system enriched his cronies, various oligarchs of his choosing, and mobsters.

American journalists were not immune. On the night of July 9, 2004, Paul Klebnikov, the forty-one-year-old editor of *Forbes Russia* and the author of *Godfather of the Kremlin: The Decline of Russia in the Age of Gangster Capitalism*, left his Moscow office at about ten p.m. He headed toward the subway when a car drove slowly by with someone firing nine shots at him. Klebnikov died in the hospital.[11]

The murder, which is still unsolved, has been described as a contract killing that, according to the publisher of *Forbes Russia,* was "definitely linked" to Klebnikov's journalism.[12] Some observers have suggested the attack was triggered by a recent *Forbes* story on the hundred richest people in Russia. Others suspected Boris Berezovsky of being behind the murder. Richard Behar, an investigative reporter with *Forbes* and a longtime friend and colleague of Klebnikov's, said the chief Russian investigator on the case told him, "I have testimony that [Boris] Berezovsky put a contract out on Klebnikov—from a person to whom Berezovsky spoke."[13]

But the case remained unsettled. Behar told Klebnikov's family that if Paul were alive today, "he'd be able to solve his own murder. That was the irony and tragedy. If he was alive, he'd be breaking more ground on Trump-Russia than any other individual reporter. I have absolutely no doubt of that. He was way, way out in front on so many things."[14]

Afterward, in 2005, with Klebnikov's murder still unsolved, Putin visited New York and invited Klebnikov's family to meet with him at the Waldorf Astoria, where he told them that journalists in Russia should be able to work without fear of violence. Without missing a beat, Behar said, Paul's widow, Musa, asked Putin if he would say that publicly. There was a long pause. Finally, Putin said he would "take that under consideration."[15]

In 2005, Richard Behar launched Project Klebnikov to develop new information on the Klebnikov murder and to pursue Paul's investigative work. Not long afterward, he met with Anna Politkovskaya, a Russian journalist and human rights activist best known for her work with *Novaya Gazeta,* hoping she could gather together investigative reporters in Russia who would work hand in hand with Project Klebnikov.[16]

In her book *Putin's Russia: Life in a Failing Democracy,* Politkovskaya accused Putin and the FSB of crushing civil liberties in order to establish a Soviet-style dictatorship. "The KGB respects only the strong," she wrote. "The weak it devours. We of all people ought to know that."[17]

"We are hurtling back into a Soviet abyss," she added, "into an information vacuum that spells death from our own ignorance. All we have left is the Internet, where information is still freely available. For the rest, if you want to go on working as a journalist, it's total servility to Putin. Otherwise, it can be death, the bullet, poison, or trial—whatever our special services, Putin's guard dogs, see fit."

———

Journalists were not Putin's only targets. There were media censorship, a crackdown on the Internet, harassment of human rights activists, and more. By 2007, Putin had revived the old Soviet practice of locking up dissidents in mental hospitals. "We're returning to this Soviet scenario when psychiatric institutions are used as punitive instruments," Yuri Savenko, president of the Independent Psychiatric Association of

Russia, told the *Chicago Tribune*.[18] "I call this not even punitive psychiatry but police psychiatry, when the main aim is to protect the state rather than to treat sick people."

As Vladimir Gusinsky and Boris Berezovsky found out, even oligarchs were at risk. In August 2000, after Berezovsky's TV station, ORT, criticized Putin's handling of the *Kursk* submarine disaster, which killed more than one hundred sailors, Putin was said to have told Berezovsky, "The show is over."[19] Berezovsky fled to London, where he was granted refugee status in 2003 and became part of a London circle of Russian exiles who hoped to bring down Putin. He died under mysterious circumstances in 2013.

As for Gusinsky, in 2001 Russian officials raided his Media Most and NTV and attempted to arrest him, but he escaped by fleeing to Israel.[20] The state broadcaster, RTR (now Russia 1), was already under Putin's control. Now he also controlled ORT (now First Channel) and NTV.[21]

Putin kept such tight control of the media that television coverage of him was almost celebratory. "Imagine you have two dozen TV channels and it is all Fox News," Vladimir Milov, a former deputy energy minister under Putin and now a critic, told the *New Yorker*.[22]

In February 2003, Mikhail Khodorkovsky, then believed to be the richest man in Russia, with a fortune of $16 billion, appeared on a television show in which he argued with Putin about widespread corruption in the Kremlin. In October, he was arrested and charged with fraud, tax evasion, and other economic crimes.[23] The message was clear: Even oligarchs had to play by Putin's rules.

Meanwhile, one of Putin's fiercest critics was FSB officer Alexander Litvinenko, who had already confronted Putin with regard to the Berezovsky assassination plot. In October 2000, Litvinenko and his family fled Moscow and applied for asylum at the US embassy in Ankara, Turkey.[24] His application was denied, but he was soon granted asylum in the UK and settled in London, reporting to MI6.[25]

In 2002, Litvinenko published *The Gang from Lubyanka*, alleging that Putin and the FSB had been in league with the Russian Mafia, specifically the Tambov-Malyshev gang, dating back to when Putin was deputy mayor of St. Petersburg. The book also charged that Putin had direct financial ties to gang leader Vladimir Kumarin.[26] Litvinenko, with coauthor Yuri Felshtinsky, also published *Blowing Up Russia: The Secret Plot to Bring Back KGB Terror,* which brought renewed interest in the KGB apartment bombings of 1999 and other fabricated "false flag" cover operations, or, as the Russians called them, "active measures." Both books were banned in Russia and in 2003 lawyer Mikhail Trepashkin said he had been told that everyone associated with *Blowing Up Russia* would be destroyed.[27]

In the meantime, Litvinenko became friends with Anna Politkovskaya, who visited him in London. His friend Alex Goldfarb, who was also a friend of Anna's, said the two were "very close" and that they shared "a natural kinship as converts," Litvinenko having been a KGB officer while Politkovskaya was the daughter of a well-placed Russian diplomat.[28]

Litvinenko had begun working with MI6 as a consultant on organized crime. At the same time, he reported his findings on Mogilevich's relationship with Putin to Mario Scaramella, an investigator affiliated with the Mitrokhin Commission, an Italian panel investigating the links between the Russian secret services and organized crime.

Litvinenko and his wife, Marina, were only too happy to provide copious amounts of material, much of it about Semion Mogilevich. Marina Litvinenko characterized Mogilevich as "one of Russia's most notorious [organized crime group] leaders . . . It is said he is responsible for contract killings and smuggling weapons."

For his part, Alexander Litvinenko described Mogilevich as "a well-known criminal terrorist" who was "in a good relationship with Russian President Putin and most senior officials of the Russian Federation." He said that Mogilevich and Putin had "a common cause, in [Litvinenko's] understanding a criminal cause," and that he knew "beyond doubt that Mogilevich is FSB's long-standing agent and that all his actions including the contacts with Al-Qaeda are controlled by the FSB . . . For this very reason the FSB is hiding Mogilevich from the FBI."[29]

Litvinenko was concerned enough about his testimony that when he returned to London, on November 23, 2005, he made a short audiotape, in broken English, about Mogilevich and Putin. "Mogilevich have good relationship with Putin since 1994 or 1993," he says on the tape, which was published ten years later by the *Telegraph* of London.[30] "Semion Mogilevich has contact with Al Qaeda. Semion Mogilevich sell weapons, sell weapons to Al Qaeda. Before I gave a lot of information about Mogilevich to Mario Scaramella."

Litivenko was also in touch with Oleg Kalugin, the ex-KGB general who had been in the US since 1995. Kalugin felt the real reason Litvinenko was getting under Putin's skin was because he had come forward with outrageous accusations about Putin and charged that the Russian leader was a pedophile.

Kalugin warned Litvinenko to keep his mouth shut. "I told him, 'Don't say that! You'll be in trouble.' Putin could not tolerate that," Kalugin told me.[31]

Nonetheless, in July 2006, Litvinenko submitted a highly provocative article to the *Chechenpress* website in which he referred to a video on the Internet that showed Putin kissing the stomach of a young boy, aged four or five. In the video, Putin's embrace of the young boy may be nothing more than harmless horsing around, but Litvinenko wrote, "Nobody can understand why the Russian president did such a strange thing as kissing the stomach of an unfamiliar small boy."[32]

Then Litvinenko explained the unusual gesture by saying that when Putin was given a very junior position in the KGB it was because "his bosses learned that Putin was a pedophile . . . The Institute officials feared to report this to their own superiors, which would cause an unpleasant investigation."

When Putin became FSB director, Litvinenko wrote, he found and destroyed videos "which showed him making sex with some underage boys."[33]

At the same time, as if he were not courting enough danger, Litvinenko remained friends with Anna Politkovskaya and collaborated with her on a project exposing the FSB. Deeply concerned about the risks she faced investigating corruption, he suggested she take various precautions for her personal security and urged her to take advantage of her American citizenship and "go write [her] articles in America." But she stayed in Russia.

In New York, Richard Behar had a box on his desk in which he kept sundry memorabilia, including a business card on which Anna had written her email address. When they had met in New York, he told her that Project Klebnikov hoped to find investigative reporters in Russia who would help solve Paul's murder. She warned Behar she could "probably count on one hand the number of Russian investigative reporters who aren't corrupt."[34] But she had vowed to help anyway.

Then, on October 7, 2006, Anna was shot dead in the elevator of her apartment complex in central Moscow. It happened to be Vladimir Putin's birthday.

In London, Marina Litvinenko gave Sasha the news, and later said "he was just broken down because for him it was absolutely devastating news." He also worried that "he could be next."[35]

On October 19, Sasha went to a meeting at the Frontline Club in London, a restaurant/gathering place for journalists, photographers, and other like-minded people, at which he made a short speech publicly accusing Putin of being responsible for Anna Politkovskaya's murder.[36]

Even after Anna's murder, however, Litvinenko didn't seem to take the threat to his own well-being too seriously. She had been in Russia, after all, but he had safely defected to the West. He took enormous pride in his newly won citizenship and seemed to regard it as an extra layer of protective covering. "Now they won't dare to touch me," he told a friend.[37] "No one would try to kill a British citizen." And if something did happen, he wrote in a statement to British officials, at least he would be a proud British citizen. "Possibly I may die," he wrote, "but I will die, as a free person, and my son and my wife are free people. And Britain is a great country."[38]

On November 1, 2006, Litvinenko had lunch with Mario Scaramella at a Japanese restaurant and Scaramella warned Litvinenko that he had received intelligence about a Russian plot to kill those involved with the Mitrokhin Commission. Later that day, after he and Scaramella finished, Litvinenko had tea at the Pine Bar in the Millennium Hotel in Mayfair at about four p.m.[39] with Andre Lugovoy and Dmitri Kovtun, two former KGB officers who had gone into private security.[40] According to *The Litvinenko Inquiry,* an official report issued by the House of Commons about the death of Alexander Litvinenko, "the forensic and other evidence strongly indicates that it was during this meeting that Mr. Litvinenko drank green tea poisoned with radioactive polonium."[41]

According to Norman Dombey, a British physics and astronomy emeritus professor at the University of Sussex, the radioactive isotope in Litvinenko's tea was made at the Avangard facility in Sarov, Russia. "One of the isotope-producing reactors at the Mayak facility in Ozersk, Russia, was used for the initial irradiation of bismuth," said Dombey.[42] "In my opinion, the Russian state or its agents were responsible for the poisoning."

From his hospital deathbed, Litvinenko told British authorities investigating his poisoning, "I have no doubt whatsoever that this was done by the Russian Secret Services. Having knowledge of the system, I know that the order about such a killing of a citizen of another country on its own territory, especially if it is something to do with Great Britain, could only have been given by one person. That person is the President of the Russian Federation, Vladimir Putin."[43]

A more than three-hundred-page report by Sir Robert Owen, chairman of the Litvinenko Inquiry, concluded that Litvinenko was given a fatal dose of polonium during his meeting with Lugovoy*[44] and Kovtun, who were identified as prime suspects. Russia has refused to extradite either of the two men.[45]

In his report, Sir Robert concluded, "the FSB operation to kill Litvinenko was probably approved by [then–FSB chief Nikolai] Mr Patrushev and also by President Putin."[46]

In a reference to the pedophilia charges, Sir Robert added, "It hardly needs saying that the allegations made by Mr. Litvinenko against President Putin in this article were of the most serious nature. Could they have had any connection with his death?"[47]

But the report also noted that Litvinenko's testimony before the

---

* On March 9, 2015, just after the UK's Litvinenko Inquiry had put together substantial evidence implicating Lugovoy in the murder, President Putin granted Lugovoy a medal for "services to the motherland." According to Ben Emmerson, the queen's counsel for Litvinenko's widow, Marina, the timing of Putin's decision was no coincidence. "[It] is clearly both a provocation from president Putin and the clearest possible message he identifies himself with Mr Lugovoy."

Mitrokhin Commission and the intelligence he furnished Mario Scaramella, the Mitrokhin Commission attorney, was "particularly sensitive" in describing Mogilevich as someone in "a good relationship" with President Putin, a relationship that included Mogilevich's sale of weapons to al-Qaeda and acting as "the FSB's long standing agent."[48]

In addition, there was the fact that Litvinenko had played a role in the transcription and publicizing of the so-called Kuchma Tapes (aka the Melnychenko tapes), including making a statement before the Mitrokhin Commission that Mogilevich "is in a very close relationship with Russian president Putin . . . At the present, Putin is Mogilevich's *krysha* [protection in criminal jargon]. This is Putin who protects Mogilevich."[49]

That provocative revelation could also have been a motive for murder. In the end, many questions remain unanswered, but a few things are certain. On November 23, 2006, Litvinenko died of polonium-210 poisoning. Anna Politkovskaya had been dead for two months. And Putin's Russia had become a Mafia state in which compliant loyalists became billionaires and telling the truth could get you killed.

CHAPTER SIXTEEN

BLOOD MONEY

Even though Litvinenko was dead, the issues he had been investigating were more alive than ever. That was especially true in Ukraine, where Prime Minister Viktor Yanukovych, a Putin partisan, advanced to the runoff election for president in 2004 amidst widespread allegations of fraud. Yanukovych's dubious tactics triggered the Orange Revolution of 2004 and 2005, and a Ukrainian Supreme Court ruling that nullified his victory.

From the Kremlin's point of view, Yanukovych's reversal created a serious problem. He had been a highly reliable pawn for Putin. The Firtash-Mogilevich money pipeline that siphoned off billions from Ukraine's energy trade was a paradigm of how Putin was able to transform control over Russia's natural resources into political power. And to keep this arrangement in place, Putin needed a reliable surrogate in charge in Ukraine.

It began with Gazprom, Russia's largely state-owned energy giant, selling enormous amounts of natural gas to RosUkrEnergo (RUE), Mogilevich's and Firtash's intermediary, at bargain-basement prices, thereby putting RUE in a position to resell it to European nations at a huge markup. Firtash became a billionaire. Putin allegedly took a sizeable share as well. The oligarchs in turn then funded Yanukovych's pro-Russian Party of Regions to keep Ukraine securely in Putin's camp and to make sure these highly profitable deals remained in place. In a diplomatic cable, then–US ambassador to Ukraine John Herbst referred to the Party of Regions as "a haven for Donetsk-based mobsters and oligarchs."[1]

All of which was ideal, except for one thing: Yanukovych was a lousy candidate, and if he was to remain the leader of the Party of Regions, he desperately needed a makeover to wipe out the image he had as a thuggish Kremlin stooge.[2]

His résumé was not much help. In his youth, Yanukovych had been twice convicted of assault.[3] In 2004, his rival Viktor Yushchenko barely survived an assassination attempt by dioxin poisoning during the campaign,[4] and blamed the poisoning on unnamed "government officials" who feared he would beat Yanukovych.[5]

Even if Yanukovych's camp had nothing to do with the dioxin, there were widespread allegations of massive vote rigging, which were echoed by Secretary of State Colin Powell, who cited "credible reports of fraud and abuse."[6] In the end, there was enough evidence that the supreme court of Ukraine annulled the election after Yanukovych was initially declared the winner. In the revote, Yushchenko won.[7]

When it came to oligarchs such as Dmitry Firtash and aluminum tycoon Oleg Deripaska, Yanukovych had known how to be wonderfully compliant, but now that wasn't enough. With a fortune of $12 billion, he had become a symbol of unbridled greed that was embodied by Mezhyhirya, his insanely extravagant estate, which was known as Ukraine's Versailles, with its private zoo with kangaroos and a herd of ostrich, a yacht club, a galleon in its pond, marble floors, $100,000 chandeliers, a collection of seventy rare cars, a helicopter pad, and more.[8] So Yanukovych was damaged goods. The Party of Regions needed a new face— or a dramatic makeover.

Enter Paul Manafort, formerly of the GOP consulting firm Black, Manafort, Stone, and Kelly and now with his new firm, Davis, Manafort and Freedman.[9] Brilliantly skewered in a memorable 1992 *Spy* magazine piece by Art Levine,[10] Paul Manafort and Roger Stone's firm, in all its various incarnations over the years, came to occupy a hallowed place in the dark, amoral domain of Washington lobbying. "Name a corrupt despot, and Black, Manafort will name the account: Ferdinand Marcos, $900,000 a year; the now deposed Somalian dictatorship, $450,000; the drug-linked Bahamian government, $800,000," *Spy* reported, before going on to rate various firms in terms of how dodgy their clients were. Black, Manafort, Stone, and Kelly won out as the sleaziest of them all.[11]

Boyhood friends who learned their craft at the feet of Richard Nixon and Roy Cohn,[12] Manafort and Stone had put together the hottest lobbying shop in Washington. Their firm had played a vital role in the 1980 election of Ronald Reagan. Their first client after Reagan's election had been Donald Trump, who retained them to help with federal issues such as getting permits to dredge the channel to the Atlantic City marina to make room for Trump's yacht, the *Trump Princess*.[13]

Of the two men, Stone was the showboat, buff from the gym, sporting bleached blond hair, the proud owner of five Jaguars, a hundred silver wedding ties, and countless designer suits, and the subject of fashion stories in *Penthouse* and *GQ*, such a dandy that he even coined aphorisms—Stone's Rules—about cuff links: "Large hub-cap types are for mafia dons from Jersey and Las Vegas lounge singers. Cufflinks should be small, understated, and tasteful."[14]

A self-proclaimed libertine, Stone displayed a photo in his Miami office of himself clad only in a banana hammock, standing poolside next to porn star Nina Hartley. If the photo had shown him from behind, you'd have seen the face of Richard Nixon tattooed on his back. All of which made him catnip to reporters, who couldn't resist the bravado of a spinmeister who walked down the aisle of press buses and called out, "I'm here. Who needs to be spun?"[15]

Next to Stone, Manafort was relatively understated, although over time, he cultivated a more lavish globetrotting lifestyle in keeping with the oligarchs he worked for. Putting on his long overcoat with a grand sweeping gesture, he cut such a swashbuckling figure that friends reportedly dubbed him "the Count of Monte Cristo."[16]

But in general, he played his cards close to his vest, befitting a protégé of George H. W. Bush's consigliere, James Baker.[17] Baker was all smoothness and charm, the Velvet Hammer, always proper, but a man no one wanted to cross. "From Baker, [Manafort] learned the art of ostentatious humility," writes Franklin Foer in the *Atlantic*,[18] "how to use the knife to butter up and then stab in the back."

Together, Manafort and Stone rewrote the rule book on lobbying, bundling political consulting, public relations, and other services into an operation that *Time* magazine called "the ultimate supermarket of influence peddling."[19]

Before long, they went global, and took an almost perverse and giddy pride in representing the most brutal tyrants on the planet—including Iraq's Saddam Hussein, Nicolae Ceaușescu of Romania, Zairean dictator Mobutu Sese Seko, and regimes that enslaved children and murdered priests. "Black, Manafort, Stone, and Kelly lined up most of the dictators of the world we could find," Stone crowed.[20] The firm's propensity to represent dictators—rulers from the Dominican Republic, Nigeria, Kenya, Equatorial Guinea, and Somalia were also clients—was such that the Center for Public Integrity included them in a report titled "the Torturers' Lobby."[21]

———

So on some level, working for Yanukovych in Ukraine was more of the same for Manafort. On the other hand, Ukraine was a real geopolitical tinderbox. At a time when the EU and NATO were inching ever closer to Russia's borders, Putin was determined that Ukraine not fall into the West's sphere of influence.

Manafort's work in Ukraine began in late 2004 when he was hired as general consultant to the Party of Regions to transform Yanukovych's image from that of the archvillain of the Orange Revolution and a pawn of Putin, to that of a pro-West reformer who was one of Ukraine's most popular politicians.[22]

And so, Manafort operatives moved into a small office for six to eight people on the first floor of 4 Sofievskaya Street in Kiev.[23] Ukrayinska Pravda described the office as mysterious and noted that the windows were curtained all day long. When journalists approached they were politely told to leave and not come back.[24]

Over the next decade, Manafort made at least 138 trips to Ukraine[25] in a spectacularly lucrative relationship that also took him into the shadowy world of flight capital, offshore shell companies, banks in Cyprus, and Russian agents.

Far more than a mere political consultant, Manafort had the kind of power in Ukraine that American intelligence operatives and oil executives had brandished back in the Cold War era, when covert operations staged coups in Guatemala or Iran. Manafort, however, had found a way to undertake his operations without being in any way attached to the United States government—indeed, often working against America's stated policies, all while making tens of millions of dollars,[26] much of which, according to an indictment that was later filed, went into foreign tax havens and then into real estate, antique rugs, expensive cars, and other instruments used to avoid taxes.[27] His deputy Rick Gates, who played a key role in Manafort's Ukraine operation, explained to a group of Washington lobbyists, "Paul has a whole separate shadow government structure . . . In every ministry, he has a guy."[28]

At the time, Russian intelligence agents had penetrated the highest levels of power in various institutions throughout Ukraine,[29] and Manafort's operation was no exception. His most trusted protégé, Konstantin Kilimnik, who was affectionately known as KK, was a case in point. Also called "Manafort's Manafort,"[30] because he was his boss's right hand, Kilimnik, though just over five feet tall next to the six-foot-plus Manafort, aped his employer in many ways, the *Atlantic* reported, driving the same BMW and wearing similar designer suits.[31] But what was most interesting about Kilimnik was that the man Paul Manafort so heavily relied on in Ukraine was a foot soldier for Russian intelligence.

Kilimnik told the *New York Times* he had no ties to Russian intelligence, but in fact he had studied at the Military Institute of the Ministry of Defense in Moscow, which trains interpreters for the Russian military intelligence agency, formerly known as the GRU and now called the Main Directorate.[32] Moreover, according to Phil Griffin, a longtime political consultant with Manafort who hired Kilimnik in the early 2000s to work at the International Republican Institute in Moscow, "he was completely upfront about his past work with Russian military intelligence. It was no big deal."[33]

Given the language barrier, Kilimnik became crucial. "Because Paul doesn't speak Russian or Ukrainian, he always had to have someone like that with him in meetings," said one operative who worked with Manafort.[34] "So KK was with him all the time. He was very close to Paul and very trusted."

Assisting Manafort covered a lot of ground. Manafort and his team launched a potent disinformation campaign to discredit Yanukovych's rivals using covert operations that could have been pulled straight out of the KGB playbook. According to the *Guardian,* Manafort worked with former *Wall Street Journal* and *Financial Times* reporter Alan Friedman to propose an ambitious strategy to discredit rival Yulia Tymoshenko all over the world.[35]

They set about smearing Ukrainian opponents of Yanukovych by rewriting their Wikipedia entries. They set up a phony think tank in Vienna called the Center for the Study of Former Soviet Socialist Republics, which proceeded to disseminate articles supporting Yanukovych. When then–secretary of state Hillary Clinton publicly supported Yulia Tymoshenko, Manafort's team allied with Breitbart, the right-wing news site, to attack Hillary for creating "a neo-Nazi Frankenstein."[36]

Thanks to his work with Yanukovych, Manafort was soon fully conversant with a network of oligarchs including aluminum billionaire Oleg Deripaska, coal and steel tycoon Rinat Akhmetov, and natural gas magnate Dmitry Firtash. "Manafort was introduced by Yanukovych's people to Firtash, Deripaska, and others and it opened up a whole new world for him," said Kenneth McCallion.[37]

Now the money began to roll in. In late 2004, Deripaska dispatched Manafort to the eastern Ukraine city of Donetsk, the *Wall Street Journal* reported, where he met Rinat Akhmetov. A billionaire financier behind the Party of Regions, Akhmetov agreed to pay Manafort's firm roughly $12 million to provide corporate strategy and branding assistance for his holding company, System Capital Management.[38]

Less than a year later, in 2005, according to the Associated Press, Manafort began a secret deal with Deripaska whereby Manafort's firm was paid $10 million[39] per year to influence politics, business dealings, and media coverage inside the US, Europe, and the former Soviet republics in a way that would benefit Vladimir Putin's government.

Deripaska was "among the 2–3 oligarchs Putin turns to on a regular basis," according to a diplomatic cable published by WikiLeaks, so Manafort clearly knew whose interests were being served.[40] "We are now of the belief that this model can greatly benefit the Putin Government," Manafort wrote in the proposal.[41] He added that his firm would "be offering a great service that can re-focus, both internally and externally, the policies of the Putin government."

Lobbyists serving the interests of foreign governments are required to register with the Justice Department under the Foreign Agents Registration Act.[42] However, Manafort did not bother to register until June 2017.[43]

In summer 2005, Manafort went to Moscow before Ukraine's parliamentary elections and met with Yanukovych, Akhmetov, and other influential Ukrainians tied to the Party of Regions. At times, Yanukovych made noises about cooperating with the US.

But Ambassador John Herbst told the Daily Beast that such sentiments stopped as soon as they infringed "upon [Yanukovych's] core interests in Ukraine, which were related—among other things—to ensuring his friends got their share of the national pie, and things that might have ticked off the Kremlin."[44]

Articulating pro-West sentiments was terrifically popular with voters, especially in the western half of the country, during electoral campaigns. But Yanukovych's heart—and wallet—were in Moscow. "He was out for the good of himself, his group, and also his country, starting with himself and his group," said Herbst. "And for that, having a good relationship with the U.S. was a counter to being overly dependent on the Kremlin."

As for Manafort, Herbst noted that the Party of Regions, "long a haven for Donetsk-based mobsters and oligarchs," had taken on Manafort for an "extreme makeover" to "transform its image into that of a democratic political force."[45]

———

Meanwhile, Manafort began to live an outrageously extravagant lifestyle commensurate with his huge income. He bought a brownstone in New York and a home in Arlington, Virginia. He got three Range Rovers and a Mercedes-Benz, and paid for expensive improvements at his homes in the Hamptons and Palm Beach, Florida.[46] But he brought in so much money from Ukraine that in order to hide it from US authorities, he allegedly laundered it through scores of United States and foreign corporations, partnerships, and bank accounts, and allegedly filed false income tax returns, failed to file foreign bank reports, and engaged in bank fraud conspiracy.*[47]

In all, Manafort is said to have deposited $75 million in offshore accounts.[48] He also allegedly laundered more than $30 million in income by purchasing property, goods, and services such as valuable antique rugs, automobiles, real estate, landscaping, and home improvements for his house in the Hamptons and hiding the income from the US Treasury.[49] Richard Gates is said to have transferred more than $3 million from the offshore accounts to other accounts he controlled.

Among the offshore companies Manafort used to wire millions of dollars to the United States was a shell company called Lucicle Consultants Limited. Among many other transactions with Lucicle, Manafort allegedly transferred more than $1.3 million to a home improvement company in the Hamptons.[50]

In the meantime, for candidate Yanukovych, the makeover had begun. Manafort and Yanukovych became friends. They played tennis together at Mezhyhirya. Manafort had the good sense to let Yanukovych win.[51] As reported by the *Atlantic*, they swam nude together outside the *banya* (sauna). Manafort was given to wearing fine Italian suits. He got Yanukovych to do the same. Manafort combed his hair back. Ditto for Yanukovych. Manafort taught him how to make small talk[52] and how to wave to a crowd. "Manafort taught Yanukovych how to speak, how to become a Western type of candidate, a media star," said Ken McCallion.[53]

Manafort introduced polling techniques, microtargeting, and voter turnout practices that were standard operating procedure in the US.[54] He even taught Yanukovych to steal lines from American politicians. "I understand your dreams," Yanukovych told supporters at a rally, before

---

* In 2017 and 2018, Manafort and Gates were indicted on a total of forty-four counts of money laundering, bank fraud, and tax charges.

he borrowed an oldie but goodie from Bill Clinton's repertoire.[55] "I feel your pain, and I share in your desire to make Ukraine a land of opportunity."

In 2006, Yanukovych's Party of Regions did far better than anyone expected in the parliamentary elections, resulting in Yanukovych's becoming prime minister. That put Manafort in a position to ask for—and get—more and more money. Every time he submitted extravagant bills, Yanukovych simply asked other oligarchs to chip in a million or so.[56] There was no end in sight.

One major source of the funds was Dmitry Firtash, whose billions, Reuters reported, grew out of "remarkable sweetheart deals brokered by associates of Russian leader Vladimir Putin, at immense cost to Russian taxpayers."[57] His money, of course, came from the billions of dollars skimmed off the top of the energy trade—principally Turkmen and Russian natural gas—in Ukraine by RosUkrEnergo at bargain-basement prices and resold at much higher Western market prices.

In March 2008, US ambassador to Russia William Burns tried to get to the bottom of what RUE really was by meeting with a representative of the company, who, he cabled, "seemed like a man who had received instructions to reveal nothing and who was very comfortable in that role. Our meeting with him helped confirm that RUE has little interest in revealing its inner workings."[58]

On paper, RUE was half owned by Gazprom and half by Firtash and Ivan Fursin. But as Yulia Tymoshenko, the braided leader of the pro-West Orange Revolution who became prime minister of Ukraine in 2005, alleged, they were just fronts for a powerful and familiar name in organized crime. "When I was the Prime Minister," she said, "we provided the President of Ukraine with documented proof that some powerful criminal structures are behind the RosUkrEnergo company. I can only say as a politician: we have no doubts whatsoever that the man named Mogilevich is behind the whole operation called RosUkrEnergo."[59]

Nevertheless, RUE continued to rake in the dough. Between 2010 and 2014 alone, according to Russian customs documents detailing the trade, Gazprom sold more than twenty billion cubic meters of gas at prices so low that Firtash and—possibly—Mogilevich made more than $3 billion.[60] In addition, bankers close to Putin gave Firtash up to $11 billion in credit, which positioned Firtash to become a dominant player in Ukraine's chemical and fertilizer industry and a major backer of pro-Putin political factions in Ukraine, and to fund Manafort. Just as Putin had used the state assets of the Russian people to enrich political allies, now he was doing the same with Firtash and Mogilevich in Ukraine, which was so vital to Putin's strategic interests.

The high stakes became more than apparent in December 2007, when Ukraine's leadership changed hands and Yulia Tymoshenko, the opposition leader, became prime minister. Suddenly, the billions of dollars being siphoned off from the Ukraine energy trade through the Mogilevich-Firtash money pipeline were at risk. And in January 2009, Prime Minister Tymoshenko finally engineered a deal that eliminated RUE as an intermediary in gas transactions.[61] RUE claimed that this amounted to a confiscation of its property.

Yanukovych too had a change in fortune on the horizon. As of 2010, Manafort had been successful in reinventing him as a pragmatic businessman and a "new-born democrat."[62] By 2013, however, that façade had been stripped away when massive nationwide protests erupted, sparked by President Yanukovych's sudden decision to suspend the promised signing of a trade agreement with the European Union and instead be closer to Russia.[63] He was doing everything Putin wanted, which sparked massive protests in Maidan (Independence) Square, the central square in Kiev. In the Orange Revolution of 2004, Yanukovych had been forced to give up the presidency in response to protests. Once again, he was the target as violence escalated during months of protests centered around Maidan Square. In the end, nearly one hundred activists and seventeen police officers were killed.

Finally, on February 21, 2014, President Yanukovych signed the Agreement on Settlement of the Political Crisis in Ukraine. The next day, Yanukovych tried to flee by charter plane but was stopped by border guards.[64] He finally escaped to Russia on February 23. Within twenty-four hours, he had been put on Ukraine's most wanted list and had become the target of a criminal case regarding the mass killings of civilians who were demonstrating.[65] Wanted by Ukraine for high treason, Yanukovych went into exile in Russia.

And what of the puppet master? What role, if any, did Paul Manafort have in all this? It was not clear exactly who was behind Yanukovych's decision to crush the protesters with force, but human rights lawyer Eugenia Zakrevskaya called on Manafort to clarify allegations that he may have played a role in the events that occurred in Kiev between February 18 and 20, 2014.

No conclusive evidence has surfaced regarding Manafort's role in the Maidan violence, but the allegations clearly struck close to home, according to text messages hacked from the phone of Manafort's daughter Andrea. In March 2015 Andrea texted her sister, Jessica, saying their father had "no moral or legal compass."

"You know he has killed people in Ukraine?" she wrote. "Knowingly. As a tactic to outrage the world and get focus on Ukraine. Remember when there were all those deaths taking place. A while back. About a year ago. Revolts and what not. Do you know whose strategy that was to cause that, to send those people out and get them slaughtered.[66]

"Don't fool yourself," Andrea texted. "That money we have is blood money."

CHAPTER SEVENTEEN

WAR BY OTHER MEANS

As the Ukraine crisis was building to a boil, a short story called "Without Sky" was published in a literary magazine called *Russian Pioneer*. Set in the future, after the "fifth world war,"[1] "Without Sky" was written by Natan Dubovitsky, whose literary endeavors would have been considerably less noteworthy were it not for the fact that his real name was Vladislav Surkov and from 2011 to 2013, as deputy prime minister to Vladimir Putin, he served as the Kremlin's chief ideologue and "gray cardinal."

As Soviet-born British author Peter Pomerantsev put it, Surkov, "'the puppet master who privatised the Russian political system' . . . is the real genius of the Putin era,"[2] a man who is essential to understanding how Putin created a new strain of authoritarianism that was far more subtle and more understated than the epic spectacles from the previous century.

On some level, it was not surprising that Surkov wrote a war story, given that life in Russia under Putin essentially means living a narrative of unending war, which is broadcast on Russian TV incessantly on programs about enemies of the state, Chechen terrorists, fascists taking over Ukraine, and the like, mixed with a dark romantic nostalgia for Russia's lost imperial past.[3]

Still, Surkov's war was fundamentally different from past wars:

This was the first non-linear war. In the primitive wars of the nineteenth, twentieth, and other middle centuries, the fight was usually between two sides: two nations or two temporary alliances. But now, four coalitions collided, and it wasn't two against two, or three against one. It was all against all.

And what coalitions they were! Not like the earlier ones. It was a rare state that entered the coalition intact. What happened was some provinces took one side, some took the other, and some individual city, or generation, or sex, or professional society of the same state—took a third side. And then they could switch places, cross into any camp you like, sometimes during battle.

The goals of those in conflict were quite varied. Each had his own, so to speak: the seizing of disputed pieces of territory; the forced establishment of a new religion; higher ratings or rates; the testing of new military rays and airships; the final ban on separating people into male and female, since sexual differentiation undermines the unity of the nation; and so forth.[4]

Perhaps what was most striking about Surkov was that he had made the stupendously unlikely journey from Moscow's dark, bohemian avant-garde art world to the highest reaches of the Kremlin. Think of an avid Lou Reed fan, an Andy Warhol devotee, or a performance art aesthete doing the job of Paul Manafort, Steve Bannon, or a master "political technician" who takes on a portfolio at the Kremlin that "include[s] ideology, media, political parties, religion, modernization, innovation, foreign relations, and modern art."[5]

A gangsta rap fan who has a Tupac Shakur photo on his desk, Surkov had run the gamut in his career from metallurgy to directing theater. All the while, he immersed himself in the netherworld of the Moscow art scene, where performance artist Oleg Kulik imitated rabid dogs "to show the brokenness of post-Soviet man" and camp drag artist Vladik Mamyshev-Monroe played out a post-Soviet Andy Warhol/RuPaul routine impersonating the likes of Marilyn Monroe, Adolf Hitler, and Rasputin.[6]

Then, in the nineties, Surkov reinvented himself and became a PR man for the dashing oil and banking billionaire Mikhail Khodorkovsky.[7] His first ad campaign for Khodorkovsky showed the oligarch holding bundles of cash and sent the message, "I've made it; so can you!" According to Peter Pomerantsev in the *Atlantic,* to the post-Soviet world, "the shape-shifting power" of PR and advertising, the magical ability to create new realities and to alter the way reality is perceived, was completely new. Surkov had discovered a new niche and had become a superstar.

By 1999, Surkov had joined the Kremlin as "political technologist," playing a role for Vladimir Putin that was akin to Karl Rove's position with George W. Bush, or the role Steve Bannon later played, albeit briefly, with Donald Trump. "I am the author, or one of the authors, of the new Russian system," Surkov asserted.[8]

As a political operative, Surkov's innovation was to merge theatrical techniques from the world of performance art with an unparalleled mastery of the dark arts of marketing and PR and apply the result in service to Putin's highly centralized, top-down bureaucracy.

Among other things, Surkov created Putin's image, much as he had done with Khodorkovsky, and when Putin arrested and jailed Khodorkovsky for fraud, the ever adaptable Surkov devised a campaign for that too, showing the formerly glamorous oligarch behind bars. Essentially, he helped turn Russia into one great reality TV show that could be reshaped on command to serve Putin's needs.[9]

To accomplish this, Surkov regularly met with the top brass of Russian TV to tell them who was to be banned from appearing on TV and who to attack or defend. He created fake far-right political parties such as the Nashi, the Russian counterpart of the Hitler Youth, that plagiarized Joseph Goebbels, the pitiless Nazi propagandist.[10] He took one rival candidate who was something of a democratic socialist and painted him, rather convincingly, as a Stalinist. He had Russian TV produce terrifying but phony TV stories about the imminent extermination and persecution of various groups. In other words, Surkov created a false reality consisting of fake news and alternative facts.

Of course, propaganda was nothing new. After all, even in the most liberal democracies, it is a truism that politicians lie. Public servants of all stripes—even the most benign—use "spin doctors" to advance their agendas. But it is also true that even the most egregious politicians usually lie in a way that advances a coherent and cohesive narrative to support their policies and agendas.

The character of Surkov's lies, however, was very different. As British documentary filmmaker Adam Curtis observed, "Surkov turned Russian politics into a bewildering, constantly changing piece of theater. He sponsored all kinds of groups, from neo-Nazi skinheads to liberal human rights groups. He even backed parties that were opposed to President Putin."[11]

Having done all that, Surkov proceeded to do something that no American political operative would ever do: Rather than fight for control of the narrative with his and Putin's adversaries, Surkov set out to destroy the very idea of reality. And by undermining the whole notion of truth, of what actually happened, Surkov was able to create a never-ending conflict about perception that helped the Putin regime's ability to control and manage Russia. The result was that the opposition was completely befuddled because the ceaseless flood of contradictory stories meant that no one knew what the enemy was up to or even who they really were, or what was really going on. Meanwhile, supporters who listened to lie after lie were allowed to choose whichever fiction they preferred to believe—and to dismiss the rest as fake news.

———

Surkov's information warfare tactics were enormously successful at home, where Russians were desperate for stability and a tough guy to stand up to the West.[12] And so the state-controlled media portrayed Putin as the head of a great civilization that would reclaim its former glory, liberate lands in the former Soviet Union, and not give in to the "gay-dominated and degraded" West.[13]

But Surkov's tactics were also exportable and as such became part of an arsenal Putin used in his quest to restore Russia's imperial glory. To understand Putin's overriding strategy, one has to look at Valery Gerasimov, the chief of the General Staff of the Armed Forces of Russia, who published a controversial two-thousand-word paper[14] in February 2013 that became known as the Gerasimov Doctrine* and concluded that costly armed invasions often fail to advance strategic goals—as Russia found out in Afghanistan in the eighties, and as the US has discovered in Vietnam, Afghanistan, and Iraq. "In the 21st century we have seen a tendency toward blurring the lines between the states of war and peace," Gerasimov wrote. "Wars are no longer declared and, having begun, proceed according to an unfamiliar template . . . The very 'rules of war' have changed. The role of nonmilitary means of achieving political and strategic goals has grown, and, in many cases, they have exceeded the power of force of weapons in their effectiveness."[15]

Gerasimov went on to assert that in today's undeclared war, the same objectives are often pursued by nonmilitary means.[16] As a result, he argued, it made sense to put conventional warfare on the same spectrum as "hybrid warfare" and "active measures" and the like. And so, after the Euromaidan protests in Ukraine, Putin launched a massive global offensive, intending to weaken not just the United States but Britain, NATO, the European Union, and, indeed, the entire Western Alliance, to roll back the gains they had made since the Cold War.

To that end, Russia began to pour money into pro-Russian parties in the former Soviet states of Georgia, Estonia, and Lithuania, all of which later came into power.[17] It began to do the same with right-wing candidates in the US and Western Europe who shared Putin's goal of dismantling the Western Alliance. There were spies, hackers, and informational warriors, sophisticated assaults on Facebook and other social media. The Mafia was just one weapon in Russia's arsenal. There were many, many more.

---

* It is worth noting that after the term "Gerasimov Doctrine" became popular in foreign policy circles, Mark Galeotti, a senior research fellow at the Institute of International Relations Prague who coined the term, disavowed it, and asserted that there is no single Russian doctrine and no single organizing principle. Instead, he wrote, "There is a broad political objective—to distract, divide, and demoralize—but otherwise it is largely opportunistic, fragmented, even sometimes contradictory."

Meanwhile, the Mafia went about ensnaring the powers that be with good old-fashioned *kompromat* that targeted their baser instincts (sex, money) and turned these would-be masters of the universe into puppets serving Russia's interests. These were the kinds of operations that were years—sometimes decades—in the making.

The biggest advantage to this new type of warfare was that it is hard to rouse opposition to an enemy no one can see. Indeed, the most striking facet of this new phenomenon may have been that a massive new global struggle had begun and barely anyone seemed to notice. Vladimir Putin had begun assaulting the sovereignty of various nations—a Virtual War, if you like—and almost no one was reporting on it in newspapers, on TV, on the radio, or on the Internet. The big unanswered question was what would happen when he took on the United States of America.

———

In early February 2013, about thirty or thirty-five guests gathered in a ballroom at the Hotel Ukraine in Moscow, aka the Radisson Royal, an immense thirty-four-story neoclassical skyscraper in the Stalinist style overlooking the Moskva River. Semion Mogilevich had taken over an entire floor of the hotel[18] to celebrate the fifty-fifth birthday of the legendary Sergei Mikhailov, aka Mikhas, presumed longtime leader of the Solntsevo crime gang. The entire restaurant had been reserved for the occasion.

Mogilevich and Mikhailov had been enjoying such revelries for three decades, through good times and bad. They first hung out at the Legendary Hotel Sovietsky in the mideighties with Viktor Averin, Alimzhan Tokhtakhounov,[19] and Vyacheslav Ivankov.[20] In 1995, there had been the horrendous assassination attempt on Mogilevich in Prague. The next year came the Mafia summit convened by Birshtein in Tel Aviv.

A lot had changed over the years. In 2009, Vyacheslav Ivankov had been gunned down by a sniper in Moscow, his murder presumably the fallout from a gang war with a Georgian crime boss, prompting a legendary funeral. A *New York Times* account of the funeral described Yaponchik as "royalty" among "these heavily tattooed crime barons," "the last of a mafia-like criminal class known as the Vory v Zakone, or Thieves-in-Law."[21]

But in general they had succeeded beyond their wildest dreams. The amount of money they had made was staggering. Mogilevich was said to be worth more than $10 billion.[22] After three decades running Solntsevo, Mikhailov had acquired a patina of respectability as a highly charitable businessman who had to fight accusations of criminal behavior by making one contribution after another to the Russian Orthodox Church, hospitals, orphanages, and the like.[23] And they were plugged in to the highest levels of the Kremlin as well as many of the former Soviet states.

And now they were gathered together for an intimate evening. The following account of that evening is based on a report[24] by Russian journalist Anastasia Kirilenko in *The Insider* and other sources including one who has had direct contact with the Russian underworld over many years, and who said the guests that evening "would not have been invited if they had not been well-known [to Mogilevich]. This was family. There were no strangers."[25]

In that context, the presence of two unnamed Americans was particularly striking, the source said, because they presented themselves as associates of Donald Trump, who was trying to build Trump Towers in Moscow and possibly Kazakhstan,[26] potentially with Mikhailov's Solntsevo gang as a partner.

Mikhailov and Viktor Averin didn't speak English, the source said, but they made sure that a third party monitored the Americans to find out whether they were full of hot air or whether there was something behind them. In other words, the leaders of the Solntsevo crime gang, one of the largest and most powerful gangs in the world, appear to have been doing due diligence to see if Trump's operation was up to snuff. As they listened attentively, the source said, they heard the Americans talking about a meeting they had had with Trump's daughter Ivanka. Then they discussed the possibility of making a return trip to Moscow "and getting together with Vova."[27]

"Vova" was said to be a reference to Vladimir Putin.

The Americans, the source said, were not introduced to everyone by name. One of them, however, was described as being five foot eight or nine, heavyset, with curly hair and a receding hairline, "definitely not slim, and having a California smile."

Later, the source thought that he was likely Felix Sater. The source maintained Sater had a connection with Mogilevich dating back to the nineties.

If true, that means that Sater really did have a triple life. If true, it means that he was not just a pump-and-dump con man/convicted felon who had reinvented himself as a government cooperator.

But Sater said that such allegations were completely false. "I wasn't [in Moscow] in 2013, and my passport doesn't have a Russian visa for that year," Sater told me.[28] "I testified before the House Intelligence Committee, the Senate Intelligence Committee, and the Senate Judiciary Committee that the only relationship I had with Mogilevich was helping the FBI figure out the scam in the YBM Magnex deal. The whole thing between Mogilevich and me is a lie, a fallacy, a falsehood."

The source had more. He claimed Mogilevich had a history with Donald Trump that dated back many years as well. "It didn't sound to me that this was the first business they did," he told me. The connection between the two men, the source said, had nothing to do with politics. "I don't think that anybody really believed that an idiot like Trump could even become mayor of a Texan village. A big businessman, let's get something on him."[29]

President Trump, of course, has denied any relationships with Russia, which presumably includes Mogilevich. There is no way to verify what relationship Trump and Mogilevich may have had—if any.

In the past, at gatherings like this one, Iosif Kobzon—aka the Russian Sinatra—had often provided the entertainment. The favored crooner of Russian TV and variety shows, Kobzon, with his all-too-noticeable hairpiece, was a favorite of Putin's, renowned for his alleged Mafia ties,[30] and straight out of central casting as a Russian version of Johnny Fontane in *The Godfather*. But now it was time to pass the torch to a younger generation. This time, according to *The Insider*, the entertainer was Emin Agalarov, an Azerbaijani-Russian singer-businessman. The son of Azerbaijani real estate billionaire Aras Agalarov, Emin could not be reached for comment and his attendance could not be verified.

Emin had been educated in the US, graduating from Tenafly High School in New Jersey and Marymount Manhattan College in New York before going on to work with the Crocus Group, a large real estate development company his father started, where he was in charge of restaurants, entertainment complexes, and a resort on the Caspian Sea.[31]

In Russia, the Agalarovs already had plenty of clout. The elder Agalarov had started out modestly enough in the late eighties, with a company called Saffron that exported Russian souvenirs—*matryoshka* Russian nesting dolls and the like—and computer equipment. In 1990, Agalarov started COMTEK Expositions Inc., a Soviet-American joint venture,[32] with, among others, Boris Kogan. A resident of Trump Tower who became a notorious arms dealer,[33] Kogan, who died in 2017, was the cofounder of a company, the Kaalbye Group, that has been accused of sending arms to President Bashar al-Assad's regime in Syria. Kaalbye has denied the charges.[34]

By the time privatization began in the early nineties, Aras was so well connected that he was able to get in on the ground floor of lucrative stock listings, including that of SurgutNefteGaz,[35] the gas and oil giant largely owned by Putin.[36] That privilege was granted only to a select few.

In an interview with the Russian daily *Moskovsky Komsomolets*, Agalarov denied having any significant ties to the underworld. "In the early 90's, I had many personal conflicts, conversations, meetings, 'arrows,' as they were then called. But we never colluded with anyone—and we never had any 'roofs' [i.e., *krysha*, or protection] . . . And how can bandits threaten such a person? Physical reprisal? But if they kill me, they will not get anything."[37]

In 2006, Emin married Leyla Aliyeva, the daughter of pro-Putin Azerbaijani president Ilham Aliyev, who, according to the Organized Crime and Corruption Reporting Project, "systematically seized shares in the most profitable businesses: banks, construction and telecommunications companies, gold mining and other deposits." President Aliyev was voted the most corrupt "person of the year" by the OCCRP in 2012, beating out Vladimir Putin and Albanian drug lord Naser Kelmendi.[38]

Not long after this politically connected marriage took place,

Crocus, which was largely known for developing upscale shopping malls, began to win massive government contracts, such as a $1.2 billion deal to develop the campus for Far Eastern Federal University in Vladivostok on Russia's Pacific Coast.[39] That was followed by enormous contracts to build part of a superhighway ringing Moscow, and two huge stadiums for the World Cup. Under Putin's reign, massive government contracts like that are awarded only to those who happen to be in Putin's good graces.

Meanwhile, the Agalarovs kept their close ties to the United States. In 2007, Emin bought a $3 million home in Alpine, New Jersey, and his father got an $8 million home there as well.[40] His sister, Sheila Agalarova, became a real estate agent nearby.

But for all the success the Agalarovs had, Emin's career as a pop star had never really taken off in the West. By 2006, he had begun releasing roughly one album per year but had never gotten traction in the US or Europe. So in 2012, he hired British-born publicist Rob Goldstone to come up with a strategy for breaking out as an international star.[41]

Before long, it became clear that partnering with Donald Trump might prove valuable for both father and son. For his part, Emin hoped Trump could line up a gorgeous woman—a Miss Universe, perhaps—for Emin's newest video. They might even get Trump himself to make a cameo appearance. Finally, the Agalarovs hoped to persuade Trump to stage the next pageant at Crocus City Hall, their 7,500-seat arena in Moscow. And if that were to take place, Aras would be sure to insist that Emin perform in front of that huge global audience.

If that couldn't make his career take off, nothing could.

––––––

On April 16, 2013, about two months after Mikhailov's fete in Moscow, police burst into an apartment on the sixty-third floor of Trump Tower on Fifth Avenue, just three floors below Donald Trump's penthouse, and rounded up suspects who were part of two gambling rings[42] that were allegedly run by Alimzhan Tokhtakhounov, a longtime associate of Mogilevich, Mikhailov, and other leaders of Solntsevo, from Uzbekistan.

Widely known as Taiwanchik, a diminutive that referred to his Asian facial features, Tokhtakhounov, according to a racketeering and money-laundering indictment before the Southern District of New York, had been designated as a *vor*, and, "as a Vor, Tokhtakhounov had substantial influence in the criminal underworld and offered assistance to and protection" to the Russian Mafia.[43] In 2011, Tokhtakhounov had made the FBI's "Ten Most Wanted" list—at number five, he was two slots behind Semion Mogilevich.

But Tokhtakhounov told the *New York Times* that he was innocent of all wrongdoing.[44] "I am not bad, like you think," he said. "I am not the Mafia, I am not a bandit."

Tokhtakhounov likely first developed ties to key figures in the Russian underworld when he was just a young boy growing up in Tashkent, Uzbekistan, through Mikhail Chernoy,[45] the metals-oligarch-in-waiting, who was a classmate of his younger brother and bestowed the nickname "Taiwanchik" on Tokhtakhounov. By the eighties, he had established good relations with Sergei Mikhailov, Vyacheslav Ivankov, and Anton Malevsky, leader of the Izmaylovskaya Organized Crime Group,[46] who appears to have been the source of the mysterious $350,000 check to Michael Cohen from Russian hockey player Vladimir Malakhov.[47]

In the early nineties, Tokhtakhounov represented Ivankov's interests in Germany, lived the high life with a spectacular nine-million-euro apartment in Paris's chic Sixteenth Arrondissement,[48] and had four villas in Italy,[49] all the while traveling the world as a cardsharp engaging in high-stakes gambling and money laundering. Then, in 2002, Tokhtakhounov allegedly fixed an ice-dancing competition at the Salt Lake City Winter Olympics.[50]

And now, in 2013, Tokhtakhounov was named as the ringleader in an indictment charging thirty-four members and associates of two Russian-American organized crime families—the Taiwanchik-Trincher organization, based in New York, Kiev, and Moscow, and the Nahmad-Trincher organization, based in Los Angeles and New York—with operating international sports books that laundered more than $100 million out of the former Soviet Union, through shell companies in Cyprus, and funneled it into investments in the United States in an

enterprise that was based in Trump Tower. The entire operation, prosecutors say, was working under the protection of Tokhtakhounov. In a
single two-month stretch, according to the federal indictment, the
money launderers paid Tokhtakhounov $10 million.[51]

This was no ordinary gambling bust. First of all, the apartment in
question, 63A-B, was one of the most sought-after units in the building and was so highly prized that Trump himself had bought it when
the building was completed in 1983.[52] In 1994, however, he personally
sold it to Oleg Boyko, an oligarch who was sometimes described as Yeltsin's personal banker.[53]

In May 2009, Boyko sold his Trump Tower apartment to Vadim Trincher, a high-stakes poker player who is a dual citizen of Israel and the
US, for $5 million. According to an FBI analysis of the purchase, the
funds used to buy the apartment moved through shell companies Trincher maintained in Cyprus.[54] By the time the gambling bust took place,
according to the Smoking Gun, the apartment, with its twenty-four-
karat-gold faucets, alabaster walls crafted by Portuguese artisans, and
$350,000 bathroom floor made of amethyst imported from Tanzania,
had become one of the most ostentatious apartments in what was already one of the most ostentatious buildings in America.[55] (Which did
not mean it was terrifically livable. A leak from the apartment upstairs
in 2012 caused $6 million in mold and mildew damage, the Trinchers
said, and was so bad they had to cancel a fund-raiser for Newt Gin-
grich's presidential race that year.)[56]

The sixty-third floor was not the only place in Trump Tower where
the ring was operating. Hillel "Helly" Nahmad, a billionaire Manhattan
art dealer who ran an eponymous New York gallery in the Carlyle Hotel
on the Upper East Side, had bought up the entire fifty-first floor of
Trump Tower[57] and used it as the site of a high-stakes gambling operation that catered to A-list celebrities and Russian oligarchs.[58]

Another key figure in the gambling ring was Anatoly Golubchik,
who owned a condo in Trump International Beach Resort in Sunny Isles
Beach, Florida.[59] As James Henry reported in the American Interest,[60]
Golubchik also owned a shell company called Lytton Ventures with a

director named Galina Telesh—who happens to have been married to Semion Mogilevich.

According to the indictment filed by United States Attorney Preet Bharara, the gambling ring had been in operation since 2006, if not earlier, and had laundered at least $100 million.[61] In the end, twenty-eight defendants pleaded guilty, including Helly Nahmad[62] and Vadim Trincher,[63] and went to jail.[64] As for Tokhtakhounov, he fled the country.

————

In June 2013, just two months after the Trump Tower gambling bust, Emin and Aras Agalarov traveled to Las Vegas to meet Trump while the Miss USA pageant was being held there.

Just as Aras had begun to position himself in the world of Russian real estate as Russia's Donald Trump, so had his son, Emin, reached out to Trump's Miss Universe Pageant in hopes of adding a bit of heat to his own career. In 2008, the Miss Universe pageant had featured entertainment by a newcomer named Lady Gaga, and Emin hoped a similar showcase might help him break through.[65] Olivia Culpo, the Miss Universe winner in 2012, ended up starring in Emin's music video for a song called "Amor."

By the time the video was released in May, Emin had become friendly with Paula Shugart, president of the Miss Universe Organization. He told *Forbes,* "And having had a few dinners and conversations with her, she said, 'We're always considering taking the contest to Russia and never really succeeded. And in the current year we have a lot of debts.'"

(A spokesperson for the Miss Universe Organization told the magazine that the issue of debt was not discussed.)[66]

And so, discussions began about presenting the next Miss Universe pageant in Moscow, specifically at Crocus City Hall, the Agalarov-owned theater.[67]

Finally, on June 15, 2013, the Agalarovs met with Trump in the lobby of the Trump International Hotel Las Vegas, where Trump's Miss USA pageant would be held in a few days. Trump greeted them warmly, chatted for ten minutes or so, and then shouted out to onlookers.[68] "Look who came to me!" Trump said. "This is the richest man in Russia!"[69]

That wasn't true, of course. The Agalarov fortune was less than $2 billion—not chump change, to be sure, but not good enough to break into Russia's top fifty oligarchs.[70]

None of which mattered to Trump. He was smitten. The Agalarovs were his new best friends. On the evening of June 15, he joined the Agalarov party of about twenty people in a private dining room at CUT, a restaurant in the Palazzo on the Strip, accompanied by Olivia Culpo; Nana Meriwether, the outgoing Miss USA; and his personal attorney, Michael Cohen.[71]

In addition to publicist Rob Goldstone, the Agalarovs brought another interesting figure to their party, Irakly "Ike" Kaveladze,[72] vice president of Aras's Crocus International, who had been working with Agalarov for nearly thirty years.

Born in 1965 in Soviet Georgia, Kaveladze had been classmates at the prestigious Moscow Finance Institute in the late eighties with Mikhail Prokhorov, now an owner of the Brooklyn Nets basketball team, and formed a partnership with him selling customized blue jeans while they were students.[73]

While he was in the US, Kaveladze had set up a company called International Business Creations, which established more than two thousand Delaware-based shell companies and hundreds of bank accounts for anonymous Russian clients. According to a congressional investigation, between 1991 and 2000, more than $1.4 billion in cash from Russia and Eastern Europe was laundered through accounts opened by Kaveladze.[74]

According to US officials, Kaveladze partnered in that operation with Boris Goldstein, a banker who attracted the attention of US officials, in a little-noticed footnote to a report by the General Accounting Office on Russian money laundering.[75] "We have obtained information that indicates that this individual has had a close relationship with companies associated with members of the former Soviet Union's intelligence agency," it read.[76] Goldstein denies any connection with shell companies founded for Russians or the KGB, and has issued libel proceedings.

Whether Trump was aware of such details or not, they did not seem to present an obstacle to him, and before long, the Agalarovs agreed to put up $20 million to produce the next Miss Universe pageant in Moscow in November.[77]

But the night was young, and there was still time for more fun. Trump's party moved on to the Act, a nightclub in the Palazzo mall. According to the *Las Vegas Sun,* acts "performed at the club were aggressively adult in nature,"[78] and were said to include simulated sex acts and naked girls pretending to urinate.[79]

———

On June 16, during the live telecast of the Miss USA pageant, Trump was joined onstage by Aras Agalarov and said he was thrilled to announce that the Miss Universe pageant would be staged in Moscow. "This will be one of the biggest and most beautiful Miss Universe events ever," Trump said.[80] "It is only fitting that the world's most iconic and premier beauty contest will take place in Russia's most premier venue, Crocus City Hall."

In fact, Trump was so excited that the next day he tweeted about the upcoming pageant. "Do you think Putin will be going to The Miss Universe Pageant in November in Moscow - if so, will he become my new best friend?" he wrote.[81]

But that wasn't enough. Trump Tower Moscow had not gotten off the ground in twenty-seven years of trying. Trump Vodka had flopped. Yet he still wanted to expand his brand into Russia, and that meant Putin had to be on board. Later that month, Trump typed a personal letter to the Russian president inviting him to attend. People familiar with the document said it showed how eager Trump was to win over Putin.[82]

According to the *Washington Post,* at the bottom, Trump added a postscript saying that he looked forward to seeing "beautiful" women during his trip.[83]

———

It was an interesting time for Trump to go back to Russia. For one thing, now that he was back on his feet again, his entire approach to money had done a 180. For years he had described himself as the "king of debt." He bragged about his ability to use it to his advantage. Trump had always loved debt. But suddenly, he had begun paying cash for almost everything.[84] Starting in 2006, he paid $12.6 million for an estate in Scotland, the *Washington Post* reported. Cash. Then came two homes in Beverly Hills. Cash again. Five golf courses on the East Coast. A winery in Virginia. All cash.

And so it went over the next few years. In 2014, he paid nearly $80 million for two golf courses, one in Ireland and one in Scotland. Where was that money coming from—at a time when no one in banking in the West would touch golf construction? Later that year, sportswriter and author James Dodson found out when he played with Donald and Eric Trump at the Trump National Golf Club in Charlotte, North Carolina.

Well aware that financing for new golf courses had been dead in the water since the 2008 recession, Dodson asked Eric where the Trumps were getting their money from.

"Well, we don't rely on American banks," Eric replied, according to Dodson.[85] "We have all the funding we need out of Russia."

Thanks to the Russians, Trump was very much back in business. In fact, things were going so well that he was once again considering running for president, in 2016. Indeed, not long after the gambling ring bust, lawyer Michael Cohen told the *New York Post* that Trump spent $1 million to research a run for the presidency. "At this point Mr. Trump has not made any decision on a political run, but what I would say is that he is exactly what this country needs," Cohen said.[86]

Trump could not have agreed more. "I made a speech in Michigan the other day, and they set their all-time record," he told Fox News. "It was a great, great event. It was an amazing event. And people in this country are just desperate for leadership. So, whether it's me or frankly let it be somebody, but somebody has to come along and straighten out this country."[87]

Every once in a while, however, Trump was apprised of the dark waters in which he was swimming. In July, Trump, who was developing a highly controversial golf resort in Scotland, was stunned when John

Sweeney, interviewing him for the BBC's *Panorama*, asked about Felix Sater and his ties to the Mafia.

"Why didn't you go to Felix Sater and say: 'You're connected with the Mafia. You're fired'?" Sweeney asked.

Clearly startled by the question, Trump lashed out. "John, maybe you're thick," he told Sweeney, "but when you have a signed contract, you can't in this country just break it. And by the way, I hate to do this but I do have that big group of people waiting, so I have to leave. I have to leave."

And so, with the camera still rolling, Trump walked out.

———

As his trip to Moscow approached, Trump became increasingly outspoken. In September, Putin wrote an op-ed in the *New York Times* calling for the US to stay out of the Syria conflict and attacking the idea of American exceptionalism. Trump adored Putin's patronizing put-down of Obama. "The way it was crafted was very, very interesting," Trump told Fox News.[88] "And it really is talking down to the president. There's no question about that. Well, absolutely amazing that he did that. And certainly, it's getting play all over the world. And it really makes him look like a great leader, frankly."

Trump couldn't wait to get to Moscow. He went on MSNBC to promote the Miss Universe pageant there, and said, "We have invited Vladimir Putin, and I know for a fact that he wants very much to come."

———

At 9:15 p.m. on Thursday, November 7, 2013, Donald Trump took a seat on a private jet owned by his friend Phil Ruffin,[89] who had married a former Miss Ukraine from the pageant.[90] They took off from Asheville, North Carolina, for Moscow and the Miss Universe pageant, and landed at Vnukovo International Airport in Moscow the next day, according to Bloomberg News.

Shortly after he landed, there was a brief business meeting.[91] Then Trump went to Moscow's Ritz-Carlton and was given the same presidential suite Barack and Michelle Obama had stayed in back in 2009. Meanwhile, a Russian approached Keith Schiller, Trump's longtime bodyguard, and offered to send five women to Trump's hotel room. Schiller, who later testified about it before Congress, said he viewed it as a joke, according to sources who were present at the interview. "We don't do that type of stuff," he responded.[92]

Putin spokesman Dmitry Peskov called to express regrets that Putin's schedule would not allow the two men to meet and Putin later sent a note and a decorative lacquered box as a gift, which was delivered by Aras Agalarov's daughter. Disappointed that Putin couldn't attend, Trump made much of the gift. "Putin even sent me a present, beautiful present, with a beautiful note," he said. "I spoke to all of his people."[93]

Sometime Friday, as shown by a photo posted by the restaurant to Facebook,[94] Trump and the Agalarovs went to a private dinner at Nobu Moscow, the famous Japanese restaurant co-owned by Emin's father and actor Robert De Niro. It was Aras Agalarov's birthday[95]—he was turning fifty-eight—but he had also organized the dinner for Trump to meet more than a dozen Russian oligarchs, including Herman Gref, the chief executive officer of state-controlled Sberbank of Russia, the nation's biggest bank.[96] Gref would be important if Sberbank were to finance any Trump-branded development with Crocus. No such project could possibly move forward without having the approval of the Russian government.

After many fruitless years of trying to develop a Trump Tower in Moscow, several real possibilities were now alive. Trump told *Real Estate Weekly* that he was in talks with Agalarov as well as three other groups. "There's no rush as far as I'm concerned," he said.[97] "The Russian market is attracted to me. I have a great relationship with many Russians, and almost all of the oligarchs were in the room."

Agalarov was developing a fifty-seven-acre site near the Crocus complex where the pageant was being held and hoped to build thousands of New York–style condos.[98] Trump's approach, however, was slightly different—sort of Trump SoHo 2.0. To that end, Tamir Sapir's son, Alex, and Rotem Rosen, both of whom had participated in the

SoHo development, had flown in from New York to meet with Agalarov and Donald to discuss replicating Trump SoHo in Moscow. "The Trump Soho has a lot of very high profile Russian visitors and they have been telling us they wish there was something modern and hip like it in Moscow," said Alex Sapir.[99] "Over the last ten years, there have been no big new hotels built in Moscow. A lot of people from the oil and gas businesses have come to us asking to be partners in building a product like Trump Soho there."

Still, it was striking that Trump had had no success developing a project in Moscow after twenty-six years of trying, at a time when there were dozens of Trump-branded towers all over the world. Donald Trump Jr.'s explanation that trust, crime, and fear got in the way was persuasive—but only *if* you believed corruption had presented an insurmountable stumbling block for Trump projects in the past.

A more convincing reason, the *Atlantic* reported, may have been that Felix Sater, in his various forays into Russia, had managed to alienate potential partners with his profligate conspicuous consumption—a substantial feat given the voracious appetite for extravagance among Russian oligarchs. "You really have to be very talented to do that," a Russian real estate consultant told the *Atlantic*. "And most people didn't take him seriously. He was ready to pay for a few bottles of Cristal in the club, but was not someone you want to make a serious deal with."[100]

Another factor—one that no one talked about—may have been the most relevant of all. In Moscow, Trump was unable to offer either his financiers or his condo buyers an amenity that had been vital to his comeback and to many of his business associates who came to his rescue after the Atlantic City fiasco. By this time, many hundreds of condo buyers had likely used shell companies and all-cash payments to purchase Trump-branded apartments. They were laundering money. Similarly, hundreds of millions of dollars in financing for various Trump-branded properties—in SoHo, Toronto, Panama, and more—had been repeatedly traced to Russians trying to get their money out of their country. And that is precisely what the Trump Moscow project could *not* offer. Laundering money for the wealthiest Russians meant getting their money out of Russia—not putting more in it.

———

Trump's second day in Moscow was Saturday, November 9, and according to Facebook posts by various onlookers, he was at the Ritz-Carlton Moscow for part of the day and spent some time getting a tour of the city. At some point that day, Trump was interviewed by MSNBC's Thomas Roberts, who was hosting the pageant that night, and asked Trump whether he had a relationship with Putin. "I do have a relationship with him," Trump said. Then he added that Putin had "done a very brilliant job. . . . He's done an amazing job—he's put himself really at the forefront of the world as a leader in a short period of time."[101]

The Miss Universe pageant had become a valuable asset for Trump, but it also served another function for him. He loved beautiful women. And, as the owner of the pageant, Trump told shock jock Howard Stern, he was entitled to do as he pleased. "I'll go backstage before a show, and everyone's getting dressed and ready and everything else," he said.[102] "You know, no men are anywhere. And I'm allowed to go in because I'm the owner of the pageant. And therefore I'm inspecting it . . . *Is everyone OK?* You know, they're standing there with no clothes. And you see these incredible-looking women. And so I sort of get away with things like that."

Not that the contestants approved. Tasha Dixon, a former Miss Arizona, told a CBS affiliate in Los Angeles that Trump barged into her dressing room in 2001 when she was a contestant. "He just came strolling right in. There was no second to put a robe on or any sort of clothing or anything. Some girls were topless. Other girls were naked," Dixon said. "Our first introduction to him was when we were at the dress rehearsal and half-naked changing into our bikinis."[103] There were other such stories. (In 2016, the Trump campaign called them "totally false.")

And so, that night, for the first time in the pageant's sixty-one-year history, with contestants from eighty-six countries on parade, the Miss Universe pageant was televised live all over the world from Moscow. Gabriela Isler of Venezuela was crowned as Miss Universe, and Emin performed two numbers.[104] Trump had told the Agalarovs that one billion people usually watched the telecast, a selling point the pageant broadcast in its press releases,[105] but in fact the audience was considerably smaller. (According to Deadline Hollywood, in 2013, about 3.8 million viewers in the US watched the show, down from 6.1 million the year before.)[106]

Trump was not the only denizen of Trump Tower to attend. It had been seven months since the FBI raid on the tower's fifty-first floor. Alimzhan Tokhtakhounov had fled the United States and was still on the lam. But here he was, a VIP guest on the red carpet near Donald Trump.[107] "We never thought we'd have a presidential candidate who was caught up with that level of criminality and corruption," said John Sipher, the former CIA agent in Moscow.[108] "We in the government knew to stay the fuck away. The fact that the Trump people were actually attracted to that is really dangerous."

———

Later on that night, the Daily Beast reported,[109] the Agalarovs and Herman Gref, the head of the giant Sberbank of Russia, threw a huge dinner party for Trump. He was thrilled by all the attention he was getting. "I was with the top-level people, both oligarchs and generals, and top-of-the-government people," he said later, on the Hugh Hewitt radio show.[110] "I can't go further than that, but I will tell you that I met the top people, and the relationship was extraordinary."

Exactly what happened next is unclear. Trump later told FBI director James Comey that he returned to New York and didn't even stay overnight. "He said he arrived in the morning, did events, then showered and dressed for the pageant at the hotel," Comey wrote in a memo. "Afterwards, he returned only to get his things because they departed for New York by plane that same night."[111]

But Trump's account, as reported by Comey, does not ring true.[112] The time of landing is unspecified in flight records, according to Bloomberg, but it was early enough to afford Trump much of Friday in Moscow during the day, all of Friday night, and all day Saturday before his flight left at 3:58 a.m. Sunday.

The bottom line was that Trump claimed not to have even spent one night in Moscow, but according to records, he had one full overnight in Moscow, and another night that went into the early hours.

That left some time, but not much, for fun. Answers to what exactly happened during that period may—or may not—be found in a report put together by former MI6 agent Christopher Steele that has become famously known as the Steele Dossier.

Steele, who is fluent in Russian, was no naïf when it came to the Kremlin. Back in the early nineties, he had worked in Moscow under diplomatic cover out of the British embassy during the turbulent ascent of the oligarchs. But he returned to London, and in November 2006, Steele was put in charge of MI6's investigation into the assassination of Alexander Litvinenko. When the official report of the Litvinenko Inquiry was released, it backed up Steele's findings that the murder was an FSB hit that was "probably approved" by Vladimir Putin.[113]

Steele soon left MI6 for the private sector and in 2009 started a small investigative-research firm called Orbis Business Intelligence. Among his clients was the FBI, which hired him to help crack Tokhtakhounov's gambling and money-laundering ring in Trump Tower. Steele became aware of Tokhtakhounov's presence at the Miss Universe pageant and was agog at his proximity to Trump. "It was as if all criminal roads led to Trump Tower," he told friends.[114]

In the spring of 2016, Orbis agreed to become a subcontractor for Fusion GPS, a research firm in Washington that had been hired by the Perkins Coie law firm, which represented both Hillary Clinton's presidential campaign and the Democratic National Committee.[115] Steele's job was to investigate Republican candidate Donald Trump.

The Steele Dossier, much of which has not been corroborated, became a sensation when it was made public by BuzzFeed in 2017 for its astonishing allegations that Trump's campaign "accepted a regular flow of intelligence from the Kremlin, including on his Democratic and other political rivals," that Russian operatives had been cultivating Trump for years, and that they had obtained *kompromat* by recording videos of Trump engaging in "personal obsessions and sexual perversions."[116]

If there was *kompromat* on Trump, it seemed likely that the Mafia would know, so I posed that question to a knowledgeable source who had direct experience with the Russian underworld: Does Mogilevich have *kompromat* on Trump? I asked. Does the Mafia know?

"Of course they do," he told me. "Everyone talks about it, Seva [Mogilevich] and Mikhas [Mikhailov]."

But my source cautioned that he had not seen any *kompromat* first-hand, only that he had heard about it. His allegations have not been corroborated.

CHAPTER EIGHTEEN

THE BATTLE IS JOINED

In March 2014, Russia allegedly conducted a massive Internet disruption in Ukraine just as it was seizing and annexing the Crimea. As usual, Roger Stone, Paul Manafort's sometime partner, seemed to know exactly what was going on and reveled in its venality, according to Politico, by sending out an email to a small group of friends.

"Where is Paul Manafort?" Stone's email asked. Among the multiple choices he suggested were the following: "Was seen chauffeuring Yanukovych around Moscow," and "Was seen loading gold bullion on an Army Transport plane from a remote airstrip outside Kiev and taking off seconds before a mob arrived at the site."

The final option was: "Is playing Golf in Palm Beach."[1]

But Manafort was merely the tip of the iceberg.

By this time, many of the leaders of the Republican Party were effectively on the payroll of the Kremlin, which had become as effective as Big Oil or Big Pharma at using K Street lobbyists to serve its agenda. The only difference was that they were essentially serving the interests of Vladimir Putin in the most heated geostrategic sector on the planet.

Russian oligarch Oleg Deripaska, who had hired former senator and Republican presidential nominee Bob Dole as a lobbyist in 2005, later tried, unsuccessfully, to woo Senator John McCain, the GOP presidential nominee in 2008. Russian conglomerate Alfa paid nearly $2 million in lobbying fees to Barbour Griffith & Rogers, the lobbying firm co-founded by former Mississippi governor Haley Barbour.[2]

Similarly, in 2014, former Senate majority leader Trent Lott (R-MS) and former senator John Breaux (D-LA) became the main lobbyists for Gazprombank, a subsidiary of Russia's largest supplier of natural gas. More recently, in 2016, millions of dollars in Russian money was funneled to Senate majority leader Mitch McConnell[3] and other high-profile Republicans to finance GOP senatorial candidates.

Foreign nationals are prohibited from contributing to Senate races, but, according to the *Dallas Morning News,* during the 2015–16 election season, Ukrainian-born oligarch Leonard "Len" Blavatnik, who has British-American dual citizenship, put a small fraction of his $20 billion fortune into GOP Senate races. McConnell, who took $2.5 million for his GOP Senate Leadership Fund from two of Blavatnik's companies, was the leading recipient. Others included political action committees for Senator Marco Rubio, Senator Lindsey Graham, Ohio governor John Kasich, and Arizona senator John McCain.

When it came to getting legal representation, Russians went to the most connected lawyers in the land. The fourth-largest law firm in the United States,[4] Jones Day, itself represented at least ten major corporations and organizations that were close to Putin's heart, a group comprising both Russia's most powerful corporations and several of the oligarchs who came to Trump's rescue.

Jones Day's Russian clients included Oleg Deripaska's Basic Element; the Alfa Group and Access-Renova Group, which jointly own billions of dollars in oil and gas assets; Alfa Bank, the largest private commercial bank in Russia and part of the Alfa Group; Letterone, a $30 billion holding company for assets in technology, oil, and gas; Rosneft, the world's largest listed oil company; the Sapir Organization, which helped fund Bayrock's Trump SoHo; the Eurasian Natural Resources Corporation, run by Alexander Mashkevich; the Russian Standard Group, whose holdings included the Miss Russia pageant; Sukhoi Civil Aircraft, a large military aircraft manufacturer in which Mogilevich had an interest; the Alfa-Access-Renova Group, a joint venture that helped make

Leonard Blavatnik one of the wealthiest people in the world; and Viktor Vekselberg's Renova Group.

Another Jones Day client, the National Rifle Association, according to McClatchy, has been the subject of a multiagency investigation into whether "the Kremlin secretly helped fund efforts to boost Trump"[5] by funneling money through the NRA.

In July 2018, Maria Butina, an alleged Russian agent in the US, was indicted by special counsel Robert Mueller on charges of being a covert agent who had infiltrated the NRA and other conservative groups, including the organizers of the National Prayer Breakfast. Butina, who pleaded not guilty, allegedly reported to Alexander Torshin, the deputy head of the Russian central bank who had ties to Russian intelligence services.

This, in effect, was the Putin lobby, putting its money into K Street and powerful white-shoe law firms to help legitimize and promote the agendas of Russian oligarchs whose billions effectively represented the theft of Russia's patrimony.

And when it came to fighting the growing power and reach of the Russian offensive, exactly how was America's national security apparatus handling this mounting threat? As John Sipher told me, the CIA had issued operational directives to stay away from the Russian mob. These issues were not in their purview. As for the FBI, under director Robert Mueller, it had made Semion Mogilevich the target of a special new task force in Budapest in 2005, at a time when Mogilevich largely based his operations there.

"As soon as the Task Force began investigating his activities, Mogilevich realized he could no longer use Budapest as his base of operations," Mueller said in a 2005 speech.[6] "He immediately fled the country, and is now hiding in Moscow. Working closely with Hungarian authorities, United States prosecutors obtained a 45-count indictment against Mogilevich and three other criminals, charging them with money laundering, securities fraud, and racketeering."

But in the end, Mogilevich eluded their grasp and settled in Moscow. The FBI closed down the Budapest outpost from which it had tracked Mogilevich. Meanwhile, the foreboding assortment of murderous gangsters and tattooed thugs known as the Russian Mafia had climbed the ladder of white-collar respectability, insinuated itself in multibillion-dollar global corporations, and taken on the protective coloring provided by K Street lobbyists and white-shoe law firms. They were now hard-wired into some of the most powerful Republican politicians in the country.

Like a slow-motion train wreck that can't be stopped, a national security catastrophe of historic proportions was in the works. And it was happening under the noses of the top figures in American law enforcement, whom the Russians were going to for criminal representation. It wasn't enough that William S. Sessions had taken on Mogilevich, the most feared mobster in the world, as a client. Sessions's successor as FBI director, Louis Freeh, was also working for the Russians.

In Freeh's case, the client in question was Denis Katsyv's Cyprus-based Prevezon Holdings, a giant real estate firm that hired Freeh to negotiate a settlement with the US government over an alleged money-laundering/tax-fraud scheme involving Kremlin officials.[7] Katsyv is a Ukrainian businessman whose company appeared to be a beneficiary of the $230 million tax fraud.

Prevezon won international attention in 2008 when its ties to the massive tax scam were uncovered by Russian tax lawyer Sergei Magnitsky, an anticorruption specialist who investigated the case on behalf of Hermitage Capital Management, an investment firm cofounded by Bill Browder. After he began investigating the case, Magnitsky was arrested and imprisoned for eleven months without trial.[8] According to the official death certificate, Magnitsky died in prison of "closed cerebral cranial injury."[9] Instead of pursuing the real criminals, Russian authorities had gone after Magnitsky. According to his prison diary, investigators kept trying to persuade him to testify against Hermitage and drop his charges against the police and tax authorities. When Magnitsky refused, he was moved to worse and worse sections of the prison.[10] During his imprisonment, he developed several serious medical conditions but was denied appropriate care, was physically assaulted, and died at the Matrosskaya Tishina Prison in 2009, at the age of thirty-seven.[11]

Back in 1997, as FBI director, Louis Freeh had warned that Russian organized crime posed a threat to the US that far transcended mere criminality and that there was now a greater danger of nuclear attack by such criminal enterprises than there was by the Soviet Union at the height of the Cold War.[12] But now he represented Prevezon, which had hired him to settle its dispute with the US government. Later, Freeh bought a $9.38 million mansion in Palm Beach, Florida, just a ten-minute drive from Mar-a-Lago.[13]

⸺

Meanwhile, relations between Russia and Western officials were approaching a Cold War–level chill. Putin's bête noire was the 2016 Democratic presidential candidate, former secretary of state Hillary Clinton. In fact, Clinton had made her feelings about Putin clear in 2008, when, as a senator, she had joked about George W. Bush's famous assessment of Putin. "I looked the man in the eye," the former president had said, "I was able to get a sense of his soul; a man deeply committed to his country and the best interests of his country."

Hillary, of course, saw things quite differently. Because Putin was a KGB agent, she said, "by definition he doesn't have a soul."[14]

Three years later, in 2011, when mass protests against Putin accused him of having rigged recent elections, Putin blamed then–secretary of state Clinton for giving aid and comfort to the demonstrators with statements of support. Even though she had gone along with and implemented Obama's reset policy to improve Russian-American relations, Putin knew that Clinton had a much tougher line toward Moscow than others in Obama's cabinet. And when Hillary joined the protesters and said the elections were "dishonest and unfair,"[15] Putin saw her assessment as a deliberate attempt to undermine his power. "We need to safeguard ourselves from this interference in our internal affairs," Putin said.[16]

Ultimately, he feared, she was such a strong supporter of "regime change" policies that, if elected in 2016, she might pose a serious threat to his survival. "[Putin] was very upset [with Clinton] and continued to be for the rest of the time that I was in government," Michael McFaul, who served as the US ambassador to Moscow until 2014, told Politico. "One could speculate that this is his moment for payback."

If Putin's hired guns went after Hillary, it would not be the first time. Starting in 2011, Paul Manafort, operating on behalf of Ukrainian president Yanukovych, placed articles critical of Hillary Clinton in the *Wall Street Journal* and on various websites, according to the *Guardian,* as part of a "black ops" operation against her.[17]

But Putin's calculus involved far more than Ukraine and Hillary Clinton, and when he intervened in the Middle East on behalf of Syria, it was because he had stumbled upon a diabolical and grandiose plan that would drive a dagger deep into the heart of the Western Alliance.

It began in September 2015, when Putin announced that he would join Syrian president Bashar al-Assad in the fight against ISIS. In addition to striking at ISIS, however, Russian air attacks hit countless civilians, so many that in 2016 Amnesty International accused the Russians of joining Assad forces in deliberately targeting hospitals. Before long, Russia, intentionally or not, was creating a massive flow of refugees into Europe. "Russia is extensively involved in the Syrian conflict but has done virtually nothing to help the 11 million people who have lost their homes and livelihoods as a result," said Bill Frelick, refugee rights program director at Human Rights Watch.[18]

According to Senate testimony in 2016 by General Philip Breedlove, the supreme allied commander of NATO, Russia's inaction, far from being an oversight, was part of a deliberate and cunning policy to use the influx of millions of refugees as a political weapon that would destabilize Western Europe. "Together Russia and the Assad regime are deliberately 'weaponizing' migration in an attempt to overwhelm European structures and break European resolve," Breedlove said.[19]

In other words, now that Russia had, inadvertently perhaps, helped spark an immigration crisis that overwhelmed the entire continent, it began a stealth campaign that aided right-wing, anti-immigrant, populist movements and politicians in Great Britain, Germany, the Netherlands, France, Italy, Austria, and more.

The more Russia inflamed the crisis in Syria, it found, the more refugees it created, and the more Russia was able to weaken the European

Union. The migration emergency served as the perfect catalyst for further action. As Great Britain prepared to vote on whether or not to exit the European Union (aka Brexit), for instance, Russia jumped into the fray. Nigel Farage, leader of the far-right UK Independence Party, fanned anti-EU sentiment while criticizing sanctions against Russia and issuing complimentary appraisals of President Putin. Hundreds of millions of dollars from dubious Russian sources were laundered in British banks.[20] Then, as the vote for Brexit approached in June of 2016, Russian cyberwarfare began. According to research conducted jointly by experts from the University of California at Berkeley and Swansea University in Wales, no fewer than 150,000 Twitter accounts linked to Russia began to tweet inflammatory and divisive messages about Brexit, Muslims, and immigrants.[21]

Quietly, almost unseen, Putin also attacked NATO's Eastern flank, through Poland—and again Mogilevich played a key role in an operation that, according to Polish investigative reporter Tomasz Piatek, succeeded in compromising NATO. The author of the bestselling *Macierewicz and His Secrets,* Piatek describes a series of convoluted scams, starting in the late eighties with David Bogatin—the same David Bogatin who laundered money through Trump Tower in 1984 and pioneered the Red Daisy gas tax scam—who moved to Poland and, according to Piatek, "robbed a lot of Poles through his creation of the infamous First Commercial Bank in Lublin," one of the first commercial banks in post-communist Poland.[22]

According to Piatek, operatives tied to Mogilevich and the Solntsevskaya crime gang were principals in a 2014 wiretapping scandal where top Polish politicians were secretly recorded at their favorite restaurants—all of which helped the pro-Russia Law and Justice Party to win the elections.[23] "The scandal was similar to the wiretapping scandal that led to the fall of Hungarian prime minister [Ferenc] Gyurcsány's government and helped Viktor Orbán [Putin's Hungarian ally] win subsequent elections," Piatek said.[24]

The upshot was that in November 2015, when the Law and Justice Party won an absolute majority in Poland for the first time, it appointed Antoni Macierewicz as minister of defense. At one time or another in his career, Piatek reported, Macierewicz had given access to classified documents to a company controlled by the Russian Mafia in Poland. Among other failings, he had given a radio interview about *Protocols of the Elders of Zion,* the fraudulent pamphlet that purports to be a Jewish plan for world domination, about which he said, "Experience shows that there are such groups in Jewish circles."[25]

Once he became minister of defense, Piatek says, Macierewicz began recruiting pro-Kremlin, neo-Nazi youngsters as soldiers to fight in his new Territorial Defense Force, which reported directly to him—that is, not to the General Command of the Polish army, with which it was in direct competition—and began transferring officers and resources from the army to the TDF. As a result, Piatek says, "Macierewicz has been accused of destroying the Polish army and its relationship with its Western Allies."[26]

And so it went—not just in the UK, Poland, or Hungary, but all over Europe. As a 2018 minority staff report by the Senate Foreign Relations Committee put it, since 2004, Putin had launched a relentless asymmetric assault on democracy in Russia, Europe, and the United States using an "arsenal that includes military invasions, cyberattacks, disinformation, support for fringe political groups, and the weaponization of energy resources, organized crime, and corruption. The Kremlin has refined the use of these tools over time and these attacks have intensified in scale and complexity across Europe."

In Eastern Europe, Russia attacked Ukraine, Georgia, Montenegro, Serbia, Bulgaria, and Hungary. In the Baltic, it attacked Latvia, Lithuania, and Estonia. In Scandinavia, it went after Denmark, Finland, Norway, and Sweden. And it went after the Netherlands, France, Germany, Spain, and Italy as well. Ultimately, Putin's goal, the Senate report said, was "to attack the democracies of Europe and the United States and undermine the transatlantic alliance upon which Europe's peace and prosperity have depended for over 70 years."[27]

Needless to say, the Russian Mafia was not the only weapon in Putin's arsenal of "active measures," a Russian term for political and economic warfare by its security services. Both domestically and with foreign adversaries, Russia hacked its foes, as it did when it captured emails from

Hillary Clinton and her allies, so it could release them and damage her presidential campaign.

Both domestically and abroad, Putin asserted ironclad control over the Russian narrative through disinformation and propaganda. Only a strong leader like Putin could remind a wronged and humiliated Russia of past glories and rebuild his country into a great superpower again. Only Putin could have annexed Crimea and pushed back against the West.

As for the opposition, by this time, dozens of journalists and dissidents had been killed, including Boris Nemtsov, the former deputy prime minister under Yeltsin, who was one of Putin's most prominent critics until February 2015, when he was shot from behind near Moscow's Red Square. To that same end, Putin also had the power to destroy media oligarchs who did not serve his agenda—as Vladimir Gusinsky and Boris Berezovsky found out when they were forced into exile.[28]

Outside Russia, where Putin didn't control the media, the Russians resorted to more sophisticated tactics. They hijacked social media and exploited algorithms to make highly provocative "fake news" go viral. They harnessed the power of social media to amplify the rabid fanaticism of the so-called alt-right, in the process turning Facebook into one of the most powerful publishers of phony news stories and propaganda from Russia and the alt-right in the world. They used third parties, such as Julian Assange and WikiLeaks, to make it seem as if leaks had emanated from heroic whistleblowers, rather than being obtained by Russian intelligence, and they deliberately used not only "alternative facts" and fake news but bogus websites that pretended to *correct* fake news, and, in the process, upended the very notion of truth, of reality itself, of what is real. In all, according to the German Marshall Fund's Alliance for Securing Democracy, "the Russian government has used cyberattacks, disinformation, and financial influence campaigns to meddle in the internal affairs of at least 27 European and North American countries since 2004."[29]

———

Within that context, the Russian Mafia played the central role in nurturing an exceptionally pliant asset who initially seemed to be more of a person of influence than a man with real political clout. It had been nearly thirty years since Trump welcomed David Bogatin to Trump Tower and facilitated the sale of five apartments, which helped launder Russian Mafia money for the first time. Since then, he had received many millions of dollars—perhaps billions—for his condos. Vyacheslav Ivankov had lived at Trump Tower and run operations for Mogilevich. Bayrock had been there from 2002 to 2008, and helped Trump rise out of the ashes of Atlantic City and become a billionaire yet again— potentially leaving him deeply, deeply indebted to the Russian Mafia.

And yet at 11:05 a.m. on June 16, 2015, Donald Trump stepped on the descending escalator in the pink-marbled six-story atrium at Trump Tower and began a journey into history by announcing his candidacy for the Republican nomination for the presidency of the United States.[30]

Trump's decision to run had been in the works for some time. In January, Emin Agalarov and Rob Goldstone, Emin's publicist, had visited Trump in Trump Tower. Having seen Emin perform at the Miss Universe pageant, and having appeared in one of Emin's music videos, Trump had told him, "Maybe next time, you'll be performing at the White House?"[31]

At about the same time, Trump had hired Corey Lewandowski as his campaign manager. In March, he had formed a presidential exploratory committee. And now, three months later, Trump was proclaiming that we had become a nation of "losers" and that America needed someone "really rich"—namely, him—to restore its lost economic primacy.[32]

Starting off by saying he would build a "great, great wall" to stop illegal immigration, and have Mexico foot the bill, he added, "Nobody builds walls better than me—believe me—and I build them very inexpensively," he said.

"I don't need anybody's money. It's nice," he said.[33] "I'm not using donors. I don't care. I'm really rich . . . I'm proud of my net worth. I've done an amazing job."[34]

At the time, Trump was still treated largely as a novelty. "Clown Runs for Prez," read the cover headline of the New York *Daily News*.[35] A 4 percent showing in a *Washington Post*/ABC News poll put him in a tie for ninth place among Republican candidates. Worse, the same poll showed him to have a 16 percent favorable and 71 percent unfavorable rating.[36] It was later revealed by the *Hollywood Reporter* that Trump even had to resort to paying $50 each to background actors—like extras in movies—to pretend they were Trump supporters cheering him on at the Trump Tower atrium.[37]

To the most seasoned political observers, Trump was an incredible long shot, and they didn't have a clue about his ties to the Russian mob. On the other hand, Putin now had a candidate of his own choosing representing one of America's two major political parties as the 2016 elections were about to get under way.

By this time, Mogilevich had done his job. He had targeted, ensnared, and compromised a powerful and influential American businessman. But now that Trump had real political prospects, Putin went ahead full bore and pulled out other weapons in his arsenal. The Kremlin's "active measures" were about to go fully operational. The battle had been joined.

CHAPTER NINETEEN

BACK CHANNELS

Just two days after announcing his candidacy, on June 18, 2015, Trump appeared on the Sean Hannity show on Fox News, where he was asked if he had had any contact with Vladimir Putin, and how he might deal with him if he were elected.

"Yes," Trump said. "So I was there two years ago. We had a tremendous success with the Miss Universe contest in—I own Miss Universe, Miss USA, all of that, and it does great. It's on NBC, but that's OK. But it does fantastically well. And two years ago, we had it in Moscow, and it was a tremendous success. And I got to meet everybody. I got to meet all . . ."

"Did you talk to him?" Hannity asked.

"I don't want to say. But I got to meet all of the leaders. I got to meet all—I mean, everybody was there. It was a massive event. And let me tell you, it was tremendous."

For an opening, it was a bit tentative and coy, especially for the bombastic Trump. Nevertheless, he had just uttered his first words as a candidate about Putin. "We can get along," Trump said.[1] It was official. The Trump-Putin connection had gone public.

A few weeks later, in July, at FreedomFest, a self-styled "festival of free minds," in Las Vegas, Trump announced he would probably reverse President Obama's policies and roll back sanctions against Russia. "I know Putin and I'll tell you what, we get along with Putin," Trump said.[2] "I don't think you'd need the sanctions. I think we would get along very, very well."

As it happened, Trump's statement was an answer to a question posed by Maria Butina, a Russian operative who was a protégé of Putin ally Alexander Torshin. No sanctions? It was everything Putin and the oligarchs wanted.

As if in response, Putin offered Trump praise in return. "He says that he wants to move to another, closer level of relations," Putin told reporters. "Can we really not welcome that? Of course, we welcome that." He added that Trump was a "colorful and talented" person, a compliment Trump said afterward he regarded as an "honor."[3]

Meanwhile, the Russian cyberwarfare campaign against the United States was already under way. According to a January 2017 report by the Office of the Director of National Intelligence (ODNI), "Assessing Russian Activities and Intentions in Recent US Elections," the Central Intelligence Agency, the Federal Bureau of Investigation, and the National Security Agency concluded with "high confidence" that "Russian President Vladimir Putin ordered an influence campaign in 2016 aimed at the US presidential election. Russia's goals were to undermine public faith in the US democratic process, denigrate Secretary Clinton, and harm her electability and potential presidency. We further assess Putin and the Russian Government developed a clear preference for President-elect Trump."[4]

To gather ammunition for that influence campaign, on an undetermined date in July 2015, a bit more than forty-three years after five burglars broke into Democratic National Committee offices at the Watergate Hotel in Washington, the DNC offices were broken into again—not by burglars, but by Russian hackers.

The Democrats first found out about it in the most indirect way imaginable. In September, an agent from the FBI's Washington field office left a phone message at the DNC office for an outsourced low-level computer technician who did not bother to return the call. "They left a phone message at the help desk of the DNC," John Podesta, then Hillary Clinton's campaign chairman, told CNN.[5] "They didn't treat it with the kind of seriousness, I think, that it deserved."

According to the DNC, the FBI repeatedly called its help desk but never reached out to DNC leaders. As a result, according to a complaint filed by the Democratic National Committee against the Russian Federation and the Trump campaign, "Russian intelligence gained access to Democratic National Committee (DNC) networks and maintained that access until at least June 2016." Consequently, the complaint said, the GRU—Russian military intelligence—was able to "exfiltrate" large volumes of data from the DNC and leading Democratic officials.[6]

The ODNI report also noted that Putin publicly said it was important the DNC data was exposed to WikiLeaks. "We assess with high confidence that the GRU relayed material it acquired from the DNC and senior Democratic officials to WikiLeaks," the report said. "Moscow most likely chose WikiLeaks because of its self-proclaimed reputation for authenticity."[7]

———

Meanwhile, Trump's candidacy took off like a rocket. In a jam-packed field of seventeen Republican candidates jostling for the nomination, Trump, ever the master showman, surged to the fore, a bombastic New York tycoon pandering to tens of millions of "forgotten" Americans, promising to "make America great again."

Having put together a base in part by falsely claiming that President Obama had been born in Kenya and therefore was not eligible to be president, Trump derided Jeb Bush as "low-energy," Senator Ted Cruz as "Lyin' Ted," Senator Marco Rubio as "Little Marco," and Hillary Clinton always, of course, as "Crooked Hillary."

By mid-July, just a few weeks after he announced his candidacy, Trump had claimed first place in two major polls.[8] He called Mexicans "rapists." He mocked war hero John McCain for getting captured. One after another, Trump trampled the widely accepted norms of American political discourse and not only got away with it, but awakened and inflamed the passions of a right-wing anti-immigrant fervor that had been the sleeping giant in American politics. He was so often compared to P. T. Barnum that a Nexis search in May 2018 found more than fifteen hundred articles in which Trump was mentioned with Barnum.

He represented something larger than life, even if that reputation never held up to scrutiny.

Opponents who underestimated the loyalty of his base did so at their peril. The more he broke the rules, the more they loved it. "I could stand in the middle of Fifth Avenue and shoot somebody and I wouldn't lose any voters, okay?" Trump told supporters in Iowa about a week before the state's caucuses.[9] "It's, like, incredible."

The mere fact that Trump was running for president did not mean he had abandoned his dreams of building a Trump Tower in Moscow. Far from it. In fact, the relationship he had cultivated with the Agalarovs was still very much alive. On July 24, 2015, Rob Goldstone, the music promoter who worked with Emin Agalarov, invited Trump to Moscow to celebrate the birthday of Emin's father, Aras Agalarov, the real estate oligarch.

In an email to Trump's assistant, Rhona Graff, Goldstone proffered an inducement. "Maybe he would welcome a meeting with President Putin," Goldstone wrote.[10]

Trump didn't take the bait, but Felix Sater was still traveling to Moscow on behalf of the illusory Trump Tower in Russia. By this time, Bayrock was so deeply entangled in litigation that it had folded its tent. Felix Sater had become a "senior adviser" to Trump and continued to work with his old pal Michael Cohen, trying to draw up deals for Trump. "We did not own real estate together, but certainly looked at a bunch of stuff together, during Trump and post-Trump," Sater told Talking Points Memo.[11] "After I left [Bayrock], I was still looking at deals for Trump, but I would think about real estate with Michael. [It] was just two real estate guys talking."

According to emails published by the *New York Times,* Sater saw the eventual realization of Trump Tower Moscow as a coup for Trump that would enhance his chances as a candidate, not conflict with them. In the emails, Sater boasted to Cohen that he had arranged financing for a Trump Tower in Moscow from VTB, a bank that was under US sanctions for undermining democracy in Ukraine.[12]

On November 3, 2015, he also emailed Cohen, "I arranged for Ivanka to sit in Putins [*sic*] chair at his desk and office in the Kremlin. I will get

Putin on this program and we will get Donald elected. We both know no one else knows how to pull this off without stupidity or greed getting in the way. I know how to play it and we will get this done. Buddy our boy can become President of the USA and we can engineer it. I will get all of Putins [*sic*] team to buy in on this, I will."[13]

In one of his emails, Sater vowed to pull out all the stops and use his connections to get Putin to praise Trump's business expertise. "If he says it we own this election," Sater wrote. "Americas [*sic*] most difficult adversary agreeing that Donald is a good guy to negotiate."[14]

According to someone familiar with the emails, the *Washington Post* reported, Sater also wrote Cohen something like, "Can you believe two guys from Brooklyn are going to elect a president?"[15]

———

Meanwhile, as the Trump campaign staffed up, Russophile policy wonks flocked to Trump's side and began solidifying their ties to Moscow. On December 15, 2015, Trump campaign foreign policy adviser Lieutenant General Michael Flynn attended a gala dinner in Moscow in honor of RT, the Russian media outlet on which Flynn appeared occasionally as an analyst, and sat next to President Putin, leading Politico to characterize him as one of the most intriguing examples of "how the Russians have recruited disaffected members" of the US political establishment.[16] Flynn, who had been fired in 2014 as director of the Defense Intelligence Agency by Obama, was paid approximately $45,000 by the Russians for a giving a speech at a related event.[17]

In early January 2016, Carter Page, who had helped open the Moscow office of Merrill Lynch, met with Trump campaign manager Corey Lewandowski at Trump Tower and became an unpaid volunteer for the foreign policy committee Trump was said to be forming.[18] In March, twenty-eight-year-old George Papadopoulos was recruited to join the foreign policy team as well, and was told improved relations with Russia would be a cornerstone of Trump's foreign policy.[19]

A week later, Papadopoulos flew to Rome and met Joseph Mifsud, a former Maltese diplomat based at the London Academy of Diplomacy.[20] On March 24, there was a follow-up meeting at which Mifsud was accompanied by a woman Papadopoulos identified wrongly as Putin's niece. (Putin does not have a niece.)

After corresponding with the woman, the professor, and others, Papadopoulos met over breakfast in a London hotel with Mifsud, who told him that the Russians had dirt on Hillary Clinton: "They [the Russians] have dirt on her . . . they have thousands of emails."[21] After this Papadopoulos "continued to communicate" with the Trump campaign and his Russian government interlocutors.

In an interview with *La Repubblica*, the Italian news outlet, Mifsud denied Papadopoulos's account and said he never stated that the Russian government had "dirt" on Hillary Clinton.[22]

Trump and Manafort weren't the only influential Americans to have questionable relations with Russians during this period. Manafort had brought with him Rick Gates, Rick Davis, and Tad Devine from his firm in DC. The lone Democrat in the operation, Devine had worked on both Al Gore's and John Kerry's campaigns, and later became the senior campaign strategist for Senator Bernie Sanders's 2016 presidential run. (Tad Devine worked for Yanukovych in the 2006 Ukraine parliamentary elections, in which Yanukovych ended up as prime minister, and the 2010 presidential election, which Yanukovych won.[23] Devine did not return a phone call from the author.)

Similarly, in 2012, the European Centre for a Modern Ukraine, a Ukrainian nonprofit representing Yanukovych's Party of Regions, employed the Podesta Group, run by Tony Podesta, whose brother, John Podesta, became the campaign chairman for Hillary Clinton.[24]

By this point, even though most Americans didn't realize it, Putin and his allies had put money, directly and indirectly, on political consultants who were tied to campaigns for the three strongest candidates for the presidency of the United States in 2016—Donald Trump, Bernie Sanders, and Hillary Clinton.

———

For all the millions he had made in Ukraine, Manafort had fallen on hard times. Oleg Deripaska's net worth had plummeted after the 2008 financial crisis, which meant he wanted Manafort to liquidate a fund

Manafort was overseeing and give Deripaska back his share—some $17 million, according to financial statements obtained by the *New York Times*.[25] But Manafort had already spent a fortune on real estate, rare antique rugs, and the like. He had blown millions investing in his son-in-law's real estate ventures and his daughter Jessica's film. He was out of cash. Rather than pay Deripaska back, according to the indictment, Manafort simply stopped responding to him.[26]

Now, with Trump's ascent, Manafort saw a chance to get back in the game. He had known Trump for decades, had worked for him on occasion, and kept a condo in Trump Tower, though he said their relationship was largely confined to small talk. So in mid-February, as recounted by Franklin Foer in the *Atlantic,* Paul Manafort reached out to real estate magnate Tom Barrack, a longtime friend who was also close to Trump.[27]

For decades, Manafort had personified the Washington insider, but now he crafted a memo portraying himself as the polar opposite, saying he was a longtime foe of Karl Rove who had "avoided the political establishment in Washington since 2005."[28]

Having charged Ukrainian oligarchs exorbitant fees, Manafort switched his approach when it came to Trump. Any remuneration he might get from the campaign, he seemed to be thinking, was nothing compared to the riches that would come with his newfound influence. As a result, he offered to be Trump's campaign manager absolutely free of charge.

Tom Barrack added a cover letter to Trump that described Manafort in terms that were certain to be appealing to the candidate, as "the most experienced and lethal of managers" and "a killer." In March, Manafort joined the campaign as an adviser, with Corey Lewandowski still in place as campaign manager.[29]

Next, Manafort called Konstantin Kilimnik, the aide-de-camp he had relied on so heavily in Ukraine and who frequently served as Manafort's go-between with Deripaska.[30] Deeply in debt to Deripaska, Manafort nonetheless saw the billionaire as his savior. If he was hired as Trump's campaign manager, Manafort was certain Deripaska would see things in a new light. Perhaps private briefings on the campaign from Trump's campaign manager himself would put him back in favor? Manafort sent a batch of press clippings to Kilimnik celebrating his new job with Trump. "How do we use [these articles] to get whole," Manafort emailed Kilimnik. "Has OVD [Deripaska] operation seen?"[31]

Kilimnik replied that he thought that they would "get back to the original relationship" with Deripaska in time. Kilimnik, meanwhile, was a year into running a political consulting firm called Begemot Ventures International (BVI) with a Washington-based operative named Sam Patten, whose relationship with Kilimnik went back nearly two decades, to when they were colleagues at the International Republican Institute, a GOP-aligned foreign policy group.[32]

In 2014, Patten had begun working with a data-mining firm called Cambridge Analytica in an effort "to introduce new technologies and methodologies to U.S. campaigns during the 2014 congressional cycle."[33] Specializing in "psychographic" profiling, the company used online data to create sophisticated personality profiles for voters, who could then be targeted with specifically tailored messages that could encourage—or discourage—them from voting one way or another.[34]

Not long after Manafort came on board, one of his daughters texted the other that Manafort and Trump were "literally living in the same building and . . . they go up and down all day long hanging and plotting together," according to a tweet by *New York Times* reporter Ken Vogel.[35]

As the Republican primaries got under way in early 2016, the "beta run" of Cambridge Analytica's efforts to microtarget voters for president was adopted by the presidential campaign for Texas senator Ted Cruz.[36] But when the Cruz campaign fizzled, Cambridge Analytica persuaded Trump's digital director, Brad Parscale, to try out the firm.[37]

As Trump won one Republican primary after another in the spring of 2016, and increasingly looked to be the presumed nominee, so the alt-right brain trust gravitated toward his candidacy, including one of the principal owners of Cambridge Analytica, billionaire Robert Mercer, an investor in Breitbart News. In addition, former Breitbart chair Stephen Bannon, a senior adviser to Trump who was sometimes viewed as the candidate's Svengali, served as vice president of CA's board until the campaign.[38]

Cambridge Analytica was created in 2013 as the American arm of a British company called Strategic Communications Laboratories Group (SCL), but, like so much of the Trump-Russia scandal, the story of Cambridge Analytica is shrouded in fog, with parts of its ownership hidden in an elaborate web of interlocking tangential relationships that are difficult to decipher.

———

Meanwhile, Trump's astounding success during the primaries had left political analysts dumbfounded. By mid-March, he had dispatched would-be standard bearers of the GOP establishment—former Florida governor and presidential brother and son Jeb Bush, Senator Marco Rubio of Florida, New Jersey governor Chris Christie, and others—so that for most of the spring, it was a three-man race, with Trump going up against Texas senator Ted Cruz and Ohio governor John Kasich.

Then, on May 3, Trump won every delegate in the Indiana primary, which meant that Senator Cruz, his leading adversary, no longer had a road to the Republican nomination. There was so much rancor between the old-guard GOP stalwarts and the Trump insurgency that there was talk about mutiny at the July convention. But the bottom line was Trump had become the presumptive nominee. And that meant he had to build a team for the general election, so he could focus on Clinton.

To that end, on June 20, Trump fired campaign manager Corey Lewandowski and replaced him with Paul Manafort. Lewandowski had never run a major campaign before, and, as Trump prepared for the possible battle on the floor of the RNC, the stated reason for the personnel shift had to do with Manafort's vast experience. In 1976, Manafort had helped manage Gerald Ford's floor fight in his showdown with Ronald Reagan. He and Roger Stone had helped perform a similar service for Reagan in 1980 and had played key roles for George H. W. Bush in 1988 and Bob Dole in 1996. "Ultimately, Paul is in charge," Barry Bennett, a senior adviser to the Trump campaign, told the *New York Times*. "He's got the experience to help get Mr. Trump across the finish line."[39]

That was the official story—and it was pretty much how the mainstream press presented it. But another way to look at it was that Team

Trump had continued to solidify its connections to Team Putin. In addition to having been paid tens of millions by Putin and his allies, Manafort was likely deeply in hock to Deripaska and had already proffered his services to the oligarch for private briefings—creating a back channel to Putin. And, of course, Manafort was still working with Konstantin Kilimnik, with his GRU ties. Foreign policy adviser George Papadopoulos had also met with his mysterious Maltese diplomat, Joseph Mifsud, about getting dirt on Hillary's emails.

In addition, there were Trump's ties to the Agalarovs. During the early stages of the primaries, Aras Agalarov had conveyed his support to Trump via an email channel that went from Aras to Rob Goldstone, Emin's publicist, to Donald Jr. On February 29, Goldstone had sent an email to Donald Jr. saying that "on the eve of Super Tuesday," with eleven states voting in GOP primaries, Emin's father had asked him to pass along Aras's attached letter along with support "from many of his important Russian friends and colleagues."[40]

The attached letter offered Trump best wishes in a conventional, anodyne manner. What was more important was that the Agalarov channel was open. It was activated again on June 3, when Goldstone emailed Don Jr.:

> Emin just called and asked me to contact you with something very interesting. The Crown prosecutor* of Russia met with his father Aras this morning and in their meeting offered to provide the Trump campaign with some official documents and information that would incriminate Hillary and her dealings with Russia and would be very useful to your father. This is obviously very high level and sensitive information but is part of Russia and its government's support for Mr. Trump—helped along by Aras and Emin. What do you think is the best way to handle this information and

---

* The title "crown prosecutor" does not exist in Russia, but in a number of jurisdictions in the British Commonwealth, it is the title given to the state prosecutor presenting a case against an individual in a criminal trial. Goldstone was presumably referring to the office of the prosecutor general, the head of Russia's judiciary.

would you be able to speak to Emin about it directly? I can also send this info to your father via Rhona,* but it is ultra sensitive so wanted to send to you first.

Best

Rob Goldstone[41]

"Very high level." "Ultra sensitive." Too sensitive for Rhona. "Official documents." "Incriminate Hillary." "Part of Russia and its government's support for Mr. Trump." Don Jr. was intrigued.

Seventeen minutes later, he responded. He was on the road and wanted to speak to Emin first, but, he added, "[I]f it's what you say I love it especially later in the summer. Could we do a call first thing next week when I am back?"

Rather than wait until the next week, however, suddenly things went into overdrive. In the midst of a spectacularly frenetic presidential campaign, three key people in the campaign—the newly appointed campaign manager Paul Manafort; son-in-law and crown prince Jared Kushner; and Don Jr.—wiped their schedules clean and set up a mysterious meeting with an unnamed Russian government lawyer.

And so, they got together at four p.m. on Thursday, June 9, in Don Jr.'s twenty-fifth-floor Trump Tower office. Don had been told the Russians would bring two people to the meeting, but instead there were five.

Leading the way was Natalia V. Veselnitskaya, a Russian lawyer who was in New York representing Denis Katsyv's Cyprus-based Prevezon Holdings. Prevezon was being prosecuted by United States Attorney Preet Bharara for allegedly laundering $230 million via the tax fraud that Sergei Magnitsky had uncovered.

Like other Russian companies, Prevezon had made a point of hiring lawyers who had lots of clout. Earlier, it had been represented by former FBI director Louis Freeh. Another Prevezon attorney, Scott Balber, also had represented Donald Trump in 2013, when Trump sued comedian Bill Maher because the comedian failed to honor a promise to pay $5

---

* "Rhona" appears to be a reference to Rhona Graff, Trump's longtime assistant.

million if Trump could prove he wasn't "the spawn of his mother having sex with an orangutan."[42]

As for Sergei Magnitsky, his death, in 2009, had led Congress to pass the Sergei Magnitsky Rule of Law Accountability Act, which became emblematic of the intensely volatile relations between the Obama administration and Putin. The bipartisan bill, which passed the Senate by an overwhelming ninety-two–to–four margin, was intended to punish Russians who were allegedly responsible for the death of Sergei Magnitsky, by prohibiting them from entering the United States and its banking system, and by allowing American officials to seize assets belonging to Russians who had been implicated in human rights cases.[43]

By sanctioning individuals close to Putin, the Obama administration was saying, in effect, that Russia was a Mafia state, and that it made sense not to strike at the Russian people with punishing economic measures, but instead to target the select group of individuals—mobsters, oligarchs, public officials—responsible and to penalize them.

It was a weapon that struck at the core of the pact Putin had with his oligarchs. After all, if he could no longer provide *krysha*—if Putin could no longer protect his oligarchs—how much longer would they pay fealty to him?

Bill Browder, who was Magnitsky's boss and who had crusaded to get the eponymous bill passed by Congress, explained the calculus to the *American Interest*. "[Putin] allows people to get rich off the proceeds of government service," Browder said, "and then he asks them to do services he's interested in for the state. . . . He asks [his subordinates] to do very terrible things—to torture people, to kill people, to kidnap people, in order for the government to seize people's properties. And in return he offers them impunity. If all of a sudden . . . he can't promise them foreign impunity, that messes up everything for him."[44]

In response to the Magnitsky Act, Russia passed the Dima Yakovlev Bill, sometimes known as the anti-Magnitsky law, part of which bans citizens of the United States from adopting Russian children, thereby reframing the Magnitsky conflict issue as a human rights issue in which the United States was undermining the welfare of abandoned Russian orphans.

To promote the cause, Veselnitskaya founded the Human Rights Accountability Global Initiative Foundation in Washington to lobby for restoring American adoption of Russian children. Which sounded like a cause no one could disagree with, but since the Kremlin promised to rescind the anti-Magnitsky law if the sanctions were lifted, the word "adoption" had become a code word that really meant lifting sanctions. This was the genius of K Street lobbying that Paul Manafort had taught the Russians. In fact, they were lobbying to provide relief to oligarchs and gangsters who had allegedly been behind the $230 million tax scam and who tortured and killed Sergei Magnitsky. But they could promote their cause under the banner of human rights with pictures of cute little orphans who were in desperate need of an American home.

Of the people in the room, Don Jr. was most interested in the so-called highly sensitive information referred to in the Goldstone emails that would supposedly incriminate Hillary. Before the meeting, Veselnitskaya had sent a four-page memo to the Trump team asserting that Democratic donors had allegedly evaded paying US taxes on Russian investments.[45] They had been donors to Obama and it was possible they were donors to Hillary Clinton as well.[46] That's what Don Jr. was interested in—if it could be tied to Hillary.

But instead Veselnitskaya launched into a spiel about Bill Browder and Hermitage Capital Management, arguing that Browder was the real architect of a massive tax fraud scheme against the Russian state—which was of little interest to Don Jr.

Then, she asked whether a Trump presidency would lift the Magnitsky sanctions.

"Looking ahead, if we come to power, we can return to this issue and think what to do about it," Don Jr. said, as she recalled.[47]

Finally Don Jr. asked her the crucial question on his mind. "This money . . . from Russia, do you have any financial documents showing that this money went to Clinton's campaign?" he asked, according to Veselnitskaya.[48]

The answer, alas, was no.

And with that, the air suddenly went out of the room. Team Trump wanted dirt on Hillary, but the Russians hadn't delivered. Don Jr. thought it was a complete waste of time. Jared Kushner had stood by vaguely throughout. He was so bored he texted his assistant, "Can u pls call me on my cell? Need excuse to get out of meeting."[49]

But if the meeting was a waste of time for the Americans, it was a triumph for the Russians. Trump Jr. may have been upset that the Russians had not come through with the promised incriminating evidence about Hillary. But to the Russians, this was not about a single transaction. Instead, it was about structuring an ongoing relationship.

Former CIA acting director Michael Morell described the email exchange between Rob Goldstone and the Trumps as "huge" given that it "shows that a senior member of the Trump team" knew in early summer of 2016 that "the Russians were working on behalf of Trump."[50] In the midst of an insanely hectic campaign, three key members of Donald Trump's inner circle had cleared the decks for Veselnitskaya and her entourage seemingly without even really understanding what the agenda was, or, for that matter, whom they were really meeting with.

For her part, Veselnitskaya later insisted that in meeting with the Trump team, she was in no way working for the Russian government, but there was more to the story than she let on. First, far from being just a private lawyer, since 2013 Veselnitskaya has also been an informant for Yuri Chaika,[51] the prosecutor general of Russia, who is close to Agalarov and has been a strong Putin loyalist.[52] Chaika, quite likely, is the man Rob Goldstone meant when he referred to the crown prosecutor.

Moreover, according to the *New York Times,* emails obtained and released by Dossier, an organization founded by Mikhail B. Khodorkovsky—the oligarch who was stripped of his holdings, put in jail, and then exiled from Russia—indicate that Veselnitskaya worked closely with a senior prosecutor on Chaika's staff to write the Russian government response to a US Justice Department request in 2014 for help with its civil fraud case against Prevezon and its owner, Denis Katsyv.[53] In other words, she was deeply connected within the Kremlin, and the case she made reflected its talking points.

Much as Don Jr. evinced a lack of interest in her sanctions presentation, it may well have met a more welcome reception by another member of the Trump team. While Don was miffed at the unfulfilled promise of dirt on Hillary, Paul Manafort was quietly taking notes on his cell phone.[54]

In full, they read:

- Bill Browder
- Offshore—Cyprus
- 133m shares
- Companies
- Not invest—loan
- Value in Cyprus as inter
- Illici
- Active sponsors of RNC
- Browder hired Joanna Glover*
- Tied into Cheney
- Russian adoption by American families

These, then, were Veselnitskaya's talking points, crafted from a memo she'd written with the staff of the Russian prosecutor general, and Donald Trump Jr.'s indifference aside, Manafort knew this was no joke. There was money on the table. All of this went back to Putin. This was the Kremlin speaking, and given the content of the meeting it seemed to be taking them seriously.

Then there was the fact that, in addition to Goldstone and an unnamed translator, Veselnitskaya had brought along two additional men. Who were they?

One was Rinat Akhmetshin, a Soviet-born American citizen from Tatarstan in his early fifties, who had become that truly Washington creature—a self-proclaimed K Street lobbyist, "spending other people's money to achieve other people's goals," as he put it.[55]

---

* As noted by the *Washington Post*, "Joanna Glover" is likely a reference to Juleanna Glover, who worked with Browder in promoting the Magnitsky Act and also worked for Dick Cheney at one time.

Akhmetshin happened to be earning his money by lobbying to get rid of the Magnitsky Act, and by his account, he ended up at Trump Tower that day by . . . sheer happenstance. As the *Financial Times* reported it, Akhmetshin says he had taken the train from DC to New York that day in order to see a Russian play that evening when Veselnitskaya called.[56]

That's why, he claims, he was dressed so casually. Regardless of his wearing jeans and a T-shirt instead of his usual suit, Akhmetshin, with his long history of ties to Russian intelligence, won instant entrée to the inner sanctum of the Trump campaign.

When the Magnitsky Act was being debated on Capitol Hill, according to two observers, Akhmetshin could be seen walking with former congressman Ron Dellums, whom he had recruited, and Paul Behrends, senior aide to Dana Rohrabacher, a Republican congressman from California, to meet with top Democrats on the House Foreign Affairs Committee, Eliot Engel and Gregory Meeks.[57]

Widely known as Putin's favorite congressman, Rohrabacher traveled to Moscow on an official congressional trip in April 2016, Politico reported, and met privately with Vladimir Yakunin, a Putin confidant who was sanctioned in 2014 after the Russians invaded Ukraine. (Yakunin has been close to Putin for more than two decades, dating to the early nineties, when he helped Putin set up the Ozero co-op dachas on the shore of Lake Komsomolskoye.)[58]

Kyle Parker, a House Foreign Affairs Committee staffer who was a driving force behind the Magnitsky Act, noticed Akhmetshin making the rounds of Congress and immediately sent out an email blast to his colleagues alerting them that Akhmetshin used to spy for the Soviets and "specialized in active measures campaigns," according to an email reviewed by Politico.

For his part, Akhmetshin insists he is not a spy, although he makes it clear he is more than familiar with that world. Others, however, are not so sure. "He is a former GRU person for sure," an attorney who worked with Akhmetshin told the *Guardian*. Then he added, "[H]e once said there is no such thing as 'former.'"[59]

If Akhmetshin's appearance didn't raise questions, there was the final member of Veselnitskaya's group. She had brought with her Irakly Kaveladze, who had worked for the Agalarovs for years and had been in Vegas with Trump and the Agalarovs in 2013.

A longtime Agalarov loyalist, Kaveladze was there to monitor the situation on behalf of his patron, but he was also a man who had moved more than a billion dollars through two thousand US corporations he created.[60]

Kaveladze's attorney's explanation for his client's presence was that he was attending the meeting as "a translator." But that made no sense; Veselnitskaya already had arranged for an unnamed professional translator.

Between Kaveladze and Akhmetshin, with his past in military intelligence; Veselnitskaya, with her ties to Chaika; and the content of the meeting, it's hard to believe the Russians were there in their stated role as lobbyists. As former acting director of the CIA John McLaughlin put it to the Cipher Brief, "it looks to me like an elaborate operation carried out through intermediaries to probe the receptivity of the Trump campaign to assistance from the Russian government during the campaign."[61]

"It is not unusual for it to be carried out through such a long chain of intermediaries, because the tradecraft objective here is to separate the original ambition as far as possible from the ultimate result so it becomes very hard to trace back, as it is in this case, exactly what happened and who did what," McLaughlin said.[62]

And what did the Russians learn? They learned that Jared, distracted as he was, didn't seem to mind participating in such dirty tricks. They had seen that Don Jr. was eager to play ball, writing back, "I love it." And how security-conscious was the scion of the future president? Don Jr. waited a mere seventeen minutes before responding to Goldstone. Then he wrote back, apparently oblivious to the fact that he was creating a paper trail directly between himself and the Russians.

All the various threads were coming together. The Russians had, in effect, activated a channel from the Trumps through the Agalarovs to the Kremlin, from Don Jr. to Emin to Emin's father to Putin, with Rob Goldstone forwarding messages as necessary. Manafort was still in touch with Kilimnik and was offering private briefings to Deripaska. Even though Bayrock was no longer operational, its presence had opened ongoing relations to the Kremlin through Chabad and through Felix Sater, who had continued to develop Russian contacts and go to Moscow on behalf of Trump. Moreover, according to a report in Christopher Steele's dossier, "a Kremlin insider with direct access to the leadership confirmed that a key role in the secret TRUMP campaign/ Kremlin relationship was being played by the Republican candidate's personal lawyer Michael COHEN."[63]

The Republican National Convention was getting under way in Cleveland in July. Never before had Russia had someone in its grasp who was so deeply compromised as Trump, with his vast array of ties to the Russian Mafia and oligarchs. Never before had Russia had someone in its grasp who was so close to power as Donald Trump, the presumptive presidential nominee of the Republican Party. Something big was bound to happen.

CHAPTER TWENTY

ENDGAME

On June 15, 2016, six days after the Trump Tower meeting, Republican leaders in the House of Representatives got together to discuss the situation in Ukraine. Two of them, Speaker of the House Paul Ryan, a representative from Wisconsin, and House Majority Leader Kevin McCarthy, from California, had just met the new Ukrainian prime minister, Volodymyr Groysman, who had come into power saying he was committed to stamping out corruption and strengthening ties to the European Union.[1]

Ryan seemed to like Groysman. "This guy's a pretty good guy," he said, according to a transcript of the conversation published by the *Washington Post*.[2] "This guy's like the anti-corruption guy . . . and he's passing all these anti-corruption laws."

The conversation piqued the interest of Representative Cathy Rodgers, the Republican Conference chairman from Washington. "How are things going in Ukraine?" she asked.

"Well, the Russians are bombing them 30–40 shells a day," Ryan said. "Crimea is gone. And they're trying to clean up their government to show that they want to be western . . . He has this really interesting riff about . . . what Russia is doing to us, financing our populists, financing people in our governments to undo our governments, you know, messing with our oil and gas energy, all the things Russia does to basically blow up our country, they're going to roll right through us and go to the Baltics and everyone else."

"Yes!" said Rodgers. She added that she had been astounded by the sophistication of Russian propaganda.

"This isn't just about Ukraine," said Ryan.

". . . It's a propaganda war," said Rodgers.

"Maniacal."

"Yes," said Rodgers.

"And guess . . . guess who's the only one taking a strong stand up against it?" said Ryan. "We are."

What? Rodgers was agog. She didn't buy it for a second. "We're not . . . we're not . . . but we're not."

All the while, House Majority Leader Kevin McCarthy had been listening and decided to join in. The second-ranking Republican after Ryan, McCarthy had a nasty habit of blurting out inconvenient truths every once in a while. In 2015, on Fox News no less, McCarthy had said that a principal reason behind the costly and interminable congressional investigations into the Benghazi tragedy had been to drive down Hillary Clinton's poll numbers. "Everybody thought Hillary Clinton was unbeatable, right?" he said. "But we put together a Benghazi special committee, a select committee. What are her numbers today? Her numbers are dropping."[3]

McCarthy had appalled fellow Republicans because he had just corroborated Democratic allegations that the Benghazi probe was not about getting to the bottom of a real scandal so much as turning Congress's investigative powers into a political weapon against Hillary.

This time, the majority leader had an opportunity to make an even bigger gaffe. The day before, a hacker using the name Guccifer 2.0 had gone public in claiming credit for breaking into the Democratic National Committee's computers, and a cybersecurity firm called CrowdStrike had attributed the operation to Russian intelligence.[4]

Now came McCarthy's eureka moment. "I'll GUARANTEE you that's what it is," he said. "[Unintelligible] . . . The Russians hacked the DNC and got the opp research that they had on Trump."

"And delivered it to . . . to who?" asks Ryan.

[Unintelligible.]

"There's two people, I think Putin pays—Rohrabacher and Trump . . . [laughter] . . . swear to God."

Ryan couldn't believe what he was hearing. Kevin McCarthy, the second most powerful Republican in the House, had said Trump and Rohrabacher were on the Kremlin payroll! How else to explain Russia's generosity to the Republicans when it came to Democratic emails?

As Speaker of the House, Ryan tried to gain control. He could not allow this to become public. "This is an off the record . . . [laughter] . . . NO LEAKS . . . [laughter] . . . Alright? . . . This is how we know we are a real family here. What's said in the family stays in the family."

When asked to comment on the exchange, Brendan Buck, a spokesman for Ryan, told the *Washington Post* that it "never happened."

Matt Sparks, a spokesman for McCarthy, said, "The idea that McCarthy would assert this is absurd and false." After being told that there was a recording, Sparks characterized the conversation as "a failed attempt at humor."[5]

———

Eight days later, on June 23, the United Kingdom became an example of what Ryan had called Russia's attempts to "basically blow up" a country, when Britain dealt an extraordinary and unexpected blow to the European Union by severing its most vital connection to Europe. To the astonishment of hundreds of millions of people all over the world, 51.9 percent of the British electorate voted to leave the European Union. And what was Russia's role? At the time, few people were aware of the extent of Russia's interference. Only later, in 2018, did a minority report from the US Senate Foreign Relations Committee conclude that "the Russian government has sought to influence democracy in the United Kingdom through disinformation, cyber hacking, and corruption."[6]

"The Kremlin has long aimed to undermine European integration and the EU, in addition to its aims to sow confusion and undermine confidence in democratic processes themselves, making Brexit a potentially appealing target," it added.

According to a research team from the University of California at

eptember 2012, Russian president
dimir Putin *(left)* meets with
sian real estate billionaire Aras
larov *(right),* head of the Crocus
up. Agalarov hosted the 2013 Miss
verse pageant with Trump in
sia and allegedly is an old drinking
dy of Sergei Mikhailov, head of the
itsevo crime gang. *(RIA-Novosti,*
ail Klimentyev, Presidential Press Service/AP)

sian president Vladimir Putin *(center);* Putin's favorite comedian,
dimir Vinokur *(right);* and billionaire Aras Agalarov *(left)* during an
rds ceremony in the Kremlin in Moscow on October 29, 2013. Vladimir
okur was pro-Trump during the 2016 US presidential election and
ted on Instagram, "We won, Congratulations," on November 9, 2016.
a Mordovets/Getty Images)

Crocus Group president Aras Agalarov *(right)* and vice president Emin Agalarov
(left) arrive with Donald Trump *(center)* for the 2013 Miss Universe beauty
pageant final at Moscow's Crocus City Hall on November 9, 2013. *(Vyacheslav*
Prokofyev/Itar-Tass/Abaca Press/Newscom)

Left to right: Crocus Group president Aras Agalarov; Gabriela Isler of Venezuela, Miss Universe 2013; and Donald Trump at the pageant's awards ceremony in Crocus City Hall on November 9, 2013. *(© RIA Novosti/The Image Works)*

Allegedly a longtime associate of Semion Mogilevich and Sergei Mikhailov, Alimzhan "Taiwanchik" Tokhtakhounov is accused of running an international gambling ring with Vadim Trincher out of Trump Tower in 2013. Shortly after he fled the US to avoid prosecution, he appeared as a VIP guest at the 2013 Miss Universe pageant. *(Oksana Yushko/The New York Times/Redux)*

Left to right: Rotem Rosen, Aras Agalarov, Donald Trump, and Alex Sapir at the 2013 Miss Universe pageant in Moscow. Rosen is the right-hand man of Lev Leviev, who is closely aligned with Putin. Alex Sapir's father, Tamir Sapir, partnered with Trump for Trump SoHo and was alleged to have Russian Mafia connections. *(Courtesy Real Estate Weekly)*

President Donald Trump *(left)* a
Stephen Bannon, who was
chairman of Trump's 2016
campaign and had been vice
president of Cambridge Analyti‹
a data-mining firm specializing
"psychographic" profiling as a w
of microtargeting voters. CA's
parent company, Strategic
Communications Laboratories,
had ties to Ukrainian oligarch
Dmitry Firtash. *(Mandel Ngan/AFP/*
Getty Images)

On October 1, 2012, Russian prime minister Dmitry Medvedev *(left)* receives a T-sh
from Facebook CEO Mark Zuckerberg during their meeting at the Gorki residence
outside Moscow, at which they discussed Facebook's role in the 2012 presidential
election. Russia used Facebook as a purveyor of huge amounts of pro-Trump,
anti-Clinton propaganda in the 2016 election. *(Yekaterina Shtukina/AFP/Getty Images)*

CEO of Cambridge Analytica Alexander Nix speaks
the 2016 Concordia Summit on September 19, 2016, i
New York City. Even before his firm had finalized a
contract with the Trump campaign, Nix reached ou‹
WikiLeaks' Julian Assange and asked him to share t
DNC emails so that CA could help disseminate then
(Bryan Bedder/Getty Images for Concordia Summit)

Shown here in Moscow, Russian lawyer Natalia Veselnitskaya was present at the Trump Tower meeting in June 2016 with Paul Manafort, Donald Trump Jr., and Jared Kushner that was reportedly arranged to provide "dirt" on Hillary Clinton. Veselnitskaya has admitted to acting as an informant on behalf of the Kremlin. *(Yury Martyanov/AFP/Getty Images)*

re the infamous June 2016 meetings with the Russians, Donald Trump Jr., shown here in an ator in Trump Tower, responded to the prospect of getting "dirt" on Hillary Clinton by iling a contact "if it's what you say I love it." *(Albin Lohr-Jones/Bloomberg, Pool/Getty Images)*

Donald Trump rides an escalator to a press event to announce his candidacy for the US presidency at Trump Tower on June 16, 2015, in New York City. *(Christopher Gregory/Getty Images)*

Trump's daughter Ivanka Trump *(center)* onstage at the Republican National Convention in Cleveland, Ohio, July 21, 2016. From left to right are campaign adviser Rick Gates, Donald Trump, campaign manager Paul Manafort, and Ivanka's husband, Jared Kushner. At a time when Russian ambassador Sergei Kislyak was meeting with various members of the Trump campaign, the Ukraine plank in the Republican platform was changed in Russia's favor. *(Mar Reinstein/Corbis/Getty Images)*

Trump Tower on Fifth Avenue. Russian Mafia money first made its way to Trump Tower when shell companies owned by David Bogatin, whose brother worked for Semion Mogilevich, bought five condos in the building. Since then, many alleged figures in the Russian Mafia have called Trump Tower home, and it has provided a base of operations for several money-laundering operations. *(Mark Lennihan/AP)*

...hael Flynn *(left)* the retired ...eral chosen by President- ...ct Donald Trump as national ...urity adviser, speaks to ...chael Cohen, Trump's ...orney and "fixer." Flynn had ...ed with Vladimir Putin at a ...scow gala in 2015 and was ...d approximately $45,000 for a ...ech at a related event. Michael ...hen was working with Felix ...er on a deal for Trump Tower ...scow, which never came to ...tion. *(Sam Hodgson/The New York ...es/Redux)*

Together at last: Trump chats with fellow president Vladimir Putin as they attend the Asia-Pacific Economic Cooperation (APEC) Economic Leaders' Meeting in Da Nang, Vietnam, on November 11, 2017. *(Mikhail Klimentyev/AFP/Getty Images)*

Berkeley and Swansea University in Wales, Russia had assembled at least 150,000 Twitter accounts to promote Brexit.[7] A report by Britain's National Bureau of Economic Research later showed that automated tweeting played "a small but potentially decisive" role that was "possibly large enough to affect the outcomes" in the 2016 Brexit vote, by adding 1.76 percentage points to the pro-"leave" vote share.[8] The bottom line: Russian interference may have made the difference.

———

In early July, Republicans began gathering in Cleveland, Ohio, prior to the Republican National Convention to hammer out their platform. The party elders had had little input from the presumptive nominee, Donald Trump, on most issues, with the striking exception of American policy with regard to Ukraine.[9] Throughout the campaign, Trump had been less than supportive of Ukraine in its ongoing battle with Russia. In August 2015, when asked by NBC's Chuck Todd on *Meet the Press* what he thought about Ukraine's joining NATO, "I wouldn't care," he replied. He also said that Ukraine was "really a problem that affects Europe a lot more than it affects us." Coupled with his prediction to Bill O'Reilly that "I would have a great relationship with Putin," Trump's remarks led anti-Russia activists in Ukraine to call Trump a "Kremlin agent."[10]

That Trump's sentiments also were directly at odds with most Republicans became readily apparent when platform committee member Diana Denman, a longtime GOP activist from Texas, called for a plank saying the US would provide lethal defensive weapons to Ukraine for its battle with Russian separatists. Denman did not expect a battle. Her proposal was very much in line with age-old GOP policies. But before long, two men who said they were part of the Trump campaign came over to her, read the language she wanted to insert, and said it needed to be reviewed.

One of the men was J. D. Gordon, a forty-eight-year-old former Pentagon spokesman who was now a foreign policy adviser on the Trump campaign. He introduced himself to Denman and said he had phoned New York about the Ukraine plank. When she asked Gordon whom he had spoken to, he told her he had discussed it with Trump.[11] Gordon has called Denman's account inaccurate.

"[Gordon] said this is the language that Donald Trump himself wanted and advocated for back in March at a meeting at the unfinished Trump hotel here in Washington, D.C.," CNN's Jim Acosta reported. "J. D. Gordon says then candidate Trump said he didn't want to, quote, 'go to World War 3 over Ukraine.' And so, as J. D. Gordon says, at the Republican convention in Cleveland he advocated for language in that Republican Party platform that reflected then candidate Trump's comments."[12]

In the end, Gordon won, and the language was changed from calling on the US to provide Ukraine "lethal defensive weapons" to the phrase "appropriate assistance." Ohio senator Rob Portman described the radical change in policy as "deeply troubling," and even Charlie Black, a veteran Washington political operative who was once a partner of Manafort's, said the "new position in the platform doesn't have much support from Republicans."[13]

Which, of course, was something of an understatement. The direction indicated by the new plank was a far-reaching and profound departure from everything the Republican Party had stood for.

———

But Trump wasn't the only person Gordon spoke to who would have approved of the change. During the convention, Gordon also had two brief encounters with Russian ambassador Sergey Kislyak, who had quietly started to pop up in secret meetings repeatedly with Trump operatives.[14] It's not clear what role Kislyak might have played in aiding the Trump campaign, but the Kremlin was always eager to know the latest on Trump's positions regarding sanctions and Ukraine.

Just two months earlier, in April, Hope Hicks, a Trump spokesperson, had said, incorrectly, that a meeting with Kislyak in Washington "never happened."[15]

"There was no communication between the campaign and any foreign entity during the campaign," Hicks told the AP.

Yet on April 27, Trump gave a major foreign policy speech sponsored by the Center for the National Interest at Washington's Mayflower Hotel, in which he called for better relations with Moscow: "I believe an easing of tensions, and improved relations with Russia from a position of strength only is possible, absolutely possible," Trump said.[16]

That Trump chose the Center for the National Interest as the forum to make his remarks was in itself of interest, in that Putin had referred to its director, former Nixon aide Dmitri Simes, as his "American friend and colleague" in 2013, and Simes had pledged his full support for Putin's aggressive stance on Syria.[17]

As it happened, however, Ambassador Kislyak was seated in the front row[18] and before the event there was a private meeting with him and Trump; Jeff Sessions, then the Republican senator from Alabama who had joined the Trump team in February; and Trump's son-in-law, Jared Kushner.[19] Sessions denied being at any such meetings.[20]

This was not a question of chance contacts occurring with Russian officials at embassy soirees in the Washington social whirl. Throughout the operation, Trump surrogates repeatedly, and deliberately, reached out to Russian officials and otherwise made clear their knowledge of ongoing Russian operations to attack Clinton's campaign.

Current and former US officials familiar with the exchanges told Reuters that Michael Flynn and other Trump advisers made at least eighteen calls and emails to Kremlin operatives during the last seven months of the 2016 presidential campaign.[21] Even before he attended the December 2015 dinner in Moscow with Putin, and before Guccifer 2.0 took credit for the DNC hacking in 2016, General Flynn and his son had met secretly with Kislyak at the ambassador's residence in Washington. And Flynn's correspondence strongly suggested that he was very much in the loop with regard to Russia's hacking operation. In mid-July 2016, he emailed an unnamed Trump communications adviser, "There are a number of things happening (and will happen) this election via cyber operations (by both hacktivists, nation states and the DNC)."[22]

In the wake of the Trump Tower meeting in June, and the weakened Ukraine plank, Russian support came pouring in—in the form of money, strategic advice, and newly forged alliances. Simon Kukes, a

Russian-born American citizen who had replaced Putin foe Mikhail Khodorkovsky as head of Yukos, gave a total of $283,283 to various Trump entities, including a joint fund-raising committee called Trump Victory, whose beneficiaries included the Trump campaign, the RNC, and several state-level committees.[23]

At about the same time, even before his firm had finalized a contract with the Trump campaign, Cambridge Analytica CEO Alexander Nix reached out to Julian Assange and asked him to share the DNC emails so CA could help disseminate them.[24] He refused.

On July 14, George Papadopoulos sent an email to a contact with Kremlin ties asserting that top Trump officials had agreed to a pre-election meeting with representatives of Putin in the UK that would include the campaign's "national chairman and maybe one other foreign policy adviser." "It has been approved by our side," Papadopoulos wrote in the email.[25]

Four days later, the Heritage Foundation staged a seminar which Jeff Sessions attended, and took the opportunity to speak with Kislyak. A number of Sessions's conversations with the ambassador were intercepted by US spy agencies, which characterized them as "substantive" discussions on US-Russia relations in a Trump administration and Trump's positions on various issues concerning Russia.[26] During the Republican National Convention, Kislyak had also met with Carter Page.[27]

Then, on July 22, three days before the Democratic National Convention was to open in Philadelphia, WikiLeaks released nearly twenty thousand hacked emails from the DNC. Though they revealed nothing illegal, the emails showed that party officials, who are meant to remain neutral, favored Hillary Clinton and had discussed ways to undermine Bernie Sanders, leading to the resignation of DNC chair Debbie Wasserman Schultz. Typical of much of the mainstream press, the New York Times mentioned allegations "that Russian hackers had penetrated [the DNC] computer system," but focused on the internal bickering within the Democratic Party. That was more important than the fact that a hostile foreign power was assaulting America's electoral system.[28] He refused.

And so, one of the most unusual political campaigns in American history was under way, with Trump putting forth a right-wing, nativist, protectionist, anti-immigrant populism, all under the umbrella of "making America great again." Again and again throughout the campaign, contrary to every expectation, Trump's transgressions worked to his advantage, not his disadvantage. Thanks to his showmanship, Trump benefited enormously from getting more free media attention than any other candidate. Indeed, according to analysis from SMG Delta, a firm that tracks television advertising, from the beginning of his campaign through February 2016—still early in the campaign cycle—it was estimated that Trump received nearly $2 billion in free media, twice what Clinton got.[29]

Mixing the aesthetics of professional wrestling and reality TV, he threw red meat to his base. It was good—not bad—to demean Mexicans as rapists; to say women who have abortions should serve time in jail; to deride Senator John McCain, a Vietnam War hero who was tortured and spent six years as a POW, because he had been captured; to ban immigrants solely on the basis of their Muslim religion; even to urge a supporter to "knock the crap out of 'em [anti-Trump protesters]."

"I promise you, I will pay the legal fees," Trump added. And the crowds loved it.

Even then, Trump upped the ante. When she was secretary of state, Clinton had used a private email address and server, rather than State Department servers, thereby raising concerns about security and the preservation of emails, and leading to an FBI probe. That had ended on July 5, with a recommendation that no charges be filed.[30]

But Trump wouldn't let go. In Doral, Florida, on July 27, Trump said he hoped Russian intelligence *had* successfully penetrated Hillary Clinton's network and stolen her emails, and urged Russia to release them, as a way of getting to the bottom of it. "Russia, if you're listening, I hope you're able to find the 30,000 emails that are missing," Trump said during a news conference. "I think you will probably be rewarded mightily by our press."[31]

Now, as the *Times* reported, Trump was explicitly encouraging "a foreign adversary to conduct cyber espionage against a former secretary of state." He had openly urged Russia to interfere on his behalf in a presidential election.

Soon, Russian support for Trump flooded in from all over. The Internet Research Agency, a Russian organization that, according to a Justice Department indictment, aims "to interfere with elections and political processes," had started producing, purchasing, and posting pro-Trump ads on American social media. By July it had hired more than eighty employees to put out ads to social media platforms such as YouTube, Facebook, Instagram, and Twitter.[32]

Not everyone was in the dark. On July 30, the *Guardian* reported on Trump's ties to Russia and Manafort's to pro-Putin forces in Ukraine as they may have related to the changed Ukraine plank in the GOP platform. In addition to the DNC hack, additional hacks against the Democratic Congressional Campaign Committee and the Clinton campaign had been reported. "The FBI is investigating, with all signs pointing to Russian involvement," the *Guardian* reported, adding that "experts argue Vladimir Putin has attempted in the past to damage western democracy, saying Russian security agencies have made cyberattacks on French, Greek, Italian and Latvian targets during elections."[33]

On September 5, the *Washington Post* published a story by Dana Priest, Ellen Nakashima, and Tom Hamburger reporting that "U.S. intelligence and law enforcement agencies are investigating what they see as a broad covert Russian operation in the United States to sow public distrust in the upcoming presidential election and in U.S. political institutions." The article added that the Russian campaign used cyberwarfare to hack computers used in politics and to spread disinformation.[34]

At about the same time, Malcolm Nance published *The Plot to Hack America*, exposing how the Russians were using cyberspies and WikiLeaks to hack the DNC, the Clinton campaign, their friends and allies in the media, and voter registration systems in no fewer than twenty-five states. In October, the *Financial Times*[35] presented evidence that Trump SoHo had multiple ties to "an international money-laundering network." But the article, which was published behind a paywall, was not widely picked up, and with so much other reporting grabbing headlines, the issue of Trump's laundering money never dominated the national conversation.

But these reports were the exceptions. The ongoing drip, drip, drip of thousands of emails being released throughout the campaign by Guccifer and WikiLeaks commandeered the news cycles far more than the revelations of the Russian intelligence operation.

Meanwhile, contacts between Russia and the Trump campaign continued unabated, under cover of news instead of night. In August, Manafort met with longtime aide Konstantin Kilimnik at a Manhattan cigar bar, the Grand Havana Room, and "talked about bills unpaid by [their] clients, about [the] overall situation in Ukraine ... and about the current news," including the presidential campaign, according to a statement by Kilimnik.[36] In Ukraine, political foes charged that Kilimnik might be working with Russian intelligence, but Kilimnik told the *Washington Post* that his meetings with Manafort were "private visits" and were "in no way related to politics or the presidential campaign in the U.S."[37]

Yet suspicions were raised when a jet linked to Oleg Deripaska landed in New Jersey within hours of a meeting between Manafort and Kilimnik.[38] (A Deripaska spokeswoman told Vice News the billionaire was not offered and did not receive briefings from Manafort.)[39]

In mid-August, Manafort resigned as campaign manager after it was revealed that he'd received secret payments from Ukraine. A few days later, however, on August 19, one of Manafort's daughters, Andrea Manafort Shand, texted a friend that the resignation was merely for show. "So I got to the bottom of it," she wrote, in texts published by the Huffington Post.[40] "As I suspected, my dad resigned from being the public face of the campaign but is still very much involved behind the scenes. He felt he was becoming a distraction."

As for the campaign staff, Trump's team merely shuffled the deck. The media spotlighted newcomers Steve Bannon and Kellyanne Conway, but Manafort continued to have influence. His deputy, Rick Gates, who had been with him in Ukraine, moved to the Republican National Committee, where he soon established himself as a player in Trump's circle.[41]

Delighting in the transgressions underlying the apparent chaos, Roger Stone broadcast his complicity, appearing by phone on the Alex Jones show, hosted by the noted conspiracy theorist/radio broadcaster in April, and predicting that "devastating" revelations would be forthcoming from WikiLeaks about the Clinton Foundation. On August 21, Stone tweeted, "Trust me, it will soon [be] Podesta's time in the barrel."[42]

In August, Stone, in an appearance at the Southwest Broward Republican Organization in Florida, answered a question about what he suspected would be the campaign's "October surprise" by saying: "I actually have communicated with [Julian] Assange. I believe the next tranche of his documents pertain to the Clinton Foundation, but there's no telling what the October surprise may be."[43]

"I expect Julian Assange and the WikiLeaks to drop a payload of new documents on Hillary on a weekly basis fairly soon," Stone said later, in September, on Boston Herald Radio. He added he was in touch with Assange "through an intermediary."[44]

Stone was not the only Trump operative working with WikiLeaks. Representatives of the site coordinated points of attack directly with Donald Trump Jr. as well, with WikiLeaks emailing him on October 12, "Hey Donald, great to see you and your dad talking about our publications." (A couple of days earlier, Donald Trump had proclaimed, "I love WikiLeaks!")

"Strongly suggest your dad tweets this link if he mentions us," WikiLeaks wrote, directing Don Jr. to a link that suggested it would help Trump supporters sort through the stolen documents.[45] "There's many great stories the press are missing and we're sure some of your follows [sic] will find it," WikiLeaks went on. "Btw we just released Podesta Emails Part 4."

Don Jr. didn't respond to that message, but as the *Wall Street Journal*'s Byron Tau pointed out, just fifteen minutes later the candidate himself tweeted, "Very little pick-up by the dishonest media of incredible information provided by WikiLeaks. So dishonest! Rigged system!"

By this time, Donald Trump's ties to WikiLeaks and the Russian bots were fully operational and more than capable of coming to Trump's rescue when necessary. That became apparent on October 7, when the *Washington Post* released the infamous video of Trump with Billy Bush, then-host of the television show *Access Hollywood,* in which Trump says about women that you can just "grab 'em by the pussy."

Within an hour of the story's release, WikiLeaks was fighting to win back control of the narrative by releasing hacked emails from the account of Clinton campaign manager John Podesta.[46] In addition, at least 2,752 Twitter accounts from Russia's Internet Research Agency went into action on Trump's behalf whenever they were necessary. On September 17, Trump reversed his lies asserting that Obama had been born in Kenya and declared instead that Obama "was born in the United States, period." Russian tweets came to the rescue, with various Russian accounts now asserting that it was Hillary who started the birther controversy.[47]

And so it went, Russian hackers and bots leading a supine press corps by its nose. After all, it is far easier to write stories about hacked emails that are delivered on a silver platter than to probe a multifarious political conspiracy to sabotage a presidential election.

———

Thanks to Cambridge Analytica, Clinton's campaign may have faced an even bigger problem with Facebook than with Twitter bots. That's because the British data-mining company had made a deal with a Russian-American academic named Aleksandr Kogan, who harvested no fewer than fifty million people's raw profiles from Facebook without their permission, roughly thirty million of which contained enough information to build psychographic profiles. The profiles had been assembled with the premise that big data enabled clients to drill into the psychology of individual voters, thereby allowing them to identify the different types of American voters and shape their behavior.[48]

It is difficult to assess the effectiveness of Cambridge Analytica's approach of microtargeting narrowly tailored messages to the electorate. But, according to the Intercept, Alexander Nix, the head of Cambridge Analytica, has claimed to "have a massive database of four to five thousand data points on every adult in America." Nix also claimed that Trump campaign online ads were seen at least 1.5 billion times.[49]

In the end, more than 126 million Facebook users were shown Russian-generated election propaganda.[50] "They were using 40–50,000 different variants of ads every day that were continuously measuring responses and then adapting and evolving based on that response," Martin Moore of King's College London told the *Guardian*.[51] "It's all done completely opaquely and they can spend as much money as they like on particular locations because you can focus on a five-mile radius or even a single demographic. Fake news is important but it's only one part of it. These companies have found a way of transgressing 150 years of legislation that we've developed to make elections fair and open."

Absurd as some fake news seemed, much of it went viral when it triggered Facebook algorithms that pushed the buttons of impassioned Trump supporters. A case in point: a story that became known as "Pizzagate" suggested that certain phrases in John Podesta's hacked emails were actually code words linked to a Democratic Party pedophilia ring based in the basement of a Washington, DC, pizza parlor. Ludicrous as the story was, it went viral on sites such as Infowars.com, parts of Reddit, and various alt-right sites.[52]

The story, like others, had first started on Facebook. Which shined a new light on a 2012 meeting Facebook CEO Mark Zuckerberg had with Prime Minister Dmitry Medvedev in Moscow. They talked about Facebook's role in politics, and according to the *Times,* they joked about its importance in the American presidential campaign.[53] Suddenly, the joke was on America, and though most Americans didn't yet realize it, it had deadly serious consequences.

———

As he campaigned across the country, Trump occasionally addressed the issue of his ties to Russia. "I mean I have nothing to do with Russia," he said told CBS Miami on July 27, 2016. "I don't have any jobs in Russia. I'm all over the world but we're not involved in Russia. . . . I have nothing to do with Russia, nothing to do, I never met Putin, I have nothing to do with Russia whatsoever."[54]

None of which placated Clinton. On September 26, when she and Trump went head to head in the first presidential debate, Hillary attacked: "I was so shocked when Donald publicly invited Putin to hack into Americans. That is just unacceptable."[55]

Nonetheless, Trump's off-kilter response was enough for his supporters. "I don't think anybody knows it was Russia that broke into the D.N.C.," Trump said. "She's saying Russia, Russia, Russia, but I don't—maybe it was. I mean, it could be Russia, but it could also be China. It could also be lots of other people. It also could be somebody sitting on their bed that weighs 400 pounds, O.K.?"

Finally, in the third debate, on October 19, about three weeks before the election, it came to a head, with Clinton asserting that Putin liked Trump "because he'd rather have a puppet as president of the United States."

Trump: No puppet. No puppet.

Clinton: And it's pretty clear . . .

Trump: You're the puppet!

Clinton: It's pretty clear you won't admit . . .

Trump: No, you're the puppet.

Clinton: . . . that the Russians have engaged in cyberattacks against the United States of America, that you encouraged espionage against our people, that you are willing to spout the Putin line, sign up for his wish list, break up NATO, do whatever he wants to do, and that you continue to get help from him, because he has a very clear favorite in this race. So I think that this is such an unprecedented situation. We've never had a foreign government trying to interfere in our election. We have 17—17 intelligence agencies, civilian and military, who have all concluded that these espionage attacks, these cyberattacks, come from the highest levels of the Kremlin and they are designed to influence our election. I find that deeply disturbing.[56]

But the Russia issue got no traction, and was buried by sensational but relatively insignificant reports of Trump's horrifying transgressions against women, Muslims, and immigrants—not to mention the never-ending reports about Clinton's emails.

For the most part, political pundits thought Clinton was so far ahead that it didn't matter, anyway. But on October 28, eleven days before the election, then–FBI director James Comey announced in a letter to Congress that as a result of an unrelated case, the FBI had obtained additional emails that might relate to its investigation of Hillary's use of a private email server. It was soon revealed that the emails were obtained as the result of an investigation into former congressman Anthony Weiner.

Suddenly, the Hillary Clinton email case—and conversation—had been reopened. In the end, after reviewing the new emails, Comey said the FBI had not changed its conclusions. But so far as the general public knew, Hillary was the only candidate being investigated.[57]

On October 27, polls were showing her with a reasonably comfortable margin of six to nine points over Trump. But Clinton later said, "Our analysis is that Comey's letter—raising doubts that were groundless, baseless, proven to be—stopped our momentum."[58]

To complicate matters further, on October 31, just nine days before the election, a *New York Times* headline—"Investigating Donald Trump, FBI Sees No Clear Link to Russia"—seemed to exculpate Trump entirely, when, in fact, the investigations were just beginning.[59]

But the electorate didn't know that. Voters only knew that Hillary was being hammered in the press, and Donald Trump always seemed to skate free. The polls tightened. By November 3, that 7 percent margin had closed to less than 3 percent.[60]

In the closing week before the election, Trump used Russia-backed WikiLeaks as a battering ram against Hillary day after day. On October 31, in Warren, Michigan, Trump told a rally, "Did you see where, on WikiLeaks, it was announced that they were paying protestors to be violent, $1,500? . . . Did you see another one, another one came in today? This WikiLeaks is like a treasure trove."[61]

Then, on November 2, in Orlando: "Out today, WikiLeaks just came out with a new one. Just a little while ago. It's just been shown that a rigged system with more collusion, possibly illegal, between the Department of Justice, the Clinton campaign and the State Department."[62]

And on November 4, in Wilmington, Ohio: "Boy, I love reading those WikiLeaks."[63]

———

On November 5, three days before the presidential election, Ivanka and Jared Kushner made a pilgrimage to the grave of the Chabad rebbe Menachem Mendel Schneerson in the old Montefiore Cemetery in Queens, New York. Known as the Ohel, the rebbe's grave is considered holy by followers of Chabad and is visited by tens of thousands of people annually. Jared and Ivanka reportedly made a special prayer for Ivanka's father there, at the grave of a man whose adherents believed he had not really died, that he was the messiah; a man who had been the leader of a movement that somehow led directly to Vladimir Putin.[64]

On November 8, Election Day, Russian hackers targeted election systems in at least twenty-one states, mostly in the form of "assaults on the vast back-end election apparatus—voter-registration operations, state and local election databases, e-poll books and other equipment."[65] Initially, the impact of these attacks was unclear. Typical of the complaints, according to an election-monitoring group called Election Protection, in a Democratic-leaning county in a swing state, dozens of voters in Durham, North Carolina, were being told they were ineligible to vote, even when they displayed valid registration cards. Others were sent from one polling station to another, only to be rejected again, or were told, incorrectly, they had already voted.[66]

Months earlier, VR Systems, which provided information about voting via ebooks for Durham, had been hacked by Russians. Without VR's information, which is used to verify voters' eligibility, voters would be unable to cast ballots at all.[67]

Still, all over America, the consensus was that Hillary would win. According to Nate Silver's FiveThirtyEight election site, nine of the top ten pollsters had Hillary winning. Silver gave Trump a 28.6 percent chance[68] of winning, but that was far more generous than most of his colleagues. Others gave Trump less than a 1 percent shot.[69]

Trump impressed friends as being relaxed and at ease with what he characterized as a no-lose situation. "He was like, 'Look, what do I have to lose?'" Pastor Darrell Scott, CEO of the National Diversity Coalition for Trump, told *GQ*.[70] "'I'm gambling with house money. You know what I mean? If I win, great, I want to win; if I lose, what's my default position? The CEO of Trump International.'"

Even WikiLeaks was making plans for President Hillary Clinton. At 6:35 p.m., WikiLeaks wrote to Don Jr., "Hi Don if your father 'loses' we think it is much more interesting if he DOES NOT conceed [*sic*] and spends time CHALLENGING the media and other types of rigging that occurred—as he has implied that he might do."[71] If Trump contested the election, WikiLeaks reportedly argued, that would help Trump discredit the mainstream press and create a new media network to serve his agenda.[72]

Uncharacteristically, the Trump campaign had booked its "victory party," if that's what the evening held, not in a Trump property but at the midtown Hilton just three blocks from Trump Tower because its massive ballroom could hold three thousand people. According to *GQ*, the setup, which was dominated by risers for camera crews and a large press pen, looked as if it had been set up for a press conference more than a celebration.[73]

By five p.m., the insiders at Fox News had begun working on the corresponding narrative: Hillary Clinton was the forty-fifth president of the United States. Within the network, all this was a closely guarded secret that was shared largely with people who had to prepare graphics and other materials. "Fox News declares Hillary Clinton elected president," read one graphic.

———

At 5:03, Fox News exit polls had Hillary winning Wisconsin and Pennsylvania, two critical states that Trump needed. Fox political anchor Bret Baier recalled, "They were saying, 'You know, this is not definitive, but it really looks like Clinton will pull it out by about 11 p.m. Eastern time.'"[74]

At 8:22, things still looked good for Clinton. As the votes rolled in, the *New York Times* tweeted that Hillary had an 82 percent chance of winning.[75]

But suddenly, the narrative changed. The exit polls, after all, were not final tallies. At 9:30, it was clear that key states like North Carolina and Florida were too close to call. By 9:40, the *Times* had lowered Hillary's chances of victory to 55 percent. Then, by 10:50, Trump had captured two of the most important swing states, Ohio and Florida. Then Utah and North Carolina went for Trump.

By 11:36, his supporters had begun chanting, "President Trump, President Trump."[76]

———

In some ways, it seemed that everything had come together better than Putin could possibly have dreamed: three decades earlier, Mogilevich and the Russian Mafia's compromising of Trump had begun by possibly using Trump real estate to launder their money. They had bailed out Trump when he was bankrupt. They had ensnared him with some form of *kompromat*, most likely, though in exactly what form is unclear. They had ensured that he was beholden to Russia's money, and its power.

Meanwhile, the Gerasimov Doctrine had been implemented, and with it a new kind of asymmetric warfare using hackers and cyberattacks, disinformation and media manipulation. All done at Putin's behest, often by thinly disguised state actors, working hand in hand with the FSB. All largely unseen. All done with deniability. Accompanied by an almost Surkovian attempt to destroy the entire notion of truth via cries of "Fake news!," pathological lies, and right-wing propaganda, fueled with the gasoline of social media, real and robotic.

As to the impact of all the "active measures" undertaken by Russia leading up to the 2016 election, it is difficult to quantify exactly how much they changed the outcome of the presidential race. However, according to the study by the University of California at Berkeley and

Swansea University in Wales, automated tweeting alone by thousands of bots added 3.23 percentage points to Trump's vote in the US presidential race.[77]

Given Trump's narrow victory in states such as Wisconsin, Pennsylvania, and Michigan—states that were predicted to vote Democratic but were won by Trump with a margin of less than 1 percent,[78] and which put him over the top in the electoral college—it is more than likely that the Russian interference made the difference.

———

As midnight neared on election night, things were going so well for Trump's forces that an unlikely personage emerged at the Hilton. Even during the campaign, Felix Sater had continued to work with Michael Cohen in an effort to get Trump Tower Moscow going well into the presidential campaign, all the while cultivating contacts ranging from intelligence officials to Arkady and Boris Rotenberg, the two billionaire brothers who had been Putin's judo sparring partners. But on July 26, Trump tweeted that he had "ZERO investments in Russia" and the Trump Tower Moscow project was dead.

Trump, of course, had claimed in a deposition that he barely knew Sater. Now, though, on the most significant night of Trump's political life, Sater was back in his good graces and was a guest at the invitation-only victory party for the next president of the United States.

At 1:50 a.m., Trump took Pennsylvania, meaning his election was all but certain. Finally, at 2:29 a.m., came Wisconsin, a state that had not gone Republican since 1984. Then, in a statement that had been unexpected only hours before, the Associated Press officially called Donald Trump the next president of the United States.

Three minutes later, at 9:32 local time in Moscow, Deputy Vyacheslav Nikonov of the pro-Putin United Russia Party, the grandson of the namesake of the Molotov cocktail, was greeted by enthusiastic applause when he announced Trump's victory in the Duma.[79] Vladimir Putin's implementation of one of the most audacious intelligence operations in history had been successful beyond his wildest dreams.

Later that day, Vladimir Vinokur, Putin's favorite comedian, posted

a collage of two photos on Instagram. One of the photos showed Vinokur chatting amiably with Putin. The other showed the Russian
comic with Trump. "We won!" it said. "Congratulations!"

A new era had begun.

TRUMP'S FIFTY-NINE RUSSIA CONNECTIONS

Donald Trump has repeatedly said he has nothing to do with Russia. Below are fifty-nine Trump connections to Russia.

1. **Roman Abramovich**
   Putin confidant/billionaire who, along with fellow oligarch Lev Leviev, created the Putin-approved Federation of Jewish Communities of Russia under the leadership of Chabad rabbi Berel Lazar, aka "Putin's rabbi." Ivanka Trump is close to Abramovich's ex-wife, Dasha Zhukova, and has taken several trips with the Abramoviches, including a trip to Russia in 2014 as their guest.[1]

2. **Aras Agalarov**
   A billionaire Russian real estate developer who is close to Putin, Agalarov partnered with Trump in bringing the Miss Universe pageant to Moscow and was a serious potential partner behind the never-built Trump Tower Moscow. Agalarov remained in contact with Trump after Miss Universe and during the 2016 presidential campaign.

3. **Emin Agalarov**
   Son of Aras Agalarov, pop singer Emin performed at the 2013 Miss Universe pageant, got Donald Trump to appear in one of his music

videos, and was a key figure in arranging the infamous June 2016 meetings in Trump Tower between Russian operatives and top Trump associates.

4. **Evsei Agron**

The first alleged boss of the Russian Mafia in Brighton Beach, Agron came to New York in 1975 and ran his crime gang out of Brooklyn's El Caribe Country Club, which was owned by Dr. Morton Levine and his family, including nephew Michael Cohen, Trump's lawyer.

5. **Rinat Akhmetshin**

Former Soviet counterintelligence officer who became a K Street lobbyist working to end sanctions. Akhmetshin attended the Trump Tower meeting with Donald Trump Jr., Paul Manafort, and others in June 2016 at which a Russian lawyer promised to provide opposition research on Hillary Clinton. According to the *New York Times,* Akhmetshin had also worked in Kiev with Konstantin Kilimnik, an aide to Paul Manafort who had a background in Russian intelligence.

6. **Tevfik Arif**

One of the billionaire oligarchs behind the Bayrock Group, the real estate development company, whose offices were in Trump Tower. Prior to the dissolution of the Soviet Union, Arif worked for the KGB-linked Ministry of Commerce and Trade.

7. **Marat Balagula**

Evsei Agron's alleged successor as head of the Brighton Beach Mafia, Balagula was suspected of having ordered the hit on Agron, but was never charged and moved into Agron's former office in the El Caribe Country Club, which was still owned by Michael Cohen and his uncle. Balagula partnered with David Bogatin, who had previously purchased five apartments in Trump Tower.

8. **Boris Birshtein**

Russian-Canadian who founded Seabeco SA in keeping with KGB guidelines to set up corporations abroad. Worked with son-in-law

Alex Shnaider (who later built Trump Tower in Toronto) and two-thirds of the Eurasian Natural Resources Corporation's Trio (Patokh Chodiev and Alexander Mashkevich). Birshtein hosted the famous 1995 summit meeting in Tel Aviv, at which Semion Mogilevich was allotted an enormous share of the Ukraine energy trade.

9. **David Bogatin**

One of the pioneers behind the Red Daisy gas tax scam, Bogatin bought five apartments in Trump Tower for $6 million in 1984, in the process becoming the first alleged Russian mobster to launder money through Trump Tower. Donald Trump personally sold the apartments to Bogatin.

10. **Jacob Bogatin**

Key member of the Mogilevich Russian organized crime family who was indicted for his involvement in Mogilevich's YBM Magnex stock scam. Brother of David Bogatin.

11. **Oleg Boyko**

Russian oligarch who was close to Boris Yeltsin and who purchased a Trump Tower apartment in 1994, which he later sold to Vadim Trincher.[2]

12. **Mikhail Chernoy**

Billionaire oligarch who ran Trans-World Group with his brother, Lev; gained control of Russia's aluminum industry; and acquired a huge stake in processing and distributing other metals and petroleum products. In the nineties, Chernoy worked with the Chodiev Group. Chernoy also worked with Semyon Kislin, who had a long relationship with Trump and who partnered with Tamir Sapir, a financier of Trump SoHo.

13. **Vitaly Churkin**

Russian ambassador to the UN. Churkin met Trump in 1986 and along with Yuri Dubinin set up the trip Trump took to Moscow in 1987. Churkin died in 2017 in New York.

14. Michael Cohen

Donald Trump's personal lawyer. Cohen and his extended family, through his uncle, owned El Caribe Country Club in Brooklyn, which provided an alleged base of operations for the Russian Mafia in Brooklyn. In 1999, Cohen received a mysterious check for $350,000. Both Cohen and his brother Bryan married Ukrainian women, and Bryan's father-in-law, Alex Oronov, partnered with Viktor Topolov, an oligarch.[3]

15. Oleg Deripaska

Russian oligarch and founder and owner of Basic Element, a huge diversified industrial group. Close to Putin. Paid Trump campaign manager Paul Manafort $10 million per year to advance Putin's global agenda. Manafort owed Deripaska nearly $19 million after a failed business deal, but that debt was said to have been forgiven after Manafort offered Deripaska secret briefings on the Trump campaign. Has admitted that, at times, he has had to collaborate with suspected mobsters because he had no choice but to work with such people. Also employed David Geovanis, who in 1996 helped arrange meetings for Trump in Moscow with key Russian figures regarding a potential Trump Tower there.[4]

16. Natalia Dubinina

Daughter of Yuri Dubinin who was already living in New York as part of the Soviet delegation to the UN when her father became Soviet ambassador to the UN in March 1986. Stated that there was a determined effort by the Soviet government to seek out Trump. At a time when KGB chief Vladimir Kryuchkov had been complaining about the failure to recruit enough American agents, Dubinina played a key role in setting up a meeting with Trump and encouraging him to come to Moscow.

17. Yuri Dubinin

As Soviet ambassador to the UN, Dubinin met Trump and invited him to Moscow in 1987. The trip was arranged by Intourist, which was essentially a branch of the KGB whose job was to spy on high-profile tourists. As a result, Trump's entire visit, including his hotel stay, would have been subject to surveillance by the KGB.[5] Dubinin later became Soviet ambassador to the US.

18. **Dmitry Firtash**
Ukrainian oligarch who is considered a front man for Semion Mogilevich in "opaque intermediary companies" that siphoned off billions of dollars from the Ukraine energy trade. Supporter of the pro-Putin Party of Regions, which backs such policies. Also partnered with Paul Manafort on an abortive deal involving New York's Drake Hotel.

19. **Michael Flynn**
Foreign policy adviser to Trump during the campaign who later became Trump's short-lived national security adviser. Met with GRU chief Igor Sergun in Moscow in 2013[6] and gave a speech to new hires at GRU headquarters. Was paid $45,000 by RT for a speech in late 2015, and was seated near Putin at an RT dinner.

20. **Rick Gates**
When Paul Manafort became Trump's campaign manager, Gates, as Manafort's partner, became the campaign's number two, after having worked closely with Manafort for pro-Putin forces in Ukraine. In 2017, Gates was charged with conspiracy against the United States, making false statements, money laundering, and failing to register as a foreign agent as required by the Foreign Agents Registration Act. In 2018, Gates pleaded guilty to one count of making false statements and one count of conspiracy against the United States.

21. **David Geovanis**
As head of real estate for a subsidiary of the Brooke Group,* Geovanis arranged meetings for Trump during his 1996 Moscow trip to explore building Trump Tower Moscow. Later went to work for Oleg Deripaska's Basic Element.

---

* In 1999, Brooke Group became Vector Group.

22. **Rob Goldstone**

Music promoter who represents Emin Agalarov. Helped arrange the infamous Trump Tower meeting in June 2016 in which representatives of the Russian government offered the Trump campaign "dirt" on Hillary Clinton. Extended an invitation to Trump in the summer of 2015 to a party for Agalarov with the possibility of meeting Putin. Attended Trump's 2013 Miss Universe pageant.

23. **Anatoly Golubchik**

Sentenced to five years in prison in 2014 for his role in the $100 million gambling ring being run out of Trump Tower.[7] Owned a condo in Trump International Beach Resort and appeared in the Panama Papers as part of a shell company that has the same corporate director as a company owned by Mogilevich and ex-wife, Galina Telesh.

24. **Vyacheslav "Yaponchik" Ivankov**

One of the last of the old-time *vory*, Ivankov took over the Brighton Beach Mafia in 1992 and became one of the most powerful mobsters in the US. Connected to Putin through Leonid Usvyatsov, Putin's judo coach who happened to be a mobster. Owned 25 percent stake in Mogilevich's company Arbat. Mogilevich flew into New York on occasion to meet with Ivankov. FBI agents looked all over Brooklyn for Ivankov—only to find that he lived in Trump Tower. Ivankov also made frequent visits to Trump's Taj Mahal casino in Atlantic City.

25. **Irakly Kaveladze**

Longtime US-based associate of Aras Agalarov's real estate firm, the Crocus Group, Kaveladze attended the June 2016 meeting in Trump Tower among Donald Trump Jr., Paul Manafort, Jared Kushner, and the Russians. At one point, he claimed he'd attended as a translator, but another translator was present. In truth, he was there as a representative of the Agalarovs. In the nineties Kaveladze's company International Business Creations established more than two thousand Delaware-based shell companies and laundered more than $1.4 billion in cash.[8]

26. **Viktor Khrapunov**

A former Kazakh energy minister and ex-mayor of Almaty, the biggest city in Kazakhstan, Khrapunov was charged with conspiring to systematically steal billions of dollars of public assets and laundering the money through shell companies, including three corresponding to apartments in Trump SoHo. Khrapunov has denied the allegations.

27. **Konstantin Kilimnik**

Started working for Paul Manafort in 2005 when Manafort was representing Ukrainian oligarch Rinat Akhmetov, a gig that morphed into a long-term contract with Viktor Yanukovych, the Kremlin-aligned hard-liner who became president of Ukraine. Studied at the First Department of the Moscow Military Red-Banner Institute of the Ministry of Defense of the USSR, which trained interpreters for the Russian military intelligence agency.[9] Made two trips to meet with Manafort during the 2016 presidential election regarding the Trump campaign, and the possibility that Manafort would give briefings to Oleg Deripaska. Also opened a consulting firm in 2015 that had ties to Cambridge Analytica, the data firm that helped elect Trump.[10]

28. **Semyon "Sam" Kislin**

In the late seventies, Trump bought hundreds of television sets for the Commodore Hotel (now the Grand Hyatt) from Kislin, a Ukrainian immigrant who became a billionaire. Partnered with Tamir Sapir, whose Sapir Organization worked with Bayrock and financed Trump SoHo. As a commodities trader, Kislin was tied to Mikhail and Lev Chernoy and, according to the FBI, to Vyacheslav Ivankov's gang in Brighton Beach.[11] Kislin has denied having ties to the Russian mob.

29. **Sergey Kislyak**

Russian ambassador to the US who had a number of secret meetings and communications with Trump campaign officials, including General Mike Flynn and Senator Jeff Sessions. During the Republican National Convention, Kislyak had two brief encounters with

Trump foreign policy adviser J. D. Gordon, who was a key figure in rewriting—and weakening—the Ukraine plank in the Republican platform.

30. Simon Kukes

Bought an apartment in Trump Parc in 2000 and contributed more than $280,000 to various Trump entities. Picked by Putin to head Yukos Oil, replacing Putin foe Mikhail Khodorkovsky. Shortly after the Trump Tower Russian meeting, Kukes started making major contributions to the Trump campaign as well as the Republican National Committee.

31. Bennett LeBow

Founder and chairman of the Brooke Group. LeBow and Howard Lorber, president of the Brooke Group, accompanied Trump on his 1996 trip to Moscow.

32. Lev Leviev

An Israeli billionaire close to Putin, Leviev made his fortune by cracking the world diamond monopoly of the De Beers cartel. Has several ties to Trump, among them a business relationship with Jared Kushner, who bought four floors of the old New York Times Building, on West Forty-Third Street, from Leviev for $295 million.[12] In addition, Leviev was closely tied to the late Trump SoHo financier Tamir Sapir through Sapir's son-in-law Rotem Rosen, who was the CEO of the American branch of Africa Israel, Leviev's holding company, and who also became CEO of the Sapir Organization. One of Chabad's biggest patrons worldwide, Leviev allied with Roman Abramovich to create the Federation of Jewish Communities of Russia under the leadership of Chabad rabbi Berel Lazar, who would come to be known as "Putin's rabbi."

33. Howard Lorber

President of the Brooke Group. Lorber and Brooke CEO Bennett LeBow accompanied Trump to Moscow in 1996.

34. Yuri Luzhkov

As mayor of Moscow, Luzhkov was criticized by John Beyrle, then US ambassador to Russia, in a 2010 cable to Washington. "Corruption in Moscow remains pervasive," Beyrle wrote. "Luzhkov oversees a system in which it appears that almost everyone at every level is involved in some form of corruption or criminal behavior." Trump's meetings in Moscow city hall to discuss major developments in Moscow took place under Luzhkov's aegis.[13]

35. Paul Manafort

Before becoming Trump's campaign manager, Paul Manafort had been hired by Ukraine's pro-Putin Party of Regions to do an "extreme makeover" of Viktor Yanukovych that succeeded in making him president—only to see Yanukovych later exiled in disgrace. Manafort worked for oligarchs Oleg Deripaska and Rinat Akhmetov. As early as 2005, Manafort proposed to influence politics, business dealings, and news coverage inside the United States, Europe, and former Soviet republics to Putin's benefit. He is alleged to have hidden $75 million in offshore accounts,[14] at least one of which has ties to Mogilevich.

36. Alexander Mashkevich

Kazakh billionaire who, with Patokh Chodiev and Alijan Ibragimov, is part of the Troika, or Trio, as they are known, major stockholders in the Eurasian Natural Resources Corporation, which controls chromium, alumina, and gas operations in Kazakhstan. Along with Chodiev, Mashkevich worked at Boris Birshtein's KGB-linked Seabeco[15] and was tied up with the Russian Mafia through their alliance with the Chernoys in the Aluminum Wars. He is listed in Bayrock's promotional literature as a primary financial backer, but it is unclear if Mashkevich actually backed Bayrock projects.

37. Sergei Mikhailov

Alleged to be the longtime head of Solntsevskaya Bratva, the biggest crime gang in Russia, and an associate of Semion Mogilevich, who is said to have laundered money for him starting in 1984. According to one denizen of the Russian underworld, Mikhailov is very much the boss and is more powerful that Mogilevich, who, as the brains of the operation, laundered vast amounts of money and came up with its most sophisticated financial scams, which is why Mikhailov has partnered in at least eight companies with Mogilevich. Mikhailov's ties to Trump largely run through Mogilevich, but in 2013 Mikhailov was said to be interested in backing a Trump Tower development in Moscow and allegedly met with Trump representatives at the Ukraine hotel in Moscow.

38. Semion Mogilevich

Ukrainian-born alleged "Brainy Don" of the Russian Mafia, with a multibillion-dollar organization allegedly involved in the sale of nuclear materials to terrorists, human trafficking and prostitution, drugs, and money laundering. In a 1995 Tel Aviv meeting, Mogilevich was awarded a controlling stake in RosUkrEnergo by fellow mobsters, thereby securing the franchise to siphon off untold riches from the Ukraine-Russia energy trade. Has close ties to Yuri Luzhkov, the former mayor of Moscow; Leonid Derkach, former head of the Security Service of Ukraine; and Vladimir Putin. In 1992, Mogilevich sent Vyacheslav Ivankov to New York to oversee expansion of the Mafia into the US.

39. Hillel "Helly" Nahmad

An art dealer who started buying apartments in Trump Tower in 1999, eventually taking over a full floor. Nahmad was a leader of the Nahmad-Trincher Organization, which operated "international sports books" that laundered more than $100 million out of the former Soviet Union, through shell companies in Cyprus, and into investments in the United States in an enterprise that was based in Trump Tower. The entire operation, prosecutors say, was protected by Alimzhan Tokhtakhounov.

40. Eduard Nektalov

A diamond dealer from Uzbekistan, Nektalov, who bought a condo in Trump World Tower directly below Kellyanne Conway, came under investigation by the US Treasury Department for mob-connected money laundering. In 2004, after rumors circulated that Nektalov might cave in and cooperate with federal investigators, he was murdered on Sixth Avenue.[16]

41. Alexandre Ventura Nogueira

Primary broker of the Trump Ocean Club in Panama, Nogueira marketed the Trump-branded units to Russians, among others with criminal pasts.

42. Carter Page

Foreign policy adviser to the Trump campaign. Traveled to Moscow in July 2016 during the presidential election and met with senior Russian officials and influential oligarchs. Was approached in 2013 by Russian intelligence officials who were trying to recruit him. Page met with a Russian spy in 2013 and supplied research materials.

43. George Papadopoulos

A foreign policy adviser to the Trump campaign, Papadopoulos triggered the FBI investigation into Trump's collusion with Russia when he told an Australian top diplomat that Russia had political dirt on Hillary Clinton. In March 2016, Papadopoulos met with Joseph Mifsud, a Maltese professor who had valuable contacts with the Russian Ministry of Foreign Affairs, in hopes of setting up a meeting between Trump and Putin.

44. Sergei Polonsky

A flamboyant six-foot-four Russian real estate oligarch, Polonsky was convicted of fraud in 2017. While still associated with Donald Trump, Felix Sater served as an adviser to Polonsky in Mirax Group, which partnered with Sistema, a conglomerate tied to Mogilevich. Polonsky also partnered with Moscow mayor Yuri Luzhkov, a Mogilevich crony.

45. Vadim Rabinovich

A pro-Russia Ukrainian oligarch and Mogilevich lieutenant who spent seven years in jail for embezzlement, Rabinovich attended the famous 1995 Russian Mafia summit in Tel Aviv at which Mogilevich was granted a generous share of the Ukraine energy trade. A year later, in 1996, Rabinovich hung around with his partners Howard Lorber and Bennett LeBow as they showed Trump around town.

46. Vladimir Rezin

In 1996, Trump began negotiations with Rezin, the first deputy mayor of Moscow, to build a $300 million luxury residential complex. Like all of Trump's proposed projects in Moscow, it never came to fruition.

47. Rotem Rosen

Chief lieutenant of real estate magnate Lev "King of Diamonds" Leviev, Rosen married Zina Sapir, daughter of Tamir Sapir, who founded the Sapir Organization, which backed Trump SoHo. Attended Trump's 2013 Miss Universe pageant in Moscow in hopes of negotiating a Trump Tower Moscow. His son's 2008 bris was touted by *New York* magazine as "the best bris invite ever." Attendees included Donald Trump, daughter Ivanka, and her husband-to-be, Jared Kushner.

48. Dmitry Rybolovlev

Russia's "fertilizer king," Rybolovlev owns a 3.3 percent stake in the Bank of Cyprus, alleged to be a haven for money laundering. In 2008, he purchased a mega-mansion from Trump in Palm Beach for $95 million, which Trump had purchased four years earlier for $40 million.

49. Tamir Sapir

An impoverished immigrant turned billionaire, Sapir partnered with Semyon Kislin, who, according to the FBI, was a "member or associate" of Vyacheslav Ivankov's mob in Brighton Beach. Like Kislin, Sapir likely made his money through ties to Uzbek oligarch Mikhail Chernoy. Lived in Trump Tower, and partnered with Bayrock and Trump on Trump SoHo. Sapir denied having any mob ties. Died in 2014.

50. Felix Sater

Bayrock's international man of mystery, Sater was born in the Soviet Union in 1966. As managing director of Bayrock Group, he partnered with Trump and made various stabs at developing Trump Tower Moscow. Cooperated with the government after pleading guilty to racketeering for his role in a $40 million stock fraud scheme in 1998. His father was said to be a lieutenant in Mogilevich's organization and did business with the Italian Mafia in New York. Childhood friend of Trump lawyer Michael Cohen. Served as a government asset who helped the US track terrorists and mobsters, but is also alleged to be working with Mogilevich. Accompanied Ivanka Trump and Donald Jr. on a 2006 Russia trip, in which he said he arranged for Ivanka to spin around in Putin's chair in the Kremlin.

51. Alex Shnaider

In the early 2000s, he began to develop the tallest building in Canada, the sixty-five-story Trump Tower and Hotel in Toronto. When it came to financing the skyscraper, Shnaider, a billionaire of Russian extraction, turned to Raiffeisen Bank International AG in Vienna,[17] whose affiliate company was linked to RosUkrEnergo. Shnaider is also the son-in-law of Boris Birshtein and worked at Birshtein's KGB-tied company, Seabeco.

52. Eric Sitarchuk

As an attorney, Sitarchuk represented Mogilevich lieutenant Jacob Bogatin during the YBM Magnex scandal and, many years later, Donald Trump himself as owner of the Trump International Hotel in DC, when a wine bar argued that the president's ownership of the hotel constituted an unfair competitive advantage.[18]

53. Roger Stone

A close Trump ally for decades, Stone represented Trump when he moved into the gambling industry in the eighties. Served as adviser to the Trump campaign during the 2016 election. Communicated directly and indirectly with WikiLeaks in order to obtain dirt on Hillary Clinton and hacked emails before the election.

54. Gennady Timchenko

Yet another judoka pal of Putin's who ended up a billionaire, in this case as chairman of the Gunvor oil-trading firm, with a net worth of $15.6 billion.[19] Cited as a member of Putin's inner circle, Timchenko has been subject to sanctions. As an owner of Sibur, a large gas company, he is one of the biggest clients of Navigator Holdings, a shipping firm partly owned by Trump's commerce secretary Wilbur Ross.[20]

55. Vadim Trincher

Along with Alimzhan Tokhtakhounov, Anatoly Golubchik, and Hillel Nahmad, Trincher was a leader of two Russian-American organized crime families—the Taiwanchik-Trincher Organization and the Nahmad-Trincher Organization—which ran "international sports books" that laundered more than $100 million out of the former Soviet Union. They operated out of the sixty-third floor of Trump Tower until they were busted in 2013.

56. Alimzhan "Taiwanchik" Tokhtakhounov

Another ringleader of the Taiwanchik-Trincher Organization, Tokhtakhounov has allegedly spent more than three decades working with Mogilevich and the Solntsevo Organization, dating back to the early eighties, when he hung out with Mogilevich and Mikhailov at the Legendary Hotel Sovietsky in the Moscow suburb of Solntsevo. He was indicted for conspiring to fix the ice-skating competition at the 2002 Winter Olympics. After the bust of the gambling ring in Trump Tower in April 2013, he surfaced in November at the Miss Universe pageant in Moscow near Donald Trump.

57. Viktor Vekselberg

A member of Putin's inner circle, Vekselberg is the largest shareholder in the Bank of Cyprus,[21] investing in it at a time when Wilbur Ross, who has since become Trump's secretary of commerce, was the bank's vice chairman.

58. Natalia Veselnitskaya

A Russian attorney for Denis Katsys's Cyprus-based Prevezon Holdings, Veselnitskaya set up the June 2016 meeting in Trump

Tower with Donald Trump Jr., Jared Kushner, and Paul Manafort, among others. Veselnitskaya has been an informant to Yuri Chaika, the prosecutor general of Russia. The meeting held forth the promise of handing over damaging information on Hillary Clinton to the Trump campaign, as well as addressing the possibility of lifting sanctions against Russia. Closely aligned with the Agalarovs.

59. Viktor Yanukovych

Elected president of Ukraine after being completely remade as a candidate by Paul Manafort. Earned a reputation as a "Putin puppet," and was ousted in 2014, and exiled to Russia. Manafort, Rick Gates, and Konstantin Kilimnik all worked for Yanukovych for more than a decade—in return for tens of millions of dollars.

ACKNOWLEDGMENTS

This book would not have been possible without the help of many people. At Dutton, I was fortunate to have wonderful editing by editor in chief John Parsley, who oversaw the book, and Brent Howard. I am also grateful to Dutton publisher Christine Ball and president Ivan Held, who assembled a terrific team that treated the book with the highest level of professionalism. They include Maria Whelan, Amanda Walker, Carrie Swetonic, Kayleigh George, Cassidy Sachs, Linda Rosenberg, Susan Schwartz, Andrea St. Aubin, Aja Pollock, Nancy Resnick, Dora Mak, Sabila Khan, Leigh Butler, and Chris Lin. I'd also like to thank Penguin Publishing Group president Allison Dobson. My thanks as well to Anke Steinecke for her comprehensive legal review.

My literary agent, David Kuhn, did a superb job of taking this project from its inception to finding a great home for it at Dutton. He and Lauren Sharp at Aevitas have been enormously supportive and were always there with valuable advice throughout the entire process.

Parts of this book grew out of articles that appeared initially in *The New Republic* and *Vanity Fair.* At *The New Republic,* I'm indebted to former publisher Hamilton Fish and editors Eric Bates and Bob Moser for editing my piece "Trump's Russian Laundromat." At *Vanity Fair* online, I'd like to thank John Homans for editing "Why Robert Mueller Has Trump SoHo in His Sights."

I'm deeply indebted to my research assistant, Olga Lautman, a wonderfully talented and resourceful investigator who opened the doors to Russian-language websites and other sources, and who often worked late into the night doing so much in so many ways to make this book better. Similarly, I'd like to thank other members of my team, including fact checker Ben Kalin, photo editor Cynthia Carris Alonso, and my friend, photographer James Hamilton, for the author photo.

I want to thank fellow investigative reporters Richard Behar and Anastasia Kirilenko for generously sharing related materials and their views on the subject. Among the many people who were either interview subjects or gave me assistance, I'd like to thank Anders Åslund, Mark Galeotti, Alex Goldfarb, Ryan Goodman, Ze'ev Gordon, Steve Halliwell, Julie Holstein, Scott Horton, Oleg Kalugin, Richard Lerner, Bernard Lown, Ken Ann Marlowe, Kenneth McCallion, James Moody, Frederick Oberlander, Nikos Passas, Tomasz Piatek, Nick Pileggi, Howard Rosenberg, Sandra Rubin, Felix Sater, Anya Schiffrin, Giannina Segnini, John Sipher, Jonathan Winer, Robert S. Wolf, Sherman Teichman, and Beverly Zabriskie.

And I would also like to thank the many sources who helped me on a background or not-for-attribution basis. Helpful as such sources have been, this book also relies extensively on declassified government documents, congressional investigations, and news accounts from thousands of newspapers and journals from all over the world. I should add that the endnotes provide a far more complete list of people and sources that have contributed to this book.

It would have been impossible to research this book without the Internet, and I am especially grateful to the people and institutions who built the Internet research tools that enabled me to search through such vast amounts of material from all over the world so quickly. Wherever possible, I have cited relevant websites in the endnotes. The reader should be advised, however, that Internet links are not eternal and some web addresses may be out of date or dead. Because I made a practice of citing original sources whenever possible, a number of extraordinarily useful resources do not appear in my endnotes nearly as often as they should. Among them, I'm particularly grateful to the Kleptocracy

Initiative Archive Project and the Organized Crime and Corruption Reporting Project.

Many friends and colleagues helped either by contributing in one way or another to the book itself or through much-needed moral support. They include John Anderson, Sidney Blumenthal, Patricia Bosworth and Doug Schwalbe, Edmundo Desnoes and Felicia Rosshandler, David Duffy and Marcelline Thomson, Michael Klebnikov and Alexandra Ourusoff, Clara Mulberry, and Cody Shearer. I'm especially grateful to Susan Letteer, whose friendship, insight, and support were so valuable.

Finally, my gratitude goes to my family—Chris, Shanti, Thomas, Marley, and Miles; and Jimmy, Marie-Claude, Adam, Mel, and Otis; Matthew and Jacelyn; Harlow and Richard Unger; and Romy-Michelle.

AUTHOR'S NOTE TO THIS EDITION

This is a book by an American author about an American president. In that sense its subject is first and foremost national. But the nature of the topic—a campaign to compromise the President of the United States run by the leader of our historic enemy, Russia—is international in its reach and impact.

It is undeniable that Donald Trump has been the subject of prolonged and malicious attention from the Russian state, both in its traditional manifestation of the security services (KGB, FSB) and also in its more recent buccaneering commercial form: through corporate vehicles and international businessmen acting as Vladimir Putin's proxies. In this book I chart the oligarchs, the crooks, the shell companies, the complex operations, the billion-dollar deals and the shady trade-offs which lead to the key question: has Donald Trump, either through willful ignorance or an unexplained lack of awareness, become a Russian asset?

The First Amendment to the US Constitution says: "Congress shall make no law respecting an establishment of religion, or prohibiting the free exercise thereof; or abridging the freedom of speech, or of the press." Other countries do not share our unqualified right to freedom of speech. In particular, libel law in the United Kingdom allows claims from people who, as public figures, would have no viable right of action in the States. This is why in 2010 the Obama administration passed the Speech Act allowing American courts to refuse to enforce overseas libel judgments.

In spite of the transatlantic gap between our libel laws my publishers and I wanted the book not only to reach a home audience but also an international one. After all, the major public interest questions raised by the unhealthy entanglement between Trump and Putin do not stop at the American frontier, with or without walls. This is a relationship which has a significant global impact, whether you look at politics, trade, economics, crime, climate change, war or peace.

Out of respect for different jurisdictions some changes have been made for this edition. But the core questions raised are the same, and I believe them to be of equal importance to anyone genuinely concerned with matters of public interest wherever they may live.

The powerful people criticized in this book will not like it, and they may disagree with what it says even though we have tried to treat them fairly. That is a risk we have to take; their opposition is not a reason to keep it from you. Our job is to get the book out. Once we have published it, you can read it and assess the evidence for yourself. Then you can make up your mind.

NOTES

EPIGRAPH

1. Robert I. Friedman, *Red Mafiya: How the Russian Mob Has Invaded America* (New York: Little, Brown, 2000).

CHAPTER ONE: (VIRTUAL) WORLD WAR III

1. https://www.youtube.com/watch?v=_HzAdP3y-k8.
2. Donald Trump (@realdonaldtrump), "Russia has never . . . ," Twitter, January 11, 2017, https://twitter.com/realdonaldtrump/status/819159806489591809.
3. James Clapper interview, "Clapper: Russia Treating Trump Like an Asset," *The Lead,* CNN, http://www.cnn.com/videos/politics/2017/12/18/james-clapper-trump-putin-russia-asset-intv.cnn.
4. Jeff Stein, "Putin's Man in the White House? Real Trump Russia Scandal Is Not Mere Collusion, US Counterspies Say," *Newsweek,* December 21, 2017, http://www.newsweek.com/trump-putin-man-white-house-russia-investigation-scandal-moscow-kremlin-755321.
5. James Comey, *A Higher Loyalty* (New York: Flatiron Books, 2018).
6. Ibid.
7. "Russian President Vladimir Putin honors Russia's intelligence network," Viral World News, June 24, 2017, https://www.worldnews.com.ng/2017/06/24/russian-president-vladimir-putin-honors.html.
8. Sandra Peddie, "At 100, Mob Underboss Sonny Franzese Gets out of Federal Prison," *Newsday,* updated June 23, 2017, http://www.newsday.com/long-island/crime/sonny-franzese-released-from-prison-1.13756776?view=print.
9. "100 Jahre alter Ex-Mafiaboss aus Knast entlassen," *Spiegel Online,* June 24, 2016, http://www.spiegel.de/panorama/justiz/new-york-sonny-franzese-100-jahre-alter-ex-mafia-boss-aus-knast-entlassen-a-1153883.html.
10. Michael Hechtman, "100-Year-Old Crime Boss Beats the Odds, Is Released from Prison," *New York Post,* June 24, 2017, http://nypost.com/2017/06/24/100-year-old-crime-boss-beats-the-odds-is-released-from-prison/.

11. Associated Press, "93-Year-Old Crime Boss Gets 12-Year Sentence," CBS News, January 14, 2011, https://www.cbsnews.com/news/93-year-old-crime-boss-gets-12-year-sentence/.

12. Michael Franzese, *Blood Covenant* (New Kensington, PA: Whitaker House, 2003).

13. Ibid.

14. Fredric Dannen, "The Born-Again Don," *Vanity Fair,* February 1991, https://www.vanityfair.com/news/1991/02/john-gotti-joe-columbo-fbi-investigation-witness.

15. Franzese, *Blood Covenant.*

16. Dannen, "Born-Again Don."

17. Russian Organized Crime in the United States, Hearing Before the Permanent Subcommittee on Investigations of the Committee on Governmental Affairs, United States Senate, 104th Congress, Second Session, May 15, 1996, https://archive.org/stream/russianorganized00unit/russianorganized00unit_djvu.txt.

18. Franzese, *Blood Covenant.*

19. Ibid.

20. United Press International, "In What Federal Prosecutors Called the Biggest Motor Fuel . . . ," UPI.com, August 7, 1995, https://www.upi.com/Archives/1995/08/07/In-what-federal-prosecutors-called-the-biggest-motor-fuel/7331807768000/.

21. Franzese, *Blood Covenant.*

22. Ibid.

23. Nicholas Horrock and Linnet Myers, "Extradition Target Says His Real Crime Is Success," *Chicago Tribune,* April 3, 1992.

24. James S. Henry, "The Curious World of Donald Trump's Private Russian Connections," *American Interest,* December 19, 2016, https://www.the-american-interest.com/2016/12/19/the-curious-world-of-donald-trumps-private-russian-connections/.

25. Ibid.

26. Russian Organized Crime in the United States.

27. Franzese, *Blood Covenant.*

28. Prepared Statement of Michael Franzese Before the Senate Governmental Affairs Permanent Investigations Subcommittee Section, Federal News Service, May 15, 1996.

29. Russian Organized Crime in the United States.

30. Ibid.

31. Ibid.

32. Norval White and Elliot Willensky with Fran Leadon, *AIA Guide to New York City,* 5th ed. (New York: Oxford University Press, 2010).

33. Ada Louise Huxtable, Letter to the Editor, "Donald Trump's Tower," *New York Times,* May 6, 1984.

CHAPTER TWO: TRUMP'S BEAUTIFUL LAUNDRETTE

1. Wayne Barrett, *Trump: The Greatest Show on Earth: The Deals, the Downfall, the Reinvention* (New York: Regan Arts, 2016).

2. Horrock and Myers, "Extradition Target Says."

3. David Cay Johnston, *The Making of Donald Trump* (New York: Melville House, 2016).

4. Author's telephone interview with Winer.

5. Barrett, *Trump.*

6. Friedman, *Red Mafiya.*

7. Ibid.

8. Edward Luce, "Russia and the West's Moral Bankruptcy," *Financial Times,* March 28, 2018, https://www.ft.com/content/feda2630-31dc-11e8-b5bf-23cb17fd1498.

9. Thomas Frank, "Secret Money: How Trump Made Millions Selling Condos to Unknown Buyers," BuzzFeed, January 12, 2018, https://www.buzzfeed.com /thomasfrank/secret-money-how-trump-made-millions-selling-condos-to.

10. Sam Howe Verhovek, "Entrepreneur Who Left US Is Back, Awaiting Sentence," *New York Times,* April 30, 1992, https://www.nytimes.com/1992/04/30/nyregion /entrepreneur-who-left-us-is-back-awaiting-sentence.html.

11. Barrett, *Trump.*

12. Dan Dorfman, "On the Trail of Baby Doc," *New York,* July 14, 1986.

13. Author's interview with Kalugin.

14. Christopher Andrew and Oleg Gordievsky, *Comrade Kryuchkov's Instructions* (Redwood City, CA: Stanford University Press, 1991).

15. Katie Sanders, "Did Vladimir Putin Call the Breakup of the USSR 'the Greatest Geopolitical Tragedy of the 20th Century'?" Punditfact, March 6, 2014, http:// www.politifact.com/punditfact/statements/2014/mar/06/john-bolton/did-vladimir -putin-call-breakup-ussr-greatest-geop/.

16. C. J. Chivers, "Editor's Death Raises Questions About Change in Russia," *New York Times,* July 18, 2004.

17. "Journalists Killed in Russia Since 1992," Committee to Protect Journalists, https:// cpj.org/europe/russia.

18. Author's interview with Kalugin.

19. Karen Dawisha, *Putin's Kleptocracy: Who Owns Russia?* (New York: Simon & Schuster, 2014).

20. David Z. Morris, "Vladimir Putin Is Reportedly Richer Than Bill Gates and Jeff Bezos Combined," *Fortune,* July 29, 2017, http://fortune.com/2017/07/29/vladimir -putin-russia-jeff-bezos-bill-gates-worlds-richest-man/.

21. Garry Kasparov, *Winter Is Coming: Why Vladimir Putin and the Enemies of the Free World Must Be Stopped* (New York: PublicAffairs, 2015).

CHAPTER THREE: MARRIED TO THE MOB

1. David Cay Johnston, *The Making of Donald Trump* (Brooklyn: Melville House, 2016).

2. Gwenda Blair, *The Trumps: Three Generations of Builders and a Presidential Candidate* (New York: Simon & Schuster, 2000).

3. Johnston, *Making of Donald Trump.*

4. Blair, *Trumps.*

5. Charles Denson, "Fred Trump's Coney Island: 50th Anniversary Exhibit," Coney Island History Project, July 5, 2016, http://www.coneyislandhistory.org/blog /news/fred-trumps-coney-island-50th-anniversary-exhibit.

6. Ibid.

7. Ibid.

8. Katherine Clarke and Will Parker, "Meet Paul Manafort's Real Estate Fixer," *Real Deal,* August 31, 2017, https://therealdeal.com/2017/08/31/meet-paul-manaforts -real-estate-fixer/.

9. Katherine Clarke, "Manafort Pal Sues PMG over LIC Clock Tower Site Deal," *Real Deal,* April 3, 2017, https://therealdeal.com/2017/04/03/manafort-pal-sues-pmg -over-lic-clock-tower-site-deal/.

10. Tom Winter, "DOJ: Ex-Manafort Associate Firtash Is Top-Tier Comrade of Russian Mobsters," NBC News, July 16, 2017, https://www.nbcnews.com/news/us-news/doj-ex-manafort-associate-firtash-top-tier-comrade-russian-mobsters-n786806.

11. Clarke and Parker, "Meet Paul Manafort's Real Estate Fixer."

12. Johnston, *Making of Donald Trump.*

13. Blair, *Trumps.*

14. Barrett, *Trump.*

15. Blair, *Trumps.*

16. Ibid.

17. Ibid.

18. Roger Dunstan, "Overview of New York City's Fiscal Crisis" (PDF), California Research Bureau, California State Library, March 1, 1995. Retrieved January 20, 2011.

19. Charles V. Bagli, "Trump Sells Hyatt Share to Pritzkers," *New York Times,* October 8, 1996, http://www.nytimes.com/1996/10/08/business/trump-sells-hyatt-share-to-pritzkers.html.

20. Michelle Dean, "A Mentor in Shamelessness: The Man Who Taught Trump the Power of Publicity" *Guardian*, April 20, 2016, https://www.theguardian.com/us-news/2016/apr/20/roy-cohn-donald-trump-joseph-mccarthy-rosenberg-trial.

21. Albin Krebs, "Roy Cohn, Aide to McCarthy and Fiery Lawyer, Dies at 59," *New York Times,* August 3, 1986, https://archive.nytimes.com/www.nytimes.com/library/national/science/aids/080386sci-aids.html.

22. Timothy L. O'Brien, *TrumpNation: The Art of Being the Donald* (New York: Warner Books, 2005).

23. Marie Brenner, "How Donald Trump and Roy Cohn's Ruthless Symbiosis Changed America," *Vanity Fair,* August 2017, https://www.vanityfair.com/news/2017/06/donald-trump-roy-cohn-relationship.

24. Michael Kruse, "He Brutalized for You," Politico Magazine, April 8, 2016, https://www.politico.com/magazine/story/2016/04/donald-trump-roy-cohn-mentor-joseph-mccarthy-213799.

25. Ibid.

26. Lana Adler, "Roy Cohn and the Shocking Jewish Mentorship That Created Donald Trump," *Forward,* October 10, 2016, http://forward.com/opinion/351591/roy-cohn-and-the-shocking-jewish-mentorship-that-created-donald-trump/.

27. David W. Dunlap, "1973: Meet Donald Trump," *New York Times,* July 30, 2015, https://mobile.nytimes.com/times-insider/2015/07/30/1973-meet-donald-trump.

28. Brenner, "How Donald Trump."

29. Barrett, *Trump.*

30. Michael S. Schmidt, "Obstruction Inquiry Shows Trump's Struggle to Keep Grip on Russia Investigation," *New York Times,* January 4, 2018, https://www.nytimes.com/2018/01/04/us/politics/trump-sessions-russia-mcgahn.html.

31. Johnston, *Making of Donald Trump.*

32. Tom Robbins, "A Brief History of Donald Trump and the Mafia," Vice, April 28, 2016, https://www.vice.com/en_us/article/ppx7b9/a-brief-history-of-donald-trump-and-the-mafia.

33. Barrett, *Trump.*

34. Robbins, "A Brief History."

35. Ibid.

36. Johnston, *Making of Donald Trump.*
37. Bill Powell and Peter McKillop, "Citizen Trump," *Newsweek,* September 28, 1987.
38. Bagli, "Trump Sells Hyatt Share."
39. Nicholas Pileggi, "The Mob and the Machine," *New York,* May 5, 1986.
40. Barrett, *Trump.*
41. Donald Trump and Tony Schwartz, *Trump: The Art of the Deal* (New York: Random House, 1987).

CHAPTER FOUR: BRIGHTON BEACH

1. Friedman, *Red Mafiya.*
2. Elisabeth Sherman, "What Brooklyn Looked Like Before the Hipster Invasion," All That Is Interesting, September 20, 2016, http://all-that-is-interesting.com/brooklyn -before-hipster-invasion.
3. Jeffrey Robinson, *The Merger: The Conglomeration of International Organized Crime* (New York: Overlook Books, 2000).
4. Oleg Kalugin, *Spymaster: My Thirty-Two Years in Intelligence and Espionage Against the West* (New York: Basic Books, 1994).
5. Author's interview with Kalugin.
6. Caleb Melby and Keri Geiger, "Behind Trump's Russia Romance, There's a Tower Full of Oligarchs," *Bloomberg Businessweek,* March 16, 2017, https://www.bloomberg .com/news/articles/2017-03-16/behind-trump-s-russia-romance-there-s-a-tower-full -of-oligarchs.
7. Ibid.
8. Keren Blankfeld, "The Money Problems of Manhattan Real Estate Mogul Tamir Sapir," *Forbes,* September 24, 2010, https://www.forbes.com/forbes/2010/1011/rich -list-10-real-estate-tamir-sapir-drenchedin-debt.
9. Caleb Melby and Keri Geiger, "Trump's Tower of Russian Oligarchs."
10. Charles V. Bagli, "Brass Knuckles over 2 Broadway; MTA and Landlord Are Fighting It Out over Rent and Renovations," *New York Times,* August 9, 2000, http://www .nytimes.com/2000/08/09/nyregion/brass-knuckles-over-2-broadway-mta-landlord -are-fighting-it-over-rent.html.
11. "HealthTech Mob Ties Charged," CNN Money, November 25, 1997, http://money .cnn.com/1997/11/25/companies/healthtech/.
12. Michael Daly and Michael Weiss, "Felix Sater: The Crook Behind the Trump-Russia 'Peace' Plan," Daily Beast, February 24, 2017, https://www.thedailybeast.com/felix -sater-the-crook-behind-the-trump-russia-peace-plan.
13. Palmer and Oberlander v. John Doe 98-CR-01101 and United States of America, "Petition for a Writ of Certiorari to the United States Court of Appeals for the Second Circuit," United States Supreme Court, docket no. 14-676, http:// c10.nrostatic.com/sites/default/files/Palmer-Petition-for-a-writ-of-certiorari-14-676 .pdf.
14. Robinson, *Merger.*
15. Friedman, *Red Mafiya.*
16. Stephen Handelman, *Comrade Criminal: Russia's New Mafiya* (New Haven: Yale University Press, 1995).
17. Michael Schwirtz, "Vory v Zakone Has Hallowed Place in Russian Criminal Lore," *New York Times,* July 29, 2008, http://www.nytimes.com/2008/07/29/world/europe /29iht-moscow.4.14865004.html.
18. Friedman, *Red Mafiya.*

19. "Solntsevskaya OPG: Full File of Interpol and Special Services," OSP-UA.info, February 2, 2016, Google Translate translation from Russian, https://translate.google
.com/translate?hl=en&sl=ru&u=http://osp-ua.info/politicas/55782-solntsevskaja
-opg-polnoe-dose-interpola-i-spetssluzhb.html&prev=search.

20. James O. Finkenauer and Elin J. Waring, *Russian Mafia in America: Immigration, Culture, and Crime* (Boston: Northeastern University Press, 1998).

21. Robinson, *Merger.*

22. Friedman, *Red Mafiya.*

23. Finkenauer and Waring, *Russian Mafia in America.*

24. Jake Pearson, "Notorious Russian Mobster Says He Just Wants to Go Home," Associated Press, January 27, 2018, https://apnews.com/3accd9e526fd4609998ddc
fa0abc418f.

25. Friedman, *Red Mafiya.*

26. Robinson, *Merger.*

27. Ibid.

28. Friedman, *Red Mafiya.*

29. Ibid.

30. Ibid.

31. Ibid.

32. Finkenauer and Waring, *Russian Mafia in America.*

33. Friedman, *Red Mafiya.*

34. Ibid.

35. Ibid.

36. Ibid.

37. Phil Williams, *Russian Organized Crime: The New Threat?* (London and New York: Routledge, 1997).

38. Friedman, *Red Mafiya.*

39. Ibid.

40. Ibid.

41. Ibid.

42. Ibid.

43. Author interview with Nick Pileggi.

44. Ralph Blumenthal with Celestine Bohlen, "Soviet Emigre Mob Outgrows Brooklyn, and Fear Spreads," *New York Times,* June 4, 1989, http://www.nytimes.com
/1989/06/04/nyregion/soviet-emigre-mob-outgrows-brooklyn-and-fear-spreads
.html?pagewanted=all.

45. Harry Hurt III, *Lost Tycoon: The Many Lives of Donald J. Trump* (Brattleboro, VT: Echo Point Books & Media, 1993).

46. Ibid.

47. Damian Ghigliotty, "Old New York: The Plaza Hotel," *Commercial Observer,* October 14, 2014, https://commercialobserver.com/2014/10/old-new-york-the-plaza
-hotel/.

48. George Hackett with Mary Bruno, "Donald Trump's Lofty Ambition," *Newsweek,* December 2, 1985.

49. Mark Bowden, "The March 1990 *Playboy* Interview with Donald Trump," *Playboy,* March 1, 1990, http://www.playboy.com/articles/playboy-interview-donald-trump
-1990.

50. Powell and McKillop, "Citizen Trump."

CHAPTER FIVE: HONEY TRAP

1. David Remnick, *Lenin's Tomb: The Last Days of the Soviet Empire* (New York: Knopf Doubleday Publishing Group, 1993).
2. Anastasia Kirilenko and Claire Bigg, "Ex-KGB Agent Kalugin: Putin Was Only a Major," Radio Free Europe Liberty, March 31, 2005, https://www.rferl.org/a/russia-ex -kgb-kalugin-putin-only-a-major/26930384.html.
3. Kalugin bio, spy museum, https://www.spymuseum.org/private-events/spy-speaker-series/oleg-kalugin/.
4. Author's interview with Kalugin.
5. John le Carré, "My New Friends in the New Russia: In Search of a Few Good Crooks, Cops and Former Agents," *New York Times,* February 19, 1995, http://www.nytimes.com/books/99/03/21/specials/lecarre-newrussia.html.
6. Ibid.
7. Ibid.
8. Český Rozhlas, "Czechoslovak Secret Police Files Reveal Interest in Trump Couple," Hello Czech Republic, December 2, 2016, http://www.czech.cz/en /Zivot-a-prace/Czechoslovak-secret-police-files-reveal-interest-i.
9. Karel Janicek, "Czechoslovakia Secret Police File: Trump Sure of Presidential Win—in 1996," *Chicago Tribune,* January 12, 2017, http://www.chicagotribune.com /news/nationworld/ct-trump-1996-presidential-race-20170112-story.html.
10. Hans-Wilhelm Saure, "Czech Secret Agents Spied on Trump: He's 'Completely Tax-Exempt for the Next 30 Years,'" *Business Insider,* December 15, 2016, http:// www.businessinsider.com/czech-secret-agents-spied-on-donald-trump-he-is-tax -exempt-for-30-years-2016-12.
11. Rozhlas, "Czechoslovak Secret Police Files."
12. Kate Connolly, "Czechoslovakia Spied on Donald and Ivana Trump, Communist-Era Files Show," *Guardian,* December 15, 2016, https://www.theguardian.com/us -news/2016/dec/15/czechoslovakia-spied-on-donald-trump-ivana-files.
13. Janicek, "Czechoslovakia Secret Police File."
14. Rozhlas, "Czechoslovak Secret Police Files."
15. Connolly, "Czechoslovakia Spied on Donald."
16. Ibid.
17. Lois Romano, "Donald Trump, Holding All the Cards," *Washington Post,* November 15, 1984, https://www.washingtonpost.com/archive/lifestyle/1984/11/15/donald -trump-holding-all-the-cards-the-tower-the-team-the-money-the-future/8be79254 -7793-4812-a153-f2b88e81fa54/?utm_term=.29ee27932b32.
18. Ron Rosenbaum, "Trump's Nuclear Experience," Slate, March 1, 2016, http://www .slate.com/articles/news_and_politics/the_spectator/2016/03/trump_s_nuclear_ex perience_advice_for_reagan_in_1987.html.
19. Author's interview with Rosenbaum.
20. Romano, "Donald Trump, Holding All the Cards."
21. Scott Feinberg, "Donald Trump Angled for Soviet Posting in 1980s, Says Nobel Prize Winner," *Hollywood Reporter,* May 26, 2017, https://www.hollywoodreporter .com/news/donald-trump-angled-soviet-posting-1980s-says-nobel-prize-winner-1006312.
22. Author's interview with Lown.
23. Kate Brannen, "A Timeline of Paul Manafort's Relationship with Donald Trump," Slate, October 30, 2017, http://webcache.googleusercontent.com/search?q=

cache:http://www.slate.com/articles/news_and_politics/jurisprudence/2017/10/a
_timeline_of_paul_manafort_s_relationship_with_the_trump_world.html.

24. Author's interview with Lown.

25. Andrew and Gordievsky, *Comrade Kryuchkov's Instructions*.

26. Kalugin, *Spymaster*.

27. Andrew and Gordievsky, *Comrade Kryuchkov's Instructions*.

28. Ibid.

29. Luke Harding, "The Hidden History of Trump's First Trip to Moscow," Politico, November 20, 2017, https://www.politico.com/magazine/story/2017/11/19/trump -first-moscow-trip-215842.

30. Tatyana Antonova, "Trump Immediately Melted: Intrigue of the First Visit of the US President to the USSR, MKRU, November 9, 2015 (translated by Google), http:// www.mk.ru/politics/2016/11/09/tramp-srazu-rastayal-intriga-pervogo-vizita -prezidenta-ssha-v-sssr.html.

31. Paula Span, "When Trump Hoped to Meet Gorbachev in Manhattan," *Washington Post,* December 3, 1988, https://www.washingtonpost.com/lifestyle/style/from-the -archives-when-trump-hoped-to-meet-gorbachev-in-manhattan/2017/07/10/3f570b42 -658c-11e7-a1d7-9a32c91c6f40_story.html?utm_term=.2137d1ae73dd.

32. Author interview with Kalugin.

33. Harding, *Collusion*.

34. Romano, "Donald Trump, Holding All the Cards."

35. Herald Staff, "Foreign Intrigue," *Miami Herald,* June 5, 1987.

36. Cameron Stewart, "Donald Trump, the Deals and the Mafia Dons," *Australian*, August 16, 2017, https://www.theaustralian.com.au/news/investigations/donald -trump-the-deals-and-the-mafia-dons/news-story/40c61d98c72c3ba10064357c047 ee8ce.

37. Barrett, *Trump*.

38. Trump, *Art of the Deal*.

39. Harding, "The Hidden History."

40. Barrett, *Trump*.

41. Harding, *Collusion*.

42. Michael Oreskes, "Trump Gives a Vague Hint of Candidacy," *New York Times*, September 2, 1987, http://www.nytimes.com/1987/09/02/nyregion/trump -gives-a-vague-hint-of-candidacy.html.

43. Span, "When Trump Hoped."

44. Harding, "Hidden History."

45. Andrew Higgins and Andrew E. Kramer, "Russia's Sexual Blackmail Didn't Die with the Soviets," *New York Times,* January 11, 2017, https://www.nytimes.com /2017/01/11/world/europe/donald-trump-russia.html?_r=0.

46. Kevin Randall, "From Tradecraft to Sexpionage, Cold War KGB and US Spies Concur: *The Americans* Actually Happened," *Vanity Fair*, May 21, 2014.

47. Author interview with Kalugin.

48. Kathleen Klenetsky, "Soviets 'Intensely Interested' in 1988 US Campaign," *Executive Intelligence Review* 14, July 24, 1987, https://www.larouchepub.com /eiw/public/1987/eirv14n29-19870724/eirv14n29-19870724_067-elephants_and _donkeys.pdf.

49. Oreskes, "Trump Gives a Vague Hint."

50. Ilan Ben-Meir, "That Time Trump Spent Nearly $100,000 on an Ad Criticizing US Foreign Policy in 1987," BuzzFeed, July 10, 2015, https://www.buzzfeed.com

/ilanbenmeir/that-time-trump-spent-nearly-100000-on-an-ad-criticizing-us?utm
_term=.qqg716kY8#.vr08wVBGy.

51. Oreskes, "Trump Gives a Vague Hint."

52. Hilary Sargent, "The Man Responsible for Donald Trump's Never-Ending Presidential Campaign," Boston.com, January 22, 2014, https://www.boston.com/news/local
-news/2014/01/22/the-man-responsible-for-donald-trumps-never-ending-presidential
-campaign.

53. Kim I. Mills, "New Hampshire GOP Activist Wants to Draft Trump for President," Associated Press, July 13, 1987.

54. Barrett, *Trump.*

55. Howard Kurtz, "Between the Lines of a Millionaire's Ad; New Yorker's Foreign-Policy Foray Follows Political Overtures," *Washington Post,* September 2, 1987.

56. Fox Butterfield, "New Hampshire Speech Earns Praise for Trump," *New York Times,* October 23, 1987.

57. Frank Clifford, "Non-Candidate Trump Talks Tough on Political Issues," *Los Angeles Times,* October 23, 1987, http://articles.latimes.com/1987-10-23/news/mn-10766
_1_speech.

58. Barrett, *Trump.*

59. Janicek, "Czechoslovakia Secret Police File."

60. Ibid.

61. Hans Wilhelm Saure, "Czech Stasi Spotted the Trumps" (translated by Google), *Bild,* December 14, 2016, https://www.bild.de/news/ausland/donald-trump/tschechen
-stasi-spaehte-trumps-aus-49320410,jsRedirectFrom=conversionToLogin.bild.html.

CHAPTER SIX: GANGSTER'S PARADISE

1. Federal Bureau of Investigation, "Top Ten Fugitives: Global Con Artist and Ruthless Criminal," FBI Archives, October 21, 2009, https://archives.fbi.gov/archives
/news/stories/2009/october/mogilevich_102109.

2. Manish Sahajwani, "8 of the Richest Gangsters of All Time," Investopedia, http://
www.investopedia.com/financial-edge/0912/8-of-the-richest-gangsters-of-all-time
.aspx.

3. Paul Lashmar and Andrew Mullins, "How Wall St Was Fleeced by the Most Evil Gangster in the World," *Independent,* August 20, 1999, http://www.independent.co.uk
/news/how-wall-st-was-fleeced-by-the-most-evil-gangster-in-the-world-1113929.html.

4. Justin Peters, "This Obese Mob Boss Is Twice the Villain Whitey Bulger Ever Was," Slate, August 5, 2013, http://www.slate.com/blogs/crime/2013/08/05/semion
_mogilevich_fbi_ten_most_wanted_list_this_obese_mob_boss_is_twice.html.

5. "The Billion Dollar Don," *Panorama,* BBC Television, produced by Toby Sculthorpe, aired December 6, 1999, https://www.youtube.com/watch?v=cqfgpLP9fm8.

6. Staff, World: Europe, "Russia's 'Mr. Big' Ridicules FBI Allegations," BBC News, August 31, 1999, http://news.bbc.co.uk/2/hi/europe/433695.stm.

7. Tony Thompson and Paul Farrelly, "Russian Mafia Target the City," *Guardian,* August 21, 1999, https://www.theguardian.com/world/1999/aug/22/paulfarrelly
.tonythompson.

8. Jeanne Meserve, "FBI: Mobster more powerful than Gotti," CNN, October 24, 2009, http://edition.cnn.com/2009/CRIME/10/21/mogilevich.fbi.most.wanted/.

9. Kashmira Gander, "Alexander Litvinenko Poisoning: Footage Emerges of Ex-KGB Spy Accusing Putin of Having Links to Businessman Wanted by FBI," *Independent,*

January 23, 2015, http://www.independent.co.uk/news/uk/home-news/alexander-litvinenko-poisoning-footage-emerges-of-ex-kgb-spy-accusing-putin-of-having-links-to-9999744.html.

10. Cathy Scott-Clark and Adrian Levy, "Why a Spy Was Killed," *Guardian,* January 26, 2008, https://www.theguardian.com/lifeandstyle/2008/jan/26/weekend.adrianlevy.

11. Federal Bureau of Investigation, "Top Ten Fugitives."

12. Intelligence Section, Organizational Intelligence Unit, "Semion Mogilevich Organization Eurasian Organized Crime," Federal Bureau of Investigation, August 1996, https://data.occrp.org/text/2554469?dq=heroin&page=40.

13. Friedman, *Red Mafiya.*

14. Nick Kochan, *The Washing Machine: Money, Crime and Terror in the Offshore System* (Mason, Ohio: Thomson, 2005).

15. Laura Radanko, *The Russian Mafia in America* (Gainesville, FL: University Press of Florida, 2011).

16. Alan A. Block and Constance A. Weaver, *All Is Clouded by Desire: Global Banking, Money Laundering, and International Organized Crime* (Westport, CT: Praeger, 2004); Friedman, *Red Mafiya*; Kochan, *Washing Machine.*

17. Friedman, *Red Mafiya.*

18. Ibid.

19. "Solntsevskaya OPG"; Seth Ferranti, "The Solntsevskaya Brotherhood by Niko," Gorilla Convict, October 1, 2015, https://www.gorillaconvict.com/2015/10/the-solntsevskaya-brotherhood-by-niko/.

20. Rumafiozi_eng, "Solntsevskaya Gang Tougher and Cleverer Than Shabalovskaya—Part 1," *LiveJournal* blog, September 12, 2011, https://rumafiozi-eng.livejournal.com/152784.html.

21. "Solntsevskaya OPG: Interpol and Special Services Dossier" (translated by Google), OSP-UA.info, February 2, 2016, http://osp-ua.info/politicas/55782-solntsevskaja-opg-polnoe-dose-interpola-i-spetssluzhb.html.

22. David Satter, *Darkness at Dawn: The Rise of the Russian Criminal State* (New Haven: Yale University Press, 2003).

23. Rumafiozi_eng, "Solntsevskaya Gang Tougher."

24. Transcript of "The Billion Dollar Don," *Panorama,* BBC Television, produced by Toby Sculthorpe, aired December 6, 1999, http://news.bbc.co.uk/hi/english/static/events/panorama/transcripts/transcript_06_12_99.txt.

25. Author's interview with source close to Mogilevich.

26. "Solntsevskaya OPG."

27. Ibid.

28. Serhii Plokhy, *The Last Empire: The Final Days of the Soviet Union* (London: Oneworld Publications, 2015).

29. Bowden, "March 1990 *Playboy* Interview."

30. Author's interview with James Moody.

31. Masha Gessen, *The Man Without a Face: The Unlikely Rise of Vladimir Putin* (New York: Riverhead Books, 2012).

32. Gordon Thomas, *Gideon's Spies: The Secret History of the Mossad,* 7th ed. (New York: Thomas Dunne Books, 2015).

33. Intelligence Section Organizational Intelligence Unit, Department of Justice, Federal Bureau of Investigation, *Semion Mogilevich Eurasian Organized Crime,* August 1996.

34. James S. Henry, "The Curious World of Donald Trump's Private Russian Connections," *The American Interest,* December 19, 2016, https://www.the-american-interest .com/2016/12/19/the-curious-world-of-donald-trumps-private-russian-connections.

35. Gordon Thomas and Martin Dillon, *Robert Maxwell, Israel's Superspy: The Life and Murder of a Media Mogul* (New York: Carroll & Graf, 2002).

36. Thomas, *Gideon's Spies.*

37. Author's interview with Winer.

38. Friedman, *Red Mafiya.*

39. Ibid.

40. Palash Galoosh, "The World's Most Powerful Mobster That You Probably Never Heard Of," *International Business Times,* December 30, 2012, http://www.ibtimes .com/worlds-most-powerful-mobster-you-probably-never-heard-980488.

41. Irina Reznik and Maria Rozhkova, "Milliarder sredney ruki," Compromat.ru, January 28, 2008, http://www.compromat.ru/page_22103.htm.

42. Kochan, *Washing Machine.*

43. Ibid.

44. "Solntsevskaya OPG."

45. Thomas Petrov and Alexey Gordon, "Nationwide Con Artist," *Russian Mafiozi* blog, July 3, 2011, http://rusmafiozi-eng.blogspot.com/2011/07/nationwide-con-artist .html?m=1.

46. Friedman, *Red Mafiya.*

47. "Uzbek, Putin, FSB i Geroin," Glavk, April 28, 2017, http://glavk.info/articles/7728 -uzbek_putin_fsb_i_geroin/%D0%BA%D0%BD%D0%B8%D0%B3%D0%B5.

48. Ibid.

49. Affidavit for Vyacheslav Ivankov wiretapping order application, District Court for the Southern District of New York, https://sethjhettena.files.wordpress.com/2017 /11/vyacheslav-ivankov-wiretap-affidavit.pdf.

50. Friedman, *Red Mafiya.*

51. Lee Hockstader, "Russia's Criminal Condition," *Washington Post,* February 26, 1995, https://www.washingtonpost.com/archive/politics/1995/02/26/russias-criminal-con dition/99b2292d-6478-4d42-8914-30589d5da224/?utm_term=.87954cc6418e.

52. Friedman, *Red Mafiya.*

53. Ibid.

54. Ibid.

55. Ibid.

CHAPTER SEVEN: THE BILLIONAIRE BOYS' CLUB

1. Johnston, *Making of Donald Trump.*

2. Ibid.

3. Robert O'Harrow Jr., "Trump's bad bet: How too much debt drove his biggest casino aground," *Washington Post,* https://www.washingtonpost.com/investigations /trumps-bad-bet-how-too-much-debt-drove-his-biggest-casino-aground/2016/01 /18/f67cedc2-9ac8-11e5-8917-653b65c809eb_story.html.

4. Friedman, *Red Mafiya.*

5. Associated Press, "Ten Atlantic City Casinos Fined $2.48 Million," January 21, 1993.

6. Reuters Staff, "Putin says grandfather cooked for Stalin and Lenin," Reuters, March 11, 2018.

7. Allen C. Lynch, *Vladimir Putin and Russian Statecraft* (Washington, DC: Potomac Books, 2011).

8. Vladimir Putin with Nataliya Gevorkyan, Natalya Timakova, and Andrei Kolesnikov, *First Person: An Astonishingly Frank Self-Portrait by Russia's President* (New York: Public Affairs 2000).

9. Gessen, *Man Without a Face.*

10. Joshua Yaffa, "Putin's Shadow Cabinet and the Bridge to Crimea," *New Yorker,* May 29, 2017, https://www.newyorker.com/magazine/2017/05/29/putins-shadow -cabinet-and-the-bridge-to-crimea.

11. Simon Shuster, "Vladimir Putin's Billionaire Boys Judo Club," *Time,* March 1, 2011, http://content.time.com/time/world/article/0,8599,2055962,00.html.

12. Zarina Zabrisky, "Wrestling and Mafia States" Medium, July 3, 2017. https://medium .com/mosaic2/wrestling-and-mafia-states-d79f1e71bb4.

13. Alexei Sobchenko, "Russia: Putin's Past Becoming a Hot Internet Topic in Moscow," Eurasianet, January 6, 2016, https://eurasianet.org/s/russia-putins-past -becoming-a-hot-internet-topic-in-moscow.

14. Damien Sharkov, "'Putin Involved in Drug Smuggling Ring,' Says Ex-KGB Officer," *Newsweek,* March 13, 2015, http://www.newsweek.com/putin-involved-drug -smuggling-ring-says-ex-kgb-officer-313657.

15. Sir Robert Owen (chairman), *The Litvinenko Inquiry: Report into the Death of Alexander Litvinenko,* issued January 2016, archived June 2016 (hereafter *Litvinenko Inquiry*), 16, http://webarchive.nationalarchives.gov.uk/20160613090324 /https://www.litvinenkoinquiry.org/report.

16. "Uzbek, Putin, FSB i Geroin."

17. "Putin starred in several films of 'Lenfilm' studio," Front News International, December 16, 2017, https://frontnews.eu/news/en/19790.

18. Tom Parfitt, "Vladimir Putin the Stuntman Played Nazi Soldier," *Times* (London), December 16, 2017, https://www.thetimes.co.uk/article/vladimir-putin-the -stuntman-played-nazi-soldier-lx52sl6ql.

19. "Uzbek, Putin, FSB i Geroin."

20. U.S. Department of the Treasury Press Release, "Treasury Sanctions Russian Officials, Members Of The Russian Leadership's Inner Circle, And An Entity For Involvement In The Situation In Ukraine," March 20, 2014.

21. Gessen, *Man Without a Face.*

22. Dawisha, *Putin's Kleptocracy.*

23. Gessen, *Man Without a Face.*

24. Special services and the mafia. Vladimir Ivanidze (Journalist "Top Secret"). Report at the VIII International Conference "KGB: Yesterday, Today, Tomorrow". 24-25 November 2000. http://grigoryants.ru/kgb-vchera-segodnya-zavtra/specsluzhby-i -mafiya-8-konferenciya/.

25. Foreign Affairs Note, "EXPULSIONS OF SOVIET OFFICIALS WORLDWIDE, 1986," United States Department of State, January 2017.

26. Zarina Zabrisky, "Mafia, KGB, Putin and Trump" Medium, November 7, 2016. https://medium.com/mosaic2/mafia-kgb-putin-and-trump-208a7c8e1a56.

27. Henry, "Curious World."

28. "KGB: Yesterday, Today, Tomorrow," III International Conference, October 1–3, 1993.

29. Author's interview with Sipher.

30. Masha Gessen, *The Man Without a Face.*

31. Author's interview with Kalugin.

32. Putin et al., *First Person.*

33. Mark Almond, "Introducing KGB PLC," *The Spectator,* July 10, 1993.

34. "Vladimir Vladimirovich Putin," Ministry of Education and Science of the Russian Federation, http://en.russia.edu.ru/russia/president/1591/.

35. Gessen, *Man Without a Face.*

36. Author's interview with Kalugin.

37. Dawisha, *Putin's Kleptocracy.*

38. *Who Is Mr. Putin?,* film by Anastasia Kirilenko, https://www.youtube.com/watch ?v=m7p4UWjVZa8.

39. Alexander Litvinenko and Yuri Felshtinsky, *Blowing Up Russia: The Secret Plot to Bring Back KGB Terror* (London: Gibson Square, 2002).

40. *Who Is Mr. Putin?,* 19:00; Gessen, *Man Without a Face.*

41. Klebnikov, *Godfather of the Kremlin.*

42. Henry, "Curious World."

43. Jürgen Roth, "Über die symbiotische Beziehung von Politik, Wladimir Putin und die Sankt Petersburger Mafia," *Jürgen Roth / Blog,* May 1, 2014, http://www.juergen -roth.com/blog/uber-das-symbiotische-beziehung-von-politik-wladimir-putin-und -die-sankt-petersburger-mafia/.

44. Sobchenko, "Russia: Putin's Past."

45. Author's interview with American businessman.

46. Dawisha, *Putin's Kleptocracy.*

47. Catherine A. Fitzpatrick, "Spanish Judge Issues Warrants for Russian Mafia Close to Putin; Was Judo Instructor Involved?" Interpreter, May 3, 2016, http://www .interpretermag.com/russia-update-may-3-2016/.

48. Zabrisky, "Wrestling and Mafia States."

49. David Taylor, "Putin's Associates Stole My Oil Company, Says Business Exile," *Times* (London), July 20, 2015, https://www.thetimes.co.uk/article/putins-associates -stole-my-oil-company-says-business-exile-kjq9fc2ktsm.

50. Catherine Belton, "New Book Links Putin to Underworld," *Moscow Times,* October 2, 2003, http://old.themoscowtimes.com/sitemap/free/2003/10/article/new-book -links-putin-to-underworld/235513.html.

51. Dawisha, *Putin's Kleptocracy.*

52. Tony Gentile, "'Putin Involved in Drug Smuggling Ring,' Says Ex-KGB Officer," *Newsweek,* March 13, 2015. http://www.newsweek.com/putin-involved-drug-smuggling-ring-says-ex-kgb-officer-313657.

53. Mark Hosenball, "A Stain on Mr. Clean," *Newsweek,* September 9, 2001. http:// www.newsweek.com/stain-mr-clean-152259.

54. Alessandra Stanley, "Russian Banking Scandal Poses Threat to Future of Privatization," *New York Times,* January 28, 1996, https://www.nytimes.com/1996/01/28 /world/russian-banking-scandal-poses-threat-to-future-of-privatization.html?page wanted=all&src=pm.

55. Ibid.

56. Marshall I. Goldman, "Putin and the Oligarchs," *New York Times,* November 23, 2004, http://courses.wcupa.edu/rbove/eco343/040compecon/Soviet/Russia/ 041123olig.txt.

57. Henry, "Curious World."

58. Paul Klebnikov, "Revenge of the Oligarchs," *Forbes,* February 23, 1998. https:// www.forbes.com/forbes/1998/0223/6104089a.html#310de932d951.

59. Dawisha, *Putin's Kleptocracy*.

60. "Gennady Timchenko, Real-Time Net Worth as of 4/25/18," *Forbes*, April 25, 2018, https://www.forbes.com/profile/gennady-timchenko/.

61. Newsmaker, "Andrei Turchak: Eight Years at the Head of the Depressed Region," Russia News Today, December 10, 2017, https://chelorg.com/2017/10/12/andrei-turchak-eight-years-at-the-head-of-the-depressed-region/.

62. Vladimir Pribylovsky, "Close to Putin," Scilla.ru, 2016, http://scilla.ru/works/knigi/CloseToPutin.pdf.

63. Dawisha, *Putin's Kleptocracy*.

64. Pribylovsky, "Close to Putin."

65. Dawisha, *Putin's Kleptocracy*.

66. Ibid.

67. Alex Goldfarb with Marina Litvinenko, *Death of a Dissident: The Poisoning of Alexander Litvinenko and the Return of the KGB* (New York: Free Press, 2007).

68. Ibid.

69. "Witness Statement of Alexander Goldfarb," *Litvinenko Inquiry*, May 20, 2013, http://webarchive.nationalarchives.gov.uk/20160613090957/https://www.litvinenkoinquiry.org/files/2015/03/INQ017567.pdf.

70. Daniel Treisman, *The Return: Russia's Journey from Gorbachev to Medvedev* (New York: Free Press, 2011).

71. Dawisha, *Putin's Kleptocracy*.

72. *Who Is Mr. Putin?*, https://www.youtube.com/watch?v=m7p4UWjVZa8.

CHAPTER EIGHT: MOGILEVICH'S BIG MOVE

1. Roman Anin, Olesya Shmagun, and Jelena Vasic, "Ex-Spy Turned Humanitarian Helps Himself," Organized Crime and Corruption Reporting Project, November 4, 2015, https://www.occrp.org/en/investigations/4565-ex-spy-turned-humanitarian-helps-himself.

2. *Litvinenko Inquiry*, http://webarchive.nationalarchives.gov.uk/20160613090305/https://www.litvinenkoinquiry.org/report.

3. Lyndsey Telford, Edward Malnick, and Claire Newell, "Is this Alexander Litvinenko's Beyond the Grave Attack on Putin?," *Telegraph*, January 23, 2015, http://www.telegraph.co.uk/news/uknews/law-and-order/11364724/Is-this-Alexander-Litvinenkos-beyond-the-grave-attack-on-Putin.html.

4. Timothy Bancroft-Hinchey, "Notorious Russian Mob to Leave US Jail," *Pravda*, July 13, 2004, http://www.pravdareport.com/hotspots/crimes/13-07-2004/6157-yaponchik-0/.

5. Ibid.

6. Selwyn Raab, "Mob-Linked Businessman Killed in Brooklyn," *New York Times*, May 3, 1989, http://www.nytimes.com/1989/05/03/nyregion/mob-linked-businessman-killed-in-brooklyn.html.

7. Author's interview with source.

8. Friedman, *Red Mafiya*.

9. Ibid.

10. Stefan Lemieszewski, "Boris Berezovsky and Badri Patarkatsishvili," Narkive, 2005, http://soc.culture.russian.narkive.com/fE6hW8hK/boris-berezovsky-and-badri-patarkatsishvili.

11. Intelligence Section, Organizational Intelligence Unit, "Semion Mogilevich Organization Eurasian Organized Crime," Federal Bureau of Investigation, August 1996.

12. Affidavit for Vyacheslav Ivankov wiretapping, https://www.deepcapture.com/wp-content/uploads/Ivankov-Case.pdf.

13. Friedman, *Red Mafiya*.

14. Ibid.

15. Ibid.

16. Ibid.

17. Affidavit for Vyacheslav Ivankov wiretapping; Friedman, *Red Mafiya*.

18. Intelligence Section, Organizational Intelligence Unit, "Semion Mogilevich Organization Eurasian Organized Crime," Federal Bureau of Investigation, August 1998.

19. Friedman, *Red Mafiya*.

20. Ibid.

21. Ibid.

22. Morgenthow and Latham et al. v. the Bank of New York Company et al., index no. 604598/00, Supreme Court of the State of New York, https://web.archive.org/web/20070701095350/http://russianlaw.org/Morgent1.htm.

23. Paul Lashmar and Andrew Mullins, "How Wall St Was Fleeced by the Most Evil Gangster in the World," *Independent,* August 20, 1999, http://www.independent.co.uk/news/how-wall-st-was-fleeced-by-the-most-evil-gangster-in-the-world-1113929.html.

24. Morgenthow v. Bank of New York.

25. Ibid.

26. Paul Farrelly, "Elite's Underworld Links Exposed," *Guardian,* September 4, 1999, https://www.theguardian.com/world/1999/sep/05/paulfarrelly.theobserver.

27. "Solntsevskaya OPG."

28. Ibid.

29. BBC, Transcript—*Panorama*.

30. Ibid.

31. Intelligence Section, Organizational Intelligence Unit, "Semion Mogilevich Organization Eurasian Organized Crime," Federal Bureau of Investigation, August 1996.

32. BBC, Transcript—*Panorama*.

33. Friedman, *Red Mafiya*.

34. 1996 FBI File on Semion Mogilevich.

35. Paul Klebnikov, "The Rise of an Oligarch," *Forbes,* September 4, 2000, https://www.forbes.com/forbes/2000/0904/6606089a.html#5a6425203dfd.

36. Henry, "Curious World."

37. Douglas Frantz and Raymond Bonner, "A Cosmetics Heir's Joint Venture Is Tainted by Ukrainian's Past," *New York Times,* April 5, 1997.

38. Raymond Bonner, "The Russians Are Coming!," *New York Review of Books,* November 16, 2000, http://www.nybooks.com/articles/2000/11/16/the-russians-are-coming/.

39. Intelligence Section, Organizational Intelligence Unit, "Semion Mogilevich Organization Eurasian Organized Crime," Federal Bureau of Investigation, August 1996.

CHAPTER NINE: TURN OF THE SCREW

1. Staff, "The Time Donald Trump Almost Lost Trump Castle," *Press of Atlantic City,* August 3, 2016, http://www.pressofatlanticcity.com/trump/the-time-donald-trump-almost-lost-trump-castle/article_3f5da17a-5983-11e6-8f48-f7350ec7ab17.html.

2. Russ Buettner and Charles V. Bagli, "How Donald Trump Bankrupted His Atlantic City Casinos, but Still Earned Millions," *New York Times*, June 11, 2016, https://www.nytimes.com/2016/06/12/nyregion/donald-trump-atlantic-city.html.

3. Ibid.

4. Douglas Feiden, "Trump Co. Buying Castle the Donald Gets $130M in Stock, 885G in Cash," *Daily News* (New York), October 1, 1996, http://www.nydailynews.com/archives/money/trump-buying-castle-donald-130m-stock-885g-cash-article-1.737340.

5. Mark Bowden, "The Art of the Donald," *Playboy*, May 1997.

6. Roffman v. Trump, 754 F. Supp. 411 (E.D. Pa. 1990), https://law.justia.com/cases/federal/district-courts/FSupp/754/411/2353559/.

7. Bowden, "The Art of the Donald."

8. Ibid.

9. Eric R. Quinones, "Trump's Empire, Act II: Stay Cocky, but Learn from Mistakes," *New Yorker*, November 5, 1996.

10. Jeffrey Toobin, "The Miss Universe Connection," *New Yorker*, February 26, 2018, https://www.newyorker.com/magazine/2018/02/26/trumps-miss-universe-gambit.

11. Ibid.

12. Monte Reel and John McCormick, "Behind Manafort's Loans, a Chopper Pilot Who Flew into Trump's Orbit," Bloomberg Politics, July 25, 2017, https://www.bloomberg.com/news/articles/2017-07-25/behind-manafort-s-loans-chopper-pilot-who-flew-into-trump-orbit.

13. Cnaan Liphshiz, "Brash Ukraine Oligarch Vadim Rabinovich Challenges Europe's Jewish Leaders," *Forward*, October 30, 2013, https://forward.com/news/breaking-news/186487/brash-ukraine-oligarch-vadim-rabinovich-challenges/.

14. Intelligence Section, "Semion Mogilevich Organization."

15. 2012-02.12. U.S. Cable, Moscow Embassy, "The Luzhkov Dilemma," WikiLeaks.

16. David Ignatius, "A History of Donald Trump's Business Dealings in Russia," *Washington Post*, November 2, 2017.

17. Mark Galeotti, "Wikileaks (3): Moscow—Luzhkov and the 'other,'" *In Moscow's Shadows* (blog), December 3, 2010, https://inmoscowsshadows.wordpress.com/2010/12/03/wikileaks-3-moscow-luzhkov-and-the-other-mafia/.

18. Ibid.

19. Luke Harding, "WikiLeaks Cables: Moscow Mayor Presided Over 'Pyramid of Corruption,'" *Guardian*, December 1, 2010.

20. TASS, "Vizity Donal'da Trampa v Rossiyu. Dos'ye" (Donald Trump's Visits to Russia: Dossier), November 9, 2016, http://tass.ru/info/3770283.

21. Jeff Grocott, "Trump Lays Bet on New Moscow Skyline," *Moscow Times*, November 12, 1996, http://old.themoscowtimes.com/news/article/tmt/316249.html.

22. Jeff Grocott, "Trump Tours Sites for Luxury Towers," *Moscow Times*, November 6, 1996, http://old.themoscowtimes.com/sitemap/free/1996/11/article/trump-tours-sites-for-luxury-towers/316474.html.

23. Steven Lee Myers, *The New Tsar: The Rise and Reign of Vladimir Putin* (New York: Knopf Doubleday Publishing Group, 2014).

24. Ibid.

25. Ibid.

26. Ibid.

27. Ibid.

28. Ibid.

29. Ibid.

30. Ibid.

31. Ann Imse, "Past Echoes in Ex-Soviet Prison: Lubyanka: Old KGB Cellblock Recalls Interrogation and Torture of Dissidents," *Los Angeles Times,* September 7, 1991, http://articles.latimes.com/1991-09-07/news/mn-1571_1_lubyanka-prison.

32. "Stalin's Depraved Executioner Still Has Grip on Moscow," *Telegraph,* December 23, 2003, https://www.telegraph.co.uk/news/worldnews/europe/russia/1450145/Stalins-depraved-executioner-still-has-grip-on-Moscow.html.

33. Myers, *New Tsar.*

34. Karen Dawisha, *Putin's Kleptocracy.*

35. Myers, *New Tsar.*

36. Ibid.

37. Ibid.

38. Ibid.

39. Ibid.

40. Cass Jones, "Boris Berezovsky: Timeline," *Guardian,* March 23, 2013, https://www.theguardian.com/world/2013/mar/23/boris-berezovsky-timeline-found-dead.

41. Goldfarb and Litvinenko, *Death of a Dissident.*

42. Ibid.

43. Myers, *New Tsar.*

44. Ibid.

45. Ibid.

46. Yuri Felshtinsky and Vladimir Pribylovsky, "Putin v Moskve," Kasparov.ru, January 21, 2010, http://www.kasparov.ru/material.php?id=4B5811FDB4E78.

47. Myers, *New Tsar.*

48. Ibid.

49. Julia Ioffe, "How State-Sponsored Blackmail Works in Russia," *Atlantic,* January 11, 2017, https://www.theatlantic.com/international/archive/2017/01/kompromat-trump-dossier/512891/.

50. Myers, *New Tsar.*

51. Felshtinsky and Pribylovsky, "Putin v Moskve."

52. *Putin's Asymmetric Assault on Democracy in Russia and Europe: Implications for U.S. National Security: A Minority Staff Report Prepared for the Use of the Committee on Foreign Relations United States Senate,* 115th Congress, 2nd Session, January 10, 2018, https://www.foreign.senate.gov/imo/media/doc/FinalRR.pdf.

53. Boris Yeltsin, *Midnight Diaries* (New York: Public Affairs, 2000).

54. David Satter, testimony before the House Committee on Foreign Affairs, Hudson Institute, May 17, 2007, https://web.archive.org/web/20110927065706/http://www.hudson.org/files/publications/SatterHouseTestimony2007.pdf.

55. Myers, *New Tsar.*

56. Litvinenko and Felshtinsky, *Blowing Up Russia.*

57. Dawisha, *Putin's Kleptocracy.*

58. Telegraph Staff, "Stalin's Depraved Executioner Still Has Grip on Moscow," *Telegraph,* December 23, 2003.

59. Celestine Bohlen, "Yeltsin Resigns: The Overview; Yeltsin Resigns, Naming Putin as Acting President to Run in March Election," *New York Times,* January 1, 2000, https://www.nytimes.com/2000/01/01/world/yeltsin-resigns-overview-yeltsin-resigns-naming-putin-acting-president-run-march.html.

CHAPTER TEN: THE MONEY PIPELINES

1. Steve Harvey, "Party to Trump: Don't Be Cruel," *Los Angeles Times,* February 24, 2000, http://articles.latimes.com/2000/feb/24/local/me-2184.

2. Geoffrey York, "Yeltsin Quits: 'I did all I could,'" *Globe and Mail* (Canada), January 1, 2000, https://www.theglobeandmail.com/news/world/yeltsin-quits-i-did-all-i-could/article1035877/.

3. Ibid.

4. John Diamond, "Yeltsin Shocker: 'I Am Leaving,'" *Chicago Tribune,* January 1, 2000, http://articles.chicagotribune.com/2000-01-01/news/0001040001_1_kremlin-russian-people-prime-minister-vladimir-putin.

5. Christopher Boian, "Eyeing Presidency, Putin Offers a Millennial Vision for Russia," Agence France Presse, December 30, 1999; see http://www.russialist.org/archives/3715.html##5. The full essay, in Russian, may be found here: http://www.ng.ru/politics/1999-12-30/4_millenium.html.

6. Garfield Reynolds, "Putin Gives People Paternal Patriotism," *Moscow Times,* December 30, 1999.

7. Author's interview with anonymous source.

8. Friedman, *Red Mafiya.*

9. Seth Hettena, *Trump/Russia: A Definitive History.*

10. Henry, "Curious World."

11. CBC News, "YBM Magnex used by mob to bilk investors," CBC, June 8, 1999.

12. Karen Howlett, "YBM officers pocketed millions, U.S. says," *Globe and Mail,* April 26, 2003.

13. Peters, "This Obese Mob Boss."

14. Robert S. Mueller, III, "Moving Beyond the Walls: Global Partnerships in a Global Age," Speech given for the 10th Anniversary of ILEA Budapest, Hungary, May 12, 2005.

15. Taras Kuzio, "A kleptocratic coalition of clans has captured the Ukrainian state," *Kyiv Post,* December 29, 2016.

16. Sandra Rubin, "My Meeting with the Most Dangerous Man in Russia," *National Post*, November 20, 1999.

17. Ibid.

18. Ibid.

19. Ibid.

20. Ibid.

21. "US Embassy Cables: Gas Supplies Linked to Russian Mafia," *Guardian,* December 1, 2010, https://www.theguardian.com/world/us-embassy-cables-documents/182121.

22. "It's a Gas: Funny Business in the Turkmen-Ukraine Gas Trade," Global Witness, July 25, 2006, https://www.globalwitness.org/en/reports/its-gas/.

23. Sobel Koshiw, "Dmytro Firtash: Exiled Political Power Broker," *Kyiv Post,* December 9, 2016, https://www.pressreader.com/ukraine/kyiv-post/20161209/281809988526501.

24. "US Embassy Cables."

25. Stefan Wagstyl and Tom Warner, "Gazprom's Secretive Ukrainian Partner Tells of Lone Struggle to Build Business," *Financial Times,* April 28, 2006.

26. "US Embassy Cables: Gas Supplies Linked to Russian Mafia," *Guardian,* December 1, 2010. https://www.theguardian.com/world/us-embassy-cables-documents/182121.

27. Wagstyl and Warner, "Gazprom's Secretive Ukrainian Partner Tells of Lone Struggle to Build Business."

28. "US Embassy Cables."

29. Wagstyl and Warner, "Gazprom's Secretive Ukrainian Partner Tells of Lone Struggle to Build Business."

30. Ibid.

31. United States of America v. Mogilevich, Fisherman, Bogatin, and Tsoura, Criminal No. 02-157, indictment, United States District Court, Eastern District of Pennsylvania, http://online.wsj.com/public/resources/documents/ruslobby-mogilevich-04172007.pdf.

32. Tom Winter, "DOJ: Ex-Manafort Associate Firtash Is Top-Tier Comrade of Russian Mobsters," NBC News, July 26, 2017. https://www.nbcnews.com/news/us-news/doj-ex-manafort-associate-firtash-top-tier-comrade-russian-mobsters-n786806.

33. "It's a Gas."

34. Koshiw, "Dmytro Firtash."

35. Walter Mayr, "Putin's Cold War: Using Russian Energy as a Political Weapon," *Spiegel Online*, January 9, 2006, http://www.spiegel.de/international/spiegel/putin-s-cold-war-using-russian-energy-as-a-political-weapon-a-394345.html.

36. Reuters Staff, "Special Report: Putin's Allies Channelled Billions to Ukraine Oligarch," Reuters, November 26, 2014, https://www.reuters.com/article/russia-capitalism-gas-special-report-pix/special-report-putins-allies-channelled-billions-to-ukraine-oligarch-idUSL3N0TF4QD20141126.

37. "It's a Gas."

38. Reuters Staff, "Special Report: Putin's Allies."

39. Ibid.

40. Ibid.

41. Malcolm Nance, *The Plot to Hack America: How Putin's Cyberspies and WikiLeaks Tried to Steal the 2016 Election* (New York: Skyhorse Publishing, 2016).

42. Dan Morrison, "Battle of the MTA," *Newsday* (New York), December 31, 2000.

43. Simon Bell, "First oligarch claims his due," *The Guardian,* June 2, 2007. https://www.theguardian.com/business/2007/jun/03/russia.

44. Knut Royce, "FBI Tracked Alleged Russian Mob Ties of Giuliani Campaign Supporter (quid pro quo Ivan?)" *Public Integrity,* December 14, 1999.

45. Ibid.

46. Ibid.

47. Spitzer, "[CTRL] Ukrainian Newsgroup."

48. Ben Schreckinger, "The Happy-Go-Lucky Jewish Group That Connects Trump and Putin," Politico Magazine, April 9, 2017, https://www.politico.com/magazine/story/2017/04/the-happy-go-lucky-jewish-group-that-connects-trump-and-putin-215007.

49. Itamar Eichner, "Report: 25% of Wealthiest Russians Are Jewish," Ynetnews, February 11, 2014, https://www.ynetnews.com/articles/0,7340,L-4587086,00.html.

50. Konstanty Gebert, "Putin's Jews," *Moment,* November 5, 2015, http://www.momentmag.com/putins-jews/.

51. *Frontline/World,* "Rich in Russia: How to Make a Billion Dollars: Vladimir Gusinsky," PBS.org, http://www.pbs.org/frontlineworld/stories/moscow/gusinsky.html.

52. Yossi Melman, "No Love Lost," *Haaretz,* December 8, 2005, https://www.haaretz.com/1.4885476.

53. Ibid.

54. Zev Chafets, "The Missionary Mogul," *New York Times Magazine,* September 16, 2007.

55. Judy Maltz, "Kushner Foundation Gives $342K to Chabad—Still Surprised About Jared and Ivanka's Synagogue?," *Forward,* January 9, 2017, https://forward.com

/news/359482/kushner-foundation-gives-342k-to-chabad-still-surprised-about-jared
-and-iva/.

56. Melman, "No Love Lost."
57. "Berel Lazar, Chief Rabbi of Russia," Interfax Religion, http://www.interfax
-religion.com/?act=bio&div=4.
58. Melman, "No Love Lost."

CHAPTER ELEVEN: EASY PREY

1. Susan Schmidt and James V. Grimaldi, "The Fast Rise and Steep Fall of Jack
Abramoff," *Washington Post,* December 29, 2005, http://www.washingtonpost
.com/wp-dyn/content/article/2005/12/28/AR2005122801588.html.
2. Ibid.
3. John Anderson, *Follow the Money* (New York: Scribner, 2007).
4. R. Jeffrey Smith, "The DeLay-Abramoff Money Trail," *Washington Post,* December
31, 2005, http://www.washingtonpost.com/wp-dyn/content/article/2005/12/30
/AR2005123001480_3.html.
5. Glenn R. Simpson and Mary Jacoby, "How Lobbyists Help Ex-Soviets Woo Washington," *Wall Street Journal,* April 17, 2007, https://www.wsj.com/articles
/SB117674837248471543.
6. Paul Kiel, "Justice Dept Probing Russian Influence Buying," ProPublica, June 10,
2008. https://www.propublica.org/article/justice-dept-probing-russian-influence
-buying.
7. Isobel Koshiw, "Dmytro Firtash: Exiled Political Power Broker," *Kyiv Post,* December 9, 2016.
8. Horrock and Myers, "Extradition Target Says."
9. Raymond Bonner, "Russian Gangsters Exploit Capitalism to Increase Profits,"
New York Times, July 25, 1999, http://www.nytimes.com/1999/07/25/world/rus
sian-gangsters-exploit-capitalism-to-increase-profits.html.
10. K&D, LLC t/a Cork v. Trump Old Post Office LLC, and Donald J. Trump, Civil
Action No. 17-731 (RJL), Defendant Donald J. Trump's Motion to Dismiss, May 10,
2017, https://www.politico.com/f/?id=0000015b-f33f-de0a-a15f-ffbf45ad0001.
11. Simpson and Jacoby, "How Lobbyists Help Ex-Soviets."
12. Ibid.
13. Friedman, *Red Mafiya.*
14. Author's interview with Moody.
15. Ibid.
16. US Department of the Treasury Financial Crimes Enforcement Network, "Fin-
CEN Fines Trump Taj Mahal Casino Resort $10 Million for Significant and Long
Standing Anti-Money Laundering Violations," press release, March 06, 2015,
https://www.fincen.gov/news/news-releases/fincen-fines-trump-taj-mahal-casino
-resort-10-million-significant-and-long.
17. Maxine Waters, Daniel Kildee, Gwen Moore, Al Green, Ed Perlmutter, House of
Representatives Committee on Financial Services letter to Steven Mnuchin, May
23, 2017, https://democrats-financialservices.house.gov/uploadedfiles/ltr_fsc
_members_to_mnuchin_re_fincen_request_russia_trump_5.23.17.pdf.
18. Department of the Treasury, "FinCEN Fines Trump Taj Mahal."
19. Melby and Geiger, "Behind Trump's Russia Romance."
20. Ibid.

21. Ben Terris, "George Conway Is at the Center of Everything," *Washington Post,* May 14, 2017, https://www.washingtonpost.com/lifestyle/style/george-conway-is-the -man-at-the-center-of-everything/2017/05/13/e0720ad6-366b-11e7-b412-62beef8121f7 _story.html?utm_term=.ef31d18bd89f; Elizabeth Elizalde, "Kellyanne Conway's New Jersey Roots Involve Grandfather's Alleged Mob Ties," *Daily News* (New York), March 22, 2017, http://www.nydailynews.com/news/national/kellyanne-conway -n-roots-involve-grandpa-alleged-mob-ties-article-1.3005919.

22. Brad Hamilton, "Diamond District's Very Own 'Godfather' Exposed," *New York Post,* November 25, 2017, https://nypost.com/2017/11/25/diamond-districts-very -own-godfather-exposed/.

23. Craig Horowitz, "Iced," *New York,* November, 29, 2004, http://nymag.com /nymetro/news/people/features/10490/.

24. Ibid.

25. Author's interview with Åslund.

26. Oren Dorell, "Why Does Donald Trump Like Russians? Maybe Because They Love His Condos," *USA Today,* December 15, 2016, https://www.usatoday.com/story /news/world/2016/12/15/donald-trump-russia-wealthy-condo-buyers/95464922/.

27. Bowden, "The Art of the Donald."

28. Ibid.

29. Melby and Geiger, "Behind Trump's Russia Romance."

30. Nathan Layne, Ned Parker, Svetlana Reiter, Stephen Grey, and Ryan McNeill, "Russian Elite Invested Nearly $100 Million in Trump Buildings," Reuters, March 17, 2017, https://www.reuters.com/investigates/special-report/usa-trump-property/.

31. Frank, "Secret Money."

32. McCallion & Associates, "The FBI Confirm That It Already Has an Ongoing Investigation of Trump and His Russian Connections," blog post, October 31, 2016, http://blog.mccallionlaw.com/the-fbi-confirm-that-it-already-has-an-ongoing-in vestigation-of-trump-and-his-russian-connections/.

33. Catherine Belton, "The Shadowy Russian Émigré Touting Trump," *Financial Times,* November 1, 2016, https://www.ft.com/content/ea52a678-9cfb-11e6-8324 -be63473ce146.

34. Ibid.

35. Andrew and Gordievsky, *Comrade Kryuchkov's Instructions.*

36. Ibid.

37. Ibid.

38. Tom Burgis, "Dirty Money: Trump and the Kazakh Connection," *Financial Times,* October 19, 2016, https://www.ft.com/content/33285dfa-9231-11e6-8df8-d3778b55a923.

CHAPTER TWELVE: INTERNATIONAL MAN OF MYSTERY

1. Clip of *The Apprentice*, NBC, 2004, https://www.youtube.com/watch?v=5ZXgzx-GyxWM.

2. Tom Gerencer, "How Much Money Does Trump Make in a Year?," Money Nation, November 12, 2016, http://moneynation.com/how-much-money-does-trump -make-in-a-year/.

3. Michael Kranish and Marc Fisher, *Trump Revealed: An American Journey of Ambition, Ego, Money, and Power* (New York: Scribner, 2016).

4. Charles V. Bagli, "Due Diligence on the Donald," *New York Times,* January 25, 2004.

5. Alessandra Stanley, "Contestants, Meet the King of the Jungle," *New York Times,* January 8, 2004.

6. Aaron Elstein, "Yet Another Reason Why Trump Doesn't Want to Release His Tax Returns," *Crain's New York Business,* May 26, 2016, http://www.crainsnewyork .com/article/20160526/BLOGS02/160529884/yet-another-reason-why-donald-trump-doesnt-want-to-release-his-tax-returns.

7. Timothy L. O'Brien, "Trump, Russia and a Shadowy Business Partnership," Bloomberg, June 21, 2017, https://www.bloomberg.com/view/articles/2017-06-21 /trump-russia-and-those-shadowy-sater-deals-at-bayrock.

8. Vladimir Kozlovsky, "Feliks Seyter: zhizn' mezhdu Trampom, FBR i russkoy mafi-yey," BBC News Russian Service, July 17, 2017, https://www.bbc.com/russian/features -40630592.

9. Author's interview with Rosenberg.

10. Email from Robert S. Wolf to the author, August 3, 2017.

11. Roe v. United States, motion to intervene and unseal judicial records, US Court of Appeals for the Second Circuit, 10-2905-cr, 11-479-cr, https://law.yale.edu/system /files/documents/pdf/motion_to_intervene.pdf; Palmer and Oberlander v. Doe and USA, "Petition for a Writ of Certiorari."

12. Author's interview with Lerner.

13. Kozlovsky, "Feliks Seyter."

14. Andrew Rice, "The Original Russia Connection," *New York,* August 3, 2017, http:// nymag.com/daily/intelligencer/2017/08/felix-sater-donald-trump-russia-investigation .html.

15. Sam Thielman, "Trump's Conduits for Capital from the Former Soviet Bloc Are Actually Old Pals," Talking Points Memo, July 25, 2017, http://talkingpointsmemo.com /muckraker/michael-cohen-felix-sater-teenage-acquaintances-trump-organization.

16. Ibid.

17. Anthony Cormier and Jason Leopold, "The Asset," BuzzFeed, March 12, 2018, https://www.buzzfeed.com/anthonycormier/felix-sater-trump-russia-undercover -us-spy?utm_term=.mcxpQkYkY#.pr6V9O8O8.

18. Salvatore Lauria and David Barry, *The Scorpion and the Frog: High Times and High Crimes* (New York: New Millenium, 2005).

19. Felix Sater Case File 26158.

20. Grant Stern, "BUSTED: Felix Sater Lied to MSNBC's Chris Hayes About His Felony Conviction," Stern Facts, March 22, 2018, https://thesternfacts.com/busted-felix -sater-lied-to-msnbcs-chris-hayes-about-his-felony-conviction-ac78dee652e7; State of New York v. Felix Sater, 201 AD2d 323, response to appeal of assault conviction, New York Supreme Court Appellate Division, https://www.scribd.com/document /374613429/People-v-Felix-Sater-201-AD2d-323-1st-of-3-Criminal-Appeal.

21. Charles V. Bagli, "Real Estate Executive with Hand in Trump Projects Rose from Tangled Past," *New York Times,* December 17, 2007.

22. ABC News, "Trump Associate Felix Sater Reveals Covert Career as US Intel Asset," video of interview with George Stephanopoulos, March 17, 2018, http:// abcnews.go.com/Nightline/video/trump-associate-felix-sater-reveals-covert-career -us-53816264.

23. Rice, "Original Russia Connection."

24. Bagli, "Real Estate Executive."

25. Rice, "Original Russia Connection."

26. Alan Feuer, "19 Charged in Stock Scheme Tied to Mob," *New York Times,* March 3, 2000, https://www.nytimes.com/2000/03/03/nyregion/19-charged-in-stock-scheme -tied-to-mob.html.

27. Cormier and Leopold, "Asset."

28. "NASA Study Reveals Gene Changes Between Twin Astronauts," http://abc.go.com /shows/world-news-tonight/episode-guide/2018-03/15-031518-nasa-study-reveals-gene -changes-between-twin-astronauts.

29. Cormier and Leopold, "Asset."

30. *ABC World News Tonight,* "NASA Study."

31. Cormier and Leopold, "Asset."

32. *ABC World News Tonight,* "NASA Study."

33. Ibid.

34. ABC News, "Trump Associate Felix Sater."

35. Cormier and Leopold, "Asset."

36. Ibid.

37. Ibid.

38. Pete Madden and Meghan Keneally, "Soviet-born Donald Trump adviser Felix Sater: 'Send 'em to jail' if Robert Mueller finds collusion," ABC News, March 16, 2018. https://abcnews.go.com/Politics/soviet-born-donald-trump-adviser-felix-sater-send /story?id=53790920.

39. Cormier and Leopold, "Asset."

40. Ibid.

41. Cheryl Collins and David Corn, "This Top Mueller Aide Once Worked on an Investigation of a Trump Associate Tied to the Russian Mob," *Mother Jones,* June 23, 2017.

42. Craig Unger, "Why Robert Mueller Has Trump SoHo in His Sights," *Vanity Fair,* August 13, 2017, https://www.vanityfair.com/news/2017/08/why-robert-mueller -has-trump-soho-in-his-sights.

43. Lauria and Barry, *The Scorpion and the Frog.*

CHAPTER THIRTEEN: BAYROCK

1. Jason Turcotte, "Arif Brings Lap of Luxury to New York City Market," *Real Estate Weekly,* September 26, 2007.

2. Gary Silverman, "Trump's Russian Riddle," *Financial Times,* August 14, 2016, https://www.ft.com/content/549ddfaa-5fa5-11e6-b38c-7b39cbb1138a.

3. Turcotte, "Arif Brings Lap of Luxury."

4. Richard Behar, "Trump and the Oligarch 'Trio,'" *Forbes,* October 25, 2016, https:// www.forbes.com/sites/richardbehar/2016/10/03/trump-and-the-oligarch-trio/#469 ab22c5314.

5. Unger, "Why Robert Mueller."

6. Wayne Barrett, "Inside Donald Trump's Empire: Why He Didn't Run for President in 2012," Daily Beast, May 26, 2011, http://www.thedailybeast.com /articles/2011/05/26/inside-donald-trumps-empire-why-he-wont-run-for-president .html.

7. Michael Idov, "Trump Soho Is Not an Oxymoron," *New York,* April 7, 2008, http:// nymag.com/news/features/45591/index3.html.

8. Barrett, "Inside Donald Trump's Empire."

9. Rosalind S. Helderman and Tom Hamburger, "Former Mafia-linked figure describes association with Trump," *Washington Post,* May, 17, 2016. https://www .washingtonpost.com/politics/former-mafia-linked-figure-describes-association-with -trump/2016/05/17/cec6c2c6-16d3-11e6-aa55-670cabef46e0_story.html?utm_term =.dc5ca682c8e8.

10. Craig Unger, "Trump's Russian Laundromat," *New Republic,* July 13, 2017, https://
    newrepublic.com/article/143586/trumps-russian-laundromat-trump-tower-luxury
    -high-rises-dirty-money-international-crime-syndicate.

11. Allan J. Lichtman, "Here's a Closer Look at Donald Trump's Disturbingly Deep
    Ties to Russia," *Fortune,* May 17, 2017, http://fortune.com/2017/05/17/donald-trump
    -russia-2/.

12. Behar, "Trump and the Oligarch 'Trio.'"

13. Ibid.

14. Alain Lallemand, "L'empereur du Kazakhstan enquête sur un trio venu de la Ré-
    publique kazakhe qui fit trembler les polices de Belgique," *Le Soir* (Belgium), July
    22, 2000, http://www.lesoir.be/archive/recup/m/l-empereur-du-kazakhstan-enquete
    -sur-un-trio-venu-de-la_t-20000722-Z0JGTU.html.

15. Bozena Rynska, "Counted Stars," *Izvestia,* June 20, 2005. https://iz.ru/news/303482.

16. Ibid.

17. Ibid.

18. Marc Champion, "How a Trump SoHo Partner Ended Up with Toxic Mining
    Riches from Kazakhstan," Bloomberg, January 11, 2018, https://www.bloomberg
    .com/news/features/2018-01-11/how-a-trump-soho-partner-ended-up-with-toxic
    -mining-riches-from-kazakhstan.

19. Rynska, "Counted Stars."

20. Champion, "How a Trump SoHo."

21. Associated Press, "Donald Trump Launches Trump University," May 24, 2005.

22. John Cassidy, "Trump University: It's Worse Than You Think," *New Yorker,* June
    2, 2016, https://www.newyorker.com/news/john-cassidy/trump-university-its
    -worse-than-you-think.

23. Nicholas Nehamas, "Before Donald Trump Attacked Foreigners, He Helped Sell
    Them Condos," *Miami Herald,* October 14, 2016, http://www.miamiherald.com
    /news/politics-government/article108150442.html.

24. Kris Hundley, "The Men Behind Trump Tower Tampa," *St. Petersburg Times,* Feb-
    ruary 17, 2005.

25. Associated Press, "Trump Scales Back Plans to Build a Taller Chicago Skyscraper,"
    March 9, 2005.

26. Glen Creno and Ginger D. Richardson, "Downtown Plan Calls for 50-Story Condo
    Tower," *Arizona Republic,* April 30, 2005.

27. Nehamas, "Before Donald Trump Attacked."

28. Author's interview with Bayrock employee.

29. Yana Pevzner and Thiya Barak, "A Billionaire in Stormy Waters," Ynetnews,
    March 29, 2011, http://www.ynetnews.com/articles/0,7340,L-4048812,00.html.

30. Ibid.

31. Associated Press, "Kazakh Businessman Tevfik Arif Denies Sex Party Allega-
    tions," April 2, 2012, https://www.theguardian.com/world/2012/apr/02/tevfik-arif.

32. Pevzner and Barak, "A Billionaire in Stormy Waters."

33. Ibid.

34. 2010/ 20648 Bill of Indictment, REPUBLIC OF TURKEY, ANTALYA CITY, SU-
    PREME REPUBLICAN PUBLIC PROSECUTORS' OFFICE, 2010.

35. Ibid.

36. Barrett, "Inside Donald Trump's Empire."

37. Lukas I. Alpert, "The Crass Menagerie," *New York Post,* May 15, 2009, https://
    nypost.com/2009/05/15/the-crass-menagerie/.

38. Paul Klebnikov, "Gangster-Free Capitalism?," *Forbes,* November 26, 2001, https://www.forbes.com/forbes/2001/1126/107.html#550f80f5a469.

39. Ivanidze, "Spetssluzhby i mafiya."

40. Zabrisky, "Mafia, KGB, Putin, and Trump."

41. Richard L. Palmer, statement on the infiltration of the Western financial system by Russian organized crime before the House Committee on Banking and Financial Services, September 21, 1999, https://data.occrp.org/documents/6523546?documentprefix=Seabeco#page=34.

42. Henry, "The Curious World."

43. Lallemand, "L'empereur du Kazakhstan."

44. Henry, "Curious World."

45. Ivanidze, "Spetssluzhby i mafiya."

46. Michael Dobbs, *Down with Big Brother: The Fall of the Soviet Empire* (New York: Vintage, 1998).

47. Ibid.

48. Dobbs and Coll, "Ex-Communists Are Scrambling."

49. Bloomberg News, "Trump Hotel Toronto Building Set to Be Sold After Developer Defaults," Financial Post, October 27, 2016, http://business.financialpost.com/news/property-post/trump-hotel-toronto-building-set-to-be-sold-after-developer-defaults.

50. Rob Barry, Christopher S. Stewart, and Brett Forrest, "Russian State-Run Bank Financed Deal Involving Trump Hotel Partner," *Wall Street Journal,* May 17, 2017, https://www.wsj.com/articles/russian-state-run-bank-financed-deal-involving-trump-hotel-partner-1495031708.

51. Natasha Bertrand, "Report: Russian bank whose CEO met secretly with Jared Kushner helped finance Trump's Toronto hotel," *Business Insider,* May 17, 2017, http://www.businessinsider.com/russian-vnesheconombank-trump-toronto-hotel-2017-5.

52. Ned Parker, Stephen Grey, Stefanie Eschenbacher, Roman Anin, Brad Brooks, and Christine Murray, "Ivanka and the Fugitive from Panama," Reuters, November 17, 2017, https://www.reuters.com/investigates/special-report/usa-trump-panama/.

53. "About Us," Global Witness.

54. *Narco-a-Lago: Money Laundering at the Trump Ocean Club Panama*, Global Witness, https://www.globalwitness.org/en/campaigns/corruption-and-money-laundering/narco-a-lago-panama/.

55. Parker et al., "Ivanka and the Fugitive."

56. Ibid.

57. Ibid.

58. Ibid.

59. Ibid.

60. Ibid.

61. Adam Davidson, "Donald Trump's Worst Deal," *New Yorker,* March 13, 2017, https://www.newyorker.com/magazine/2017/03/13/donald-trumps-worst-deal.

CHAPTER FOURTEEN: MOTH, FLAME

1. Author's interview with Sipher.

2. Luiza Ch. Savage, "Valerie Plame on juggling romance, babies, identities," *Macleans,* October 26, 2011. https://www.macleans.ca/news/world/not-agent-99-but-close/.

3. O'Brien, "Trump, Russia."

4. Unger, "Why Robert Mueller."

5. O'Brien, "Trump, Russia."

6. Rice, "Original Russia Connection."

7. Michael Daly and Michael Weiss, "Felix Sater: The Crook Behind the Trump-Russia 'Peace' Plan," Daily Beast, February 24, 2017, https://www.thedailybeast.com/felix-sater-the-crook-behind-the-trump-russia-peace-plan.

8. Charles V. Bagli, "Real Estate Executive with Hand in Trump Projects Rose from Tangled Past," *New York Times*, December 17, 2007, https://www.nytimes.com/2007/12/17/nyregion/17trump.html.

9. CASE NO. 09-21406-CIV-WILLIAMS/TURNOFF, Trilogy Properties v. SB Hotel Associates, US District Court, Southern District of Florida, November 26, 2013. https://www.washingtonpost.com/wp-stat/graphics/politics/trump-archive/docs/nov-13-djt-depo.pdf.

10. Unger, "Trump's Russian Laundromat."

11. Carol D. Leonnig, Tom Hamburger and Rosalind S. Helderman, "Trump's Business Sought Deal on a Trump Tower in Moscow While He Ran for President," *Washington Post*, August 27, 2017, https://www.washingtonpost.com/politics/trumps-business-sought-deal-on-a-trump-tower-in-moscow-while-he-ran-for-president/2017/08/27/d6e95114-8b65-11e7-91d5-ab4e4bb76a3a_story.html?noredirect=on&utm_term=.b932465e6bfa.

12. David Cay Johnston, *The Making of Donald Trump* (Brooklyn and London: Melville House, 2016, 2017).

13. David Cay Johnston, "Donald Trump and Kids Named in $250M Tax Scam," Daily Beast, July 14, 2016, https://www.thedailybeast.com/donald-trump-and-kids-named-in-dollar250m-tax-scam.

14. Ben Schreckinger, "The Happy-Go-Lucky Jewish Group That Connects Trump and Putin," Politico Magazine, April 9, 2017, https://www.politico.com/magazine/story/2017/04/the-happy-go-lucky-jewish-group-that-connects-trump-and-putin-215007.

15. *New York Magazine*, Bar Listing, Kiss and Fly.

16. Eli Saslow, "Trump Accuser Keeps Telling Her Story, Hoping Someone Will Finally Listen," *Washington Post*, February 19, 2018, https://www.washingtonpost.com/news/national/wp/2018/02/19/feature/trump-accuser-keeps-telling-her-story-hoping-someone-will-finally-listen/?utm_term=.cf5b888a2b82.

17. Ibid.

18. Hazel Heyer, "Executive Talk: Donald Trump Jr. Bullish on Russia and Few Emerging Markets," eTurboNews, September 15, 2008, https://www.eturbonews.com/9788/executive-talk-donald-trump-jr-bullish-russia-and-few-emerging-ma.

19. Megan Twohey and Steve Eder, "For Trump, Three Decades of Chasing Deals in Russia," *New York Times*, January 16, 2017, https://www.nytimes.com/2017/01/16/us/politics/donald-trump-russia-business.html.

20. Mark Abadi, "Former Trump Adviser Says in Email That He 'Arranged for Ivanka to Sit in Putin's Private Chair' During a Trip to Moscow," Business Insider, August 28, 2017, http://www.businessinsider.com/ivanka-trump-putin-chair-felix-sater-russia-2017-8.

21. Twohey and Eder, "For Trump, Three Decades."

22. Richard Behar, "Donald Trump and the Felon: Inside His Business Dealings with a Mob-Connected Hustler," *Forbes*, October 25, 2016, https://www.forbes.com

/sites/richardbehar/2016/10/03/donald-trump-and-the-felon-inside-his-business
-dealings-with-a-mob-connected-hustler/#2c9c96bc2282.

23. Heyer, "Executive Talk."

24. Reuters Staff, "Russian Tycoon, Symbol of Excess, Convicted of Fraud but Walks
Free," Reuters, July 12, 2017, https://www.reuters.com/article/us-russia-court
-polonsky/russian-tycoon-symbol-of-excess-convicted-of-fraud-but-walks-free-
idUSKBN19X1MZ.

25. Julia Ioffe, "Why Didn't Trump Build Anything in Russia?," *Atlantic,* September
14, 2017, https://www.theatlantic.com/international/archive/2017/09/why-didnt
-trump-build-anything-in-russia/539274/.

26. Mark Franchetti, "'Lightning' Lebedev: I Pulled My Punches," *Times* (London),
October 9, 2011, https://www.thetimes.co.uk/article/lightning-lebedev-i-pulled-my
-punches-qf96pvvggft.

27. Adam Smith Conferences, "Drivers for International Investment in the Russian
Real Estate Sector," June 2008, captured by Wayback Machine. http://web.archive
.org/web/20080604203635/http://www.adamsmithconferences.com:80/html/2008
/realestate/src006.html.

28. Reuters Staff, "Russian Tycoon."

29. Construction.ru Staff, "Three More Arrested in Real Estate Tycoon Sergei Polonsky Criminal Case," Construction.ru, May 26, 2016, http://russianconstruction
.com/news-1/23875-three-more-arrested-in-real-estate-tycoon-sergei-polonsky
-criminal-case.html.

30. Ioffe, "Why Didn't Trump Build."

31. Janusz Bugajski, *Dismantling the West: Russia's Atlantic Agenda* (Washington, DC:
Potomac Books, 2009).

32. "Fisher MB LLC," CorporationWiki, https://www.corporationwiki.com/New
-York/New-York/fisher-mb-llc-3635472.aspx.

33. Unger, "Why Robert Mueller."

34. Ibid.

35. Author's interview with Lerner.

36. Unger, "Why Robert Mueller."

37. Ibid.

38. Author's interview with Oberlander.

39. Author's interview with Winer.

40. Barrett, "Inside Donald Trump's Empire."

41. "Trump Soho Developers Settle Fraud Suit, Give Buyers 90% Refunds," Real Deal,
November 3, 2011, https://therealdeal.com/2011/11/03/bayrock-group-and-sapir
-organization-settle-federal-lawsuit-at-trump-soho-at-246-spring-street-give-buyers
-refunds/.

42. Tom Burgis, "Dirty Money: Trump and the Kazakh Connection," *Financial Times,*
October 19, 2016, https://www.ft.com/content/33285dfa-9231-11e6-8df8
-d3778b55a923.

43. Unger, "Why Robert Mueller."

44. Christopher Brennan, "Trump Associate Received More Than $21M in Kazakh Oli-
garchs' Alleged Money Laundering Scheme," *Daily News,* April 25, 2018, http://beta
.nydailynews.com/news/national/trump-associate-received-21m-alleged-oligarch
-scheme-article-1.3953189.

45. Unger, "Why Robert Mueller."

46. Brennan, "Trump Associate."

47. FL Group, "Investment of $50m in US-Based Real Estate Development Projects," press release, West, May 22, 2007, https://globenewswire.com/news-release/2007/05/22/96900/0/en/Investment-of-50m-in-US-based-real-estate-development-projects.html.

48. Henry, "Curious World."

49. Ibid.

50. O'Brien, "Trump, Russia."

51. Timothy L. O'Brien, "Hey, Mueller, You Should Check Out Iceland," Bloomberg, June 23, 2017, https://www.bloomberg.com/view/articles/2017-06-23/hey-mueller-you-should-check-out-iceland.

52. Clyde H. Farnsworth, "KGB Runs Commerce Unit, US Says," *New York Times,* October 28, 1987, https://www.nytimes.com/1987/10/28/world/kgb-runs-commerce-unit-us-says.html.

53. Henry, "Curious World."

54. Behar, "Trump and the Oligarch 'Trio.'"

55. Topousis, "Rudy Donor."

56. Friedman, *Red Mafiya.*

57. Ben Schreckinger, "The Happy-Go-Lucky Jewish Group That Connects Trump and Putin," Politico Magazine, April 9, 2017, https://www.politico.com/magazine/story/2017/04/the-happy-go-lucky-jewish-group-that-connects-trump-and-putin-215007.

58. Ibid.

59. Yossi Melman, "No Love Lost," *Haaretz,* December 8, 2005, https://www.haaretz.com/1.4885476.

60. Ibid.

61. Ibid.

62. Will Parker, "Jared Kushner Looks to Be Still Tied Up in 229 West 43rd Street Retail Condo," Real Deal, March 6, 2017, https://therealdeal.com/2017/03/06/jared-kushner-looks-to-be-still-tied-up-in-229-west-43rd-street-retail-condo/.

63. Schreckinger, "Happy-Go-Lucky Jewish Group."

64. Maltz, "Kushner Foundation Gives $342K."

65. Schreckinger, "Happy-Go-Lucky Jewish Group."

66. Rabbi Shalom M. Paltiel, "A word From the Rabbi," May 2015.

67. Shalom Patiel, speech, 2014. https://www.youtube.com/watch?v=xSpFtCmoD5o.

68. Schreckinger, "Happy-Go-Lucky Jewish Group."

69. Ibid.

70. Ibid.

71. "High-Profile Bris on Sunday—You're Invited," *New York,* May 30, 2008, http://nymag.com/daily/intelligencer/2008/05/highprofile_bris_on_sunday_you.html.

72. Michael Schwirtz, William K. Rashbaum, and Danny Hakim, "Michael D. Cohen Goes from Trump's Inner Circle to Scrutiny in Russia Investigation," *New York Times,* July 3, 2017, https://www.bostonglobe.com/news/politics/2017/07/02/michael-cohen-goes-from-trump-inner-circle-scrutiny-russia-investigation/lUEDybovhAnRnOs3WLFwyI/story.html.

73. Sam Thielman, "Trump's Conduits for Capital from the Former Soviet Bloc Are Actually Old Pals," Talking Points Memo, July 25, 2017, http://talkingpointsmemo.com/muckraker/michael-cohen-felix-sater-teenage-acquaintances-trump-organization.

74. MSNBC, "Felix Sater on President Donald Trump, Russia, and Being a Spy," *All In with Chris Hayes,* March 16, 2018, https://www.youtube.com/watch?v=3Dqhxwo1ZNI.

75. Josh Marshall, "Understanding the Trump-Russia Money Channel," Talking Points Memo, July 26, 2017, http://talkingpointsmemo.com/edblog/understanding-the-trump-russia-money-channel.

76. William K. Rashbaum, Danny Hakim, Brian M. Rosenthal, Emily Flitter and Jesse Drucker, "How Michael Cohen, Trump's Fixer, Built a Shadowy Business Empire, *New York Times,* May 5, 2018. https://www.nytimes.com/2018/05/05/business/michael-cohen-lawyer-trump.html.

77. Jerry Capeci, "Mobsters Throw Fund-Raisers To Help Pay Legal Fees, *New York Sun,* January 26, 2006. https://www.nysun.com/new-york/mobsters-throw-fund-raisers-to-help-pay-legal-fees/26525/.

78. John Marshall, "Understanding the Trump-Russia Money Channel," Talking Points Memo, July 26, 2017. https://talkingpointsmemo.com/edblog/understanding-the-trump-russia-money-channel.

79. Alison Frankel, "Underemployed Cooley Law grads lose the war, but win the battle," Reuters, July 30, 2013. http://blogs.reuters.com/alison-frankel/2013/07/30/underemployed-cooley-law-grads-lose-the-war-but-win-the-battle/.

80. Anthony Cormier and Chris McDaniel, "How Trump's Lawyer Placed a Big Casino Bet That Left Dozens Empty-Handed," BuzzFeed, March 15, 2017, https://www.buzzfeed.com/anthonycormier/trumps-lawyer-launched-an-offshore-casino-and-left-a-wake?utm_term=.svRElM8xR#.ueBE0MbV5.

81. Laura Figueroa Hernandez, "LI's Michael Cohen: Trump's Fixer and Secretary of Loyalty," *Newsday,* April 14, 2018, https://www.newsday.com/news/nation/donald-trump-michael-cohen-1.18020585.

82. Ilya Marritz and Andrea Bernstein/ProPublica, "Michael Cohen's Long History of Shady and Criminal Associations," Alternet, April 18, 2018, https://www.alternet.org/news-amp-politics/michael-cohens-long-history-shady-and-criminal-associations.

83. Ibid.

84. Ibid.

85. Anthony Cormier, Chris McDaniel, John Templon, and Tanya Kozyreva, "Michael Cohen Pitched Investors for a Powerful Ukrainian Oligarch's Company," BuzzFeed, June 9, 2017, https://www.buzzfeed.com/anthonycormier/michael-cohen-pitched-investors-for-a-powerful-ukrainian?utm_term=.ilq0xjbE5#.oxYBQoPmM.

86. Anthony Cormier, John Templon, Chris McDaniel, and Jason Leopold, "Robert Mueller Is Asking About This Little-Known Chapter of Michael Cohen's New York Life," BuzzFeed, April 10, 2018, https://www.buzzfeed.com/anthonycormier/michael-cohen-taxi-business?utm_term=.ikBK95lDM#.xjXOBpWz2.

87. Ben Fractenberg, "Michael Cohen May Have Had Taxi Business in Russia—and Shady Ties," *Forward,* April 25, 2018, https://forward.com/news/world/399745/michael-cohen-may-have-had-taxi-business-in-russia-and-shady-ties/?utm_content=daily_Newsletter_MainList_Title_Position-1&utm_source=Sailthru&utm_medium=email&utm_campaign=Daily%20-%20M-Th%202018-04-26&utm_term=The%20Forward%20Today%20Monday-Friday.

88. Ilya Marritz and Andrea Bernstein, "The Company Michael Cohen Kept—'Trump, Inc.' Podcast," ProPublica, April 18, 2018, https://www.propublica.org/article/trump-inc-podcast-michael-cohen.

89. Rashbaum et al., "How Michael Cohen Built."

90. Yuri Felshtinsky, "Who Is Mr. Cohen? Trump's Attorney Received $350,000 for the Izmaylovskaya Criminal Group," GordonUA, April 12, 2017, http://m.gordonua .com/english/news/exclusiveenglish/who-is-mrcohen-trumps-attorney-received -350000-for-the-izmaylovskaya-criminal-group-felshtinsky-181620.html.

91. Ibid.

92. Josh Marshall, "'Says Who?'—Piecing Together the Michael Cohen Story," Talking Points Memo, March 1, 2017, https://talkingpointsmemo.com/edblog/says-who -piecing-together-the-michael-cohen-story.

93. Seth Hettena, "A Brief History of Michael Cohen's Criminal Ties," Rolling Stone, April 10, 2018, https://www.rollingstone.com/politics/news/michael-cohens -ties-to-russia-crime-and-trump-w518941.

94. Lauren Price, "Upping the Ante," New York Post, February 22, 2007, https://nypost .com/2007/02/22/upping-the-ante/.

95. Marritz and Bernstein, "Company Michael Cohen Kept."

96. Hernandez, "LI's Michael Cohen."

97. Ibid.

98. Author's interview with McCallion.

99. Ibid.

100. Author's interview with Sipher.

101. Nick Allen, "New-Look KGB, Your Partner Against Crime," Moscow Times, March 21, 1997.

102. Glenn R. Simpson and Mary Jacoby, "How Lobbyists Help Ex-Soviets Woo Washington," Wall Street Journal, April 17, 2007, https://www.wsj.com/articles/SB117 674837248471543.

103. Author's interview with McCallion.

CHAPTER FIFTEEN: PUTIN'S REVENGE

1. Andrew Osborn, "Putin, before vote, unveils 'invincible' nuclear weapons to counter West," Reuters, March 1, 2018. https://www.reuters.com/article/us-russia -putin-nuclear/putin-before-vote-unveils-invincible-nuclear-weapons-to-counter -west-idUSKCN1GD514.

2. Uwe Klussmann, Matthias Schepp, and Klaus Wiegrefe, "NATO's Eastward Expansion: Did the West Break Its Promise to Moscow?," Spiegel Online, November 26, 2009.

3. "Member Countries," NATO, last updated: March 26, 2018. https://www.nato.int /cps/ua/natohq/topics_52044.htm.

4. Michael Posner, "The Invisible Man," Globe and Mail, May 27, 2005, https://www .theglobeandmail.com/report-on-business/rob-magazine/the-invisible-man/article 18228210/?page=all.

5. "Georgy Gongadze," Committee to Protect Journalists, https://cpj.org/data /people/georgy-gongadze/index.php.

6. Matthias Williams, "Murdered journalist buried in Ukraine 16 years after beheading," Reuters, March 22, 2006. https://www.reuters.com/article/us-ukraine-gongadze -idUSKCN0WO2LH.

7. Taras Kuzio, "Understanding Mykola Melnychenko," Ukrainian Weekly, June 1, 2003, http://www.ukrweekly.com/old/archive/2003/220305.shtml.

8. Roman Kupchinsky, "The Strange Ties Between Semion Mogilevich and Vladimir Putin," Eurasia Daily Monitor, Jamestown Foundation, March 25, 2009, https://

jamestown.org/program/the-strange-ties-between-semion-mogilevich-and
-vladimir-putin/.

9. Roman Kupchinsky, "The Gongadze Case," Radio Free Europe/Radio Liberty, August 6, 2004, https://www.rferl.org/a/1342344.html.

10. "70 Journalists Killed in Russia, Ukraine, Between 1992 and 2018," Committee to Protect Journalists, https://cpj.org/data/killed/?status=Killed&motive-Confirmed%5B%5D=Confirmed&type%5B%5D=Journalist&cc_fips%5B%5D=RS&cc_fips%5B%5D=UP&start_year=1992&end_year=2018&group_by=year.

11. Otto Pohl, "The Assassination of a Dream," *New York,* November 1, 2004, http://nymag.com/nymetro/news/people/features/10193/.

12. Sri Jegarajah, "Forbes' Russian Editor Klebnikov Shot Dead Near Moscow Office," Bloomberg, July 10, 2004. (archived at Archive.today) https://archive.li/eYpwd.

13. Email from Richard Behar to author.

14. Ibid.

15. Ibid.

16. Ibid.

17. Anna Politkovskaya, *Putin's Russia: Life in a Failing Democracy,* trans. Arch Tait (New York: Metropolitan Books/Henry Holt, 2007).

18. Alex Rodriguez, "Russian Dissidents Called Mentally Ill," *Chicago Tribune,* August 7, 2007, http://articles.chicagotribune.com/2007-08-07/news/0708070053_1_vladimir-bukovsky-soviet-labor-camps-asylum.

19. Duncan Gardham, "Vladimir Putin Told Boris Berezovsky 'the Show Is Over,'" *Telegraph,* November 14, 2011, https://www.telegraph.co.uk/news/worldnews/europe/russia/8889970/Vladimir-Putin-told-Boris-Berezovsky-the-show-is-over.html.

20. "Russian media baron held in Spain," BBC, December 12, 2000. http://news.bbc.co.uk/2/hi/europe/1067025.stm.

21. Eline Gordts, "Putin's Press: How Russia's President Controls the News," Huffington Post, October 24, 2015, https://www.huffingtonpost.com/entry/vladimir-putin-russia-news-media_us_56215944e4b0bce34700b1df.

22. Evan Osnos, David Remnick, and Joshua Yaffa, "Trump, Putin, and the New Cold War," *New Yorker,* March 6, 2017, https://www.newyorker.com/magazine/2017/03/06/trump-putin-and-the-new-cold-war.

23. Seth Mydans and Erin Arvedlund, "Police in Russia Seize Oil Tycoon," *New York Times,* October 26, 2003. https://www.nytimes.com/2003/10/26/world/police-in-russia-seize-oil-tycoon.html.

24. Alan Cowell, "Alexander Litvinenko lived and died in world of violence and betrayal," *New York Times,* November 3, 2006. https://www.nytimes.com/2006/12/03/world/europe/03iht-spy.3760139.html.

25. Gordon Corera, "Litvinenko death: Russian spy 'was working for MI6'" BBC News, December 13, 2002. https://www.bbc.com/news/uk-20715187.

26. "Hearings," *Litvinenko Inquiry,* http://webarchive.nationalarchives.gov.uk/20160613090328/https://www.litvinenkoinquiry.org/hearings.

27. Dmitry Volchek, "Conversation with Mikhail Trepashkin," Radio Free Europe / Radio Liberty, December 1, 2007.

28. *Litvinenko Inquiry.*

29. Ibid.

30. Lyndsey Telford, Edward Malnick, and Claire Newell, "Alexander Litvinenko: Murdered for Unmasking 'Kremlin-Backed' Mobsters?," *Telegraph,* January 23,

2015, http://www.telegraph.co.uk/news/uknews/law-and-order/11366469/Alexander-Litvinenko-Murdered-for-unmasking-Kremlin-backed-mobsters.html.

31. Author's interview with Kalugin.

32. *Litvinenko Inquiry.*

33. Ibid.

34. Email to the author from Richard Behar.

35. *Litvinenko Inquiry.*

36. Ibid.

37. Alexander Litvinenko and Yuri Felshtinsky, *Blowing Up Russia: The Secret Plot to Bring Back KGB Power* (London: Gibson Square, 2012).

38. *Litvinenko Inquiry.*

39. Ibid.

40. Luke Harding, "Alexander Litvinenko poisoning: move to extradite second murder suspect," *Guardian*, February 29, 2012, https://www.theguardian.com/world/2012/feb/29/alexander-litvinenko-polonium-suspect-charged

41. *Litvinenko Inquiry.*

42. Norman David Dombey, supplementary report to *Litvinenko Inquiry*, http://webarchive.nationalarchives.gov.uk/20160613091249/https://www.litvinenkoinquiry.org/files/2015/03/INQ020031.pdf.

43. *Litvinenko Inquiry.*

44. Luke Harding, "Russian Honour for Andrei Lugovoi Is Provocation, Litvinineko [*sic*] Inquiry Told," *Guardian,* March 10, 2015, https://www.theguardian.com/world/2015/mar/10/russian-honour-andrei-lugovoi-provocation-litvinineko-inquiry.

45. Paul Peachey and Lizzie Dearden, "Vladimir Putin 'Probably' Approved Poisoning of Alexander Litvinenko, Finds Inquiry," *Independent,* January 21, 2016, https://www.independent.co.uk/news/uk/crime/vladimir-putin-probably-approved-poisoning-of-alexander-litvinenko-inquiry-finds-a6824676.html.

46. *Litvinenko Inquiry.*

47. Ibid.

48. Ibid.

49. "ML's Closing Submissions on the Evidence," *Litvinenko Inquiry,* July 31, 2015, 45, http://webarchive.nationalarchives.gov.uk/20150902162845/https://www.litvinenkoinquiry.org/wp-content/uploads/2015/07/ML-Closing-Submissions.pdf.

CHAPTER SIXTEEN: BLOOD MONEY

1. Mark Rachkevych, "WikiLeaks: Nation's Businessmen Tell Tales on Each Other in Chats with US Ambassadors," *Kyiv Post,* September 15, 2011, https://www.kyivpost.com/article/content/business/wikileaks-nations-businessmen-tell-tales-on-each-o-112933.html.

2. Adrian Blomfield, "Ukraine's PM gets a Western makeover," *The Telegraph,* September 29, 2007. https://www.telegraph.co.uk/news/worldnews/1564588/Ukraines-PM-gets-a-Western-makeover.html.

3. Andrew E. Kramer, Mike McIntire and Barry Meier, "Secret Ledger in Ukraine Lists Cash for Donald Trump's Campaign Chief," *New York Times,* August 14, 2016. https://www.nytimes.com/2016/08/15/us/politics/paul-manafort-ukraine-donald-trump.html.

4. Franklin Foer, "The Plot Against America," *Atlantic,* March 2018, https://www.theatlantic.com/magazine/archive/2018/03/paul-manafort-american-hustler/550925/.

5. Peter Finn, "Yushchenko Was Poisoned, Doctors Say," *Washington Post,* December 12, 2004, https://www.washingtonpost.com/archive/politics/2004/12/12/yushchenko-was-poisoned-doctors-say/38b08066-c0b6-4c82-bb87-f109592fd390/?utm_term=.0eaf82aafc49.

6. William Branigin, "U.S. Rejects Tally, Warns Ukraine," *Washington Post,* November 24, 2004. http://www.washingtonpost.com/wp-dyn/articles/A10212-2004Nov24.html.

7. Foer, "Plot Against America."

8. Sergii Leshchenko, "Yanukovych, the Luxury Residence and the Money Trail That Leads to London," Open Democracy, June 8, 2012, https://www.opendemocracy.net/od-russia/serhij-leschenko/yanukovych-luxury-residence-and-money-trail-that-leads-to-london.

9. Steven Mufson and Tom Hamburger, "Inside Trump adviser Manafort's world of politics and global financial dealmaking," *Washington Post,* April 26, 2016. https://www.washingtonpost.com/politics/in-business-as-in-politics-trump-adviser-no-stranger-to-controversial-figures/2016/04/26/970db232-08c7-11e6-b283-e79d81c63c1b_story.html?utm_term=.594ffcd37a37.

10. Art Levine, "Publicists of the Damned," *Spy,* February 1992.

11. Ibid.

12. Steven Harper, "A Timeline: Everything We Know About Paul Manafort's Ties to Russia," Moyers, April 8, 2018.

13. Marie Brenner, "How Donald Trump and Roy Cohn's Ruthless Symbiosis Changed America," *Vanity Fair,* August 2017, https://www.vanityfair.com/news/2017/06/donald-trump-roy-cohn-relationship.

14. Matt Labash, "Roger Stone, Political Animal," *Weekly Standard,* November 5, 2007, https://www.weeklystandard.com/matt-labash/roger-stone-political-animal-15381.

15. Ibid.

16. Michael Kranish and Tom Hamburger, "Paul Manafort's 'Lavish Lifestyle' Highlighted in Indictment," *Washington Post,* October 30, 2017, https://www.washingtonpost.com/politics/paul-manaforts-lavish-lifestyle-highlighted-in-indictment/2017/10/30/23615680-bd8f-11e7-8444-a0d4f04b89eb_story.html?utm_term=.8c811d08c5a7.

17. Franklin Foer, "The Quiet American," *Slate,* April 28, 2016, http://www.slate.com/articles/news_and_politics/politics/2016/04/paul_manafort_isn_t_a_gop_retread_he_s_made_a_career_of_reinventing_tyrants.html.

18. Foer, "Plot Against America."

19. Evan Thomas, "The Slickest Shop in Town," *Time,* March 03, 1986. http://content.time.com/time/subscriber/article/0,33009,960803-1,00.html.

20. Devin Maverick Robins, "Should I Stay Or Should I Go?" Ken Rudin's Political Junkie, August 13, 2015. https://www.krpoliticaljunkie.com/episode-89/.

21. Pamela Brogan, "the Torturers' Lobby" The Center for Public Integrity, 1992. https://cloudfront-files-1.publicintegrity.org/legacy_projects/pdf_reports/THETORTURERSLOBBY.pdf.

22. Alexander Burns and Maggie Haberman, "Mystery Man: Ukraine's U.S. Fixer," Politico, March 5, 2014, http://www.politico.com/story/2014/03/paul-manafort-ukraine-104263.

23. Mustafa Hayem, "Amerikanskiye tekhnologi na sluzhbe u Yanukovycha," *Ukrayinska Pravda,* March 19, 2007, https://www.pravda.com.ua/rus/articles/2007/03/19/4414941/.

24. Ibid.

25. Peter Stone and Greg Gordon, "Exclusive: Manafort Flight Records Show Deeper Kremlin Ties Than Previously Known," McClatchy DC Bureau, November 27, 2017, http://www.mcclatchydc.com/news/nation-world/article186102003.html.

26. Foer, "Plot Against America."

27. Ibid.

28. Ibid.

29. Andrew E. Kramer, "He Says He's an Innocent Victim. Robert Mueller Says He's a Spy," *New York Times,* April 6, 2018, https://www.nytimes.com/2018/04/06/world/europe/robert-mueller-kilimnik-ukraine-russia-manafort.html.

30. Kenneth P. Vogel, "Manafort Man in Kiev," Politico, August 18, 2016. https://www.politico.com/story/2016/08/paul-manafort-ukraine-kiev-russia-konstantin-kilimnik-227181.

31. Franklin Foer, "The Astonishing Tale of the Man Mueller Just Indicted," *The Atlantic,* June 6, 2018.

32. Kramer, "Innocent Victim."

33. Rosalind S. Helderman, Tom Hamburger, and Rachel Weiner, "At Height of Tensions, Manafort Met with Associate from Ukraine," *Atlanta Journal-Constitution,* June 20, 2017, https://www.myajc.com/news/height-tensions-manafort-met-with-associate-from-ukraine/lLnB46poEpw5yyJPRKGAgK/.

34. Vogel, "Manafort's Man."

35. Luke Harding, "Former Trump Aide Approved 'Black Ops' to Help Ukraine President," *Guardian,* April 5, 2018, https://www.theguardian.com/us-news/2018/apr/05/ex-trump-aide-paul-manafort-approved-black-ops-to-help-ukraine-president.

36. Ibid.

37. Author's interview with McCallion.

38. Brett Forrest, "Paul Manafort's Overseas Political Work Had a Notable Patron: A Russian Oligarch," *Wall Street Journal,* August 30, 2017, https://www.wsj.com/articles/paul-manaforts-overseas-political-work-had-a-notable-patron-a-russian-oligarch-1504131910.

39. Jeff Horwitz and Chad Day, "Before Trump Job, Manafort Worked to Aid Putin," Associated Press, March 22, 2017, https://www.apnews.com/122ae0b5848345faa88108a03de40c5a.

40. Wire from FCS MOSCOW/SBOZEK/DPEARCE, "EXTRANCHECK: POST-SHIPMENT VERIFICATION: FEDERALNAYA SLUZHBA OHRANY, MOSCOW, RUSSIA, LICENSE NO: D348852" November 2006.

41. Horwitz and Day, "Before Trump Job."

42. Jeff Horowitz and Dustin Butler, "AP Sources: Manafort tied to undisclosed foreign lobbying," Associated Press, August 17, 2016. https://apnews.com/c01989a47ee5421593ba1b301ec07813.

43. Tom Hamburger and Rosalind S. Helderman, "Former Trump campaign chairman Paul Manafort files as foreign agent for Ukraine work," *Washington Post,* June 27, 2017. https://www.washingtonpost.com/politics/former-trump-campaign-chairman-paul-manafort-files-as-foreign-agent-for-ukraine-work/2017/06/27/8322b6ac-5b7b-11e7-9fc6-c7ef4bc58d13_story.html?utm_term=.5007332d1b0e.

44. Betsy Woodruff, "When Mueller Worked with Manafort's Dictator Client," Daily Beast, April 6, 2018, https://www.thedailybeast.com/when-mueller-worked-with-manaforts-dictator-client.

45. "Ukraine: Extreme Makeover for the Party of Regions?," US embassy in Ukraine diplomatic cable 06KIEV473_a, WikiLeaks, February 3, 2006, https://wikileaks.org/plusd/cables/06KIEV473_a.html.

46. Kranish and Hamburger, "Paul Manafort's 'Lavish Lifestyle.'"

47. United States of America v. Paul Manafort Jr. and Richard W. Gates III, case 1:17-cr-00201, indictment, https://www.politico.com/f/?id=0000015f-6d73-d751-af7f-7f735cc70000; Andrew Prokop, "Read: Mueller's New Indictment of Paul Manafort and Rick Gates," Vox, February 22, 2018, https://www.vox.com/2018/2/22/17042254/robert-mueller-paul-manafort-indictment.

48. "Read the New Indictment of Paul Manafort and Rick Gates," CNN, February 22, 2018, https://edition.cnn.com/2018/02/22/politics/manafort-gates-new-indictment/index.html.

49. Paige Lavender, "Read the Special Counsel's Indictment Against Paul Manafort and Richard Gates," Huffington Post, October 30, 2017, https://www.huffingtonpost.com/entry/manafort-gates-indictment_us_59f7259de4b03cd20b82f2c5?ncid=inblnkushpmg00000009.

50. Betsy Woodruff, "Mueller Reveals New Manafort Link to Organized Crime," Daily Beast, November 2, 2017, https://www.thedailybeast.com/mueller-reveals-new-manafort-link-to-organized-crime.

51. Foer, "Plot Against America."

52. Ibid.

53. Author's interview with McCallion.

54. Vogel, "Manafort's Man in Kiev."

55. Clifford J. Levy, "Ukrainian Prime Minister Reinvents Himself," *New York Times,* September 30, 2007, https://www.nytimes.com/2007/09/30/world/europe/30ukraine.html.

56. Foer, "Plot Against America."

57. Reuters Staff, "Special Report—Putin's Allies Channelled Billions to Ukraine Oligarch," Reuters, November 26, 2014, https://www.reuters.com/article/russia-capitalism-gas-special-report-pix/special-report-putins-allies-channelled-billions-to-ukraine-oligarch-idUSL3N0TF4QD20141126.

58. "RUE Head Exemplifies Company's Lack of Transparency," US embassy in Moscow diplomatic cable 08MOSCOW722, March 14, 2008, https://data.occrp.org/documents/1357287.

59. "The High Price of Gas," *Panorama,* BBC Television, November 5, 2006, http://news.bbc.co.uk/2/hi/programmes/panorama/6121508.stm.

60. Reuters Staff, "Putin's Allies Channelled Billions."

61. Will Englund, "Gas Deal Disputed in Ukraine," *Washington Post,* December 11, 2010, http://www.washingtonpost.com/wp-dyn/content/article/2010/12/10/AR2010121007029.html.

62. Taras Kuzio, "President Yanukovych Threatens Ukraine's Democracy," GlobalPost, April 12, 2010.

63. Richard Balmforth, "Kiev Protesters Gather, EU Dangles Aid Promise," Reuters, December 11, 2013, https://www.reuters.com/article/us-ukraine/kiev-protesters-gather-eu-dangles-aid-promise-idUSBRE9BA04420131212.

64. "President Yanukovych's Plane Stopped Before Taking Off," *NBC News,* February 23, 2014. https://www.nbcnews.com/storyline/ukraine-crisis/president-yanukovychs-plane-stopped-taking-n36551.

65. "Yanukovich Ob"yavlen v Rozysk—Avakov," Ukrainian Independent Information Agency, February 24, 2014, https://www.unian.info/politics/910019-how-yanukovych-ran-from-ukraine-investigation.html.

66. Natasha Bertard, "Hacked text messages allegedly sent by Paul Manafort's daughter discuss 'blood money' and killings, and a Ukrainian lawyer wants him to explain," *Business Insider,* March 21, 2017. http://www.businessinsider.com/paul-manafort-daughter-text-messages-ukraine-2017-3.

CHAPTER SEVENTEEN: WAR BY OTHER MEANS

1. Natan Dubovitsky, "Without Sky," *Russian Pioneer,* May 2014.

2. Peter Pomerantsev, "Putin's Rasputin," *London Review of Books* 33, no. 20 (October 20, 2011), https://www.lrb.co.uk/v33/n20/peter-pomerantsev/putins-rasputin.

3. Pomerantsev, "Non-Linear War."

4. Dubovitsky, "Without Sky."

5. Peter Pomerantsev, "The Hidden Author of Putinism," *Atlantic,* November 7, 2014, https://www.theatlantic.com/international/archive/2014/11/hidden-author-putinism-russia-vladislav-surkov/382489/.

6. Ibid.

7. Ibid.

8. Ibid.

9. Ibid.

10. Andrew Osborn, "Pro-Kremlin youth group accused of plagiarising Goebbels," *The Telegraph,* November 10, 2010. https://www.telegraph.co.uk/news/worldnews/europe/russia/8134688/Pro-Kremlin-youth-group-accused-of-plagiarising-Goebbels.html.

11. Tim Hains, "BBC's Adam Curtis: How Propaganda Turned Russian Politics Into Theater," Real Clear Politics, October 12, 2016, https://www.realclearpolitics.com/video/2016/10/12/bbcs_adam_curtis_how_propaganda_turned_russian_politics_into_a_circus.html.

12. Kasparov, *Winter Is Coming.*

13. Dawisha, *Putin's Kleptocracy.*

14. Molly K. McKew, "The Gerasimov Doctrine," Politico Magazine, September/October 2017, https://www.politico.com/magazine/story/2017/09/05/gerasimov-doctrine-russia-foreign-policy-215538.

15. Ibid.

16. Mark Galeotti, "I'm Sorry for Creating the 'Gerasimov Doctrine,'" Foreign Policy, March 5, 2018. https://foreignpolicy.com/2018/03/05/im-sorry-for-creating-the-gerasimov-doctrine/.

17. McKew, "Gerasimov Doctrine."

18. Anastasiya Kirilenko, "Gangster Party Candidate: Trump's Ties to Russian Organized Crime," Insider, April 7, 2018, https://theins.ru/uncategorized/98190?lang=en.

19. "Solntsevskaya OPG"; Ferranti, "Solntsevskaya Brotherhood."

20. Rumafiozi_eng, "Solntsevskaya Gang Tougher."

21. Michael Schwirtz, "For a Departed Mobster, Wreaths and Roses but No Tears," *New York Times,* October 13, 2009, https://www.nytimes.com/2009/10/14/world/europe/14mobster.html.

22. "People of Interest," Reporting Project, "Semion Yudkovich Mogilevich."

23. Sergey Mikhailov website, "Charitable Foundation 'Participation.'"

24. Anastasia Kirilenko, "Gangster Party Candidate: Trump's Ties to Russian Organized Crime," *Insider,* https://theins.ru/korrupciya/97595/.

25. Author's interview with anonymous source.

26. Author's interview with anonymous source.

27. Ibid.

28. Author's interview with Felix Sater.

29. Author's interview with anonymous source.

30. Yuri Zarakhovich, "Viewpoint: Closing the Door," *Time,* February 26, 2001, http://content.time.com/time/magazine/article/0,9171,99921,00.html.

31. Krishnadev Calamur, "Who Is Emin Agalarov?," *Atlantic,* July 10, 2017, https://www.theatlantic.com/politics/archive/2017/07/who-is-emin-agalarov/533127/.

32. Comtek Expositions, Inc. v. Commissioner, United States Tax Court, docket no. 5130-00, filed May 13, 2003, https://www.leagle.com/decision/2003136585eetcm128011231.

33. "Notorious Arms Dealer with Links to Russia's Military Industry Suddenly Dies in Ukraine," UAWire, October 8, 2017, https://uawire.org/notorious-arms-dealer-suddenly-dies-in-odessa#.

34. Joby Warrick, "Ukrainian port eyed as analysts seek Syria's arms source," *Washington Post,* September 7, 2013.

35. Nikolai Krotov, *Andrey Kozlov: Ekonomicheskaya istoriya i sud'ba cheloveka* (International Relations, Economic Chronicle, 2015), http://letopis.org/project/andrei-kozlov-ekonomicheskaya-istoria-i-sudba-cheloveka/.

36. Luke Harding, "Putin, the Kremlin Power Struggle and the $40bn Fortune," *Guardian,* December 20, 2007, https://www.theguardian.com/world/2007/dec/21/russia.topstories3.

37. Mikhail Rostovsky, "Araz Agalarov, milliarder s chelovecheskim litsom," MKRU, August 11, 2015, http://www.mk.ru/social/2015/11/08/araz-agalarov-milliarder-s-chelovecheskim-licom.html.

38. "OCCRP Names Aliyev 'Person of the Year,'" Organized Crime and Corruption Reporting Project, December 31, 2012, https://www.occrp.org/en/announcements/41-press-box/1772-occrp-names-aliyev-qperson-of-the-year-q-86373901.

39. Neil MacFarquhar, "A Russian Developer Helps Out the Kremlin on Occasion. Was He a Conduit to Trump?," *New York Times,* July 16, 2017, https://www.nytimes.com/2017/07/16/world/europe/aras-agalarov-trump-kremlin.html.

40. Jennifer Gould Keil, "Billionaire Linked to Trump Email Scandal Selling His NJ Mansion," *New York Post,* July 11, 2017, https://nypost.com/2017/07/11/billionaire-linked-to-trump-email-scandal-selling-his-nj-mansion/.

41. Mollie Simon and Jim Zarroli, "Timeline of Events: The 2013 Miss Universe Pageant," NPR, July 17, 217. https://www.npr.org/2017/07/17/536714404/timeline-of-events-the-2013-miss-universe-pageant.

42. David Corn and Hannah Levintova, "How Did an Alleged Russian Mobster End Up on Trump's Red Carpet?," *Mother Jones,* September 14, 2016, http://www.motherjones.com/politics/2016/09/trump-russian-mobster-tokhtakhounov-miss-universe-moscow.

43. United States of America v. Tokhtakhounov et al., 1:13-cr-00268, indictment, United States District Court, Southern District of New York, https://www.justice.gov/sites/default/files/usao-sdny/legacy/2015/03/25/Tokhtakhounov%2C%20Alimzhan%20et%20al.%20Indictment_6.pdf.

44. Ibid.

45. Rumafiozi_eng, "Ambassador Plenipotentiary and Extraordinary of the Russian Mob, Mr. Little Taiwanese," LiveJournal blog, August 27, 2011, https://rumafiozi -eng.livejournal.com/149072.html.

46. Roger Boyes, "From Extortion to Prostitution," *Times* (London), July 9, 2012, https://www.thetimes.co.uk/article/from-extortion-to-prostitution-gk9rwzssrc2.

47. Yuri Felshtinsky, "Who Is Mr. Cohen? Trump's Attorney Received $350,000 for the Izmaylovskaya Criminal Group—Felshtinsky," GordonUA.com, April 12, 2017, http://english.gordonua.com/news/exclusiveenglish/who-is-mrcohen-trumps-attorney-received-350000-for-the-izmaylovskaya-criminal-group-felshtinsky-181620.html.

48. Rumafiozi_eng, "Ambassador Plenipotentiary."

49. "Tayny Tayvanchika," Compromat.ru, August 7, 2002, http://www.compromat.ru /page_12105.htm.

50. Jeffrey Toobin, "Trump's Miss Universe Gambit," *New Yorker,* February 26, 2018, https://www.newyorker.com/magazine/2018/02/26/trumps-miss-universe -gambit.

51. Press Release, "Manhattan U.S. Attorney Charges 34 Members And Associates Of Two Russian-American Organized Crime Enterprises With Operating International Sportsbooks That Laundered More Than $100 Million," Department of Justice, U.S. Attorney's Office, Southern District of New York, April 16, 2013.

52. William Bastone, "Trump Tower House Arrest For Racketeer," The Smoking Gun, March 22, 2017.

53. "The Global Intelligence Files," WikiLeaks, https://wikileaks.org/gifiles/docs/54 /5481746_re-oleg-boiko-.html.

54. William Bastone, "Trump Tower House Arrest for Racketeer," Smoking Gun, March 22, 2017, http://www.thesmokinggun.com/documents/crime/house-arrest -in-trump-tower-378095.

55. Ibid.

56. Confidential, "High Roller Vadim Trincher Sues for $6 Million over Mildew Damages at Trump Tower," *Daily News* (New York), October 8, 2012, condohttp://www .nydailynews.com/entertainment/gossip/confidential/6-million-suit-mildew -damages-trump-tower-article-1.1177189.

57. Kim Velsey, "Art Dealer Hillel Nahmad Completes His Trump Tower Collection, Buys Out Entire 51st Floor," *Observer,* January 23, 2013, http://observer.com/2013/01 /art-dealer-hillel-nahmad-completes-his-trump-tower-collection-buys-out-entire -51st-floor/.

58. Megan Willett, "Meet the Billionaire Art-Dealing Playboy Who Was Arrested in a Massive Gambling Ring This Week," Business Insider, April 18, 2013, http://www .businessinsider.com/the-life-of-hillel-helly-nahmad-2013-4.

59. Oren Dorell, "Trump's Business Network Reached Alleged Russian Mobsters," *USA Today,* March 28, 2017, https://www.usatoday.com/story/news/world/2017/03 /28/trump-business-past-ties-russian-mobsters-organized-crime/98321252/.

60. Henry, "Curious World."

61. United States of America v. Tokhtakhounov et al., indictment.

62. Alec Luhn, "Billionaire US Art Dealer Hillel 'Helly' Nahmad Admits to Running $100m Global Gambling Ring," *Independent,* November 14, 2013, http://www .independent.co.uk/news/world/americas/russian-mobsters-a-hollywood-poker -princess-and-the-billionaire-us-art-dealer-who-admits-to-running-8940423.html.

63. US Attorney's Office, Southern District of New York, "Two Defendants Sentenced for Participating in Racketeering Conspiracy with Russian-American Organized Crime Enterprise Operating International Sportsbook That Laundered More Than $100 Million," press release, FBI.gov, April 30, 2014, https://www.fbi.gov /contact-us/field-offices/newyork/news/press-releases/two-defendants-sentenced -for-participating-in-racketeering-conspiracy-with-russian-american-organized -crime-enterprise-operating-international-sportsbook-that-laundered-more-than -100-million.

64. Ibid.

65. Michael Isikoff and David Corn, "Miss Universe in Moscow: How Trump's Beauty Contest Spawned a Business Deal with Russians and a Bond with Putin," Yahoo!, March 8, 2018, https://www.yahoo.com/news/miss-universe-moscow -trumps-beauty-contest-spawned-business-deal-russians-bond-putin-100026386 .html.

66. Noah Kirsch, "The Full Exclusive Interview: Emin Agalarov, Russian Scion at Center of Trump Controversy," *Forbes,* July 12, 2017, https://www.forbes.com/sites /noahkirsch/2017/07/12/the-full-exclusive-interview-emin-agalarov-russian-donald -trump-jr-controversy/#3ee9ff9569d0.

67. Isikoff and Corn, "Miss Universe in Moscow."

68. Jeremy Diamond, "Exclusive: Video shows Trump with associates tied to email controversy," CNN, July 13, 2017. https://www.cnn.com/2017/07/12/politics/video -trump-relationships-russian-associates/index.html.

69. Kyle Cheney and David Herszenhorn, "The Would-Be President and the Oligarch," *Politico,* July 12, 2017, https://www.politico.com/story/2017/07/12/trump-russia -agalarov-240434.

70. Kuisa Kroll and Kerry Dolan, "The World's Billionaires 2018," *Forbes,* March 6, 2018. https://www.forbes.com/billionaires/#40264de1251c.

71. Isikoff and Corn, "Miss Universe in Moscow."

72. Ibid.

73. Jon Swaine and Shaun Walker, "Trump in Moscow: What Happened at Miss Universe in 2013," *Guardian,* September 18, 2017, https://www.theguardian.com /us-news/2017/sep/18/trump-in-moscow-what-happened-at-miss-universe-in-2013.

74. Raymond Bonner, "Laundering of Money Seen as 'Easy,'" *New York Times,* November 29, 2000, http://www.nytimes.com/2000/11/29/business/laundering-of -money-seen-as-easy.html.

75. Jon Swaine, "Russian man at Trump Jr meeting had partner with Soviet intelligence ties, US investigators said," *The Guardian,* July 21, 2017. https://www.theguard ian.com/world/2017/jul/21/donald-trump-jr-russia-meeting-eighth-person-soviet -intelligence.

76. United States General Accounting Office, "Suspicious Banking Activities: Possible Money Laundering by US Corporations Formed for Russian Entities," Report to the Ranking Minority Member, Permanent Subcommittee on Investigations, Committee on Governmental Affairs, United States Senate, October 31, 2000, https://www.gao.gov/assets/240/230932.pdf.

77. Swaine and Walker, "Trump in Moscow."

78. John Katsilometes, "Final Act: Nightclub at Palazzo Closes After Run-ins with Parent Company," *Las Vegas Sun,* October 13, 2013, https://lasvegassun.com/blogs /kats-report/2013/oct/13/act-palazzo-closes/.

79. Isikoff and Corn, "Miss Universe in Moscow."

80. TV News Desk, "Donald J. Trump Announces Miss Universe 2013 to Take Place in Moscow, Russia," Broadway World, June 17, 2013, https://www.broadwayworld.com/bwwtv/article/Donald-J-Trump-Announces-MISS-UNIVERSE-2013-To-Take-Place-in-Moscow-Russia-20130617.

81. Donald J. Trump (@realDonaldTrump), "Do you think Putin . . . ," Twitter, June 18, 2013, https://twitter.com/realDonaldTrump/status/347191326112112640.

82. Shane Harris, Rosalind S. Helderman and Karoun Demirjian, "In a personal letter, Trump invited Putin to the 2013 Miss Universe pageant," The Washington Post, March 9, 2018. https://www.washingtonpost.com/world/national-security/in-a-personal-letter-trump-invited-putin-to-the-2013-miss-universe-pageant/2018/03/09/a3404358-23d2-11e8-a589-763893265565_story.html?utm_term=.66c727791cd8.

83. Ibid.

84. Jonathan O'Connell, David A. Fahrenthold and Jack Gillum, "As the 'King of Debt,' Trump borrowed to build his empire. Then he began spending hundreds of millions in cash," The Washington Post, May 5, 2018.

85. Bill Littlefield, "A Day (and a Cheeseburger) with President Trump," WBUR.org, May 5, 2017, http://www.wbur.org/onlyagame/2017/05/05/james-dodson-donald-trump-golf.

86. Page Six Team, "Trump Researching 2016 Run," Page Six, May 27, 2013, https://pagesix.com/2013/05/27/trump-researching-2016-run/.

87. Neil Cavuto, "Is Donald Trump exploring a 2016 presidential run," Fox News, May 29, 2013.

88. Greta Van Susteren, "Trump: 'Embarrassing' how Putin has 'played' Obama," Fox News, September 12, 2013. http://www.foxnews.com/transcript/2013/09/13/trump-embarrassing-how-putin-has-played-obama.html.

89. Vernon Silver, "Flight Records Illuminate Mystery of Trump's Moscow Nights," Bloomberg, April 23, 2018. https://www.bloomberg.com/news/articles/2018-04-23/flight-records-illuminate-mystery-of-trump-s-moscow-nights.

90. "Phil Ruffin and Aleksandra Nikolaenko," Forbes, https://www.forbes.com/pictures/mfg45hgme/phil-ruffin-and-aleksandra-nikolaenko/#113ef323105d.

91. Corn and Isikoff, "What Happened."

92. Ken Dilanian and Jonathan Allen, "Trump Bodyguard Keith Schiller Testifies Russian Offered Trump Women, Was Turned Down," NBC News, November 9, 2017, https://www.nbcnews.com/news/us-news/trump-bodyguard-testifies-russian-offered-trump-women-was-turned-down-n819386.

93. Andrew Kaczynski, "Trump Boasted in 2014 of Receiving Gift from Putin and Meeting His Advisers," BuzzFeed, July 31, 2016, https://www.buzzfeed.com/andrewkaczynski/from-russia-with-love-trump?utm_term=.gr46OnNxm#.mgv8n29d3.

94. Nobu Moscow, "Donald Trump and Emin Agalarov . . . ," Facebook, November 8, 2013, https://www.facebook.com/nobumoscow/photos/a.163105327043858.30788.158786840809040/656802097674176/?type=3&theater.

95. Silver, "Flight Records Illuminate."

96. Evgenia Pismennaya, Stephen Kravchenko and Stephanie Baker, "The Day Trump Came to Moscow: Oligarchs, Miss Universe and Nobu," Bloomberg, December 21, 2016. https://www.bloomberg.com/news/articles/2016-12-21/the-day-trump-came-to-moscow-oligarchs-miss-universe-and-nobu.

97. Konrad Putzier, "Hotel Trio Aims to Bring Manhattan to Moscow," Real Estate Weekly, May 28, 2018, http://rew-online.com/2013/11/12/hotel-trio-aims-to-bring-manhattan-to-moscow/.

98. Seth Hettena, *Trump/Russia: A Definitive History* (New York: Melville House, 2018).

99. Putzier, "Hotel Trio."

100. Ibid.

101. Swaine and Walker, "Trump in Moscow."

102. Tessa Stuart, "A Timeline of Donald Trump's Creepiness While He Owned Miss Universe," *Rolling Stone,* October 12, 2016, https://www.rollingstone.com /politics/features/timeline-of-trumps-creepiness-while-he-owned-miss-universe -w444634.

103. "Former Beauty Queen: Contestants Were Forced To Greet Trump Even When Not Fully Dressed," CBS LA, October 11, 2016. https://losangeles.cbslocal.com/2016/10/11 /former-beauty-queen-she-other-contestants-were-forced-to-greet-trump-even-when -not-fully-dressed/.

104. David Corn, "The Trump-Russia Conspiracy Is Now Very Simple," *Mother Jones,* July 11, 2017. https://www.motherjones.com/politics/2017/07/the-trump-russia -conspiracy-is-now-very-simple/.

105. Miss Universe Organization, "Donald Trump Announces Miss Universe 2013 to Take Place at Crocus City Hall in Moscow, Russia," press release, June 16, 2013, https://data.occrp.org/documents/6308844?documentq=Agalarov#page=1&mode =view.

106. Nellie Andreeva, "Ratings Rat Race: Miss Universe Down in Saturday Move, College Football Tops Night," Deadline, November 10, 2013, http://deadline.com/2013 /11/ratings-rat-race-miss-universe-down-in-saturday-move-college-football-tops -night-631871/.

107. "Aras Agalarov did not let Donald Trump to his beauties," Minval.az, 2013. https:// minval.az/news/26073.

108. Author's interview with Sipher.

109. Anna Nemtsova, "Behind the Scenes at Trump's Infamous Night in Moscow—and How It Led to Twitterdammerung," Daily Beast, July 12, 2017, https://www.thedai lybeast.com/behind-the-scenes-at-trumps-infamous-night-in-moscowand-how-it -led-to-twitterdammerung.

110. Hugh Hewitt Show, "Donald Trump Returns," September 21, 2015.

111. Silver, "Flight Records Illuminate Mystery."

112. Ibid.

113. Jane Mayer, "Christopher Steele, the Man Behind the Trump Dossier," *New Yorker,* March 12, 2018, https://www.newyorker.com/magazine/2018/03/12/chris topher-steele-the-man-behind-the-trump-dossier.

114. Ibid.

115. Ibid.

116. Ken Bensinger, Miriam Elder and Mark Schoofs, "These Reports Allege Trump Has Deep Ties To Russia," BuzzFeed News, January 10, 2017.

CHAPTER EIGHTEEN: THE BATTLE IS JOINED

1. Alexander Burns and Maggie Haberman, "Mystery Man: Ukraine's US Fixer," Politico, March 5, 2014, https://www.politico.com/story/2014/03/paul-manafort -ukraine-104263.

2. Glenn R. Simpson and Mary Jacoby, "How Lobbyists Help Ex-Soviets Woo Washington," *Wall Street Journal,* April 17, 2007, https://www.wsj.com/articles /SB117674837248471543.

3. Ruth May, "GOP Campaigns Took $7.35 Million from Oligarch Linked to Russia," *Dallas News,* August 3, 2017, https://www.dallasnews.com/opinion /commentary/2017/08/03/tangled-web-connects-russian-oligarch-money-gop-cam paigns.

4. Staci Zaretsky, "The Largest Law Firm in The United States," Above the Law, April 16, 2018.

5. Peter Stone and Greg Gordon, "FBI Investigating Whether Russian Money Went to NRA to Help Trump," McClatchy DC Bureau, January 18, 2018, http://www .mcclatchydc.com/news/nation-world/national/article195231139.html.

6. Robert S. Mueller III, speech commemorating the tenth anniversary of the International Law Enforcement Academy, Budapest, Hungary, May 12, 2005, FBI.gov, https://archives.fbi.gov/archives/news/speeches/moving-beyond-the-walls-global -partnerships-in-a-global-age.

7. Natasha Bertrand, "Former FBI Director Represented Russian Firm at Center of Major Money-Laundering Probe," Business Insider, November 16, 2017, http:// www.businessinsider.com/fbi-director-louis-freeh-russia-prevezon-money-launder ing-2017-11.

8. Anna Aruntuntan, "The Magnitsky Affair and Russia's Original Sin," Foreign Policy, July 21, 2017. https://foreignpolicy.com/2017/07/21/the-magnitsky-affair -and-russias-original-sin-putin/.

9. "Lies of Nekrasov-Phraya anti-Magnitsky Documentary," June 2016, http://russian- untouchables.com/docs/Nekrasov%20Lies%20Presentaion%20June%20(ENG)% 20NEW%20JUNE%202016%20v%202.pdf.

10. Owen Matthews, "There's Something Rotten in the State of Russia," *Spectator,* January 6, 2010, https://www.spectator.co.uk/2010/01/theres-something-rotten-in -the-state-of-russia/.

11. Luke Harding, "Hermitage lawyer's death in Russian jail a crime, says colleagues" *The Guardian,* November 18, 2009. https://www.theguardian.com/business/2009 /nov/18/moscow-death-lawyer-magnitsky.

12. Jonathan Power, "Threat of the Russian Nuclear Mafia," *Baltimore Sun*, October 14, 1997, http://articles.baltimoresun.com/1997-10-14/news/1997287146_1_russian -mafia-nuclear-weapons-nuclear-bomb.

13. Darrell Hofheinz, "Deed: Ex-FBI Head Louis Freeh Linked to $9.38M Home Purchase," *Palm Beach Daily News,* May 5, 2017, https://www.palmbeachdailynews .com/news/local/deed-fbi-head-louis-freeh-linked-38m-home-purchase /1nLZ9zH3y1hXrspMix3FjI/.

14. Amber Phillips, "18 not-so-nice things U.S. politicians have said about Vladimir Putin," *The Washington Post,* June 10, 2015.

15. Ibid.

16. Michael Crowley and Julia Ioffe, "Why Putin Hates Hillary," Politico, July 25, 2016, https://www.politico.com/story/2016/07/clinton-putin-226153Ibid.

17. Luke Harding, "Former Trump Aide Approved 'Black Ops' to Help Ukraine President," *Guardian*, April 5, 2018, https://www.theguardian.com/us-news /2018/apr/05/ex-trump-aide-paul-manafort-approved-black-ops-to-help-ukraine -president.

18. Human Rights Watch, "Russia: Failing to Do Fair Share to Help Syrian Refugees," press release, September 14, 2016, https://www.hrw.org/news/2016/09/14/russia -failing-do-fair-share-help-syrian-refugees.

19. Lizzie Dearden, "Russia and Syria 'Weaponising' Refugee Crisis to Destabilise Europe, Nato Commander Claims," *Independent,* March 3, 2016, https://www.independent.co.uk/news/world/middle-east/russia-and-syria-weaponising-refugee-crisis-to-destabilise-europe-nato-commander-claims-a6909241.html.

20. *Putin's Asymmetric Assault on Democracy in Russia and Europe: Implications for U.S. National Security A Minority Staff Report Prepared for the Use of the Committee on Foreign Relations United States Senate,* 115th Congress, 2nd Session, January 10, 2018, https://www.foreign.senate.gov/imo/media/doc/FinalRR.pdf.

21. Alexi Mostrous, "Russia used Twitter bots and trolls 'to disrupt' Brexit vote," *The Sunday Times,* November 15, 2017. https://www.thetimes.co.uk/article/russia-used-web-posts-to-disrupt-brexit-vote-h9nv5zg6c.

22. Author's correspondence with Tomasz Piatek.

23. Ibid.

24. Ibid.

25. Rajeev Syal, "Polish Defence Minister Condemned over Jewish Conspiracy Theory," *Guardian,* November 10, 2015, https://www.theguardian.com/world/2015/nov/10/polish-defence-minister-condemned-over-jewish-conspiracy-theory.

26. Author's correspondence with Tomasz Piatek.

27. *Putin's Asymmetric Assault on Democracy in Russia and Europe: Implications for U.S. National Security A Minority Staff Report Prepared for the Use of the Committee on Foreign Relations United States Senate.*

28. Lizzie Dearden, "Boris Nemtsov shot dead: What we know and what we may never find out about his murder," *The Independent,* March 3, 2015. https://www.independent.co.uk/news/world/europe/boris-nemtsov-shot-dead-what-we-know-and-what-we-may-never-find-out-about-his-murder-10081897.html.

29. *Putin's Asymmetric Assault on Democracy in Russia and Europe: Implications for U.S. National Security A Minority Staff Report Prepared for the Use of the Committee on Foreign Relations United States Senate.*

30. Philip Bumb, "If Trump never got off that escalator, where would he be now?" *The Washington Post,* June 16, 2017. https://www.washingtonpost.com/news/politics/wp/2017/06/16/if-trump-never-got-off-that-escalator-where-would-he-be-now/?utm_term=.02cd1cb92f0c.

31. David Corn and Michael Isikoff, "What Happened in Moscow: The Inside Story of How Trump's Obsession with Putin Began," *Mother Jones,* March 8, 2018, https://www.motherjones.com/politics/2018/03/russian-connection-what-happened-moscow-inside-story-trump-obsession-putin-david-corn-michael-isikoff/.

32. Alexander Burns, "Donald Trump, Pushing Someone Rich, Offers Himself," *New York Times,* June 16, 2015, https://www.nytimes.com/2015/06/17/us/politics/donald-trump-runs-for-president-this-time-for-real-he-says.html.

33. *Washington Post* Staff, "Full text: Donald Trump announces a presidential bid," *The Washington Post,* June 16, 2015. https://www.washingtonpost.com/news/post-politics/wp/2015/06/16/full-text-donald-trump-announces-a-presidential-bid/?utm_term=.bdcf72fe2648.

34. Ibid.

35. Erin Durkin and Adam Edelman, "Donald Trump Enters 2016 Presidential Race with Bizarre Speech Insulting Mexican Immigrants, Lambasting Obama," *Daily News,* June 17, 2017, http://www.nydailynews.com/news/politics/donald-trump-entering-2016-presidential-race-article-1.2259706.

36. Emily Ngo, "Donald Trump: As President, I'd Restore America's 'Brand,'" *Newsday,* June 16, 2016, https://www.newsday.com/news/nation/donald-trump -announces-he-s-running-for-president-1.10548619.

37. Aaron Couch and Emmett McDermott, "Donald Trump Campaign Offered Actors $50 to Cheer for Him at Presidential Announcement," *Hollywood Reporter,* June 17, 2015, https://www.hollywoodreporter.com/news/donald-trump -campaign-offered-actors-803161.

CHAPTER NINETEEN: BACK CHANNELS

1. Sean Hannity, "Exclusive: Donald Trump on what made him run for president on 'Hannity,'" June 17, 2015, http://www.foxnews.com/transcript/2015/ 06/18/exclusive-donald-trump-on-what-made-him-run-for-president-on-hannity .html.

2. Denise Clifton and Mark Follman, "The Very Strange Case of Two Russian Gun Lovers, the NRA, and Donald Trump," *Mother Jones,* May/June 2018, https://www .motherjones.com/politics/2018/03/trump-russia-nra-connection-maria-butina -alexander-torshin-guns/.

3. Tom Hamburger, Rosalind S. Helderman, and Michael Birnbaum, "Inside Trump's financial ties to Russia and his unusual flattery of Vladimir Putin," *Washington Post,* June 17, 2016, https://www.washingtonpost.com/politics/inside-trumps -financial-ties-to-russia-and-his-unusual-flattery-of-vladimir-putin/2016/06/17/db dcaac8-31a6-11e6-8ff7-7b6c1998b7a0_story.html?utm_term=.5ca5b7092e19.

4. US Office of the Director of National Intelligence, "Background to 'Assessing Russian Activities and Intentions in Recent US Elections': The Analytic Process and Cyber Incident Attribution," January 6, 2017, https://www.dni.gov/files/docu ments/ICA_2017_01.pdf.

5. Jim Sciutto, "How One Typo Helped Let Russian Hackers In," CNN, June 27, 2017, https://www.cnn.com/2017/06/27/politics/russia-dnc-hacking-csr/index.html.

6. Ibid.

7. Office of the Director of National Intelligence, "Background to 'Assessing Russian Activities.'"

8. Colin Campbell, "Donald Trump Has Surged to the Top of 2 New 2016 Polls," Business Insider, July 9, 2015, http://www.businessinsider.com/polls-donald-trump -in-first-place-2015-7.

9. Mary Troyan, "Trump: I could shoot a person and not lose votes," *USA Today,* January 23, 2016, https://www.usatoday.com/story/news/politics/onpolitics/2016 /01/23/trump-could-shoot-person-and-not-lose-votes/79232258/.

10. Donald Trump Jr. emails, exhibit in Justice Department inquiry into the June 9, 2016, Trump Tower meeting, https://www.judiciary.senate.gov/imo/media/doc/ Trump%20Jr%20Exhibits_redacted.pdf.

11. Sam Thielman, "Trump's Conduits for Capital from the Former Soviet Bloc Are Actually Old Pals," Talking Points Memo, July 25, 2017, http://talkingpoints memo.com/muckraker/michael-cohen-felix-sater-teenage-acquaintances-trump -organization.

12. Matt Apuzzo and Maggie Haberman, "Trump Associate Boasted That Moscow Business Deal 'Will Get Donald Elected,'" *New York Times,* August 28, 2017, https:// www.nytimes.com/2017/08/28/us/politics/trump-tower-putin-felix-sater.html.

13. Ibid.

14. Ibid.

15. Leonnig, Hamburger, and Helderman, "Trump's Business Sought Deal."

16. Michael Crowley, "The Kremlin's Candidate," Politico, May/June 2016, https://www
.politico.com/magazine/story/2016/04/donald-trump-2016-russia-today-rt-kremlin
-media-vladimir-putin-213833.

17. Ken Dilanian, "Russians Paid Mike Flynn $45K for Moscow Speech, Documents
Show," NBC News, March 16, 2017, https://www.nbcnews.com/news/us-news/rus
sians-paid-mike-flynn-45k-moscow-speech-documents-show-n734506.

18. Kyle Cheney and Randy Lemmerman, "Carter Page testimony highlights: Trump
aide dismisses Russian interference," Politico, November 6, 2017, https://www
.politico.com/story/2017/11/06/carter-page-russia-testimony-244628.

19. Sharon LaFraniere, Mark Mazzetti, and Matt Apuzzo, "How the Russia Inquiry
Began: A Campaign Aide, Drinks and Talk of Political Dirt," New York Times,
December 30, 2017, https://www.nytimes.com/2017/12/30/us/politics/how-fbi
-russia-investigation-began-george-papadopoulos.html.

20. Luke Harding, Stephanie Kirchgaessner, and Shaun Walker, "Trump Adviser
George Papadopoulos and the Lies About Russian Links," Guardian, October 31,
2017, https://www.theguardian.com/us-news/2017/oct/30/george-papadopoulos
-donald-trump-russia-charge-putin.

21. Ibid.

22. Paolo G. Brera, "Russiagate, mystery professor Joseph Mifsud speaks out: 'Dirt on
Hillary Clinton? Nonsense,'" La Repubblica, November 1, 2017, http://www.
repubblica.it/esteri/2017/11/01/news/russiagate_mystery_professor_joseph_mifsud_
speaks_out_dirt_on_hillary_clinton_nonsense_-179948962/.

23. "Thomas A. (Tad) Devine."

24. Tom Hamburger and Carol D. Leonnig, "Amid Swirl of Controversy, Democratic
Power Lobbyist Tony Podesta Steps Down," Washington Post, October 30, 2017,
https://www.washingtonpost.com/politics/amid-swirl-of-controversy-democratic
-power-lobbyist-podesta-steps-down/2017/10/30/14c4bb0a-bd97-11e7-97d9-bdab5
a0ab381_story.html?utm_term=.6fc99e262c2b.

25. Mike McIntyre, "Manafort Was in Debt to Pro-Russia Interests, Cyprus Records
Show," New York Times, July 19, 2017, https://www.nytimes.com/2017/07/19/us
/politics/paul-manafort-russia-trump.html.

26. Foer, "Plot Against America."

27. Ibid.

28. Ibid.

29. Glenn Thrush, "To Charm Trump, Paul Manafort Sold Himself as an Affordable
Outsider," New York Times, April 8, 2017, https://www.nytimes.com/2017/04/08
/us/to-charm-trump-paul-manafort-sold-himself-as-an-affordable-outsider.html.

30. Lachlan Markay, "Accused Russian Intel Asset Teamed Up with GOP Operative,"
Daily Beast, April 4, 2018, https://www.thedailybeast.com/accused-russian-intel
-asset-teamed-up-with-gop-operative-3.

31. Foer, "Plot Against America."

32. Markay, "Accused Russian Intel Asset."

33. Ibid.

34. Sue Halpern, "Cambridge Analytica and the Perils of Psychographics," New
Yorker, March 30, 2018, https://www.newyorker.com/news/news-desk/cambridge
-analytica-and-the-perils-of-psychographics.

35. Ken Vogel (@kenvogel), Twitter, June 3, 2018, https://twitter.com/kenvogel/status
/1003296131059765248?lang=en.

36. Markay, "Accused Russian Intel Asset."

37. Nicholas Confessore and Danny Hakim, "Data Firm Says 'Secret Sauce' Aided Trump; Many Scoff," *New York Times,* March 6, 2017, https://www.nytimes.com /2017/03/06/us/politics/cambridge-analytica.html.

38. Ibid.

39. Alexander Burns and Maggie Haberman, "Donald Trump Hires Paul Manafort to Lead Delegate Effort," *New York Times,* March 28, 2016, https://www.nytimes.com /politics/first-draft/2016/03/28/donald-trump-hires-paul-manafort-to-lead-delegate -effort/.

40. Donald Trump Jr. emails, exhibit in Justice Department inquiry into the June 9, 2016, Trump Tower meeting, https://www.judiciary.senate.gov/imo/media/doc /Trump%20Jr%20Exhibits_redacted.pdf.

41. Ibid.

42. Staci Zaretsky, "Bill Maher Goes Apesh*t on Donald Trump's Lawyer," Above the Law, February 11, 2013, https://abovethelaw.com/2013/02/quote-of-the-day-bill -maher-goes-apesht-on-trumps-lawyer/.

43. Elias Groll, "Here's the Memo the Kremlin-Linked Lawyer Took to the Meeting with Donald Trump Jr.," *Foreign Policy,* October 16, 2017, http://foreignpolicy.com /2017/10/16/heres-memo-kremlin-lawyer-took-to-meeting-donald-trump-jr/.

44. Damir Marusic and Karina Orlova, "All the Dots, Connected," *American Interest,* July 25, 2017, https://www.the-american-interest.com/2017/07/25/all-the-dots -connected/.

45. Linley Sanders, "Donald Trump Jr. Told Russian Lawyer 'If We Come to Power' an Anti-Russia Law Would Be Reconsidered," *Newsweek,* November 6, 2017, http:// www.newsweek.com/donald-trump-jr-told-russian-lawyer-if-we-come-power-anti -russia-law-702516.

46. Irina Reznik and Henry Meyer, "Trump Jr. Hinted at Review of Anti-Russia Law, Moscow Lawyer Says," Bloomberg, November 6, 2017, https://www.bloomberg.com /news/articles/2017-11-06/trump-jr-said-anti-russia-law-may-be-reviewed-moscow -lawyer-says.

47. Ibid.

48. Sanders, "Donald Trump Jr."

49. Peter Jacobs, "We Now Know How Jared Kushner Politely Excuses Himself from Meetings He Thinks Are a Waste of Time," *Business Insider,* July 24, 2017, http:// www.businessinsider.com/kushner-got-assistant-to-fake-call-to-get-out-of-trump -jr-meeting-with-russian-lawyer-2017-7.

50. Mackenzie Weinger, "Clapper: Trump Jr. Emails 'Only One Anecdote in a Much Larger Story,'" Cipher Brief, July 11, 2017, https://www.thecipherbrief.com/clapper -trump-jr-emails-only-one-anecdote-in-a-much-larger-story.

51. Andrew E. Kramer and Sharon LaFraniere, "Lawyer Who Was Said to Have Dirt on Clinton Had Closer Ties to Kremlin Than She Let On," *New York Times,* April 27, 2018, https://www.nytimes.com/2018/04/27/us/natalya-veselnitskaya-trump -tower-russian-prosecutor-general.html.

52. Marusic and Orlova, "All the Dots"; Karmer and LaFraniere, "Lawyer Who Was Said to Have Dirt."

53. Ibid.

54. Philip Bump, "What Paul Manafort's Trump Tower Notes Mean," *Washington Post,* May 16, 2018, https://www.washingtonpost.com/news/politics/wp/2018/05 /16/what-paul-manaforts-trump-tower-notes-mean/?utm_term=.c7fa3476ae0f.

55. Katrina Manson, "Russian lobbyist Rinat Akhemetshin on that notorious meeting at Trump Tower," *Financial Times,* September 1, 2017. https://www.ft.com/content /540354a4-8e4c-11e7-a352-e46f43c5825d.

56. Ibid.

57. Isaac Arnsdorf and Benjamin Oreskes, "Vladimir Putin's Favorite US Congressman," Politico, November 23, 2016, https://www.politico.eu/article/vladimir -putin-favorite-us-congressman-dana-rohrabacher-magnitsky-act-russia/.

58. Bill Powell, "How the KGB (and Friends) Took Over Russia's Economy," *Fortune,* September 10, 2008, http://archive.fortune.com/2008/09/04/news/international /powell_KGB.fortune/index.htm.

59. Stephanie Kirchgaessner, "Who Is Rinat Akhmetshin? The Mystery Man at Trump Jr's Russia Meeting," *Guardian,* July 14, 2017, https://www.theguardian.com /us-news/2017/jul/14/rinat-akhmetshin-russia-intelligence-donald-trump-jr.

60. Daniella Diaz, "Eighth Person in Trump Team Meeting Linked to Money Laundering Investigation," CNN, July 20, 2017, https://www.cnn.com/2017/07/19 /politics/ike-kaveladze-linked-to-money-laundering-investigation/index.html.

61. Mackenzie Weinger, "Clapper: Trump Jr. Emails 'Only One Anecdote in a Much Larger Story,'" Cipher Brief, July 11, 2017, https://www.thecipherbrief.com/clapper -trump-jr-emails-only-one-anecdote-in-a-much-larger-story.

62. Ibid.

63. Ryan Goodman, "What Could Michael Cohen Tell Mueller about Russian Collusion?" Just Security, June 13, 2018, https://www.justsecurity.org/57734 /michael-cohen-mueller-russia-collusion/.

CHAPTER TWENTY: ENDGAME

1. Adam Entous, "House Majority Leader to Colleagues in 2016: 'I Think Putin Pays' Trump," *Washington Post,* May 17, 2017, https://www.washingtonpost.com/world /national-security/house-majority-leader-to-colleagues-in-2016-i-think-putin-pays -trump/2017/05/17/515f6f8a-3aff-11e7-8854-21f359183e8c_story.html?utm_term=.66a f450a2f06.

2. "Read the Transcript of the Conversation Among GOP Leaders Obtained by the Post," *Washington Post,* https://www.washingtonpost.com/apps/g/page/national /read-the-transcript-of-the-conversation-among-gop-leaders-obtained-by-the-post /2209/?tid=a_mcntx.

3. "Rep. Kevin McCarthy how he would differ from John Boehner," Fox News, September 29, 2015, http://video.foxnews.com/v/4519442873001/?#sp=show-clips.

4. Dmitri Alperovitch, "Bears in the Midst: Intrusion into the Democratic National Committee," *CrowdStrike Blog,* June 15, 2016, https://www.crowdstrike.com/blog /bears-midst-intrusion-democratic-national-committee/.

5. Entous, "House Majority Leader."

6. "Putin's Asymmetric Assault on Democracy in Russia and Europe: Implications for U.S. National Security," minority staff report prepared for the US Senate Committee on Foreign Relations, January 10, 2018, https://www.foreign.senate.gov /imo/media/doc/FinalRR.pdf.

7. Alex Hern, "Russian Troll Factories: Researchers Damn Twitter's Refusal to Share Data," *Guardian,* November 15, 2017, https://www.theguardian.com /world/2017/nov/15/russian-troll-factories-researchers-damn-twitters-refusal-to -share-data.

8. Jeanna Smialek, "Twitter Bots Helped Trump and Brexit Win, Economic Study Says," Bloomberg, May 21, 2018, https://www.bloomberg.com/news/articles /2018-05-21/twitter-bots-helped-trump-and-brexit-win-economic-study-says?wpmm =1&wpisrc=nl_daily202.

9. Brian Naylor, "How the Trump Campaign Weakened the Republican Platform on Aid to Ukraine," NPR, August 6, 2016, https://www.npr.org/2016/08/06/488876597 /how-the-trump-campaign-weakened-the-republican- platform-on-aid-to-ukraine.

10. Michael Birnbaum and Jose A. DelReal, "Trump Tells Ukraine Confer- ence Their Nation Was Invaded Because 'There Is No Respect for the United States,'" *Washington Post,* September 11, 2015, https://www.washingtonpost.com /news/post-politics/wp/2015/09/11/trump-tells-ukraine-conference-their-nation -was-invaded-because-there-is-no-respect-for-the-united-states/?utm_term=.e89 f0b0a85aa.

11. Carrie Johnson, "2016 RNC Delegate: Trump Directed Change to Party Platform on Ukraine Support," NPR, December 4, 2017, https://www.npr.org/2017/12/04 /568310790/2016-rnc-delegate-trump-directed-change-to-party-platform-on-ukraine -support.

12. Transcript of *The Situation Room,* CNN, aired March 2, 2017, http://transcripts. cnn.com/TRANSCRIPTS/1703/02/sitroom.02.html.

13. Peter Stone, David Smith, Ben Jacobs, Alec Luhn, and Rupert Neate, "Donald Trump and Russia: A Web That Grows More Tangled All the Time," *Guardian,* July 30, 2016, https://www.theguardian.com/us-news/2016/jul/30/donald-trump -paul-manafort-ukraine-russia-putin-ties.

14. House Permanent Select Committee on Intelligence, "Report on Russian Active Measures," March 22, 2018, https://static01.nyt.com/files/2018/us/politics /20180427%20Intelligence%20Committee%20Report.pdf?authuser=1.

15. Rosalind S. Helderman, "Despite Early Denials, Growing List of Trump Camp Contacts with Russians Haunts White House," *Washington Post,* March 4, 2017, https://www.washingtonpost.com/politics/despite-early-denials-growing-list-of -trump-camp-contacts-with-russians-haunts-white-house/2017/03/03/a5b196d8 -002d-11e7-8f41-ea6ed597e4ca_story.html.

16. "Jeff Sessions Calls Russia Claims a 'Detestable Lie,'" Al Jazeera, June 13, 2017.

17. "Transcript: Donald Trump's Foreign Policy Speech," *New York Times,* April 27, 2016, https://www.nytimes.com/2016/04/28/us/politics/transcript-trump-foreign -policy.html.

18. James Kirchick, "Donald Trump's Russia Connections," Politico, April 27, 2016 (updated April 29, 2016), https://www.politico.eu/article/donald-trumps-russia -connections-foreign-policy-presidential-campaign/.

19. Tom Batchelor, "Donald Trump Met Russian Ambassador Sergey Kislyak During Election Campaign," *Independent,* March 8, 2017, https://www.independent.co.uk /news/world/americas/us-politics/donald-trump-russian-ambassador-sergey-kislyak -meeting-election-campaign-a7617261.html.

20. Ken Dilanian, "Did Trump, Kushner, Sessions Have an Undisclosed Meeting with Russian?," NBC News, June 1, 2017, https://www.nbcnews.com/news/us-news/did -trump-kushner-sessions-have-undisclosed-meeting-russian-n767096.

21. Ned Parker, Jonathan Landay, Warren Strobel, "Exclusive: Trump Campaign Had at Least 18 Undisclosed Contacts with Russians: Sources," Reuters, May 18, 2017, https://www.reuters.com/article/us-usa-trump-russia-contacts-idUSKCN18E106. Sessions Have an Undisclosed Meeting with Russian?," NBC News, June 1, 2017,

https://www.nbcnews.com/news/us-news/did-trump-kushner-sessions-have-un
disclosed-meeting-russian-n767096.

22. Nicholas Fandos and Sharon LaFraniere, "Republicans on House Intelligence Panel Absolve Trump Campaign in Russia Meddling," *New York Times,* April 27, 2018, https://www.nytimes.com/2018/04/27/us/politics/house-intelligence -committee-russia-investigation-report.html.

23. Robert Maguire, "Could This Russian-Born Trump Donor Be the Key to a Cryptic Manafort Note?," OpenSecrets.org, September 1, 2017, https://www.opensecrets .org/news/2017/09/russia-born-trump-donor-be-the-key-to-a-cryptic-manafort-note/.

24. Rebecca Ballhaus and Julie Bykowicz, "Data Firm's WikiLeaks Outreach Came as It Joined Trump Campaign," *Wall Street Journal,* November 10, 2017, https://www .wsj.com/articles/data-firms-wikileaks-outreach-came-as-it-joined-trump-campaign -1510339346.

25. Greg Farrell, David Voreacos, and Henry Meyer, "Papadopoulos Claimed Trump Campaign Approved Russia Meeting," Bloomberg, October 31, 2017, https://www .bloomberg.com/news/articles/2017-10-31/papadopoulos-claimed-trump-campaign -approved-russia-meeting.

26. Adam Entous, Ellen Nakashima, and Greg Miller, "Sessions Discussed Trump Campaign-Related Matters with Russian Ambassador, U.S. Intelligence Intercepts Show," *Washington Post,* July 21, 2017, https://www.washingtonpost.com/world /national-security/sessions-discussed-trump-campaign-related-matters-with-russian -ambassador-us-intelligence-intercepts-show/2017/07/21/3e704692-6e44-11e7-9c15 -177740635e83_story.html?utm_term=.6f7b751ff5a3.

27. Scott Shane, Mark Mazzetti, and Adam Goldman, "Trump Adviser's Visit to Moscow Got the F.B.I.'s Attention," *New York Times,* April 19, 2017, https://www .nytimes.com/2017/04/19/us/politics/carter-page-russia-trump.html.

28. Michael D. Shear and Matthew Rosenberg, "Released Emails Suggest the D.N.C. Derided the Sanders Campaign," *New York Times,* July 22, 2016, https://www .nytimes.com/2016/07/23/us/politics/dnc-emails-sanders-clinton.html.

29. Nicholas Confessore and Karen Yourish, "$2 Billion Worth of Free Media for Donald Trump," *New York Times,* March 15, 2016, https://www.nytimes.com/2016/03 /16/upshot/measuring-donald-trumps-mammoth-advantage-in-free-media.html.

30. Press Briefing, "Statement by FBI Director James B. Comey on the Investigation of Secretary Hillary Clinton's Use of a Personal E-Mail System," July 5, 2016, https://www.fbi.gov/news/pressrel/press-releases/statement-by-fbi-director-james -b-comey-on-the-investigation-of-secretary-hillary-clinton2019s-use-of-a-personal -e-mail-system.

31. Ashley Parker and David E. Sanger, "Donald Trump Calls on Russia to Find Hillary Clinton's Missing Emails," *New York Times,* July 27, 2016, https://www .nytimes.com/2016/07/28/us/politics/donald-trump-russia-clinton-emails.html.

32. United States of America v. Internet Research Agency LLC et al., case number 1:18-cr-00032-DLF, indictment, United States District Court for the District of Columbia, https://www.justice.gov/opa/press-release/file/1035562/download.

33. Stone et al., "Donald Trump and Russia."

34. Dana Priest, Ellen Nakashima, and Tom Hamburger, "Russia Suspected of Election Scheme," *Washington Post,* September 6, 2016.

35. Tom Burgis, "Dirty Money: Trump and the Kazakh Connection," *Financial Times,* October 19, 2016, https://www.ft.com/content/33285dfa-9231-11e6-8df8-d3778b55a923.

36. Rosalind S. Helderman, Tom Hamburger, and Rachel Weiner, "At Height of Russia Tensions, Trump Campaign Chairman Manafort Met with Business Associate

from Ukraine," *Washington Post,* June 19, 2017, https://www.washingtonpost.com
/politics/at-height-of-russia-tensions-trump-campaign-chairman-manafort-met
-with-business-associate-from-ukraine/2017/06/18/6ab8485c-4c5d-11e7-a186-60c031
eab644_story.html?utm_term=.afd6aa642763.

37. Ibid.

38. Greg Walters, "Paul Manafort, a Mysterious Russian Jet, and a Secret Meeting,"
Vice News, March 30, 2018, https://www.nytimes.com/2016/07/28/us/politics
/donald-trump-russia-clinton-emails.html.

39. Spencer S. Hsu and Rosalind S. Helderman, "Manafort Associate Had Russian
Intelligence Ties During 2016 Campaign, Prosecutors Say," *Washington Post,*
March 28, 2018, https://www.washingtonpost.com/politics/manafort-associate
-had-russian-intelligence-ties-during-2016-campaign-prosecutors-say/2018/03/28
/473228e8-3231-11e8-8bdd-cdb33a5eef83_story.html?utm_term=.1e1c36fd3f9b.

40. Ashley Feinberg, "Paul Manafort's Daughter Texted Friends About How Tight Her
Dad Was With Trump," *Huffington Post,* November 1, 2017, https://www
.huffingtonpost.com/entry/paul-manafort-daughter-trump-texts_us_59f748b6e4
b03cd20b832fe0.

41. Nicholas Confessore and Barry Meier, "How the Russia Investigation Entangled
Rick Gates, a Manafort Protégé," *New York Times,* June 16, 2017, https://www
.nytimes.com/2017/06/16/us/politics/rick-gates-russia.html.

42. Philip Bump, "The Confusing Timeline on Roger Stone's Communications with
WikiLeaks," *Washington Post,* March 13, 2018, https://www.washingtonpost.com
/news/politics/wp/2018/03/13/the-confusing-timeline-on-roger-stones-communi
cations-with-wikileaks/?noredirect=on&utm_term=.85e045835c03.

43. Media Matter Staff, "Roger Stone Confirms That He's In Communication With
Julian Assange," Media Matters for America, August 9, 2016, https://www
.mediamatters.org/video/2016/08/09/roger-stone-confirms-hes-communication-ju
lian-assange/212261.

44. Boston Herald Radio, "Roger Stone Joins Herald Drive Discussing 2016 Election,"
Soundcloud, https://soundcloud.com/bostonherald/roger-stone-joins-herald
-drive-discussing-2016-election-1.

45. Julia Ioffe, "The Secret Correspondence Between Donald Trump Jr. and
WikiLeaks," *Atlantic,* November 13, 2017, https://www.theatlantic.com/politics
/archive/2017/11/the-secret-correspondence-between-donald-trump-jr-and-wikileaks
/545738/.

46. Ryan Nakashima and Barbara Ortutay, "AP Exclusive: Russia Twitter Trolls De-
flected Trump Bad News," Associated Press, November 10, 2017, https://apnews
.com/fc9ab2b0bbc34f11bc10714100318ae1.

47. Ibid.

48. Matthew Rosenberg, Nicholas Confessore, and Carole Cadwalladr, "How Trump
Consultants Exploited the Facebook Data of Millions," *New York Times,* March 17,
2018, https://www.nytimes.com/2018/03/17/us/politics/cambridge-analytica
-trump-campaign.html?hp&action=click&pgtype=Homepage&clickSource=story
-heading&module=first-column-region&region=top-news&WT.nav=top-news.

49. Mattathias Schwartz, "Facebook Failed to Protect 30 Million Users from Having
their Data Harvested by Trump Campaign Affiliate," Intercept, March 30, 2017,
https://theintercept.com/2017/03/30/facebook-failed-to-protect-30-million-users
-from-having-their-data-harvested-by-trump-campaign-affiliate/.

50. Elliot Hannon, "Once Dismissive, Facebook Now Says 126 Million Users Shown
Russian-Generated Election Propaganda," Slate, October 30, 2017, http://www

.slate.com/blogs/future_tense/2017/10/30/facebook_now_says_126_million_users
_were_shown_russian_election_propaganda.html.

51. Cadwalladr, "Google, Democracy."

52. Paul Fahri, "Conspiracy theorist Alex Jones backs off 'Pizzagate' claims,"
Washington Post, March 2, 2017, https://www.washingtonpost.com/lifestyle/style
/conspiracy-theorist-alex-jones-backs-off-pizzagate-claims/2017/03/24/6f0246fe-1
0cd-11e7-ab07-07d9f521f6b5_story.html?utm_term=.ea35ab720daf.

53. Andrew E. Kramer, "Zuckerberg Meets with Medvedev in Key Market," *New York
Times,* October 1, 2012, http://www.nytimes.com/2012/10/02/technology/zucker
berg-meets-with-medvedev-in-key-market.html.

54. Jim DeFede, "CBS4 News Exclusive: Trump Denies Ties to Russia," CBS Miami,
July 27, 2016, http://miami.cbslocal.com/2016/07/27/cbs4-news-exclusive-trump
-denies-ties-to-russia/.

55. Aaron Blake, "The First Trump-Clinton Presidential Debate Transcript, Anno-
tated," *Washington Post,* September 26, 2016, https://www.washingtonpost.com
/news/the-fix/wp/2016/09/26/the-first-trump-clinton-presidential-debate-transcript
-annotated/?utm_term=.1c1c9b9cc88f.

56. Ibid.

57. Matt Apuzzo, Michael S. Schmidt, Adam Goldman, and Eric Lichtblau, "Comey
Tried to Shield the FBI from Politics. Then He Shaped an Election," *New York
Times,* April 22, 2017, https://www.nytimes.com/2017/04/22/us/politics/james
-comey-election.html.

58. Ibid.

59. Eric Lichtblau and Steven Lee Myers, "Investigating Donald Trump, F.B.I. Sees No
Clear Link to Russia," *New York Times,* October 31, 2016, https://www.nytimes
.com/2016/11/01/us/politics/fbi-russia-election-donald-trump.html.

60. "National Polls, President," FiveThirtyEight, November 8, 2016, https://projects
.fivethirtyeight.com/2016-election-forecast/national-polls/.

61. Presidential Candidate Donald Trump Rally in Warren, Michigan, C-Span video,
October 31, 2016, https://www.c-span.org/video/?417729-1/donald-trump-campaigns
-warren-michigan&start=242.

62. Donald Trump Campaign Rally in Orlando, Florida, C-Span, November 2,
2016, https://www.c-span.org/video/?417871-1/donald-trump-campaigns-orlando
-florida.

63. Chuck Todd, Mark Murray, and Carrie Dann, "Trump Has Been Strikingly Consist-
ent in Denying Russian Hacking Role," NBC News, January 6, 2017, https://www
.nbcnews.com/politics/first-read/trump-has-been-strikingly-consistent-denying
-russian-hacking-role-n703866.

64. Maltz, "Kushner Foundation Gives $342K."

65. Nicole Perlroth, Michael Wines, and Matthew Rosenberg, "Russian Election
Hacking Efforts, Wider Than Previously Known, Draw Little Scrutiny," *New York
Times,* September 1, 2017, https://www.nytimes.com/2017/09/01/us/politics/russia
-election-hacking.html.

66. Ibid.

67. Ibid.

68. "Who Will Win the Presidency?," FiveThirtyEight, November 8, 2016, https://
projects.fivethirtyeight.com/2016-election-forecast/.

69. Nate Silver, "The Real Story of 2016," FiveThirtyEight, January 19, 2017, http://
fivethirtyeight.com/features/the-real-story-of-2016/.

70. Ben Schreckinger, "Inside Donald Trump's Election Night War Room," *GQ,* November 7, 2017, https://www.gq.com/story/inside-donald-trumps-election -night-war-room.

71. Julia Ioffe, "The Secret Correspondence Between Donald Trump Jr. and Wikileaks," *Atlantic,* November 13, 2017, https://www.theatlantic.com/politics/archive/2017/11 /the-secret-correspondence-between-donald-trump-jr-and-wikileaks/545738/.

72. John Haltiwanger, "WikiLeaks Told Trump Jr. to Tell His Dad to Not Concede If He Lost on Election Day," *Newsweek,* November 13, 2017, http://www.newsweek.com /wikileaks-told-trump-jr-tell-his-dad-not-concede-if-he-lost-election-day-710147.

73. Schreckinger, "Inside Donald Trump's."

74. Ibid.

75. Edward B. Colby, "Trump vs. Clinton: Relive the Drama of Election Night 2016," *Newsday,* November 8, 2017, https://projects.newsday.com/nation/trump-clinton -relive-election-night-2016/.

76. Ibid.

77. Smialek, "Twitter Bots Helped Trump."

78. Philip Bump, "Donald Trump will be president thanks to 80,000 people in three states," *Washington Post,* December 1, 2016, https://www.washingtonpost.com/news /the-fix/wp/2016/12/01/donald-trump-will-be-president-thanks-to-80000-people-in -three-states/?utm_term=.f1bc96a13817.

79. "Russia: State Duma Applauds Trump's Victory in US Elections," YouTube, published November 9, 2016, https://www.youtube.com/watch?v=_HzAdP3y-k8.

TRUMP'S FIFTY-NINE RUSSIA CONNECTIONS

1. Ben Schreckinger, "The Happy-Go-Lucky Jewish Group That Connects Trump and Putin," Politico, April 9, 2017, https://www.politico.com/magazine/story/2017 /04/the-happy-go-lucky-jewish-group-that-connects-trump-and-putin-215007.

2. Alessandra Stanley, "Russian Tycoon Finds Politics Good Business," *New York Times,* July 4, 1995, https://www.nytimes.com/1995/07/04/world/russian-tycoon -finds-politics-good-business.html.

3. Anthony Cormier, Chris McDaniel, John Templon, and Tanya Kozyreva, "Michael Cohen Pitched Investors for a Powerful Ukrainian Oligarch's Company," Buzzfeed, June 9, 2017, https://www.buzzfeed.com/anthonycormier/michael -cohen-pitched-investors-for-a-powerful-ukrainian?utm_term=.ilq0xjbE5#.oxY BQoPmM.

4. Sonam Sheth, "A Putin Ally's Jet Arrived in the US Within Hours of a Meeting Between Trump Campaign Chairman Paul Manafort and a Russian Operative," Business Insider, March 30, 2018, http://www.businessinsider.com/oleg-deripaska -jet-arrived-in-us-after-manafort-kilimnik-meeting-2018–3.

5. Luke Harding, "The Hidden History of Trump's First Trip to Moscow," Politico, November 19, 2017, https://www.politico.com/magazine/story/2017/11/19/trump -first-moscow-trip-215842.

6. Peter Zwack, "Death of the GRU Commander," Defense One, February 1, 2016, https://www.defenseone.com/ideas/2016/02/death-gru-commander/125567/.

7. US Attorney's Office, Southern District of New York, "Two Defendants Sentenced for Participating in Racketeering Conspiracy with Russian-American Organized Crime Enterprise Operating International Sportsbook That Laundered More Than $100 Million," press release, April 30, 2014, https://www.fbi.gov/contact-us/field -offices/newyork/news/press-releases/two-defendants-sentenced-for-participating

-in-racketeering-conspiracy-with-russian-american-organized-crime-enterprise
-operating-international-sportsbook-that-laundered-more-than-100-million.

8. Raymond Bonner, "Laundering of Money Seen as 'Easy,'" *New York Times,* November 29, 2000, http://www.nytimes.com/2000/11/29/business/laundering-of
-money-seen-as-easy.html.

9. Andrew E. Kramer, "He Says He's an Innocent Victim. Robert Mueller Says He's a Spy," *New York Times,* April 6, 2018, https://www.nytimes.com/2018/04/06
/world/europe/robert-mueller-kilimnik-ukraine-russia-manafort.html.

10. Lachlan Markay, "Accused Russian Intel Asset Teamed Up with GOP Operative," Daily Beast, April 4, 2018, https://www.thedailybeast.com/accused-russian-intel
-asset-teamed-up-with-gop-operative-3.

11. Tom Topousis, "Rudy Donor Linked to Russian Mob," *New York Post,* December 22, 1999, http://nypost.com/1999/12/22/rudy-donor-linked-to-russian-mob/.

12. David B. Green, "Who Is Lev Leviev, the Israeli Billionaire with Ties to Jared Kushner and Putin," *Haaretz,* July 25, 2017, https://www.haaretz.com/us-news/who-is-the
-israeli-billionaire-with-ties-to-kushner-and-putin-1.5435007.

13. Anna Nemtsova, "Trump's Rep with Russian Gambling Bosses," Daily Beast, November 30, 2016, https://www.thedailybeast.com/trumps-rep-with-russian-gambling
-bosses.

14. Jeff Horwitz and Chad Day, "AP Exclusive: Before Trump Job, Manafort Worked to Aid Putin," Associated Press, March 22, 2017, https://apnews.com/122ae0b
5848345faa88108a03de40c5a.

15. James S. Henry, "The Curious World of Donald Trump's Private Russian Connections," *American Interest,* December 19, 2016, https://www.the-american-interest
.com/2016/12/19/the-curious-world-of-donald-trumps-private-russian-
connections/.

16. Caleb Melby and Keri Geiger, "Behind Trump's Russia Romance, There's a Tower Full of Oligarchs," Bloomberg Businessweek, March 16, 2017, https://www.bloomberg
.com/news/articles/2017–03–16/behind-trump-s-russia-romance-there-s-a-tower
-full-of-oligarchs.

17. Bloomberg News, "Trump Hotel Toronto Building Set to Be Sold After Developer Defaults," Financial Post, October 27, 2016, http://business.financialpost.com
/news/property-post/trump-hotel-toronto-building-set-to-be-sold-after-developer
-defaults.

18. K&D LLC t/a Cork v. Trump Old Post Office LLC and Donald J. Trump, Case 1:17-cv-00731-RJL, United States District Court for the District of Columbia, https://www.politico.com/f/?id=0000015b-f33f-de0a-a15f-ffbf45ad0001.

19. "Gennady Timchenko, Real-Time Net Worth as of 4/25/18," *Forbes,* April 25, 2018, https://www.forbes.com/profile/gennady-timchenko/; Mark Galeotti, "Putin and His Judo Cronies," *Foreign Policy,* May 15, 2014, http://foreignpolicy.com/2014/05
/15/putin-and-his-judo-cronies/.

20. Dina Khrennikova and Irina Reznik, "Ross-Linked Firm Expanded Ties to Russia's Sibur After Sanctions," Bloomberg, November 9, 2017, https://www
.bloomberg.com/news/articles/2017–11–09/ross-linked-firm-expanded-ties-to-russia
-s-sibur-after-sanctions.

21. Adam Goldman, Ben Protess, and William K. Rashbaum, "Viktor Vekselberg, Russian Billionaire, Was Questioned by Mueller's Investigators," *New York Times,* May 4, 2018, https://www.nytimes.com/2018/05/04/us/politics/viktor-vekselberg
-mueller-investigation.html.

ABOUT THE AUTHOR

Craig Unger is the author of the *New York Times* bestselling *House of Bush, House of Saud*. He has appeared frequently as an analyst on MSNBC, CNN, the ABC Radio Network, and many other broadcast outlets. The former editor-in-chief of *Boston Magazine*, Unger has written about this subject for *Vanity Fair* and *The New Republic*. He is a graduate of Harvard University and lives in New York City.